Lake Baikal

U.S.S.R.

HEILUNG

Dong bei
(Manchuria)

Harbin

REPUBLIC OF
MONGOLIA

Undur Khan
(Ondor Haan)

KIRIN

Desert

INNER MONGOLIA

Shenyang
(Mukden)

LIAONING

Anshan

Sea of
Japan

Yin Mts.
Paotow

HUANG

PEKING

YONG
DING R.

Peitaiho

Liao-tung
Pen.

YALU

Pyongyang

KOREA

Zhoukoudian

DAIREN
(LUTA)

Port Arthur

NINGSIA

GREAT WALL

SHANSI

Tientsin

HOPEI

Pohai

NORTH

Taihang Mts.

HUANG

Tsinan

SHANTUNG

Tsingtao

Yellow
Sea

JAPAN

anchow

Sian

SHENSI

HONAN

CHINA
(YELLOW)

PLAIN

HUAI

KIANGSU

SHENSI

HAN

HUPEI

ANHWEI

Nanking

Wusih

SHANGHAI
HANGCHOW

ZECHWAN

Chengtu

WUHAN

Hankow—
Hanyang

Wuchang

Tayeh LOWER YANGTZ

HSINAN R.
RES.

Shaohsing

Chungking

YANGTZE

UPPER

Tungt'ing
hu

(Lake Grotto Hall)

CHEKIANG

East
China Sea

KWEICHOW

Changsha

HUNAN

HSIANG

KIANGSI

FUKIEN

Taipei
TAIWAN

KWANGSI

Nanning

KWANGTUNG

Canton

Hong Kong

YANGTZE

Woosung

WOOSUNG R.

WHANGPU RIVER

NAN

PEILUN
R.

Hanoi

VIETNAM (ANNAM)

Gulf
of
Tonkin

HAINAN

South China Sea

Soochow Creek

SHANGHAI

0 2 4 6
KILOMETERS

Saml H. Bryant

.

Books by Ross Terrill

800,000,000: The Real China, 1972
Socialism as Fellowship: R. H. Tawney and His Times, 1973
Flowers on an Iron Tree, 1975

China Profile (editor and contributor), 1969
Who We Are (contributor), 1969
China and Ourselves (editor and contributor), 1970
China and the World Community (contributor), 1973
Faces of China (with Pat Fok), 1974

FLOWERS ON AN IRON TREE

FLOWERS ON

鐵
樹
開
花

AN ATLANTIC MONTHLY PRESS BOOK

AN IRON TREE

Five Cities of China

ROSS TERRILL

LITTLE, BROWN AND COMPANY   BOSTON – TORONTO

FIRST EDITION

T 10/75

"Peking" appeared, in slightly different form, in *The Atlantic*.

LIBRARY OF CONGRESS CATALOGING IN PUBLICATION DATA

Terrill, Ross.
  Flowers on an iron tree.

  "An Atlantic Monthly Press book."
  Bibliography: p.
  Includes index.
  1. China — Description and travel — 1949–
I. Title.
DS711.T465 915.1'04'5 75-17944
ISBN 0-316-537628

ATLANTIC-LITTLE, BROWN BOOKS
ARE PUBLISHED BY
LITTLE, BROWN AND COMPANY
IN ASSOCIATION WITH
THE ATLANTIC MONTHLY PRESS

Designed by Janis Capone

*Published simultaneously in Canada
by Little, Brown & Company (Canada) Limited*

PRINTED IN THE UNITED STATES OF AMERICA

To my mother

FLOWERS ON AN IRON TREE

The Chinese saying 鐵樹開花 conveys the idea of a rare or marvelous happening. Kwangsi province produced a short, purplish tree, with very hard wood; it was known as an iron tree. People said it bloomed only once every sixty years, so a flower on an iron tree was a remarkable thing.

ABOUT THIS BOOK

We have shaken off the idea of China as a threat to America. We can look at Chinese life on its own terms and for what it may have to offer. One-quarter of mankind, perched on the earth as we are, grappling with problems that bother many lands.

China's solutions to problems are often novel. We finally learned that because China is different from us does not make it a threat to us. But because the Chinese are no threat does not mean their way of life is the same as ours.

Flowers on an Iron Tree offers work and play in five cities of an elusive land which has two of the world's seven most populous cities.

There are nations, like the United States, which have depth, with numerous cities of substance widely scattered. There are other nations, like France, where each nerve seems hooked up to a key center. On the whole China is of the first kind; it has depth. After a visitor thinks he has seen the essence of the nation, China can throw before him a dozen fresh cities. Even urban China is a rainbow of diversity.

Why do I give you these five cities; not others, not the countryside? Urban China is the cutting edge of tomorrow's China. And I happen to be an escapee from a village boyhood who feels at ease in cities. I went to these five and liked them. I found that the face, style, and business of each differs in intriguing ways from the others.

Shanghai is China's New York. Dairen is a kind of Seattle, damp and sparse and on the fringes. Hangchow as a pool of beauty's self-indulgence might raise a bid from San Francisco. Wuhan is an inland giant that answers to Chicago. In the mirror of Peking an American might make out the features of Washington.

These cities are big. Their combined population exceeds that of the five U.S. cities mentioned. But they are not "advanced"; their fine points are not ours. China is poor as well as vast. A Chinese home has

xi

no phone, car, fridge, TV, or washing machine. Gadgets stop at an electric radio and a bicycle. A Shanghai family may be saving up for a transistor radio, or have its eye on a second bicycle as a U.S. family eyes a second car.

The monthly income of a couple is around a hundred yuan, one-third of which goes on food. It is hard to put a real value on the yuan, which can be changed for just over fifty U.S. cents. A family of four need spend only twelve yuan (U.S. $6.25) for a month's rest, school fees, health care, entertainment, and transportation. Yet in the pursuit of luxuries·the yuan is a snail. A TV would take four months of the couple's wages, a car just cannot be bought, nor may goods be ordered from abroad.

The United States used to bare its fangs at China because Peking was the sponsor of an "unstable" world. Today China seems an island of stability in a post-1973 world of energy crisis, monetary mess, shaky morale. China has no inflation, exports oil, feeds herself. She leans on almost no cultural resources other than her own, has no troops abroad to snarl her up in far-off fights.

China has its tensions, mainly different from the kind we have. People are not gnawed by economic insecurity, but personal hopes and values come up against Communist Party priorities. Where the United States is strong — its political system allows for change within settled rules — China is weak.

I give you five exposures of the Chinese people in their setting. No balance sheet is drawn up. I am Australian enough to be oblique rather than frontal. I try to show you China rather than aspire to tell you what to conclude about China.

I have found that to learn more about the diverse universe which is China is to become cautious about summing up the whole. This book is not a bullhorn, but a window; here are glimpses, facts, conversations, which will speak to you for themselves.

TERMS AND NAMES

CCP	Communist Party of China
CYL	Communist Youth League
catty	one-half kilogram, about 1.1 pounds
dong bei	northeast China (once known as Manchuria)
fen	a hundred fen make one yuan
Five Anti Movement	campaign in early 1950s against businessmen who practiced bribery, tax evasion, stealing state property, cheating on government contracts, and stealing economic secrets from the state
the "four olds"	traditional customs, habits, culture, and social thought, against which the Cultural Revolution was aimed
Great Leap Forward	accelerated drive toward socialism begun in the spring of 1958, only partially successful
July 21 College	factory-based school named after Mao's statement on education of July 21, 1968
Liberation	the revolution of 1949
May Fourth Movement	nationalistic cultural and political upsurge started by students in 1919
neighborhood	subdivision of a city district

xiii

PLA	People's Liberation Army (all branches of the military)
PRC	People's Republic of China
residents' area	a section of a neighborhood
revolutionary committee	standard term since the Cultural Revolution for the administrative leadership of any unit, from province down to factory or school
south China	generally means south of Yangtze River
taipan	("big boss"), foreign businessman in treaty ports
yuan	about fifty U.S. cents

CHINESE WORDS

Most Chinese place-names are translated into English, to give the reader a sense of the name as it rings in a Chinese ear.

Chinese words are sometimes given in parentheses after the English, to enable a reader who knows Chinese to check my translation, or to help identify a name or saying.

In romanizing Chinese words I use *pin-yin wen-zi* (the PRC's phonetic system) for common speech and local place-names; Wade-Giles (an older system) for historical names, people, and places already well known in their Wade-Giles form; Wade-Giles also in the note on sources, since most libraries use this older system.

In a few cases the name of a local interviewee is fictitious, either because it was not recorded or because permission to use it was not sought or granted, and in one case the name of a neighborhood is fictitious (pp. 179 ff.).

CONTENTS

xvii

CONTENTS

武汉

Wuhan

231

北京

Peking

327

SHANGHAI

上海

AMONG GREAT CITIES OF THE WORLD Shanghai is not blessed with beauty of setting. Its name means "to the sea" but the city is not within sight of the sea. It is built on a mud flat close to the estuary of the Yangtze River. No hill or dale gives Shanghai an angle on itself; no nearby forest lends respite from the urban array. Its only natural wonders are a couple of dirty rivers. Shanghai owes little to nature, everything to quirks of modern history, and to a key location at the edge of the Yangtze Valley.

Come to Shanghai from another part of China, and the pulse quickens, for here is the hubbub of the biggest nation's biggest city. The measured ways of Peking are absent from this metropolis of action. By China's standards the Shanghainese step briskly; few traditions from a distant yesterday intrude upon the rhythm of today. There is none of the languidness of serene Hangchow; the Shanghai smile comes and goes with shutterlike speed. The city lacks the spaciousness of Dairen, for inner Shanghai alone packs in 5.7 million people. At the same time, external bustle has not robbed the smooth and voluble Shanghainese of style.

Approaching the city by water you leave the quick yellow waves of the Yangtze and turn south into the Whangpu River, Shanghai's muddy path to the Pacific. You meet Shanghai at its vital entrails, the docks. Gliding past the outskirt town of Woosung, your ship comes upon a geometry of wharves on both sides of the Whangpu.

Railway yards and belching chimneys lie in the background. Fewer farms are visible than when tourist ships called at old Shanghai, giving well-insulated European passengers glued to their portholes the nearest thing to a sight of a Chinese village on their itinerary. Industry's tentacles have taken a grip on the Whangpu. The low old straw ice-houses of the fishing organizations remain — ice taken off creeks in

3

winter is stored in them and used on fishing boats in summer — but they are dwarfed now on either side by hulks of steel and concrete.

Tankers, cargo boats, and bulk carriers of several dozen nations ply the water, though a good proportion bear the red and gold flag of China. What makes this port unusual among world ports is the endless scatter of sailing boats, emerging from side creeks to take advantage of the Whangpu current, nipping around the liners like minnows among pike.

Coming from the airport at Rainbow Bridge (Hong qiao) — to which French, Pakistani, Japanese, Swiss, and Ethiopian airlines now fly — the visitor sees first the flat lush market-garden suburbs to the west. Before the revolution the Rainbow Bridge area was an aristocratic hideaway, and the site of a golf course for foreigners tired of the clatter of the "Chinese" city.

In those days — when Pan Am and Northwest Orient airlines flew into Shanghai — the commercial airport was at Dragon Brilliance (Long hua), a southern neighborhood named after Shanghai's one Buddhist pagoda. For a while Rainbow Bridge field was used exclusively by General Claire Chennault's money-spinning airline, Civil Air Transport.

Rainbow Bridge became a battlefield when Communist forces reached Shanghai from the Yangtze in 1949. The Kuomintang commander suddenly withdrew from his artillery emplacements and pillboxes at its outer rim. He built a wooden fence at its inner rim — with timber sent from the United States — that would have been excellent had the Communists been armed with bows and arrows. When fighting erupted the nice foreign villas suffered so much ravage that few are now recognizable (government officials live in them). But Chiang Kai-shek's concrete pillboxes still dot the vegetable plots of what is today a people's commune.

Leaving the cream brick and glass airport building, you head downtown by crossing Sun Yat-sen Road, a ring road thrown around the city during the Great Leap Forward of 1958. The urban honeycomb of gray buildings and white-shirted crowds grows denser by the block; no surprise that this is now one of the world's three most populous cities.

Abruptly one's course is halted at Shanghai's cool and open veranda, the Whangpu River. Here colorful boats replace dull buildings. White shirts no longer dart about but lean on the parapet, bent toward the yellow ripples.

A passenger may come in by train, either on the Nanking "Passenger Rapid" (*ke kuai*) from the northwest, or from the south via Hangchow. He arrives at what used to be Shanghai's slum area, North of the Watergate (Chapei). The gate was in Soochow Creek, which empties into the Whangpu from the west. North of the Watergate, sardine-packed, stretches in a long strip north of the creek. Adjacent on the eastern side is another crowded district, Mouth of the Rainbow (Hongkew).

You step off a train at Shanghai Station (formerly North Station) and sense the bubbling of a riot, so raucous and teeming is the panorama. Arriving travelers laden with bundles, babies, and birds clamor to get out of the ramshackle terminal, as those who have come to greet family or friends clamor to get in. There is always tumult and sweaty confusion.

Often there are tears as well, because the Chinese family is still a close-knit affair: tender partings when middle-school graduates depart for "reeducation" in the remote countryside; ebullient scenes when they return for a break or to enroll at college.

In North of the Watergate tens of thousands used to live under oil cans, matting, even newspapers pasted into a roof. Thousands had nowhere to live but the dirty alleys which punctuate the winding streets. Hundreds by the month died on the stinking pavement where they had battled to live.

Today parts of North of the Watergate are still a slum, but a cleaned-up slum. There are lanes which are mournful with flimsy houses of bamboo and boxwood. (These shacks have a picturesque name: "Dragons rolling on the ground.") But young trees sprout, water and gas are piped into the meanest home, children squat in the gutter studying books — all this is new since the Liberation of 1949.

Not all new are the scramble of street noises which grate on the foreigner but go unnoticed by most Chinese. More bicycle bells and radio loudspeakers echo in the street than before Shanghai turned red.

5

There are no cries of hopeful hawkers or clack of *mahjong* pieces, and far fewer auto horns. Chinese songs still whine persistently, though if you listen carefully — as no one seems to do — the lyric is about socialism and not about love. Smells are rich but the industrial ones nowadays subdue those of man and nature. If the "honey cart" (for night soil) was once Shanghai's acutest smell, today it may be burning coal.

Much of Mouth of the Rainbow district used to be the Japanese Concession, and its brown wooden shops and homes with dark gray roofs still look half-Japanese. Standing sentry over the southern tip of the district is seventeen-story Broadway Mansions, a former American building now called Shanghai Mansions. On its top floor foreigners and their White Russian mistresses used to dance the sultry Shanghai night away. Today there are no dances, but you can get a good view of the old Japanese Concession.

From on high you see few right angles or parallels among the streets; the pale smooth roadways run wild like a scatter of ivory chopsticks on a brown floor. Buildings at each street corner have rounded edges which also give the intersections a nongeometric look. Commercial establishments are two or three stories high. Their somber vertical boards are brightened here and there by a striped canvas awning shading the almost-melting asphalt. The area used to lack foliage but fledgling trees now line the wider roads. They nicely contrast with the serried roofs in brown and gray, like bright rows of parsley on a trout.

Set into the roofs are trapdoors which resemble the landing flaps on the wings of an aircraft. They bring a puff of air to top-floor living quarters where air-conditioning is unknown. Window frames in natural wood open outward over the street, and there are narrow second-floor balconies. On these, half-naked men fan themselves and watch the scene below, while laundry dries on poles above their heads.

✦ ✦ ✦

Shanghai is one of three Chinese cities (with Peking and Tientsin) which has become a city-state. Not part of one of China's twenty-two provinces, or five autonomous regions, it governs itself as a "municipality" of eleven million people. In the scale of wealth and power,

6

weighs more heavily than many a province. As a municipality Shanghai runs about seventy kilometers wide and ninety kilometers long. It has three sectors, each with a different beat. I will call them rural Shanghai, new Shanghai, ex-imperial Shanghai.

When the present boundaries were fixed in 1958–1959, the total area of Shanghai was divided into ten city districts and ten outlying counties. The city districts cover 160 square kilometers; the outlying counties sprawl over 6,000 square kilometers.

The counties, where five million people live and farm, are hardly part of Shanghai city except that they feed its bottomless belly. It is the rural unit of people's communes, not the urban unit of neighborhoods, into which the counties are divided. Nearest the city are vegetable communes. Further out it is rice that predominates, and cotton is a major second crop. All told there are 199 communes in the counties of rural Shanghai. That Shanghai's suburbs are modernizing fast is proved by the number of schools: five hundred middle schools and thirty-five hundred primary schools in the ten counties.

The ten districts contain the five to six million people of Shanghai city proper. Their outer reaches make up a distinctive belt of new Shanghai which before Liberation was a sleepy farming region. In the 1970s this outer belt of districts, starting some eight kilometers from the downtown hub, is made up of a string of planned satellite towns. These are self-contained communities which center on a single large factory, or group of factories, and house their workers in modern blocks of four to six stories.

It is here, among the smoky chimneys, transistor radios, brick apartment oblongs, supermarkets, parklands, construction sites without number, that the new creation of Communist Shanghai is seen. All this is proof, I feel, that among the things which red rule is doing to China the most basic is *modernization*. Odd maybe, but true, that a Marxist regime knocks the corners off China's particularity, that revolutionaries, once in power, narrow the gap between Chinese city life and modern city life elsewhere. It is also true, and impressive, that Shanghai has built new homes for 1.1 million people since 1949.

A third sector of Shanghai is the old body of the ex-imperial city, theater of mingled romance and brutishness in the days when for-

7

eigners ruled the roost. Here are districts bordering the west of the Whangpu River. Their names are unchanged since before 1949; Whangpu (Yellow Banks), Nanshih (Southern Town), Hongkew (Mouth of the Rainbow), Chapei (North of the Watergate).

An old Shanghai hand can easily find his way through these dense areas, once "foreign settlements" in the epoch of Empire borrowed from China's weakness. Here are two-storied pre-Liberation houses: some wooden, dark and mellow, bamboo poles of clothes sticking out across the cobbles from the second floor; some in red brick or fawn stone, rows of attached tenements as in Manchester or Leeds, bedspreads airing on the windowsill, bikes leaning against the shabby walls, children gamboling on the stone steps.

The main streets of Yellow Banks are still named for Chinese towns, if they run east-west, like Peking Road, or for Chinese provinces, if they run north-south, like Fukien Road. But those in the French Concession which honored notable men (Avenue Foch, Rue Courbet) have all been given local names. The streets are noisy with the rumble of Shanghai's blue trolleybuses and the incessant trill of bicycle bells, like an orchestra of mechanical cicadas echoing through the sultry day.

Here are the tall British- and American-built hotels, more sober at night than they used to be; the comfortable cinemas with their gaudy billboard scenes of revolutionary passion; the big pulsing department stores pitched to the good taste of the Shanghai shopper.

The drab office blocks that used to house foreign banks and companies have seen a spiritual but not a physical conversion. Now bureaus of Shanghai municipality, they still look like oaks from Victorian England planted by error in the tropical garden of the China coast.

Off the main arteries are numerous back-street factories, making tiles or paper or bolts. Their relaxed but not lazy workers labor in an environment of organized mess. Supplies and finished products come and go on tricycles with a platform attached. Bamboo scaffolding marks a spot where new construction is under way. Building materials lie about in unashamed heaps at inconvenient places.

Snack shops serve a bowl of noodles to the hungry; a postman picks his way through the clutter with his bag of letters; a girl carries a piece of pork she has just bought, open to the air on a small strip of news-

8

Buildings are decked in the red and white garments of socialist propaganda paper. A few traffic policemen in white uniforms, leather belts, and stiff caps sharpen the workaday scene. I notice that most of the bicycles leaning against rails and walls are padlocked.

On side streets and boulevards alike, buildings are decked in the red and white garments of socialist propaganda. The white characters presumptuously seek to make explicit and unified the thoughts of this catholic network: "The Working Class Must Lead All"; "Ten Thousand Years to Our Glorious and Correct Communist Party"; "Carry Through the Cultural Revolution to the End."

Preindustrial China did not lack great cities. Before Europe's Industrial Revolution, indeed, China was *the* land of cities; around 1800, six of the world's ten largest cities were in China. But Shanghai has no place in the rich story of urban China under the dynasties.

You see at a glance that the city of Shanghai, like most cities of America, is younger than the Industrial Revolution. Its arterial structure is that of a trading and manufacturing port. There are no broad geometric perspectives, jeweled with palaces and gates, as in a city of emperors like Peking. The squares are hardly more than intersections; Shanghai never took time out from business to make them otherwise. The monuments have a nineteenth-century look, at once heavy and perfunctory.

Religion has not shaped the features of Shanghai, as it has those of Hangchow. You may walk for an afternoon through new Shanghai and ex-imperial Shanghai and not see a single feudal relic. Where signs of religion exist they are integral with the bones of the industrial city. Churches of the Christian faith, which in Shanghai was the businessman's religion, nestle in stylistic accord with banks and commercial houses.

It is not that the Shanghai area has no history, or that it was entirely a foreign creation. A map drawn in the year 1010 depicts a town of moderate size. Plowing, weaving, salt making, and fishing were the chief sources of livelihood. By the Yuan dynasty in the fourteenth century, the district of Shanghai — an area larger than today's municipality — counted 72,000 families, or about 250,000 people. It was during this Mongol dynasty that Shanghai got a charter and its name ("to the sea" — after a nearby river of the same name). But the town itself was small and without distinction, nothing to compare with the great city of Hangchow 190 kilometers to the south.

During the Sung and Yuan dynasties, Japanese brought tribute to Shanghai port, sailing their vessels as far inland as Bright Dragon (Qing long), thirty kilometers west of Shanghai. Periodically the Japanese attacked and overran the area, and this led a Ming period district magistrate to have town walls and gates erected in 1552.

It was also during the Ming dynasty that the Whangpu River got its name: Yellow Banks. But the rivers of the Shanghai area were once curiously different in size than they are today. The Whangpu, a tiny stream in 1010, was still in 1300 but "a bow-shot" wide in central Shanghai where it is now eight hundred meters wide. On the other hand the Woosung River, which enters the Whangpu north of Shanghai, used to be much bigger than the Whangpu. Today it is much smaller, a quiet stream for minor craft, while the Whangpu receives ocean liners.

Shanghai manners changed no less through medieval times than Shanghai rivers. Chang Chih-hsiang, a historian of Ming times, wrote of Shanghai: "Being a secluded place, at one corner of the sea-coast, the manners of the inhabitants are rude and simple." But when "barbarians from the islands" (Japanese) invaded late in the sixteenth century, "distressing the villages," the manners of the people grew looser. "The townspeople became light and vain," one Chinese history book noted. "Fellows that had not a bushel of corn at home would wear elegant clothes and beautiful shoes abroad. . . . Inferior families contended for superiority in extravagance and luxury." This new smooth style seems an intriguing anticipation of a Shanghai yet to be.

A far greater jolt to Shanghai manners occurred when European traders reached the China coast in the nineteenth century. It was under European influence that Shanghai turned from a town into China's largest city and port, and, for the Chinese Communists, one of China's largest political problems.

Canton had been the first base for the penetration of European trade and religion. After Britain won the Opium War in 1842, China agreed in the Treaty of Nanking to let the eager barbarians into five treaty ports. One of them was Shanghai, "opened" to foreign trade and residence in 1843. Within twenty-five years Shanghai displaced Canton as China's number one trading post. Its hundred-year career as symbol of undeflectable Western pressure on reluctant China had begun.

Came the *taipan* ("big bosses") to set up "godowns" (warehouse-offices) on the banks of the Whangpu. Came the arrogant gray gunboats, to sink some junks and shoot a few Chinese whenever Peking balked at a fresh European demand for access or control. Came the gentle, numb-to-history missionaries who lived well off Shanghai's body while ministering to its soul. And came peasants from all over a disordered China, to try their luck in a burgeoning city that offered action if not justice.

Shanghai grew at a pace matched by no other Chinese city. In Opium War days it had about 250,000 people; by the end of the nineteenth century it had at least five times that number. From World War One Shanghai emerged with a population of more than two million, and ever since it has been China's biggest city. By World War Two there were five million residents, the city handled half of China's foreign trade, and boasted half of China's mechanized factories. (Manchuria was at that time in Japan's hands.)

Today Shanghai is comfortably conscious of its position as the nation's number one economic city. The leading Shanghai newspaper, *Literary Currents (Wen-hui pao)*, uses a national rather than a merely provincial tone of voice. City officials refer with satisfaction to Shanghai's premier role in China's sea, air, and telecommunications links with the foreign world. They observe that Shanghai's sixteen institutes of higher learning include students from every province of China.

On political issues Shanghai tends less than any other city to defer automatically to Peking's views. The Cultural Revolution, it is noted with pride, began in Shanghai. Chairman Mao, thwarted by the Peking establishment in his desire to throw new questions in the air, left the capital for several months in 1965 and turned his attention on Shanghai.

In November 1965 a Shanghai literary politician, prompted by

Mao, fired the first shot of the Cultural Revolution with a Delphic piece in *Literary Currents.* This celebrated article had been prepared with the cunning care of a coup d'etat; it was revised no fewer than eleven times. In form it was a literary critique of a Peking playwright; in substance it was a political attack on a congeries of "rightists."

Since *Literary Currents* fired that reverberating journalistic shot, Shanghai has often carried itself like the spiritual guardian of Cultural Revolutionary principles. Its officials note that Shanghai has been acclaimed by various provinces as a model in sticking closely to socialist values. During 1973 the city even started a sharp-edged monthly journal of politics, *Study and Criticism,* which does not always take the same point of view as the national Party monthly, *Red Flag.*

Shanghai's leaders have in recent years played a more prominent role on the national stage than those of any province. The city has three seats at China's inner circle of power, the Politbureau of the Chinese Communist Party (CCP). No province has as many. A handsome young cotton-mill worker, Wang Hung-wen, who cut his teeth in the Shanghai Cultural Revolution, rose above senior national figures who had taken part in the Chinese revolution to become China's number three man at the Tenth Congress of the CCP in August 1973.

The most fascinating aspect of Shanghai's character is the way the new socialist order has redirected the city's old impulses. People said of Shanghai in treaty port days that money was its god. It was a "City for Sale," as Ernest Hauser termed it in his memoir of that title, a bit of China set apart from the rest of the nation for the unencumbered service of commerce. You sense in Shanghai of the 1970s a commercial spirit, yet it pales beside the religion of commerce which gripped old Shanghai.

I ask a Shanghai friend who has recently been living in Peking what the good points of each city are. "Peking has a more dry and healthy air," she replies, "and it has space and grandly laid out streets." On Shanghai her tone is a shade fonder. "In Shanghai the customs are more agreeable, and clothes and tailoring are much better than in Peking."

On a trip from Shanghai to Tsinan, the plane stops at Nanking and two Shanghai cadres head for the airport shop. Until the last mo-

13

ment before reboarding they concentrate on shopping. They select six pairs of socks which meet their fancy, from among dozens laid out by the patient Nanking shopkeeper.

The Shanghai CCP from time to time criticizes the attitude to clothes of some of its people. During 1973 bell-bottom pants were condemned as "bizarre." At other times tight pants and longish hair have been criticized — which almost means forbidden — as hankerings after foreign fashions no longer worthy of Shanghai. That the Party feels the need for these broadsides suggests that my Shanghai friend's regard for the tailoring of her hometown is still an entrenched Shanghai trait.

Shanghai folk have a sharp eye for the detail of prices and wages. They can tell you in a flash how much a neighbor earns. They have ready views on what is good value and what is less so at the nearest department store. They know the complex rationing schedule for cloth and grain and cooking oil and how it will affect any type of citizen.

Rewi Alley, the New Zealand veteran of forty-seven years in China, was chatting with some Shanghai people about the great improvements in conditions of life since Liberation. "In the old days we went to the pawnshop with tears in our eyes," they summed up. "Now we go to the bank with joy to put in deposits."

This remark to Alley points up a paradox about the fate of the commercial spirit in Shanghai. Life is better and more secure for the ordinary man than it was thirty or fifty years ago. This is an achievement of the Communist government of China, over and above the harder work which each Shanghai citizen may have contributed. Yet the improvement is laid hold of by each man and woman as a material thing — deposits in the bank. Today, after all, there is still just socialism, whose maxim is, to each according to his work — not yet communism with its more ambitious maxim, to each according to his need.

The coming of socialism gets measured, then, in prosaic ways. Pride in socialist Shanghai is ultimately an intangible thing, yet it also takes the form of satisfaction with a better range of goods and services. The very success of socialism, at the collective level, can produce a paradoxical esteem for material things, at the individual level.

All that, if true, describes a certain "consumerism" in Shanghai.

But it is just a trapping of the city's life. There are touches of avarice at the level of consumption; in the nature of the system there can be no avarice over the means of production. A woman may save up in order to deck herself out with nice clothes. But she cannot use her money to hire the labor of others and make more money by exploiting that labor. The man-eating commercialism of old Shanghai has gone without a trace. Today's commercial spirit is a gloss on Shanghai; no longer the motive force of its life.

Year by year the eye can mark modernity's march in Shanghai. Almost nothing is as prestigious among the city's youth as science and technology. It fascinates them and provides a vehicle for their ambition. Many bookshops and magazine stands stock little else than technical literature. Engineering and biology manuals and periodicals like *Scientific Experimentation* come in and out of libraries like yo-yos.

In 1970 the city set up a highly successful Science and Technology Center. It helps factories solve tricky technical problems, popularizes new equipment and methods, mounts periodic exhibitions. By 1973 the center employs fourteen teams of thirteen hundred researchers, technicians, and experienced workers. Its exhibitions have drawn a million visitors since early 1972. During my visit the center is showing personnel from city factories two machines newly developed in Shanghai: an all-automatic lathe with hydraulic control, a gas cementing furnace with a silicon-controlled rectifier.

No doubt it is because science and technology are given high priority that they advance swiftly. A few years ago a visitor would be shown with pride a 100,000-kilowatt turbogenerator made in Shanghai (between 1914 and 1949, the biggest electric motor built in Shanghai was 50 kilowatts). In 1973 I am pointed to one of 300,000 kilowatts (with inner water-cooled stator and rotor). On the textile front, synthetics have made miracle strides. Shanghai now produces more polyester in nine days than it produced for the entire year of 1965.

Replanting of limbs and fingers is now a commonplace at leading Shanghai medical institutions, such as Number Six People's Hospital.

15

Legs can even be replanted so as to permit the return of stable and sensate feet. An intact foot has been transferred from an irreparably damaged left leg to replace a crushed foot on a salvageable right leg.

In small ways that nevertheless influence daily life the role of the machine has expanded. Here is a post office in Mouth of the Rainbow district. People hurry in and out and silently buy gummed stamps from shiny new green dispensers. Other machines cough out envelopes already stamped for a standard inland letter. This is not the Chinese corner post office of yesterday, with its pots of paste for sticking on the ungummed stamps, and long lines waiting to be served by a gossipy postal assistant. Near the post office, as all over the city, there are smart new public phones (curiously they are called "public use phones" in Shanghai but "people's phones" in Peking).

Here is a snack bar in Yellow Banks district. Fruit drinks are bought from a whirring machine which is a popular attraction not only for the thirsty but for a crowd who simply like to watch this new trick. A coin is put in and a coconut drink pours into the customer's waiting bowl (but no paper cups as yet; girls wash the bowls and issue fresh ones). At a nearby food counter a pair of chopsticks pops down for each diner from an automatic chopstick machine. Solar-energy stoves — a dish-shaped reflector catches the sun's rays — are starting to appear in Shanghai kitchens.

Television enters Shanghai life as a source of information and distraction. People are watching evening programs in fairly large numbers for the first time in China. Shanghai TV goes on till 11:00 P.M. (six nights a week), which is very late by Chinese standards. In casual conversations TV is a fruitful topic for an exchange of views. I find a couple of wharf workers enthusiastic about experimental programs in color TV that they have recently seen. Shanghai also uses color in newspaper printing. *Literary Currents* and *Liberation Daily* (the two main papers) sometimes print excellent color photographs, using multi-color rotogravure presses.

Television was a force in the ebb and flow of Shanghai's Cultural Revolution. Still memorable to many, for instance, was a TV speech made by the city's leading politician, Chang Ch'un-ch'iao, in the stormy month of February 1967. An ambitious "Shanghai Commune" had been proclaimed and left-wing forces were riding high in their assault on the city's pre-1965 order. Mr. Chang, considered a left-winger himself, had just returned from Peking and three talks with Chairman Mao.

It was announced that he would speak at Culture Square, just off Shensi Road in Black Bend district. But only a fraction of those eager to hear the latest turn of events could squeeze into the square. The two-hour speech was carried on live TV. Millions watched Chang's every gesture, caught each idiosyncratic nuance from this man who was subtly signaling a new policy, and needed a very personal appearance before the people in order to do it effectively in a city jumpy with contention.

He explained that it was too soon to have a commune. He submitted that not *all* pre-1965 things were bad. He reasoned that army men and tested cadres were indispensable for running Shanghai's complex affairs. The speech marked the consolidation of Chang's power as a center-left leader in Shanghai. It had reached its mark via television.

The acids of modernity eat away at customs evolved in rural and isolated China — as devastatingly as do the direct blows of CCP propaganda — and new social customs quickly get a foothold. A senior cadre gives me 1973 figures on Shanghai's birthrate which show a massive slowdown compared with twenty and thirty years ago: a natural increase rate of 0.7 percent; a crude birthrate of 1.2 percent. This is low even by the standards of many Western countries, not to speak of developing countries with economies comparable to China's.

On the handling of death, as of birth, the Shanghainese are becoming moderns at a rate to startle anyone who fondly believed in some innate Chinese tendency to stagnant ways. Cremation, once objectionable to the ordinary Chinese, is all but universal in Shanghai (it costs about twenty yuan — one yuan is just over fifty United States cents). In rural Shanghai the last of the grave mounds have disappeared. They got in the way of tractors.

There used to be at Dragon Brilliance, not far from the famous pagoda in the southwest corner of the city, a forwarding station for coffins going off to the countryside. Many Shanghai people have rural origins and tradition required the return of an encoffined corpse for

17

burial in the home village. But the Cultural Revolution was not kind toward "old customs" like this. The forwarding station came under attack; its morbid work was wound up. Today the building houses a factory for cutting up metal ingots and steel plate.

Nearer central Shanghai is another former coffin house. This was a storage depot where the dead but not yet departed were left until relatives saved enough money to send the coffin to its far-flung destination. This custom was squeezed into extinction even before the Cultural Revolution. Today the former coffin storage depot is part of the Shanghai Machine Tools Plant.

The Shanghai worker hears and reads more news about the world beyond China than ordinary Chinese workers have ever received before. Newspaper and magazine sales have been going up by about 10 percent each year. Two hundred fifty thousand Shanghainese learn English, with the aid of radio lessons beamed four times a day by the Spare Time English Broadcast Forum. A textbook for the lessons, written at Shanghai Teachers' University, sells out within hours whenever it goes into the shops.

It seems ironic that the CCP, politically so anti-Western, should introduce English to the Chinese masses when the CCP's Kuomintang predecessors, so grovelingly pro-Western in politics, tried nothing on a similar scale. Once more it is the Communists who are the modernizers. No American city, one also notes, has 250,000 citizens, or even one-quarter that number, who study Chinese.

One little bonus is that plenty of compositors are now able to set type in English. At the Foreign Languages Press, there are no more of the spectacular errors on the non-Chinese printed page that used to tickle or enrage foreign Shanghai veterans. One British editor of former days learned in a jolting way how Chinese compositors set English words letter by letter, without knowing the meaning of the word or sentence. He was checking the page proofs of an annual Shanghai directory which his newspaper published. Noticing the name of a man who had recently died (and whom he disliked), he wrote beside the man's name, in reproof to the compiler of the entry, "This silly ass is dead." The Linotype man, alas, was not in a position to realize that

18

the five added words were not to be set; the directory was published complete with its stunning little editorial.

Sometimes a compositor who knew a little English was as lethal as one who knew none. Under a smattering of missionary influence, one Shanghai compositor of the 1870s, when setting the name of Lord So-and-so, would always put "The Lord." Another tried conscientiously but with bad effect to set a report on a Shanghai military ball which spoke of ladies adorned in their husbands' sashes. He possessed enough English to know that "ashes" was an English word, but he had never seen "sashes." He dropped the first *s;* the elegant ladies were said to be "adorned with their husbands' ashes."

Today it is almost unknown for the Foreign Languages Press to serve up a typographical error. The only one I recall was in an English edition of Mao Tun's novel about Shanghai life, *Midnight*. Intending to refer to "maxims" (of the ancient *Book of Rewards and Punishments*), the text says "marxisms." No doubt the compositor's English vocabulary was stronger on communism than on the classics.

For all its signs of modernity, Shanghai often has the air of a sprawling village rather than a big city. There is no fashionable quarter. Babies, bundles, casual clothes are as common in downtown Nanking Road as in the residential district of Lengthy Peace (Chang ning). You see flat baskets of beans spread out to dry on the sidewalks of city streets, fruit piled up for sale at the curb. There is virtually no organized distraction, however innocent, after nine-thirty at night.

The key traits of Shanghai's modernity are its youthfulness and its social character. Beside the rows of European bank and insurance buildings, the neat green trees are small and fresh. Many things in socialist Shanghai are, like the trees, in their early stages. The CCP is trying to remake Shanghai, yet it is not working on a tabula rasa but grafting new features on an old frame. Children are asked by the CCP to do things with their lives which their parents, however, are dubious about. The industry of new Shanghai is being dovetailed with the agriculture of rural Shanghai, but the link is not yet stable. Fights swirl around the class-analysis line on culture — as the Chinese press admits.

19

For all its signs of modernity Shanghai often has the air of a sprawling village. . . . You see flat baskets of beans spread out to dry on a city sidewalk

All the years of the three million Shanghai children who
are in school today have been post-Liberation years. . . .
How *he* turns out will define Shanghai's modernization

Veterans with long memories sometimes give a quiet, enigmatic
smile when asked in private if the Communists are achieving a truly
new Shanghai. There are clearly enormous improvements, they seem
to say; but remember human selfishness is a tough flint; in the end,
won't we have to wait and see?

The veterans cannot really answer this question. The scale of values
and experience on which they weigh it is itself part of what the CCP
is trying to get rid of. Only the young people of Shanghai can give an
answer, and it will come primarily in the pattern of their lives. All the
years of the three million Shanghai children who are in school today
have been post-Liberation years. Old Shanghai has cast little shadow
on a boy now at middle school. How *he* turns out in deed and thought
will define Shanghai's modernization.

Nor will we see Shanghai's real modernity if we use only the lens of
economy and technique (though it is striking that one month of industrial output today is far more than one *year*'s output in the 1940s).
What emerges slowly but rather surely in China is a social modernity
almost never found in a country still poor. Shanghai is unique in China
because no other city is at once such a center of advanced industry

21

and communications, high wages, and cultural activity. Shanghai is unique in the world for a different reason.

The social ligaments of its modernizing process were torn away after 1949 and replaced by new ligaments. Each step in the city's development now issues from the political line, which is mediated by priests of power, the generalist cadres of the CCP. The ethic which the cadres seek to plant in the eleven million souls of the municipality is "serve the people." Your chief concern is supposed to be how you relate to other people, rather than how you can get on. A kind of politics, or moral philosophy, outweighs what we in the West call economics.

This amounts to a sharp double take for Shanghai's modernization. The imperial city never let politics determine economics. It was not disposed to give social relationships priority over marketplace relationships. So although Shanghai was a quite modern city in many respects by the 1940s, its modernity has since then been refounded, with social morality as its keystone.

In Hong Kong there is held each year a "ghost festival." It is an affair of ritual and superstition (yet leading Chinese businessmen back it). Although there is a layer of substantial economic modernization on Hong Kong society, the spirit of most people is little touched by this modernization. In Taiwan there is a similar gap. Vigorous economic development, led by Japanese and others, has transformed the face of Taipei. Yet on another level altogether is the family life of most of the Taiwan people.

These two hanging hems of China's garment remind us of a truth. Economic modernization can roar ahead without social modernization. In China itself, by contrast, economic modernity is taking its place within a context of social modernity. From the people, much dedication is asked. From the side of government, much is offered (Shanghai industry spends on social welfare 20 percent of the amount of its total wage bill).

As impossible to find a ghost festival in Shanghai as to find a stock exchange. Semifeudal superstition can coexist with purely economic modernization (as in Hong Kong). But it stands directly in the path of social modernization. Traditions melt in Shanghai as they do everywhere, but less from the sparks of economic development than under the hot rays of a Promethean social vision. The chimneys and machines of Shanghai multiply, but they are not running away with the future. They are the furniture of a new moral house.

In the summer of 1973 I seek out an editor of my acquaintance to gain an overview of trends in Shanghai. Wang Cheng-lung, aged thirty-two, is a bright new son of the Cultural Revolution. He was only twenty-three when the review in *Literary Currents* began that storm. Over the next few years he swam strongly with the tide of Shanghai organizational politics. Of wider experience and higher education he did not have much; but in 1972 he became number two man at the same *Literary Currents*.

I had seen Mr. Wang early in 1973 in Boston, where he traveled as a member of the first-ever delegation of journalists from the People's Republic of China (PRC) to the United States. It was his first trip outside China. He proved a rather quiet visitor with a vacuum-cleaner avidness for drawing in facts and impressions.

Some months later it is a different Mr. Wang who strides in with a broad smile to my suite at the Hotel of Peace. Two staff aides come in his wake as befits a major editor. We are now on Mr. Wang's home ground and he is nothing if not enormously proud of Shanghai. The obvious fondness of his memories about the United States, too, puts him in buoyant spirits to welcome a return visit from a Harvard friend.

The sparkle of his mood and his good looks make him a dashing figure. The face is square with full lips, the wiry hair is cut short, the eyes have the glint of a man with few complaints about life. He smokes without stopping, clears his throat without restraint, and taps the toe of his leather sandal against the floor. There is a thrusting, no-nonsense, can-do style about Mr. Wang.

He reminds me of a cadre I dined with in Sian in 1971, also a man who came to the fore during the Cultural Revolution. This Sian cadre talked in blunt, almost juicy terms about the struggles of 1966–1968, stubbing cigarette butts into the white tablecloth as he went along. Mr. Wang uses an ashtray, but if one were not available he might use the tablecloth. When turning to an aide for a fact, or more often, for confirmation of an opinion, his tone is like the Sian cadre's: crisp but brotherly, a touch of self-importance in its confidentiality.

When the session is over I ask my Travel Service aide, a young married woman, her impression of Mr. Wang. As we sit in a theater waiting for the curtain to go up she replies: "Wang is very handsome and very able and he was very frank with you."

Like any editor, Mr. Wang talks of his newspaper as fondly as of his child, with intermittent efforts to be detached. *Literary Currents* sells 920,000 copies of its daily four-page edition (80 percent are delivered by post to subscribers). Mr. Wang estimates that four or five people read each copy. If so, the paper reaches about one-third of Shanghai municipality's eleven million people. This far exceeds the circulation of *People's Daily* in Shanghai, where it is read mainly by an elite of Party members. (*People's Daily* prints 3.4 million copies, 1.5 million in Peking, 1.9 million in ten other cities, to which page matrixes are flown or the copy transmitted by facsimile.)

Mr. Wang did not say so, but his paper was founded after World War Two with some assistance from the United States Information Service. Odd as it now may seem, some USIS personnel in China felt that this private newspaper (as it then was) would be a useful channel for pro-American opinions.

Nor did I raise with editor Wang the irritating fact that a foreigner is not permitted to buy a copy of *Literary Currents*. Like other non-Peking ("local") newspapers it has for some years been available only for internal use. If you try to buy it at a newsstand an attendant will suggest with a nervous smile that *People's Daily* would surely interest you more. The Peking paper certainly gives you an authoritative picture of the CCP line. It is partly because local papers may sometimes blur the picture that their circulation is restricted.

However, *Literary Currents* is available in two other ways to the foreigner. Many of its articles are broadcast over Shanghai radio (and monitored by certain foreign governments). When traveling in China I rent a radio set in my hotel room. Local newspapers are also pinned to notice boards on streets and in parks. Hundreds of thousands of Shanghai people who do not subscribe to *Literary Currents* stand and read it at these notice boards on the way to or from work.

During the week of Henry Kissinger's first shock visit to China in the summer of 1971, I watched a large crowd reading *Literary Currents* in a downtown Shanghai park. Attention was focused on two articles about the United States, one describing Long Island, one tracing the expansion of the original thirteen states to the present fifty. Both stories were sober, factual, without propaganda.

The paper is a morning one and in China morning papers are produced late. Unlike Western morning papers which are usually finalized in the early evening, *Literary Currents* is not put to bed until the early hours of the morning. The paper is usually printed after dawn and few people can read it with breakfast. Mr. Wang is used to being a night owl and he sleeps from 2:30 A.M. until 9:30 A.M.

The picture of Shanghai trends which Mr. Wang gives me has more engineering in it, and less rhetoric about it, than the one I get by reading documents at Harvard. What has been going on since my visit of two years before? Mr. Wang begins with a recital of the city's new construction projects. A forest of new factories rises in parts of new Shanghai such as Minhang satellite town; they make steam turbines, automobiles, boilers, and electrical equipment.

As a general policy, the editor explains, new factories are built on the site of old factories. In this way industrial growth does not disfigure the contours of the city. But plants are being built — as part of the satellites — on some land that only yesterday was agricultural.

So much major construction is slated that a recent technical breakthrough has been especially welcomed. The Shanghai Mechanized Building Company has long worked with a two-to-six-ton tower crane; very mobile but lacking guts for heavy jobs. Now the two-to-six-ton tower crane has been transformed into a fifty-ton mast-tower crane. It has three separate jibs which can hoist loads of varying weights to various heights. Mast cranes with a big capacity are generally not easy to shift about, but the new mast-tower crane is said to possess both merits. Five months of work, by a three-in-one team of workers, cadres, and technicians, produced the new crane. It has just been tested in hoisting 100,000 square meters of prefabricated building items.

Wang Cheng-lung warms to his theme that Shanghai has a new body as well as a new soul. A big new railway station has been started;

25

a TV tower is well on the way; a tunnel has been gouged under the Whangpu. No, an underground train system is not practicable. Shanghai, after all, lies on a bed of mud. To avoid sinking into it, some of Shanghai's skyscrapers float on concrete rafts set on top of the spongy mass.*

I was later to learn that the tunnel is not for ordinary traffic and cannot be inspected. It has never been mentioned, to my knowledge, in the press or in any public statement. It is probably considered an item of defense significance.

The absence of a means of crossing the Whangpu other than by ferry has long been an anomaly — the more so in recent years, with new housing growth on the eastern side of Yellow Banks district (the river bisects the present Yellow Banks district). As workers stream home in the afternoon, the hard-pressed ferries resemble those which link Hong Kong island and Kowloon. A busy one in Yellow Banks district is called "Extension of the Land" (*lu yan*); another in Mouth of the Rainbow rejoices in the name "Happy and Just" (*tai gong*).

Given the hazards of crossing the Whangpu in old Shanghai, it is ironic that a ferry was ever called Happy and Just. According to a nineteenth-century source, "the ferry-men, being greedy of gain, will not set out to cross over, until their boats are quite full, however boisterous the weather may be, so that the boats are frequently overturned." Beyond the danger of being spilled into the water there was a second problem. "The fishermen also fix stakes in the river, and stretch their large nets from one to the other, in consequence of which those who have to cross at night get by mistake into the net, and being engulfed in the stream are made fishes of." The ferries are no longer a hit-and-miss affair. Two daily crossings of the Whangpu are a bland routine for hundreds of thousands of Shanghai workers — pending the full opening of the mysterious tunnel.

---

* Between 1921, when the problem was first noticed, and 1965, Shanghai sank more than two meters. Dykes were built along riverbanks to hold back the tide, but only in the 1960s was the cause of the sinking hit upon and tackled. A cotton mill discovered — by noticing that pipes in its deep wells kept rising — that drawing out underground water caused the ground to sink. Now water is pumped back into the ground every year from October to April. Since 1966 Shanghai has stopped sinking — has actually risen by nearly two centimeters.

As a Shanghai cadre tuned in to modern ways, Mr. Wang is fairly conscious of pollution problems — certainly more so than cadres in smaller Chinese cities. Shanghai municipality, he reports, has set up an office devoted to the issue. One member of the revolutionary committee heads it full time. Each bureau and factory has been required to appoint a special team to deal with "the three wastes."

The Chinese always try hard to divide any matter into three parts. Gas, water, and slag have been named the three wastes which together make up the pollution problem. There is a policy of "double use." Waste is not discarded but turned into value. Dye works use the waste gas from producing hydrogen sulfide to make sodium sulfide. Caustic soda from textile mills is used in papermaking. Waste slag is turned into cement. Leather and paper scraps become fertilizer.

These days in Shanghai, Mr. Wang tells me, black smoke from the chimneys can be turned into "white smoke." But what of Soochow Creek; I just walked by the creek and it looks murky; does it still contain fish? Mr. Wang confesses that it does not. But he brightens and says this may not be true forever. "We think the fish can return in the future" (shades of purged cadres coming back after a mental cleanup!).

I do not think any foreign visitor can understand the Cultural Revolution. Some Chinese have told me even they cannot fully understand it. Mr. Wang's points about the Cultural Revolution, though, are not difficult to understand. He does not talk about it as a movement that touched men's souls. The Cultural Revolution, to Mr. Wang, was a source of fresh policies for Shanghai's development ("socialist construction"). Also important, if not stated by Wang, is the way the Cultural Revolution plucked him from the rank and file and set him among the elite ("responsible persons").

A hard fact is that since the Cultural Revolution more children than before can get a middle-school education. When the new school year began in August 1973, no fewer than three million of Shanghai's eleven million people sat down to full-time study in primary and middle schools.

Mr. Wang documents how the burden of basic education on the family has been lightened. Before the Cultural Revolution, the tuition fee for a primary-school pupil was six yuan for each of the year's two

27

terms; now it is three yuan. For middle school, too, the fee was halved from twelve yuan a term to six yuan. Such concrete gains affect millions who have to weigh every yuan.

Mr. Wang also speaks of new steps ahead in workers' and spare-time schools (*ye-yu xue-xiao*). He points with pride to the "July 21 Workers' College." It is an experiment in practical study at Shanghai Machine Tools Plant (a factory which grew out of a farm tools plant founded by the UN's Relief and Rehabilitation Administration).

Workers who missed out on an education are given instruction, without fee, to help them make a greater contribution to the factory. The name comes from a maxim Chairman Mao wrote on July 21, 1968, summing up the education line of the Cultural Revolution. Over the past six years the Machine Tools Plant has selected 150 workers from its workshops to study full-time at the July 21 College.

Crucial is the rule that after graduation the educated worker does not "escape" to distant pastures but stays at the plant and applies his new skills. This is education as a collective bootstrap operation for industry, rather than education as a path to individual glory.

It is characteristic of the Chinese way of establishing socialism that one heroic model is supposed to inspire emulators. Twenty-three full-time July 21 workers' colleges have cropped up, and tens of spare-time colleges, as well as full-time and spare-time general schools (equivalent to secondary level). All told, Shanghai has about 230,000 workers pursuing serious further education.

When he speaks of reshuffling of Shanghai personnel since 1966, Mr. Wang is implicitly explaining why colts like himself are now in senior positions. "More than ninety-five percent of the previous cadres came through the Cultural Revolution experience." Yet the gist comes in the editor's next statement: "Some cadres went up to higher positions, some dropped to lower."

Mr. Wang's figures in fact depict a thorough reshuffling. Fifty percent of the cadres at municipal level are new since the Cultural Revolution. Seventy percent of those at units below the municipal level are new. A lot of old cadres "came through" only in the sense that they were not banished. Clearly they are not doing jobs of similar responsibility to those they did before 1966. New blood pounds through the main arteries of the Shanghai body politic.

The new men are rather leftist (though this is not the most important thing about them). Fewer are military personnel than in any other big city of China. They are cadres who take for granted that technical advance is a central part of what is meant by socialist construction.

They are by no means only "new men"; more often than before 1966 they are "new women." And they are young; more alert with hope and ambition than laden with memory and experience. Of the 150 members of Shanghai Revolutionary Committee in 1973, a quarter are under twenty-five years of age.

Mr. Wang alludes to "two lines" but this partly means two generations. He recounts a "struggle between revisionists and true socialists," but this can also be seen as the circulation of elites.

When the affair of Lin Piao enters the conversation I get a similar impression. It is Lin's power-hungry scheming which exercises Mr. Wang. We are still one month away from the CCP's Tenth Congress — only after the congress is Lin denounced by name in the press. Cadres at lower levels do not use his name at this stage; they say instead "swindlers like Liu Shao-ch'i." But Mr. Wang talks freely of Lin Piao.

It is startling to hear the editor spell out how Lin "tried more than once to murder Chairman Mao." One attempt was made on September 12, 1971, as Mao traveled by train from Shanghai to Peking. Wang also describes, in a tone more excited than grave, Lin's night flight to Russia and the crash of his plane at Undur Khan in Mongolia. It is all recounted as an adventure story in which a bad set of men, after committing frightful deeds, lost out in the end.

No picture emerges that is both clear and convincing of wrong policy ideas embraced by the Defense Minister. And a fundamental question about Lin's apostasy brings a puzzling answer. Who were Lin's followers *in Shanghai* and what did they try to do? "It is not clear that Lin Piao had many serious followers in this city."

What exactly does Chairman Mao mean, I ask Mr. Wang, by his arresting new maxim: "Dig tunnels deep, store grain everywhere, never

29

seek hegemony." The sentence draws, I find, on an eight-hundred-year-old Chinese saying. And it extends an earlier slogan coined by the Chairman: "Prepare for calamities, protect the fatherland, do all for the people."

Mr. Wang does not say which country the tunnels are being dug as defense against. But the press is clear on the matter. Like the United States, the Soviet Union is today imperialist. It is "even more dangerous" than imperialist America, because it rises while the United States sags. Yet I wonder how deeply Wang feels about the threat from Moscow; certainly he fails to stress it. The imperialism Shanghai people knew and felt, one reflects, was from the West and Japan, not from Russia.

The storage of grain is a self-help measure to guard against calamities both natural and man-made. It expresses in a striking way how much weight the CCP puts on mobilizing people. For the government, Mao's directive is a spur to increase grain reserves. At the national level some 40 or 50 million tons of grain have been stored away (yearly grain output is about 250 million tons).

But the directive also has a message for each citizen: do not waste, and store grain in the house. According to Mr. Wang: "In most of China, half to one year's supply of grain is now stored at the household level."

To renounce hegemony is to renounce being a Superpower. But why does Mao address the exhortation to ordinary Chinese people? Can they affect whether Peking seeks hegemony in the world? Mr. Wang thinks that "never seek hegemony" is the other side of the coin from "do all for the people." The workers of Shanghai know from daily experience what hegemony means. They saw cadres get arrogant and lord it over workers during the 1960s; that is hegemony. They make products for Vietnam and other lands bullied by imperialism; this is serving the people.

In other words, says Mr. Wang, to avoid being a Superpower means to avoid slipping back from socialist ways in China's internal life. Here is Lenin's idea that imperialism is part and parcel of an entire social system. And Mao's idea that the *basic* causes of any event in international politics are internal.

30

What about the foreign students, from Vietnam, Laos, Africa, who used to study in Shanghai? Has this method for China to serve the oppressed peoples been abandoned? Mr. Wang furrows his brow yet seeks to reassure me. "It is true that we no longer have foreign students in Shanghai." But like the fish of Soochow Creek they are not gone forever. "We will have them again in the future."

On Joyful Undertaking Street in Black Bend district — a part of the old French Concession, north of a bend in the Whangpu — stands the stylish brick home of a former capitalist. It is surrounded by Shanghai landmarks. To the west is the villa where Sun Yat-sen lived. The Huaihai Park (named after a famous battle against the Kuomintang in 1948) is a little to the east. One of the city's modest skyscrapers, Brocade River Hotel, rises twelve stories over the hard brown streets.

The house itself, flush on the street without a garden, is gray brick with rows of pink bricks for decoration. Above each door is a semi-circular design in pink tile. It is a discreet house; only the second floor has windows.

In this solid bourgeois retreat the Chinese Communist Party was born in 1921. As the Communists prepared for their first congress, a local Sun Yat-sen follower, Li Han-chun, helped out with a meeting place. Li's elder brother, Shu-ch'eng, owned this gray and pink home.

Sessions were held in its living room, while the Li Shu-ch'eng family followed a domestic routine upstairs. One congress delegate representing Shanghai — Li Ta, later a famous educator — was a friend of the principal of a nearby school for refined girls. He made it possible for the delegates to sleep in the school's dormitory.

I walk into the historic living room of Li Shu-ch'eng's house, find it set up much as in 1921. Black doors with gold handles lead in from a sun-baked street to the high white walls and red screens of a cool salon. Near the entry the floor is stone; further in it is dark wood.

The room is dominated by a table, sacred bench of the First Supper of the original disciples of Chinese communism. It is arranged as for the 1921 meeting: teacups; a heavy cloth; round wooden stools. A few pictures of Mao, Marx, Engels, Lenin, and Stalin have been added, as

31

The table in a villa on Joyful Undertaking Street at which
the Chinese Communist Party launched itself in 1921

if to bless what was achieved here. But no leaping slogans break an atmosphere which remains that of a well-off Shanghai home.

Into this room a spy rushed at the start of the sixth session of the congress. He had chosen the wrong moment to snoop around; the twelve or thirteen* delegates were sitting at the table. Having to explain himself, the intruder mumbled that he had mistaken the house for another. But suspicions were aroused and plans were made to shift the meeting out of Shanghai (see page 177).

The house is now a museum, which I inspect in company with several People's Liberation Army (PLA) men. It is a sticky Shanghai July afternoon and the green uniforms cling to the unburly bodies of the soldiers. They keep their caps on but fan themselves incessantly in a way that does not seem military.

A tape recording recounts for them in rapid Chinese the events of the summer of 1921. I wonder to myself, do they ponder that the 1921 congress was totally civilian, that soldiers then served warlord and not left-wing causes?

The museum manager tells me the Cultural Revolution brought on a crisis at the museum. Red Guards came and found shortcomings in the exhibition of Party history which was previously a component of the museum. Pressed for examples, comrade Wang points out two errors that the "influence of Liu Shao-ch'i" had spawned. The exhibition was not harsh enough toward Ch'en Tu-hsiu, a founder of the CCP who later lost his way. It prettified Liu Shao-ch'i.

Omitted was any clue that Ch'en failed to attend the congress because he had given higher priority to working for a warlord in Canton. "Later, after three months of upsurge, he could see things were going better than he expected, so he returned belatedly to Shanghai." Nor did the exhibition say in plain terms that Ch'en disagreed with the revolutionary line of the CCP. It failed to make clear that by 1923 Ch'en felt the CCP had been founded too soon, and that it was too weak to lead a revolution.

This differs a little from the opinion of Ch'en held by many scholars outside China. It jibes ill with the fact that the congress thought well

* New research suggests thirteen delegates, rather than twelve as has often been thought; see reference in Sources.

33

enough of Ch'en to elect him secretary-general of the CCP. It omits the fact that the passionate scholar did organize in Canton a Communist group and magazine, and that he took there his journal *New Youth,* brightest jewel of leftism at that time.

Manager Wang confesses that even people in Shanghai have spoken up for Ch'en Tu-hsiu. "Some said, 'Well, after all, Ch'en was a founder of the CCP.' " Indeed. "Such a view, we now see, was put forth with the ulterior motive of stimulating a capitalist restoration in China." Could the link be made clearer . . .? "Liu Shao-ch'i said Ch'en was not a good Marxist. In fact Ch'en was a *sham* Marxist."

The exhibition had not drawn attention to the smallness of the early role of Liu Shao-ch'i in the CCP. It hadn't said Liu was not a Party member in the summer of 1921 — but only a Youth League member — and that he did not join the CCP until the end of 1921, in Moscow. It had glossed over Liu's betrayal of the Party in 1925.

Stepping out into sunlit Joyful Undertaking Street, I carry from the historic house two odd thoughts. It is hard to put oneself back in time and realize how weak those thirteen men seemed in 1921. Did any of them expect the Party to go, within one man's lifetime, from nothing to firm leadership of China?

The Shanghai authorities of the 1920s set a trap for them; yet half-hearted it was indeed, by the standards of Communist authority in Shanghai of the 1970s.

The original band were socialist dissenters in a capitalist world where freedom to *be* or *do* anything existed for very few. Yet they managed to run up a heavy bill against the account of capitalist freedom. The world in which they operated — the house, the press, the financial arrangements — was a capitalist one. Even the method of discussion around that table owed little to Communist formalism. They took advantage of it all in order to kill the system.

Such bold and brilliantly successful dissent! And now Shanghai is a city apparently so placid that no dissent is called for. A maelstrom of competing options has become a concrete plateau of settled triumphs — unless the apparent set pattern of things in socialist Shanghai is an illusion. One of history's direst messes has been cleaned up — unless history should stir itself to raise the same old issues in new forms.

Beside the gray and pink walls a crowd waves and my companion waits patiently for me to get into the car. I am turned inward on a second nagging thought. Many Communists from the early maelstrom failed to make it to the concrete plateau. Many, of course, died by a right-wing sword; five of the thirteen were fairly soon martyred. But of the six who survived the 1920s, four turned out to be what manager Wang calls "speculators" (the other two are CCP leaders today: Mao Tse-tung and Tung Pi-wu*).

The path from certainty in dissent to certainty in power is a perilous one, and the issues sometimes get lost on the way. So Ch'en Tu-hsiu suspected the Chinese working class was too small to make a revolution? Mao ultimately treated Ch'en's suspicion as observed fact and built his doctrine of revolution on it. And what of Li Ta the educator, a long survivor among the thirteen, appointed in 1921 the first propaganda chief of the CCP? He was harassed to death at Wuhan in 1967 by Red Guards. Fiery children of the plateau, who had never *seen* a capitalist society, accused Li Ta, who had fought for socialism in capitalist Shanghai of the 1920s, of being a capitalist!

As I drive away with my two odd thoughts, a remark of the brooding English revolutionary William Morris floats in the mind: "Men fight and lose the battle, and the thing they fought for comes about in spite of their defeat, and when it comes turns out not to be what they meant, and other men have to fight for what they meant under another name."

Another bit of sacred Communist history, also part of capitalist Shanghai's history, gathers around the former house of Lu Hsün. It is the last house the writer lived in, before he died of tuberculosis in 1936. I visit the house to reflect on Lu Hsün and see what Shanghai of the 1970s thinks of a rebel of the 1930s.

There was a knife-edge of glory and risk about the 1930s for Shanghai's radical writers. They passed a satiric rapier through the ribs of Chiang Kai-shek's reactionary order. Chiang in turn laid a heavy paw

* Mr. Tung died in Peking on April 2, 1975.

35

on many fine flowers of China's literary talent. Lu Hsün had to sarcastically entitle his polemical essays with a weather image — "Moon Chatter about Predicting the Winds" — because it was permitted to talk about the state of the heavens but not about the state of the earth. And he had to disguise his place of living.

In Mouth of the Rainbow a whitewashed shop front houses a branch of the Chinese People's Bank. Situated on busy Mountain Pass Road, it used to be a Japanese bookshop, serving the surrounding Japanese Concession. Lu Hsün bought books here (he had studied in Japan and learned its language) and he used the shop as a cover. An employee of the bookshop was the tenant, on paper, of a nearby house which Lu Hsün rented from 1932 until his death.

Last of the hunted writer's three Shanghai abodes, it is not large but poured over three levels. Its nooks and crannies have all been freshly painted in healthy green and cream. The rent, says a guide whose own house-rent in the same district today is a mere four yuan a month, used to take one-third of Lu Hsün's income. But the household could afford a maid, who slept in the boxlike third-floor attic.

There is a sedate old Gramophone; his wife's sewing machine; candles for use in the frequent power failures. Tables are covered in a homely way with linoleum, worn shabby-smooth and smelling faintly bitter in its old age.

It looks like a writer's house, with occasional signs of being also a depot of clandestine politics. On the study wall hangs a calendar which stops at the date of its owner's death. The picture for that month of October 1936 is a sentimental one of two lovers against the sunset. At the desk is a manuscript written in the left-to-right fashion that only much later became usual in China. Lu Hsün's books are curtained off in a cabinet, not available for inspection (as those in his Peking house are).

The house was opened as a Lu Hsün museum in 1950, but reorganized in 1956, on the twentieth anniversary of Lu Hsün's death. The museum was moved from the house to a site by Mouth of the Rainbow Park. Lu Hsün's ashes were moved from a cemetery in western Shanghai to the same park.

Chairman Mao wrote an inscription in his own hand for this tomb of the contemporary writer he most admired. Lu Hsün's son planted pine trees to the left and right of the seated statue. The precarious man of irony became an establishment man of stone. Not far from the park I even notice a "Lu Hsün Cinema."

Mao's handwritten words, "Mr. Lu Hsün's Tomb," catch the eye since no one (except a foreigner) is referred to as "Mr." in China these days. It would not have been right, I suppose, to say "Comrade," since Lu Hsün never joined the CCP. The bronze Lu Hsün is wearing a scholar's gown, which is also now a thing of the past.

Mouth of the Rainbow Park is a pool of quiet verdure at the far end of the old Japanese Concession. The railroad to Woosung runs hard by its westward fence. Beyond it to the north the crammed city districts give way to the semirural counties.

This park was a favorite of the *taipan* in imperial days. One clucking missionary account of Shanghai published in 1916 called it a "genuine godsend to foreigners remaining in the city during the summer." To its forty-five acres they went "for golf and tennis, securing the exercise so necessary to health in this Eastern climate."

Today, under the same cypresses and maples, folk from Mouth of the Rainbow read, chat, watch cultural shows. In the early morning many do *tai-ji-quan,* the rhythmic, snakelike exercise which is good for health. People are apparently so familiar with Lu Hsün's tomb that none look at it. But children scamper along the granite blocks which surround the statue.

The memory of Lu Hsün became a political football in literary circles during the 1960s. One reason for this was the role of Chou Yang, a literary tsar of the CCP from the early 1930s until he was pushed out in 1966. On Lu Hsün's desk when I visit the house is the manuscript of an angry piece called "Reply to Hsu Mou-yung and the Question of a United Front Against Japan." This piece criticized Chou Yang.

Lu Hsün felt that Chou Yang and his friends were being too rigidly purist about who was worthy of the struggle and who was not. Chou Yang stood for literature that would serve "national defense." Lu Hsün adopted a more flexible, yet more radical, slogan: "a people's literature of national revolutionary struggle." Looking back, it is an interesting irony that Mao eventually purged Chou Yang, a Party faithful, and made a hero of Lu Hsün, a non-Party rebel.

Another character in the churning drama of literary politics from the 1930s to the 1960s was Mao Tun, one of the two or three finest novelists of twentieth-century China. Child of Chekiang province and long-time resident of Shanghai — like so many Chinese writers — Mao Tun helped Lu Hsün found the League of Left-wing Writers in 1930. During 1932 he wrote *Midnight,* a mirror to the bittersweet life of Shanghai when money was king and socialism no more than a dark cloud on the horizon.

From 1949 until 1965 Mao Tun was Minister of Culture. Chou Yang was his important lieutenant. Since Chou was a Party member, while Mao Tun was not, the lieutenant sometimes acted as a general. Mao Tun was presiding over a sphere so studded with dilemmas that after the Cultural Revolution the Ministry of Culture did not resume operations until 1975.

Today Mao Tun is not considered a shining case of what a writer in socialist China should be like. My English copy of *Midnight,* published in Peking in 1957, has a frontispiece with the author's autograph and photo (dressed in a Western suit). Since the Cultural Revolution, Mao Tun is published no more, and never is *any* novel adorned with a smooth studio portrait of its author, wearing a Western tie.

These ructions of the past hover like ghosts in the trees as I survey Lu Hsün's tomb in green and calm Mouth of the Rainbow Park. The statue is dour (the Chinese are not very good at statues) but better than it used to be. When first erected, I find, this image of China's great son was in concrete. Whether it was Chou Yang who chose such a utilitarian mode is not clear. But a cadre from the Lu Hsün Museum, Mr. Yao, says it was not Mao Tun's fault.

Anyway, a fresh voice prevailed five years later. On the eightieth anniversary of Lu Hsün's birth, in 1961, the concrete statue was hauled down and a bronze statue went up in its place. Mr. Yao throws dust in the eagle eye of my speculation. "The decision to change from concrete to bronze was not taken by the Ministry of Culture alone, but by the whole government." I look closer and indeed the new monument has the stamp of the highest state authority.

The gold letters say the Shanghai city government erected it, but under the terms of a proclamation by the State Council of the central government China's cabinet). Maybe Chou En-lai took the matter out of the hands of the nest of snakes which was the Ministry of Culture. The 1961 gold letters do not reproduce Mao's surprising "Mr." They read not "Mr. Lu Hsün's Tomb" but simply "Lu Hsün's Tomb."

During the Cultural Revolution fresh storms burst over the dead Lu Hsün and also over the living Chou Yang and Mao Tun. A shocking discovery was made by Red Guards who came sniffing at the museum. Lu Hsün's angry piece against Chou Yang, "Reply to Hsu Mou-yung and the Question of a United Front Against Japan," was absent from the list of his works. Indeed, the museum exhibit — says Mr. Yao — stated that this essay was not really Lu Hsün's, because it had been transcribed by an unfit colleague, Feng Hsüeh-feng, who had twisted its meaning. Big-character posters went up on every available wall. There was hell to pay and Chou Yang had to pay it — his opportunistic past caught up with him.

Criticism came to verge on rampage; the Lu Hsün Museum closed to lick its wounds. "Historical sites have to be protected." From this remark of Mr. Yao's I gather the closing in 1966 had a double purpose: not only to correct errors in the exhibit, but to keep ultraleftists from expressing their rage in a physical way.

It seems that even Lu Hsün was criticized by Red Guards in Shanghai (though not in Peking). When I ask Mr. Yao about this he makes a sparse reply: "*Everyone* was criticized during the Cultural Revolution" (did the Red Guards find fault that he sometimes wore a Western suit and tie, and sometimes a scholar's gown?).

When the museum reopened, the staff, curiously enough, was unchanged from pre-1966. Only the big fish Chou Yang had to atone; the little fish swam on into post-1969 political waters.

In downtown Yellow Banks district, on Foochow Street which features cultural shops, new editions of the works of Lu Hsün are on sale. Cuts are restored and errors smoothed out, compared with the editions done under Chou Yang's aegis in the late 1950s. Now all may freely read the "Reply to Hsu Mou-yung," and weigh Lu Hsün's irritation with Chou's party formalism. The volumes I buy, put out by Shanghai People's Publishers, enjoy a print run of one million copies.

Lu Hsün is a famous institution in new China. His former houses in Shaoshing (his hometown in Chekiang), Canton, and Peking are also museums; parks in Dairen and Tsingtao (a big port north of Shanghai) are named after him; there is a Lu Hsün Institute of Art in northeast China. You may buy postcards of him and his homes at Nanking Road stores. He is quoted whenever a sharp phrase free of current jargon is desired. His opinions are a stick to beat cultural workers who are thought wayward.

But what do the Chinese people today think of Lu Hsün? How to tingle to a satirist, if there is no longer much evil and folly to satirize? And an audacious question: can there be another Lu Hsün in late-twentieth-century China?

A museum curator is asked if there exist successors to Lu Hsün. "Every Chinese person who reads Lu Hsün," she answers, "is a kind of successor to Lu Hsün." That can only be true in a very limited sense. A reader today may be gripped by an extension of the feelings which gripped Lu Hsün during his own historical epoch. But does Lu Hsün ring more than the bell of historical memory? I put this question to Kuo Mo-jo, one of China's best-known writers. Mr. Kuo answers that Lu Hsün's *method* remains valid. Its expression in present-day China, however, cannot be the same as in the 1930s.

This eminent veteran of many struggles recalls that Lu Hsün wrote in a revolutionary and critical period; "he used his pen as a dagger." Were Lu Hsün alive today, the tone of his writing, Mr. Kuo feels, would certainly be different. "His weapon would not be a dagger but a spiritual atom bomb." I think Mr. Kuo means by spiritual atom bomb the ideas of Mao.

There are two themes, Kuo the writer who is also a government leader reflects, which Lu Hsün would surely press in the 1970s. "He would write in praise of the new culture of workers, peasants, and soldiers, who are taking hold of the philosophy of Chairman Mao." A second theme seems in tune with Lu Hsün's debunking cast of mind.

"He would certainly seek to puncture the arrogance of the two nuclear Superpowers."

Shanghai today has writers who spin out at least the first of these themes, but Kuo Mo-jo does not make high claims for their work. The novel in particular, he thinks, is well below the level of great Chinese novels of the past such as *Dream of the Red Chamber.* On the other hand some quite good shorter works have been written and "await publication."

Another foreigner asks Mr. Kuo in private conversation who is the best writer of fiction now at work and being published in China. "Hao Ran is very popular these days," comes the reply. The foreigner inquires how good Hao Ran is and Mr. Kuo says: "He is very good." The foreigner raises a comparison between Hao Ran and Lu Hsün. Kuo Mo-jo looks at him sharply and declares: "You are talking of two entirely different questions."

It is not easy for a Chinese writer of the 1970s to match the quality of Lu Hsün. Nor is it easy to describe and explain the gap. Kuo says the trouble is that authors still come from the ranks of intellectuals. They do not heave and sweat and laugh and cry with the masses. But does he really mean that Chinese writers are more divorced from the people after Liberation than they were before?

Look around Lu Hsün's house, see what kind of life he led, and you realize there is another reason. Lu Hsün's pen was a dagger because his own life was often that of a conspirator. He shared with the Shanghai masses around him an outrage at the existing order of things. His style had a truculent pride; he murmured as he died: "People ask to be forgiven, but I ask no one to forgive me." Here is the daring defiance of a crusader.

It is not that Lu Hsün wrote for the masses. His essays reached an elite of a few thousand, not to be compared with the millions who have read Hao Ran's *Bright Sunny Days,* a novel about peasant life under socialism. Lu Hsün's writing was important as tissue nerving the resistance to an *obviously unjust* order.

Hao Ran, by contrast, is a purveyor of political food to the masses. He offers back to the people skillful images of their own bland life in the new China. There is no dagger on his desk because there is, among

41

the people around him, no widely shared outrage at an obviously un-just order. Irony finds no soil in blast furnaces and housing schemes. Only a neurotic socialist remains alienated after the capitalist enemy has given in.

Yet there are dark patches to China's life; why are authors seldom the ones who uncover them? I see two reasons. The printed page, even more in socialist China than in dynastic China, is thought of as a positive norm. Only now and then is it a place where current battles about what is right and wrong are fought out. The public prints crystallize the way.

A reinforcing factor is the way conflict is dealt with in China's political system. Major political squabbles, like birds which fly over from behind, are known about — by ordinary people — only after they have gone by. Political tension does not stalk the country in Watergate style. It is bottled up at the top in a few (literally) smoke-filled rooms. When a conflict is more or less resolved, the new line — or lineup — is offered in the press and plays and stories as a finished garment of public policy.

The writer cannot readily join in a live political controversy. Fiction in China deals with a settled recent past. It popularizes lessons about past episodes that politicians have already drawn. Hao Ran writes about dark patches in China's life, but only after they have been diagnosed as dark patches. Even the arrogance of the Super-powers is not a safe target for a writer's dagger. Today's friend can become tomorrow's Superpower. China's enemy in the morning can lie with her in the evening.

No writer to my knowledge has set a story in the future. In the nature of things it would not be easy for him to do so; the future is untouchably golden until it turns into a packaged past. Writers may well be more important in today's China, because there is a massive literate audience, than ever before. (When a recent Shanghai novel, *Spring Breeze Through Willow Branches,* had a first print run of 200,000 copies, that was only par for the course.) But they can only be taillights on the locomotive of public policy, not headlights for its path.

So a bronze image is the nearest thing to Lu Hsün that we are likely to see in Shanghai. He sits there dead and cold; high in the air as if he is on a ladder rather than a chair. There are no pens which are daggers, and if there were they would sink not into flesh but into the cotton wool of abstract error.

As I walk away from Lu Hsün's granite bed Mr. Yao intones that here lies China's greatest literary man of the century. It is true, yet I wish he were singled out less. To quote ever and again only Lu Hsün, which is the custom of the Chinese literary press, is to draw a black curtain over quiet dozens of brilliant modern Chinese writers. The official literary scene is like a landscape from Kweilin in southwest China; one dazzling sheer mountain on a flat plain. Above is Lu Hsün; in the marshes are amateur writers and writing groups.

Lu Hsün was a brilliant man yet also a participant in a dialogue. Could he feel happy as a Kweilin mountain? (Rewi Alley, a friend of Lu Hsün's, once showed me the last photo ever taken of him. He was chatting with a student and autographing a book, a few hours before his death.) Nor did Lu Hsün equate literature with propaganda. "All literature is propaganda," he remarked, "but not all propaganda is literature."

It is amazing how often socialist Shanghai talks about capitalism, how insistently a visit to Shanghai evokes thought about the bitch-goddess of capitalism. Twenty-five years of Liberation, yet not quite liberated from this specter. You see no sign of capitalism, but it remains a psychic dragon, to be looked in the eye and slain.

Three images of the strange and intimate bond this dragon has with Shanghai: Lu Hsün, great foe of capitalism, yet whose frame of reference was the capitalist era and not this socialist era. The big gray and pink house where the CCP had its first congress, where socialism was hatched in the nest of capitalism. And Wang Cheng-lung of *Literary Currents,* confessing that Lin Piao tried to "restore capitalism." The number two man in China wanting to tear off the new tunic of socialism and put on that sweaty nightdress of a past affair!

Innocently I had thought capitalism lost years ago the power to attract the minds of men. But the socialist world's biggest urban

43

bastion is not only a concrete child of capitalist activity, but takes seriously capitalism in its most wispy form, *as an idea.* Can I understand the dialogue which Shanghai in its young bones has even now with the whore who happened to be its mother?

Imperialism has become a verbal chip in China today, but it used to be a matter of naked power in Shanghai. To call someone tinged with capitalism is as easy in the China of the 1970s as it was to call someone tinged with communism in the America of the 1950s. Yet in old Shanghai, capitalism was not an epithet but almost a religion.

Capitalism in China was too serious a matter (in the foreign view) to be left to the Chinese. That is why twenty boardrooms in the forty square kilometers of the foreign settlements became the control tower of Shanghai's money-making life.

To recall the flavor of settlement life, start with the racecourse, on Bubbling Well Road a few kilometers west of the Whangpu. The British imperial elite could never feel at home without a racecourse, and they presumed to feel at home in Shanghai. The smooth green racetrack, fenced off a decent distance from the smelly crush of Tibet Road to the east, expressed their serene confidence in the future of European power on the China coast. The mellow and racist clubrooms, not open to Chinese though financed in part from Chinese taxes, bespoke their gentle contempt for the people whose country they had chosen as a place for business and sport.

Chinese ponies were welcome but not Chinese people (except in the "Public Stand"). The rule did not spring from simple race prejudice; Japanese, Filipinos, blacks were members. Rather was the rule a subtly woven institution of imperialism, which Britons refined into an art. It was because Shanghai belonged to China that the *taipan* could not afford to look Chinese in the eye.

Division into two moral worlds was, in fact, the psychological secret of the foreign settlements. The Chinese and the foreigners could effectively coexist at business. They used each other — though the bargain was lopsided. But had the two elements ceased to be oil and water and tried to blend, the settlements would have been doomed. The two sides had to lie to each other in order to live with each other.

44

Settlement Shanghai had a hit-and-run economy and a kiss-and-run society.

A Chinese who played along smoothly with a *taipan* had to inwardly suspend — or pretend to — his existence as a Chinese in a time of swelling Chinese nationalism. He had to make a fiction out of Shanghai; to carry on as if it were not part of his homeland, but some chariot of commerce in the clouds.

The foreigner was not only a willing partner in the lie but its creator. He had been strong enough to turn this fiction into an established fact. Shanghai was run by a municipal council controlled by foreigners. It was not that Shanghai was a Western city; less so than is Hong Kong a Western city today. Even within the settlements the population was more than 90 percent Chinese. Shanghai was simply a Chinese city which, for the time being, had to sing to a tune played by foreign power.

The fiction of Shanghai became an export and the world heard about a city that was the "Paris of the Orient." A Shanghai newspaperman noticed an ad in the *New York Times* for a stunning new product called *parfum de Shanghai.* The irony itself was pretty stunning and the Shanghai paper commented: "Sniff! Smell that lotus in the languorous Shanghai breeze? Well, you may be trying from the wrong spot." It really seemed as if that Shanghai perfume could better be sniffed at Sterns in New York. A true *parfum de Shanghai,* the local man felt, would combine the essence of "garbage, sweat, pig-pen, garlic godown, kitchen-midden, whale's innards, and the gent's room at North Station."

So much did the foreigner need to believe in the fiction of his "international Shanghai" that he dug himself in as if for the ages. The European commercial houses were more solid than any buildings the Chinese had ever bothered to put up. The British imported bearded Sikhs from India to police the International Settlement with solid blackjacks. The French brought in smiling Annamese (Vietnamese) to patrol the boulevards of their concession. Gardens were laid out with English horticultural passion. Perfect Tudor mansions appeared. Churches went up, bricked in as if with eyes averted from the infidel temples around them. Foreigners went about the arrangements of imperialism, in short, as if they were erecting a granite monument, not just burglarizing an outhouse of the Chinese nation.

During the earlier decades of the settlements it was possible for the *taipan* to live as if Chinese society did not exist. A British description of the settlements, Maclellan's *Story of Shanghai,* could sum up and conclude its section on the later 1880s this way: "The only event worth noting, which has occurred in these years, is the celebration of the Jubilee of Her Majesty Queen Victoria, which was held on the 21st. June, 1887. But the weather was so rainy that the illuminations, fire works and procession were postponed till the following Saturday" (meanwhile France and China fought a war over Annam).

If the British love parks and created some nice ones in Shanghai, they did not love to see a Chinese enter one. The frightful but famous phrase, "Dogs and Chinese Not Admitted," arose because of regulations posted (until the late 1920s) at the gate of the Bund Garden. I have not seen any old signboard with these exact words, but the phrase sums up the meaning of regulations at the Bund Garden. Among a list of forbidden actions — like picking flowers — one was taking a dog into the park. Another, further down the list, read: "No Chinese, excepting work coolies, are admitted."

Of a different Shanghai park a foreign memoir noted in 1916: "Chinese are not admitted to the Gardens, except nurses with foreign children, unless dressed in foreign clothes or accompanied by a foreigner." A crisp explanation was given for this rule: "This is to keep the grounds from being overrun by the coolie class."

The creaky but vital mental bridge between the *taipan* and the Chinese around him was pidgin English. The foreigner very seldom tried to learn China's language; it was up to the Chinese to learn a bit of his. They did it by selecting a salad of key English words, salted with Portuguese and Indian words, forgetting all syntax — including tense, which hardly exists in Chinese — and uttering them in the up-and-down tones of their own monosyllabic tongue. The result (first in Canton) came to be famous as pidgin English. It was one of the more raffish bastards to issue from the intercourse of two civilizations on the China coast.

The term itself richly reflects the kind of traffic the mental bridge was built to carry. "Pidgin" is a pidgin-English pronunciation of the word "business."

If the presence of Filipinos and Japanese in the Race Club suggested that imperialism was more than a question of race, so did the rather humble position in Shanghai society of the White Russians. Some twenty thousand of the sixty thousand foreigners living in the city by the 1930s were refugees thrown adrift by the Soviet revolution. They had sailed down with their bundles and trinkets from Vladivostock in 1923. Or they had drifted in later via Harbin, then Tientsin, to fish with unaggressive hopefulness in the wider waters of Shanghai.

As the British topped the hierarchy of foreigners — though they never numbered more than ten thousand — the unbusinesslike Russians formed its bottom layer. They did not have the sharp commercial edge to enter fully into the fiction of imperial Shanghai. The former aristocrats among them sold their rings and watches and bracelets to get funds for daily needs. None had the capital for big enterprises. Some opened bakeries, flower stalls, restaurants, beauty shops. A few took their place among yellow faces as beggars in the street.

But the White Russians (to be distinguished from a small band of Red Russians at the Soviet consulate by Soochow Creek) became famous mostly for the glamour-pathos of their female half. Detached and practical Shanghai had great need for a prostitution market. Already by 1864 it sported 664 brothels. In 1934 *Reporter* (*Shen pao*) judged that one person in 130 in Shanghai was a prostitute (compared with one in 960 in London, one in 430 in Chicago, one in 580 in Berlin). By 1949, the CCP said it found thirty thousand prostitutes at work in the city. The British did not officially permit brothels in their settlement; the French licensed them.

Thousands of White Russian ladies were among the favorite prostitutes at the brothels on Foochow and Szechwan streets. They were available as companions for a dinner dance at the Cathay Hotel, or hostesses at a loud, gushing evening in one of Shanghai's one hundred ballrooms. It was not that they were prettier than the willowy girls with almond eyes from Soochow (though their busts were bigger). But

47

should a *taipan* crave white flesh — and balk at closing with another man's wife — he would take a plump, pale, powdered Russian miss. There was a category for all occasions in old Shanghai — and a price.

During the earlier years Europeans seldom ventured beyond the settlements into what they called the "Chinese City." But it was considered fun to watch Chinese houses go up in flames within the settlement boundaries. Here is a feature story from the *Shanghai Mercury* of 1881.

The writer recalls from his childhood a Sunday school magic-lantern show of "Celestials struggling to extinguish a fire" raging in a pagoda (in those days foreigners with a sense of style called Chinese people "Celestials"). Then he bids to rouse his readers: "But such a scene as that was a very poor representation of what a fire in a Chinese quarter really is, and of course it did not include the best half of the scene which we witness frequently here — the work of our Volunteer Fire Brigade."

Two maxims are suggested to the foreign resident of Shanghai who wishes to enjoy himself at a Chinese fire. "It is not always at the biggest fire that the most fun is to be seen." And much depends on the weather and time of day: "If there is not a breath of wind blowing, it is very aggravating to turn out to a small affair where there is no chance of its assuming interesting and exciting proportions, and a small fire at midnight comes to be reckoned as a fraud and a delusion, as it is scarcely worth going to see."

By a good Chinese fire, bear in mind, the writer means a fire in a crowded part of Shanghai. He describes one in Mouth of the Rainbow to which he had recently rushed in high hope. It began in a stack of reeds, "situated in the heart of a number of small Chinese houses." The Volunteer firemen in red jackets came streaming over Soochow Creek, the less agile ones in rickshas. "Hundreds of Celestials" were milling about.

But alas, circumstances were not favorable. "There was not a breath of wind, else the bamboo shanties all round would have fed the flames." The fire remained rather small, though some houses were wrecked, either by the flames or by the "heavy boots" of the doughty volunteers.

48

A number of Chinese occupants "frantically" tried to save what they could of their furniture and possessions.

In the end the sporting instinct found little outlet. The foreign spectators gathered around the ruins, "expressing in forcible terms their opinion that the thing wasn't worth coming to see . . . wishing they had not come out to see a pile of reeds blazing without a breath of wind."

The *taipan* seemed to treat their Chinese helpers like children, and to view the society around them less as part of human history than as one of nature's spectacles. An American missionary at the time of World War One describes the "unique charm" of the boat life along the "Chinese Bund" (the Whangpu riverbank south of the French Concession).

Miss Mary Gamewell moves delicately along the waterfront and applies her lens. "Each tiny sampan swarms with life as if it were an ant-hill. The occupants are permanent house-holders and their habitations are anchored." Certainly a smooth way to characterize these desperate refugees from famine in northern China. Notes this stroller on the Bund who has a nice job in Methodism: "The wives add a little to the [family] income by gathering rags to make into shoe soles and by patching and darning old garments for coolies without families." (On another page of her memoir Miss Gamewell reassures us that the coolies have not been forgotten: "There is a Christian mission for the ricsha coolies. It was started four years ago by a Scotch business-man on whose heart had been laid the spiritual needs of this neglected class.")

"Planks set on stakes serve as footpaths to connect the boats with the shore, and little toddlers run about on the narrowest of them at will, yet rarely tumble into the water or soft mud below." A happy whim of Providence that only an occasional toddler gets drowned or buried in mud.

One should not be too gloomy, anyway, about spasmodic disaster. "Births, marriages, and funerals lend variety to the life of the boat people." Marriages and births, you might suppose, had a slight edge over funerals as a favorite spice of variety. But Miss Gamewell has the faith to detect a silver lining in any of God's clouds. "Two or three empty coffins usually stand about on the wharf ready for an emergency, and are meanwhile useful as benches, especially for the women when they sew."

Miss Gamewell apparently found no direct place in her conscience for the Celestials. Here is what she calls a "quaint scene":

> An old Chinese woman, with all her winter padding on, tried to cross a downtown street through the maze of traffic. Ten yards or so from the pavement an electric tram car caught her full in the chest and propelled her neatly on to the further track, where another car caught her in the back. The second car pushed her staggering under the feet of a ricsha coolie drawing a Chinese cook home from market with a load of vegetables, a ham and two live ducks. By the time the old lady had disentangled a flapping duck from her elaborate head-dress and the coolie had wiped the ham clean with his dirty sleeve, all the traffic of motor-cars, wheelbarrows, and broughams had been held up, and it took some minutes more of hard work to get the innocent cause of the trouble safely back to the spot from which she started.

It is easy to make fun of this prim missionary's view of things in settlement Shanghai. Yet she was less, not more, callous than the ordinary Shanghai foreigner. On the other hand, her well-meaning instincts do not raise her above the moral level of a harsh *taipan*.

She did not view the Chinese people as full human brothers and sisters, so she did not apply to them the same scale of values that she applied to the Imperial Race. Her morality was not permitted to irrigate at all the bleak plateau of her perspective on the Chinese — except in the worse-than-nothing sense that she sought to save their souls. This aspiration made her, if anything, more contemptuous of the Chinese as she found them; the better to justify her divine mission to turn them into Christians.

If there were moral flaws in the foreign settlement arrangement, there was also the practical flaw that it could not last long. *Taipan* Shanghai's first assailant was a steadily rising tide of nationalism.

Shanghai had not been an early bastion of Chinese nationalism. It was a city where individuals relied on their wits to do what they could for themselves, more than a city where collective Chinese moods found expression. This was because Shanghai was on forced loan to foreigners. The *taipan* was indeed able to divide and rule Shanghai. Most Chinese lacked the power to challenge the foreigner. Some — the compradors who worked for Europeans — were too entangled with imperialism's uneven bounties to want to try.

One old Shanghai hand of Australian origin speaks of Christmas Eve, 1936, as his sharpest memory. A holiday cabaret was unrolling at the Metropole Ballroom. The well-to-do crowd was 80 percent Chinese and out for a lark. Suddenly the dancing stopped and the Filipino bandleader turned to the microphone. A telegram had been brought to him and he read it to the gaudy assembly. Its gist was that Chiang Kai-shek had just been released from captivity (at the hands of his own colleagues from Manchuria, who wanted him to fight Japan more and the CCP less).

The several thousand dancers rose and cheered. Fresh music began and the Australian then heard a song he had never heard before in all his years in Shanghai. The pleasure-seekers fervently sang the national anthem of China — twice.

Unusual for Shanghai to show national emotion and salute a national figure. But it did not remain so much longer. Resentment against the foreigner had been deepening since World War One. A sense of China's need to pull itself together as a modern nation in a competitive world had been growing behind the Bund. The ripples became a tidal wave when Shanghai was attacked by Japan (second assailant of the *taipan* setup).

Before the storm, the Japanese had been quiet junior partners in the fiction of Shanghai. They had their neat and mannered "Little Tokyo" in Mouth of the Rainbow. They had about two hundred million U.S. dollars invested in the city. On the municipal council they had a voice, though it was a whisper compared with that of the British.

The Japanese assault on Shanghai — limited in 1932, massive in 1937 — was the beginning of the end for the foreigners. Japanese soldiers slayed and brutalized. Mouth of the Rainbow Park they degraded into a fortress, drilling there as they shouted tuneless songs. They became the strong men of Shanghai and not even the Sikh policemen dared apply the traffic laws to their brown trucks. Every shop run by a Japanese subject had a guard posted outside it, to defend it against "anti-Japanese sentiment." The Japanese had broken ranks with the *taipan,* called the bluff on the Shanghai fiction.

The other foreigners were caught in an impossible position between the Japanese and the Chinese. Tokyo had shattered the delicate balance of imperial Shanghai by doing with blunt directness what the British had more or less done in a back-door way. They took Shanghai by the throat. Both their violence and the passion it aroused from the Chinese were altogether outside the range of the settlement harmony's agreed tones.

If there were now two worlds, it was no longer the Chinese and the foreigners, but aggressive Japan and outraged China. In this confrontation the *taipan* had no role. He could only lower his profile and look to his chests and his ledger.

After the shock of 1932, the British tried to edge a bit closer to the Chinese (who now had a government, based in Nanking, that took more interest in Shanghai than had previous Chinese governments). But the new openness was too little and too late. None of the governments standing behind the Shanghai foreigners was prepared to resist Japan. On the other hand, the world of the *taipan* was still far too separate from the world of the Chinese people to permit any effective solidarity between the two.

The European could not start looking the Chinese in the eye now, when his life in Shanghai had long hinged on avoiding exactly that. He probably knew, in his heart, that the Japanese had torn away the decorous drapery from hard realities which could no more be hidden. Shanghai had sunk to its unhappiest state ever; curse the Japanese for that. But Shanghai was also stirring with a new and political spontaneity. This held the promise of Shanghai's finding its true Chinese self; the *taipan* could only be a victim at such a dawn.

After the defeat of Japan in 1945 the Nanking government of Chiang Kai-shek took over Shanghai. The foreigners had to step back from the front rank of control. Within five years the third and final assailant of the imperial order struck. This time the foreigners stepped out of Shanghai, body, soul, and probably forever.

It was a measure of *taipan* Shanghai's fiction that most foreigners were only half-aware of the CCP during the 1920s and 1930s. Mao Tse-tung must have been just a piece of the quaint furniture of the city for Miss Gamewell, when he came to Shanghai in 1919 to help friends who were sailing to France as foreign students; and again in 1920, to study Marxism with Ch'en Tu-hsiu, while supporting himself by working in a laundry.

When he worked in Shanghai from 1923, as a member of the Central Committee of the infant CCP, Mao was no more than an irritating mosquito of subversion, buzzing without consequence on the tough hide of imperial Shanghai. How few foreign residents of Shanghai knew that the CCP held its Second Congress (1922) and its Fourth Congress (1925) in their city!

Even the massacre of left-wing workers by the newly arrived Kuomintang forces in 1927 did not ruffle the tenor of business and missionary life. It was hardly more than a sideshow for the *taipan*, a proof, for the few who had reason to cast an eye, that extremism had no future in Shanghai.

There were some left-wing Westerners, above all Edgar Snow, who followed very closely the gathering cloud of the CCP. But these people were outside the mental world of the settlement lords, who considered them, too, to be buzzing mosquitoes.

It was rated a joke when the CCP declared war on Japan in 1932 (while Chiang's government prevaricated). Yet it was the CCP's attitude to the Japanese attack on China that clinched Shanghai for socialism. Mao tapped the tide of nationalistic feeling against Japan for his Communist cause. The three assailants of the *taipan*'s world merged into one — and Mao got the booty. He then faced the enormous task of replacing the capitalist blood in Shanghai's veins with socialist blood (of this more in a moment).

✿ ✿ ✿

I walk about the city to see if any ghosts remain from settlement days. But I am a Western man picking through the ashes of Shanghai's Western past. Not much less than the *taipan* was, I am caught in a trap of cultural difference. I admire this new Shanghai; yet my bones respond with indecent excitement to trappings of the old Shanghai.

I am defensive about this fondness for Shanghai. A Shanghai woman says one day as we drive through the ex-imperial city: "Many foreigners like Shanghai best of all the Chinese cities; what about you?" I feel an odd resistance to expressing the liking for Shanghai which she wants to hear. With studied vagueness I murmur that Sian and Hangchow are fascinating cities . . .

A Westerner in Shanghai sees how the new broom of socialism has swept away unlamented debris from the past. But he may also feel that the broom jabs at his own feet. He is forced to ask how much of his reaction to China is the cultural particularity of a Westerner, how much the political sympathy of a socialist. He wonders if there are *any* universal values, stronger even than culture's bonds, than the divisive memory of the West's wrongs against China.

The Bund has been deimperialized as Sun Yat-sen Road. Its old name was an Anglo-Indian term; "bunding" was the embanking of a muddy foreshore. The new name is a safe wrap-up term to express the united Chinese people's emergence from subjugation by foreigners.

The esplanade is surely prettier than it has ever been. Once during the settlements there was a pleasant park between road and river; the municipal orchestra entertained foreigners there each Saturday night. But later the embankment became a mess, clogged with streetcar and railway lines, cargo depots, ricksha stands, parked cars. The CCP government has turned it into an ornamental garden, full of strollers and sportsmen both morning and evening. The northern segment is enclosed as Whangpu Park, popular for its shady seclusion with couples in search of peace and privacy.

At 5:00 A.M. I slip out of the Hotel of Peace and find the waterfront alive with early birds doing *tai-ji-quan* and other exercises. Beyond the hotel steps, there extends on each side a long raised ledge where the sidewalk meets the building. Their small black work bags laid to one side, dozens of people are doing push-ups, feet on the ledge,

I find the waterfront alive with early birds doing *tai-ji-quan* and other exercises

The experts have spectators, the beginners are by themselves

hands at the curb edge of the sidewalk. The heart of Shanghai is not for show, it is clear, but for benefit and use. What a change is this zeal for sport! In old Shanghai Chinese used to look with pity and humor at Westerners who went in for physical exercise.

One row of trees hugs the Whangpu parapet; six more run through the gardens; yet another row lines Sun Yat-sen Road. Their branches mingle, the red and green like a public Christmas tree, with vast crimson signboards that urge new efforts for even greater victories. Around the garden beds are fences in fan-shaped concrete pieces, a row of white hands with fingers straining toward the leaves. The golden morning light is as vivid as theater lights, reflected on the green leaves and the greasy brown shoulders of sweating youths.

The *tai-ji-quan* goes on in decentralized clusters up and down the esplanade. The experts have spectators, the beginners are by themselves. Some wield swords, spears, sticks with a flag on the end, and wide knives like scimitars, in versions of *wu-shu* (martial arts). There is a special sand-covered arena for *wu-shu,* its fifteen-foot walls dwarfed by a huge oblong block, like a giant's matchbox, on which are painted revolutionary tableaus from CCP history.*

Two girls are gently entangled, like necking deer, in a slow duet that is half dance, half gymnastics. A boy leans against a tree watching their every twist, his liquid yellow arms joined in a handclasp behind his back. Three old men raise their arms in a flourish, as if they are orchestra conductors, spurring invisible musicians to richer tones. Children too small or timid to join in squat on concrete blocks along the garden paths, lending a family touch to the purposeful scene.

I sit on an oblong block myself, to watch at closer range a youth who has found a quiet corner for his exercises. He prepares himself with leg movements, bouncing his head down to his ankles which rest on the fence. Then he launches into rapid *tai-ji-quan,* springing in the

---

* Later, during a theater intermission, a Shanghai official asks me whether I notice any changes in Shanghai since two years ago. After I mention a few, he points out that *tai-ji-quan* is more popular. The same official did not agree with my usage of *wu-shu* to describe the sword and scimitar play seen by the river. He prefers to think of it as just one branch of *tai-ji-quan.* This is not the custom, however, among people met at random in the street, who refer frequently to *wu-shu.*

air, crossing arms and legs like scissors, turning a warrior's brow now to the river, now to a cluster of technicolor palms behind us.

His trousers are spotless white cotton, his singlet is dappled in two blues, from the sweat exacted by the heavy summer air. A small boy who gravely watches volunteers that this youth is his elder brother and a dock worker. In a neat pile on the parapet are the docker's canvas belt, tunic, and helmet, to be donned in an hour or so. Beside them is a plastic-covered manual of mechanical engineering.

Through the trees the skyline of the old Bund tapers toward the former French Concession (where the Bund was called Quai de France). These domes, ornate cornices, and Greek pillars used to dignify the steady throb of commerce. Now they seem mocked, for they enclose organs of working-class political power.

There is the heavy edifice that once housed the Hong Kong and Shanghai Banking Corporation. Two shiny bronze lions with paws neatly aligned still flank the important-looking doorway. But a red star is mounted high above the door, like a Mao badge on a dull tunic. The bank has become the seat of socialist power in Shanghai: office of the municipality's CCP committee and revolutionary committee. Its door is now guarded not only by the bronze lions but by two armed soldiers of the PLA.

And there is the pivotal Customs House, which seems to have *taipan* Shanghai written on its solid features. Its famous bell tower still stares out over the muddy waters which link Shanghai in trade with the world. The chimes are no longer a single baritone chord, but the self-conscious phrases of a political song, "The East is Red."

Listening to this pervasive tune at 6:00 A.M., I recall a moment during a banquet at the Hotel of Peace two years before. Gough Whitlam, since 1972 prime minister of Australia, was being entertained by Wang Shao-yung, vice-president of the Shanghai revolutionary committee, craggy-faced veteran of political work in China's Third Army. Mr. Whitlam had passed a disturbed night, partly due to the Customs House clock. He quipped to Mr. Wang: "That clock is indeed an imperialist relic which should be got rid of."

I look down to earth again and beside me in the garden is an artist.

In meticulous charcoal strokes this young man is sketching the high anachronistic skyline. The former German Club (now a Chinese bank). Sir Victor Sassoon's Cathay Hotel, one of nineteen hundred buildings the British tycoon owned in Shanghai (now Hotel of Peace). The old Palace Hotel in homely English brick, which was bombed in the Japanese attack (now the Chinese-guests section of the Hotel of Peace). The Shanghai Club, which used to be very British and claimed the world's longest bar (now, I think, a gymnasium). The American Club building (now housing trade organizations). A cluster of British, European, and Japanese banks. Some are still banks but festooned with banners that say "Ten Thousand Years to the Chinese Communist Party."

I want to ask the silent artist a string of questions. Why does he choose to draw these archaic aunties of imperialism? What feelings do such buildings evoke in him? Does he know what went on in each building before Liberation? But there are several people besides myself looking over his shoulder. I don't want to embarrass him or disturb his concentration. The questions are not uttered.

Beyond Whangpu Park toward Soochow Creek the prework crowds are no thinner. The old British consulate stands as before amid its velvet lawns near the confluence of the two rivers. But there are no longer British diplomats in Shanghai (nor any others except Poles). The building is now a pleasant club for sailors. North of the club is an open space bordering on Soochow Creek which is a favorite spot for morning *tai-ji-quan* and evening gossip.

A group of youngsters from a middle school are practicing the martial arts (*lian wu-shu*). Their bright singlets and loose white trousers are dazzling in the yellow shafts of morning light. A fresh kind of shirt must recently have gone on sale, for several wear the same new crimson T-shirt with a white *V* across the chest. Many have the stylish stance, expressive, flattish faces, and long legs which mark them as youth of Shanghai.

Along the stone wall lapped by Soochow Creek, a row of smooth yellow legs are perched, a hand grasping each ankle as heads pop up and down in disciplined exertion. The thud of badminton games carries from Soochow Road, which borders the creek on one side and the high wall of the old British consulate on the other. This street is brightened with young maples, tied with skeins of cotton to supporting stakes, like docile tethered ponies.

Flat brown transport boats with protective covers are moored on the adjacent water. When the covers come off, green motor cabins are revealed at each bow, which gives the boats the appearance of trucks skimming half-submerged in the water. At the first bend of the creek, the central post office flaunts its serried Greek columns and green-capped clock tower. It is a faithful sample of nineteenth-century British Empire style. At the top of each column sits a massive white Chinese character. The row of twenty-two of them is like a wide grinning mouth of teeth, calling out the message of ten thousand years to Mao and the CCP.

A half-timbered structure in the Tudor manner on the south bank has lost its power to attract attention. It blends now with the grimy, functional buildings that service the boats. Few among the morning crowd would know, either, that a nearby building once housed part of the United States Navy.

From the top of Shanghai Mansions, urban and industrial areas fill the horizon. Where the Soochow enters the Whangpu the waters are marbled in dissenting shades. The blue currents of the creek give way, after a struggle, to the steady caramel flow of the larger stream. There are war boats, ferry boats, and boats with ribbed sails like maroon shells. There are passenger liners, fishing trawlers, freighters by the dozen, small barges tied together like beads on a string that snakes its heavy-pressed way from one dock to another. The boats that are *not* to be seen are foreign military boats, a fixture in these waters from 1843 until 1949. .

On the far bank stretch the roofs and chimneys of the dock area, East of the Bank (Pu dong), formerly a district of its own, now part of Yellow Banks. It is softened by trees planted since Liberation, and by the large East of the Bank Park. Upstream on the Whangpu, adjacent to Sun Yat-sen Road and separated from it by a triangle of trolley-bus wires that seem, from on high, to be scratches on the earth, a row of foreign and Chinese cargo ships are tied up. Gantry cranes swing back and forth with bales that once broke the back of coolies.

The blue currents of Soochow Creek give way to the
steady caramel flow of the Whangpu

It is nearly breakfast time and I head back across the former Garden Bridge* to the Hotel of Peace. These street crossings have automatic traffic lights, which are far rarer than traffic policemen (just as often policewomen) in Chinese cities. On the metal girders of the bridge are pasted some simple notices which are striking for their random appearance. They do not resemble the red and white slogans on other fences and buildings. Looking closer I sample some informal citizen exchanges.

One small notice in handwriting, stenciled or carbon-copied for multiple use, is by a citizen who wants to shift house. He gives details of where he lives; the street, how many square meters of space, the facilities in his apartment. He explains that he wishes to reside nearer his place of work. He appeals to anyone who may see this notice and be interested in swapping apartments to phone him at a given number. This simple sheet is an unusual sight in China: a message and appeal which issues from no Party or other institutional unit but from a lone individual.

At the northern end of the bridge I come upon a similar black and white notice the size of a page in this book, pasted on a telephone pole. It is also an unauthorized plea from an ordinary man with a problem. Its business is stated in a quickly scrawled heading: "Missing Person." A thirty-nine-year-old woman disappeared from her house some two weeks ago (maybe it is the wife of the writer of the notice). It is earnestly desired that she return safe and sound. An address and telephone number are appended. "Revolutionary comrades are please asked to make contact if they know anything about this case." Amid the tight network of organization which is Shanghai today, it is strangely moving to see that rough little cry for help. A minnow has slipped through the net.

Back in the dining room of the Hotel of Peace I meet the first real live imperialist relic of a morning which seems old at 8:00 A.M. The breakfast menu contains a surprise in the form of "Jam Soufflé." My

---

* Now called Wai bai du qiao, an interesting name which means "Bridge on the Site of the Free Ford on the Outskirts (of the City)." When Shanghai was small, and its inskirts of today were outskirts, this bridge offered a toll-free crossing of Soochow Creek.

resistance to a jam soufflé is low, at any hour of the day, and I order it. The dish is large, light, and scrumptious. I ask the waitress to compliment the chef. His response, alas, is to send out a second soaring soufflé. A further move on my part seems required — beyond eating the succulent monster — so I inquire where the chef picked up the recipe. The reply comes back from the kitchen as surely as had the second soufflé. The chef acquired it in the early 1940s, when he was an employee of the Hotel of Peace's previous incarnation, Sassoon's ugly but fabled Cathay Hotel. But for *breakfast* . . . ?

Nanking Road was never broad or grand enough to be the Champs Élysées of the Orient, as someone once termed it, but it was Shanghai's great road. It remains so in the 1970s; the narrow sidewalks bear one million shoppers a day. Today no one calls it Great Horse Road (Da ma-lu), the popular name during earlier settlement years. It has been widened in spots and trolleybuses have replaced the trams (moved to the outer city belt).

Traffic is mostly the bicycle and the bus, and it moves down the right, whereas it used, under British influence, to move on the left. Long gowns and dresses no longer swish against the pavement; trousers have taken their place. The sidewalks are wider, smoother, and better designed against the rains. Concrete slabs have replaced the old mixture of broken stones and clay.

Though the buildings are still mainly of two stories — dwarfed now and then by a department store — curved roofs in traditional style are rare. The department stores are much as they were from the 1930s onward, except that foreign and luxury goods are virtually absent. There is no admission fee to get in — and keep sightseers away — as there once was at Sincere's Store. No more shop signs written vertically in gold paint on black boards. They are functional, nearly all horizontal, and often duplicated in romanized letters of the CCP's *pin-yin* system.*

* *Pin-yin* simply means "spelling"; the full term, *pin-yin wen-zi* (phonetic system), refers to Peking's official mode of turning Chinese characters into romanized words.

Maybe there is more order and less variety to Nanking Road than in settlement days. Gone are the professional letter writers who sat at tables with brushes at the ready, to put on paper what most people could express only in speech. Portrait painters no longer create, from an oral description given them, the likeness of a dead person. Today there are municipal-run photo shops.

No more old-style portable cookshops, made of bamboo with a tin firebox and ingenious compartments for the food, which the cook carried on his back from place to place. Nor the ever-present smell of sandalwood, burned as incense in the temples. It is the paper and glue and plastic of commercial life that you smell in Nanking Road today.

I take a long walk from the waterfront to the former racecourse. It is the bright, hot midday hour. Cane matting is drawn across upper-floor windows of the shops, to give shade in a part of Shanghai where trees are sparse. Only one oasis of greenery do I come across in these business blocks of eastern Yellow Banks district. It is a small street garden with benches and shrubs. The spectacle here is quite moving. Cripples are at exercise. They have come through the streets in their wheelchairs. Some now struggle out on crutches; others stretch a limb here, test a limb there. Nurses supervise these efforts, helped by folk who seem to be volunteers from the crowd.

Shoppers — even some on bicycles — hold black umbrellas against the sun. Older men wear straw hats of standard Western shape. Arms and legs are mostly bare to the golden rays. Now and then a black armband stands out against a white shirt; its wearer is in mourning, and may leave it on for a week or more.

At a "people's market" the service has been streamlined. It might shock some Western students of Chinese cooking — if they seek to be more pure about the art than the Chinese — that ingredients can now be bought in pre-cut-and-blended combinations. You just take the package home and put it in the pan. This is Shanghai's first giant step toward the TV dinner.

There are sample tables near the entrances which save a lot of trampling and pushing. Inspection is done at these tables, where everything available that day is represented. Choices made, the customer is ready to order when he reaches the appropriate counter. It's a great help in Shanghai's really big markets, where up to ten thousand people shop at once.

Among the quick Shanghai faces and neat Shanghai clothes, you readily notice country folk who are on a visit to the city. They gape at things in the street (as do I). Their skin is generally darker from work in the fields. Their posture is less erect and their gait more shambling. They wear broad hats and carry enormous bundles.

I am approaching the Number One Department Store, near the crossing of Chekiang Road and Nanking Road. Suddenly comes a nudge in the ribs, which is not common in China. A rough-hewn character who is very tall indeed is grinning at me as I turn to face him. "You're pretty tall, eh?" he repeats loudly. It is true that both of us are taller than the average pedestrian. Maybe this disarming card is an out-of-towner, warming to a comradeship of size with another obvious out-of-towner.

Strolling through busy streets you inevitably see trifling incidents, a reminder that new China is alive with fallible humans, not decorated with smiling saints. Against the glass window of a "cultural products store" a schoolboy in a hurry wrongly rests his bicycle. A uniformed traffic policeman strides across, lays a hand on his shoulder as he enters the store, and ticks him off with a flush of anger. Hardly anyone notices this, but another incident draws a large circle. A cyclist has apparently approached the corner of Fukien Road at too high a speed, and nearly hit two heavily laden women shoppers. The frowning women angrily accuse him, drawing a traffic policeman who does the same. Sixty people watch, a few murmuring opinions to anyone interested.

On a different occasion I see a quiet little dispute, right by the Hotel of Peace, which does not come to any policeman's attention. A large middle-aged woman on a bicycle sharply bumps the elbow of a man with two children. The man protests quietly but earnestly to the woman, but she is for some reason rather petulant. Eventually she just wheels her bicycle off, while the man with a child in each hand steadily repeats that she should come back and reason the matter out.

West of the cultural products store, opposite the International Hotel, I am riding one of the loping, creaking trolleybuses. Off the Number Twenty bus steps a rather self-possessed man of middle age, with silver hair and a brown portfolio under his arm. Both the bus and the sidewalk are thick with lunchtime crowds. Still the bus conductor has noticed that Silver-hair did not pay his fare.

The young conductor sticks his head out the window toward the offender and says loudly: "Hey, you with the bag. Come back and pay. You're robbing the state." Silver-hair has been identified at least to those close by. He looks uncomfortable yet at the same time defiant. He moves steadily down the sidewalk, his lips moving in some swallowed remark. As the bus starts to move the agitated conductor cries again: "You shouldn't do that. You're robbing the state." I look around at the faces of my fellow-straphangers. Quite impassive; no strong feelings toward the little drama. Nor did anyone on the sidewalk take any physical step to get Silver-hair to come back and pay (the conductor did not ask their help, and they had but ten seconds in which to give it).

Yellow Banks district and its backbone, Nanking Road, are sufficiently anonymous that an odd sight causes no murmur from passersby. I am near the corner of Nanking Road and Sun Yat-sen Road, an eye on six elderly women who approach in single file. Something they are carrying glistens like orange peel in the sunshine. They come nearer and I see their pale flat faces. They look bored. Some chew mechanically on gum. Each of the six carries eight fine violins, four clutched in each hand like so many lobsters. But hardly a soul looks twice as the forty-eight mute violins bob along the sidewalk.

A sight very odd for a Westerner meets me at the bottom of Foochow Road. Nestling with hilarious incongruity behind the Shanghai CCP headquarters is a Tudor mansion! It looks like a large and comfortable English inn. Cozy half-timbered walls; steep tiled roofs at diverse angles; windowpanes in diamond-shape design; flower boxes built into the windowsills.

When the British brought their civilization and unpacked it on the China coast, they did not rest content with a selection of contemporary glories alone. As if in guilty awareness that their money-making bent was not John Bull's only aspect, they included this salute to England's

65

own preindustrial quaintness. It belonged to McGreggors', a liquor firm.

The Tudor mansion has not been as big a problem for the CCP to deal with as have churches (see pages 68 and 380 to 383). It has only a body, hardly a soul. The building is now a service adjunct to the CCP offices, and never gets a second glance from people who walk by. It is the transportation depot, where the use of cars and trucks for official purposes is regulated.

The courtyard — built into the mansion's belly as in stagecoach days — is a parking lot where vehicles await the need of Shanghai officials. Early in the morning you see many cars leaving to fetch their passengers. Some are small; others are larger with curtains to shield an important figure from sun and stare; most but not all are Chinese made. In 1971 the Tudor mansion was red with Mao quotations, as if blushing at being found in unsuitable company. By 1973 most of them have gone.

Among the specialty stores on Nanking Road are well-stocked TV shops, though sales assistants say — one knows this from visiting homes — that a sale to a private individual is rare. Pricing forays permit a strong, double general impression. Daily necessities are cheap (and stable). It's not strange, then, that people look well supplied with basic needs, despite their low wages. But goods which are out of the ordinary are pricy. A nice pullover for 18 yuan, a basketball for 20 yuan, a good pair of gym shoes for 5½ yuan, a TV for 350 yuan. No mystery, either, that the people of Shanghai cannot blast the trumpet of conspicuous consumption.

My camera is not working so I go into a large dark shop given over solely to cameras. A man in his thirties examines the shutter release, which has stuck. The camera is Japanese and I am doubtful that he can fix it. But in ten minutes the job is done, and he explains exactly what has occurred. I say he must be a true *nei-hang* (insider). He smiles and a few customers cheer. Japanese cameras, the man observes with modesty, are not very different from Chinese cameras.

Unlike this *nei-hang*, many younger Shanghai shop assistants are newly placed "educated youth." They are middle-school graduates who may hope for further study, but who for the time being serve as

66

envoys to help crossbreed intellectuals with workers. You find them cleaning and waiting in the hotels, and in the inns (*lü-guan* or *lü-she*) where ordinary Chinese travelers stay. You are served by them in magazine shops, laundries, barbershops, restaurants, bathhouses, photo studios.

One can understand the need for new recruits at the photo shops, for there are a staggering number of studios in this area of Shanghai. Here is a family all dressed up for a studio portrait. A girl stands shyly at the counter waiting for the finished shots of her boyfriend. Sample photos of class groups or work groups hang against soft curtains in the display windows.

My eye is caught by a portrait of a PLA man in the window of this Nanking Road shop. He holds himself stiffly and his mouth looks stern. A warrior, a member of China's 2.5-million-strong PLA, maybe a veteran of the Korean War. I glance toward the counters of the photo shop where a score of people press their orders. A middle-aged woman in a bright floral dress, three friends who may be industrial workers, two girls who seem to be twins.

I return my gaze, as if with fresh eyes, to the portrait in the window. The uniform is rather striking in green with red touches; the eyes are soft when you look into them; are the features not squarely handsome? The man is a warrior of the PLA, to be sure . . . But see his picture as a moment set on paper from the human hubbub of that photo shop. You then recall that he is also a husband, a neighbor, a grandfather.

After a glimpse of the shops in Shanghai of the 1970s, glance back at Miss Gamewell's chapter, "The Lure of the Shops." Here she is on Nanking Road shops at the time of World War One.

"On a bright morning nothing is more delightful than a leisurely stroll up and down Nanking Road for a study of the shops. . . . Coffin shops are of necessity very numerous. . . . Phonographs are commonly found in the better class barber shops . . . the work-day [for apprentices] is from sixteen to nineteen hours a day. . . . A 'tenderloin' district centers about Nanking and Foochow Roads; men shake their heads at the mention of it and women avoid it if possible" (did men shake their heads sideways or up-and-down?).

Just off Nanking Road in Tibet Road stands the former Moore

Memorial Church, a center of Shanghai Methodism. Its brick tower stares out toward the racecourse, as if in reproach, or to mark a tacit agreement that religion and money would share authority in *taipan* Shanghai.

Until the Cultural Revolution worship services were regularly held here. During 1971 I found it closed for a period of "struggle, criticism, and transformation." On each side of its elegant arched gate there rose a huge red billboard with yellow headings and white characters. They were faded — having been painted at least four years before — but the message was clear. The Cultural Revolution must be carried through to the end.

In the different atmosphere of 1973, the Tibet Road church is also different. The two red billboards, like oversized eyes beside the arched nose of the gate, have disappeared without a trace. The gate itself is no longer heavily boarded up. Push-out windows are open and there are other signs of life within the precincts. But worship services have not resumed at this relic of one world which stays on to vex the next.

In the surrounding streets I detect another change, to the humble pedestrian an improvement, from two years before. The defense shelters have nearly all been completed, so the sides of the road are no longer torn up like fields after plowing. Yet many Shanghai streets are still tricky to negotiate for another reason: building materials lie stacked at the curb and on the sidewalks.

In nearby Foochow Street the hunter for books also finds a distinct improvement between 1971 and 1973. The Foreign Literature Bookstore is open, which it was not before, and well stocked. Here Shanghai residents buy textbooks to accompany the English radio lessons. The Shanghai Bookshop is being renovated, but will soon reopen. Close by is the Antiquities Bookshop, rich in old books and scrolls (such items had a bad season during the Cultural Revolution). Residents say all this marks a big change since pre-Liberation, when foreign books and sex pamphlets were the only literature you could buy in this part of Shanghai.

A temporary notice at the Shanghai Bookshop refers buyers to various branches of the New China (Hsinhua) Bookstore. I move a couple of blocks north and find the East Nanking Road branch. Inside its spacious halls is a novel feature of new Shanghai.

Several floors are crowded with as many customers as you will see anywhere except in a department store. The ground floor has various kinds of books for sale. To one side is a new section with no books for sale yet more popular than any other. Three Chinese characters hanging over it say: "Book Rental Division."

A notice dated June 1973 explains the reasons for this innovation, which seems strange, even suicidal, for a bookshop. The huge demand for new books, "from workers, peasants, and soldiers," cannot be met by the publishing houses. So a shop whose business is selling books now also rents books — for one fen daily (a hundred fen make one yuan) over a maximum period of fifteen days. Today ten branches of the New China book chain in Shanghai offer lending-library service. Six to seven hundred people each day check out books or pamphlets from this East Nanking Road branch.

The ground-floor rental section is only for comics and other light items. It operates in two ways. Benches are provided and the comics may be read on the spot without charge. Or they may be checked out of the store at the low rental fee. Curiously, there is not a single female among the rows of eager comic-readers of all ages, nor among the lines waiting to check out items for home use.

I mount the echoing stone staircase of what must be — in floor space but not in number of volumes — one of the largest bookstores in the world. One whole floor, a hundred feet or more in length, is devoted to technical books. Another of similar size houses works on social science. Maps and posters abound as well. There is one counter for braille editions of basic works by Chairman Mao — vast tomes like family photograph albums.

Many shelves contain books by Marx, Engels, Lenin, and Stalin, reflecting the fact that some fourteen million copies of their works have been published in Shanghai over the past two years. But the four European sages attract few customers the day of my visit.

On the top floor of this literary beehive is a rental section far more extensive than the one for comics on the ground floor. Here are works of politics, science, and literature (all in Chinese). They are being snapped up, both in place and for loan, mainly by young readers. Survey books on world geography are popular among users of the reading room, as are thumbnail political sketches of foreign countries. One boy with a big white bandage on his head is lost in *Dream of the Red Chamber*. A girl furrows her brow over the *Communist Manifesto* (it is striking to watch a Chinese student devouring this German classic with a spoon so archaic, and so different from the heavy fork of the German language, as the picturelike Chinese characters).

One workingman, his tool kit on the table beside the book, is reading an *Outline History of the United States*. I peruse a copy of this forty-seven-page booklet by Shi Zhan. Published in 1972, it has seven chapters, beginning with "The Semi-colonial Era" and ending with "The Falling of the Star of U.S. Imperialism." Four pictures have been selected to illustrate the work: portraits of Washington, Lincoln, and Jack London, and a photo of New York dock workers on strike.

The East Nanking Road branch began its rental service, according to bookshop officials, over the opposition of Liu Shao-ch'i followers. These tightfisted revisionists could not see past the point that a bookshop should sell books and make a profit. They forgot that the spreading of a "socialist new culture" is the true business of a bookshop.

Further west along Nanking Road, where the road used to change its name to Bubbling Well Road, I reach the racecourse. It is now a quiet cultural shadow of its former sporting self.

The main grandstand has been refitted as part of the Shanghai Central Library. People's Square has been built on the southern side; it is now the favorite spot for a large rally. The rest of the racecourse grounds have been laid out with trees, pools and rocks, as People's Park. Thanks to the British passion for racing, residents of central Shanghai enjoy one large oasis of greenery.

The mellow old clubrooms look shabby and deserted, proof that splendor is not intrinsic but a thing of fleeting circumstance. No more horses wearing woolen blankets in winter, silk in summer, eating eggs and drinking champagne while their grooms half starved. In recent years, the smooth green racetrack has been torn up to make way for underground defense shelters.

To the south in the former French Concession, the old greyhound stadium has also been liberated from its past ways. This Canidrome — as the French called it — is now a cultural center with a hall that seats twelve thousand. If you see dogs cavorting here now they will be "running dogs of imperialism" — characters in a revolutionary play.

Nanking Road is one of the few streets in Shanghai which does not fall dead after 10:00 P.M. One evening I go to an acrobatic show at the Children's Art Theater, in Tranquillity district (which it isn't). The theater lies a few miles west of Yellow Banks district and the waterfront, but still in downtown Shanghai. It used to be a film house. During the 1950s an American, Gerald Tannebaum, took the lead in converting it for stage shows.

The air is warm and dry and my host agrees to let our driver go and to return to the hotel on foot. The last part of our ninety-minute walk will take us eastward along Nanking Road.

A Westerner who feels instinctively afraid of cities at night would not stroll here because the sidewalks are quite dark. The street was never well lit, but that was made up for by bright illumination of shops and night spots. These days the streetlights are the smart mercury-vapor type, but they are few. Establishments which are open are lit only for bare necessity, not for show. The result can seem eerie until you realize that everyone except you is used to it.

For the first half hour the streets are quite busy. Many people are, like us, returning from theater or cinema. Toward midnight activity slackens but does not stop. Country folk are bringing their vegetables into town for sale tomorrow morning. The buses continue to slouch along all night on a reduced schedule.

There are quite a lot of day-and-night (ri ye) stores which are open twenty-four hours. We see restaurants, barbershops, medicine shops, food supply shops, even a large department store, all of which are ri ye. At these stores, people can also ask directions, buy monthly bus tickets and postal supplies.

My host, Mrs. Wang, is a relaxed Shanghai girl. Her mother, who slipped in beside us at the acrobatics, has gone home on the bus, and Mrs. Wang is not counting the minutes. She is a conscientious cadre who also loves Shanghai and enjoys immensely her work of showing

71

it to visitors. She has enough confidence in me and/or the people of her city to welcome random encounters. We stop here and there to chat with Nanking Road's night people. Many of them are on the way to or from shift work. But there are folk who do not fall into this category.

One *ri ye* barbershop has a few clients and also several chain-smoking barbers, who sit around amid mirrors and hair clippings playing Chinese chess. We wander in and the late hour seems to bestow informality. They do not interrupt the game, except for breezy introductions, but a young barber who has been sweeping up offers to explain the chess moves to me. So here we sit, at midnight in a hair-cutting shop, poring over the chariots and ministers of a game which has been played in China since the T'ang dynasty.

Boys whom you would expect to be in bed at this hour stand and watch. Their arms are folded in the boneless Chinese manner; hands not tucked in behind the arm muscles but hanging out loosely. They whisper to each other in rapid Shanghai dialect of which the only words I understand are "foreigner" and a reference to my sandals (which I am wearing without socks).

Spurred to better my knowledge of the thousand-year-old game, I buy a set five minutes later at a general store. It has been made in Black Bend, just south of where we stroll, by a company with an interesting name: Factory for Bakelite Products of Residents Returned from Abroad.

There is no more of the gambling of all kinds which used to electrify the Shanghai nights. The card game *bai-fen* is being played by groups on little stools or on the steps of a building, but not for money as far as can be found. It is more common in Shanghai than it was during and soon after the Cultural Revolution (though less so than in the night alleys of Dairen).

Occasionally someone comes by who looks a bit of a swinger or even a modified hippie. Tight pants on a boy; a touch of makeup on a girl; eyes that cruise around. Some of these strollers may be overseas Chinese on a visit to China, but it is a mark of nighttime Shanghai that you cannot always be sure of the distinction.

At the tall, ornate Hotel for Overseas Chinese we linger with a dozen young people. Here the distinction is clear; these gay youths are Hong Kong residents up for a week's stay in Shanghai. It is not surprising that they find Nanking Road a bit tame after the nonstop availability of their own city's Tsimshatsui district. But one youth praises Shanghai with a remark that hangs in the mind. He is eighteen years old, works in Yuk Tak Bathhouse on Prince Edward Road in Hong Kong, and has come here to visit relatives. How does he find the way of life in Shanghai?

"The standard of living is not very high. But, oh, the people have freedom." It is not an answer that I expect and I inquire what kind of freedom he means. "Shanghai is a big city, yet its residents can play every kind of sport. The facilities, the clubs are very numerous. They can also go fishing in streams not far from here." Freedom has many modes, some of them more straightforward for a boy in cluttered Hong Kong than for an agonizing Western intellectual.

Shanghai's landmark palace of fun and entertainment, "Great World," has fallen silent. It is a rambling complex on Yenan Road (which used to be Edward VII Road). From 1916 until Liberation, its galleries and courtyards offered puppets, dancing, peep shows, and other diversions to meet the far from feeble Chinese love of pleasure and noise.

During the early 1950s the CCP took Great World in hand. Blue things were pushed off the stages of its fourteen theaters; red things came in their place. The Cultural Revolution proved too much even for a Great World turned chaste and didactic. The palace closed its doors in 1966. You may still go and see the echoing galleries, casualty of one of history's sharpest twists in prevailing ethics. Our walk proves, too, that the "tenderloin district" has melted away under the hot winds of communism. Casanova himself would find it hard to make out now at the corner of Foochow and Nanking roads.

Anyone looking for the after-dark diversions of imperial Shanghai will most nearly find them in Hong Kong. The painted singsong girls, daring dresses, bodies with no dress. The movies whose only aim is to soothe or thrill or shock. Boys at a nightclub who expect you to

73

tip them for watching you put your coat on a hook. Lilting love songs with no message but that the individual has one short life in which to find happiness for himself. A sweating ricksha man who plays the beast for the convenience of a toff in silk.

Quite a few capitalist enterprises moved from Shanghai to Hong Kong when the CCP took over. They brought the pieces of their past life and tried to set them up in the Crown Colony, where little is barred as long as it is paid for. A number of foreign establishments, from missionary groups to the American bistro Jimmy's Kitchen, also moved down the coast to try and keep old Shanghai alive in Hong Kong.

On this pretty toenail of China, the well-padded refugee found four welcome things which Shanghai had lost: a money-making way of thinking; a tolerant law that had no single scale for every human act; foreign rule and foreign capital; a Chinese population suspended outside the Chinese national experience.

❁ ❁ ❁

The Western *view* of Shanghai was a casualty of the CCP victory no less than was the Western presence in Shanghai. It was thought by a lot of foreigners that Shanghai was more a Western than a Chinese city. They overestimated the foreign component in what made the city tick. They overdrew the likely consequences for Shanghai of a foreign exit. In fact Shanghai made the transition to life without John Bull and Uncle Sam quite smoothly.

The "Shanghai problem" was much discussed over whiskey and soda during the 1930s and 1940s, yet no such separate problem existed. "International" solutions for the Shanghai problem were put up by foreigners; a trusteeship of several nations acting with joint and grave responsibility was a favorite. All this was nonsense. Shanghai was going to go where China went. When the crunch came Shanghai was no more exempt from the march of China's history than any other major Chinese city.

Foreigners also thought Shanghai was the key to China's destiny, which has not proved to be so. The *taipan* had a tendency to see the hinterland of China as a supporting cast for the leading roles played by international business on the coast. It was true that Shanghai had a marvelous location: the port, the inland waterways linked with it, the heavy population of the Yangtze delta.

But other reasons why Shanghai seemed the key to modern China were fleeting ones: its dominance in foreign trade, its close links with the world outside China, its resident foreign expertise, the disarray of many other parts of China. It was hardly true (though a leading Western scholar said so in 1952) that Shanghai was "modern China in microcosm." Even less was Shanghai after Liberation China's model niche of modernity.

Shanghai's relative importance in China's economy slightly declined after 1949. This was not because the city failed to carry through on its potential — though the Kuomintang blockade and U.S. embargo hindered this for a while. It was because China as a whole began to develop in an even, planned way for the first time in the post–Opium War era. Shanghai turned its face inward, toward its own kin. Instead of being a magnet drawing people from China's hinterland, Shanghai has become a source of people who go to the hinterland. A score of dialects were once heard in Shanghai; now you hear Shanghai dialect in China's far regions.

In a final way the Western view of Shanghai fell victim to events. Although the sunset *taipan* thought Shanghai was the key to modern China, he felt that Shanghai cut off from intercourse with the West would be the key to nothing but decay. How could Shanghai go ahead without capital from abroad? How could industry prosper without cotton from the United States, wool from Australia, metals from all over? How indeed could Shanghai feed itself without food brought in by water?

Shanghai today is fed entirely (except for a little grain) from the people's communes in its own counties. Its factories use mostly Chinese raw materials (it is easier to bring them from other parts of China than before). The interior rural Chinese market has provided a more than adequate demand for Shanghai's products, even without export outlets. At the same time, exports from Shanghai have exploded. Foreign trade exports (volume) in 1972 were up 1,000 percent on 1950, up 100 percent on 1965.

Shanghai in the 1970s is China's biggest city and leading industrial center. Its gross industrial output has increased seventeen times since 1949. Industrial output value goes up 9 to 10 percent each year. But Shanghai does not *tower* over the rest of China in output or level of skills. There was a period after 1949 when the city was downgraded a little by the CCP; it had slept too much with the whore of imperialism to be given top priority in investment and other matters. That mood passed and Shanghai's remodeled modernity came to be a source of pride for all of China. But no CCP official would incline to call today's Shanghai the key to modern China.

In things which the eye can see, Nanking Road is a mixture of much that is old and some that is post-Liberation. But in social attitudes the change is drastic; take service jobs. In *taipan* Shanghai a lot of people had a tough time, while a few people had an exciting time and could make a real art out of life. In the first group were those who served others: ricksha men, household servants, coolies of all kinds, mill hands who toiled from dawn until after dark.

Because of the jungle character of society and its vast inequalities, these lowly people at the bottom could feel no pride. They were not full members of a society with a purpose. They were on their own, so far as economic life went, in a free-for-all that placed them at the bottom.

A free-for-all holds out hope for everyone to climb up and get a better deal. So the social attitude the *taipan* saw among the coolies was not a straightforward one. It was seldom an open militant anger at the injustice of society; more often a calculated obsequiousness toward those who happened to be on top.

There is hardly a trace of this obsequiousness left in new Shanghai. A collective purpose grips the city. In pursuit of it everyone has a role. There is no more of the vast inequality between those for whom life glittered, and those who served them with a flicker of hope that something better would turn up one day. Instead there is a self-confidence that cuts across the spectrum of humility on the one side and haughtiness on the other. This is because the moral and psychological frame of reference has changed from the individual and his money to the whole society.

The humility and the haughtiness were two extremes of personal conduct in a world of jostling individuals. But the self-confidence of the bus conductor today is more than a response at the level of personal relationships. He is self-confident because he feels he has an equal role in a larger social purpose which is worthwhile. There is no one very wealthy for him to be obsequious toward. And the rationale of a Shanghai run for, and even by, the working class is one he can feel part of.

A room boy in the hotel serves you carefully but without awe. He no more looks up to you than to a picture on the wall. He gives every appearance of feeling that his job is as worthy and important as those of the hotel guests. Raise a topic of current interest with a waiter in a restaurant. He looks you in the eye and gives his opinion — not an opinion designed to please the diner, but one which he as a citizen of China believes is correct. Taxi drivers rib you and joke, just as your "professional colleagues" might do in Boston. Think of the same situation in Hong Kong and you see the depth of the social change that has hit Shanghai.

I am sure there are many exceptions to this pattern. The change toward foreigners, too, is greater than the change purely within Chinese ranks. The bus conductor may not feel entirely without envy before the film star or the PLA officer. Yet the general impression is strong and I think it is a key to understanding how Shanghai ticks today.

❁ ❁ ❁

How did the CCP change Shanghai? What exactly did they set out in 1949 to make of the city? Is what exists in the 1970s the intended result of their efforts?

Beyond the asphalt crisscross of Mouth of the Rainbow lies a quarter less old and more sparse. This is Shanghai's easternmost district, Willow Banks (Yang pu). It borders the Whangpu at the place where the river bends away from the city and snakes north toward the Yangtze. At the edge of Willow Banks begins the first of the counties, Precious Mountain, its ambience semirural.

I drive into Willow Banks to see a new workers' village.* It is called Windy City, one of four "villages" at the northern rim of the district, one of several score in Shanghai. Begun in 1952, it is testimony to what the CCP has done to and for Shanghai. Before Liberation the area was a wasteland; now it is a slab of created modernity. If life here is not what the West calls prosperous it does seem serene and healthy.

Windy City is overseen by a neighborhood revolutionary committee (*jie-dao ge-ming wei-yuan-hui*), guided by a neighborhood Party committee.† Within it there are nine residents' areas; each has its own revolutionary committee. Informal groups, serving as a social radar for the CCP, operate within the residents' areas.

Forty-four thousand people, divided into ninety-nine hundred families, live in Windy City. Their brick and concrete apartment blocks (brushed by the leaves of maple trees) are of a kind that hardly existed before Liberation. Early ones were only two stories high, but later ones are four or five stories. The blocks number no fewer than 744; total floor space is 317,000 square meters. That means an average of thirty-two square meters for each household, which averages 4.5 persons. This is a little more generous than a few years ago, when six square meters was the maximum living space allowed to each person.

These homes are small by Western standards but quite spacious by

* A "new village" covers the same area as a "neighborhood" (see next note). Shanghai's 10 districts are broken up into 110 neighborhoods, and again into about 1,000 residents' areas.
† The literal translation of *jie-dao,* and that given by many Western scholars before the Cultural Revolution (which changed the terminology of city organizations), is "street." But "neighborhood" is a more suitable word for an overall rendition of *jie-dao ge-ming wei-yuan-hui,* "neighborhood revolutionary committee." The smaller unit, *ju-min ge-ming wei-yuan-hui,* is best rendered "residents' committee," and the territory it looks after, a "residents' area."

These are also the usages in Peking's own translations; see for example a report in the English-language *China Reconstructs,* August 1973 ("The Neighborhood Revolutionary Committee"), on the famous Fengsheng *jie-dao ge-ming wei-yuan-hui* in Peking; and a Hsinhua dispatch describing neighborhood and residents' committees, September 29, 1974. Also letters to the author from two Peking officials who deal with translation matters: Wang Hsi (March 28, 1975) and Chia Ai-mei (April 23, 1975).

the standards of Asian cities. Windy City's strong point, however, is communal facilities. Its own schools — four kindergartens, nine primary schools, three secondary schools — are no more than a short bicycle ride from any apartment block. A cultural center is equipped with TV, movies, and a library. People in new Shanghai (the young above all) seem to study as relentlessly as people in old Shanghai used to battle for a dollar.

Windy City does not have its own hospital; there is one for all of Willow Banks district. But its clinic, open twenty-four hours a day, can perform an appendectomy, and its x-ray equipment includes a machine that can expose the inner walls of bronchial tubes. Under the clinic's supervision are nine medical stations (one per residents' area) and each of these employs three or four "barefoot doctors" (paramedical personnel).

The neighborhood has a sports complex, two small parks, and full shopping and banking services which any housewife can reach without having to cross an outside street. The housing blocks have a metropolitan touch, yet the setting has a suburban spaciousness. Just down the road from Windy City is a large public park which serves several new workers' villages. Nearby rises the Willow Banks Sports Stadium, a district facility which would do any small city proud. It is another social world entirely from the Shanghai of twenty-five years ago.

I go into one household that is a little larger than the norm. Six people live in four rooms plus kitchen and toilet. Mr. Ch'iao is a senior technician in a cotton mill and his wife is a primary-school teacher. The son is a printer; his wife is a clerk at the docks. Two more members of the household are grandchildren who attend primary school.

The four who work bring in a total of 240 yuan a month. About 25 percent of it goes on food; only 7.5 yuan on rent. Calls on other residents at random suggest that the Ch'iaos' place is typical of surrounding blocks in rent rate, furnishings, style, and facilities. The average monthly wage in the family (sixty yuan) is also exactly the average for Windy City as a whole. Industrial workers and technicians predominate in Windy City, with a heavy sprinkling of teachers, doctors, and other "professionals."

Glance back at how the CCP organized this brilliant network of social participation and control. In 1951 Shanghai became one of the first two Chinese cities (Tientsin was the other) to set up neighborhood organizations. It was the CCP's way of fitting people into the demands of the new order.

Final conquest of the city had been full of drama but rather easy. During May 24, 1949, the Kuomintang organized a brittle victory parade through the city streets. More to the point was a quiet event the same night that was noticed by only a few. It happened outside City Hall on the corner of Foochow and Kiangsi streets.

Boxes and steel cabinets were loaded onto army trucks, which lumbered off to Kiangwan airfield. A little after midnight another set of trucks pulled up at City Hall and the nearby police building. Troops in uniforms of a lighter shade than the others, and with soft shoes rather than boots, jumped out and entered the buildings.

Next morning the inhabitants of Hamilton House, opposite City Hall, awoke to see boyish soldiers in mustard-green cottons asleep under the victory banners of their fleeing adversary. Shanghai had changed hands — though a few Kuomintang troops resisted from concrete urinals near the Whangpu.

So much did the Communists feel they had heaven's mandate to grasp Shanghai that they went about the job laconically. They even permitted the free departure for Taiwan of those Kuomintang troops (holed up in Mouth of the Rainbow) who did not wish to join the Communist cause!

After the slaughter, incredible inflation, and sheer incompetence of Kuomintang rule, most of Shanghai was either passive or welcoming toward the peasant boys of the PLA. Above all, the coming of the Reds had for some time seemed inevitable. Chiang's men had been edging in fear toward the wharves and the airport. Having proclaimed that they would defend the city from the CCP, they had lately given the impression of trying to get the city to defend *them* from the CCP.

Shops and cinemas remained open, newspapers kept appearing, the singsong girls were not for the moment deterred by the prospect of a stiffer (or would it be less stiff?) clientele. The British School decided with a slight shake of the head to delay a sports program; the announcement said it was "postponed due to unavoidable circumstances."

The CCP under General Ch'en Yi (later Foreign Minister) also began on a calm and practical note. It rode the weary mood and kept in the background its real goals for Shanghai. The city was allowed to slow down after its recent distracted rushing in circles.

The long summer afternoon of foreign prestige in Shanghai drew to an end. Notices in French and English came down as Chinese businessmen read the signs of the times. A forest of controls — "as many regulations as there are hairs on a cow," runs the Chinese saying — began to limit the foreigner's freedom of action. He could hardly drive his car any more since gasoline suddenly cost three U.S. dollars a gallon (two dollars of it tax).

Foreign journalists drifted out of China to other assignments. The Foreign Correspondents Club in Broadway Mansions unraveled. Its Chinese staff were paid off; waiters were given leftover mustard, pickles, and ketchup. These arbitrary remnants they used as a foundation to start their own restaurant at the top of the building.

Foreign businessmen found CCP officials under instructions to do business only in the Chinese language; interpreters were used even if they did not seem necessary. Chinese culture was asserting itself and the Westerner felt left out in the cold.

The trend to self-reliance was clear though it took the CCP machine, inexperienced as it was in urban affairs, months to get itself in order. One young cadre went to a French monastery to ask a priest about some of his foreign contacts and their activities. The serious young man knew little of the West or its religion. When his detailed inquiries were finished he asked if the priest was pro-American. The Frenchman said he was not. Was he pro-Communist? When the priest again said no the CCP man seemed puzzled. The priest volunteered a clarification: "We work for Christ." The cadre responded simply: "I don't know him but I suppose he is a capitalist."

If the conquest of the levers of power was easy, the conversion of the minds of men was endlessly tough. Shanghai had no soul, but the CCP wanted to give it one. A young journalist who had worked for a foreign company was taken in hand by the CCP, which thought he had the potential to be useful. Two cadres devoted several weeks to remolding his way of thinking. But the old Adam popped back to the surface when the journalist was given a long oral test. He was asked to name history's key motivating force. Too quickly he blurted out, "Money." The answer was supposed to be "Class struggle."

The CCP was determined to replace Shanghai's free-for-all, motored by each individual's calculation of his interests. In its place would come planned and shared social purpose, its philosophic cogwheel "serve the people."

Four sources of influence had to be dethroned (for the CCP did not intend to share power with anyone else): foreigners; the private business of Shanghai's quite large middle class; government officials and professionals who had served the Kuomintang; Taoism, Buddhism, and lesser religions like Christianity.

The control over Shanghai sought by the CCP was quite different from that which the Kuomintang attempted after the Japanese defeat. It was systematic rather than haphazard; based on a philosophy; part of a nationwide effort; and designed for the interests of the ordinary workingman.

The CCP chose to move in careful, soft-hard-soft stages. For a couple of months there was economic austerity and the People's Government asked that "three people's rice be shared by five." Then in August the government threw a five-day public party at Renaissance Park. There was dancing, traditional opera, and good food. There were movie actresses signing autographs for all, and booths where citizens could let off steam by "shooting" effigies of the beaten Kuomintang leaders.

The Communists also chose to use the back door of social persuasion rather than the archway of state coercion. Their two aims were to gain full control of the body and mind of Shanghai, and to restore and swell production. The neighborhood organizations were crucial for both of these.

Was the city still plagued with petty thieves? Residents'-area guardians soon tracked them down, by a method no more draconian than noticing who had money to spend beyond what his wage would permit. Were there drifters who were sponging off relatives and not doing a useful job of work? The local household-register cop (*hu-ji jing*) ran into them, and overnight these sons of old Shanghai became living symbols of the city's conversion from adventure to production. There are few twilight characters left in new Shanghai, few hangers-on, few misfits who are allowed to remain so, few restless types with an eye on the main chance.

By the time Windy City was created the neighborhood network was fairly complete in Shanghai (though only in 1954 did national legislation make it part of China's state organization). The inner-city districts were wrapped in a package of residents' ties.. In the new workers' villages, where more than one million people now live, it was possible to install the system from the start.

There is nothing haphazard about Windy City, and less that is distinctive of Shanghai than in the old districts of Black Bend or Mouth of the Rainbow. If anything remains of the old free-for-all it is invisible. No one is engaged in private business; residents speak of it as a historical relic which normal people no longer practice, as Europeans might speak of witchcraft.

Only among Windy City's one thousand retired workers do you find an old stick whose life was rooted in the private business of pre-Liberation. He recalls how the CCP threw a lasso around the neck of *taipan* and comprador Shanghai. The initial method was not to seize foreign private business, but to tax it to the sky, and get workers to make wage demands against it (using the lock-in as weapon) until most firms begged to be allowed to close, or to be taken over by the Bureau of Industry and Commerce.

While foreign private business was quickly cut back, Chinese private business continued to operate, under close supervision. Businessmen were much scared by a Five Anti Campaign which began near the end of 1951 (the targets: bribery, tax evasion, contract cheating, stealing state economic secrets, stealing state property). Private business as its own moral world had lost all sense of mission — though it was 1956 before most Chinese private business was taken over by the state.

Here is a Windy City veteran who used to be a waiter in a luxury dining room. He looks back on the CCP's ways of cutting the decorative fat off Shanghai's productive bones. All private establishments were required to secure new licenses. By declining to renew licenses, the Bureau of Industry and Commerce quietly weeded out nonessential enterprise.

No fewer than eight hundred restaurants closed. Not many people could now eat out in lavish style. Hotel rooms fell vacant by the hundred as foreign visitors stopped coming to Shanghai. Room boys left the Bund to work in outlying cotton mills, became dutiful members of new workers' villages.

Modest cadres without experience in economic management paid pointed visits to lingerie shops, beauty parlors, funeral establishments, nightclubs. They had a quiet chat with the owners about what could be judged an appropriate business in liberated Shanghai. Were these exotic spots serving the people? Or were they catering to a moneyed few, pandering to silly traditions, aiming at the lush pocket of the foreigner?

In the supermarkets of Windy City you see what the CCP put in place of the pre-1949 glitter of commercial Shanghai. Essentials are there; frills are not. The canteens serve good food but the menu, chalked on a blackboard, is neither long nor wide in its price range. Most dishes are ten fen, a bowl of plain rice is five fen, the priciest offering is twenty fen. There are no waiters; you line up at a window in the kitchen wall and carry back your own meal.

At the clothing counters colors, if not styles, are in full array. But the brassiere and the petticoat have lost their grip, it seems, over the bodies if not the minds of women. As for the elaborate and costly coffin and funeral shops of old, they are as obsolete in Windy City as a blacksmith in Manhattan. Ninety people died in the village during the first six months of 1973. Every single corpse was cremated.

There is no sign of a Buddhist or Taoist temple, much less a Christian church, in the neat alignment of Windy City. After 1949 the CCP moved firmly against Taoism — a religion that was intertwined with underworld secret societies — by propaganda shows and curtailment of the activities of Taoist priests. Buddhism was treated more gently since it was at once a more popular and a less rebellious faith. But it had to give up its property, and there could be no question of expansion.

Christianity had its wings clipped because it was a bridgehead for foreign influence. The CCP skillfully drove a wedge between Western missionaries and Chinese Christians. The former were pressured first; the latter generally were not pressured until later. In this way the local flocks were isolated from their spiritual roots in the international church.

The Dean of the Anglican Holy Trinity Cathedral was presented with a land-tax bill for U.S. $56,000. He said, "There must be some mistake." But there was no mistaking the CCP's will to uproot the social base of the church. For none of these three religions was there any prospect of a foothold in the new workers' villages of Shanghai. They were heterodox; they saw the world at an irritating tangent; they had alien loyalties which the CCP could not encompass.

You can no more find a singsong girl (or an opium pipe) in Windy City than in a Boy Scout Camp. This is less the result of suppression than of a drastic change of social system. Since there is a driving social purpose, the female half of society is naturally part of it.

As in all the new areas of Shanghai, the vast majority of women have jobs (in the city as a whole, more than 500,000 housewives have taken jobs since 1958). There is a principle of equal pay for equal work. Since many women do lighter work than men, however, and many work in neighborhood factories where wages are lower than in factories at higher levels, most women earn less than most men.

I watch housewives at work in Windy City's own factories, making electronic parts, knife handles, and light bulbs. Children are cared for at kindergartens — striking for their luxurious toys, and the teaching of politics to tots just able to walk — and most mothers get two half hours off to nurse their babies during each working day. It is obvious from physical appearances that the general health level of women and children is high — maybe a little higher than that of folk in the downtown districts.

I find women to the fore among doctors at Windy City's clinic, a substantial force on the neighborhood committee, and the real power holders on the nine residents' committees. But it is the birth control section at Windy City's clinic which exhibits best the new deal for women. The lady doctor in charge describes the rising popularity of the pill, which is given out free of charge to all married women.

I see propaganda materials used by barefoot doctors in the nine medical stations which the clinic supervises. Three reasons for having a small family are pressed: each person is better able to contribute to socialist construction; the health of women and children is protected; the family is in better shape economically. The leaflets and posters also point out that smaller families are an integral part of the total vision of a new Shanghai. Since better health care is pushing the mortality rate down, they say, overall resource planning demands that the birthrate must keep going down too.

The birthrate figures for Windy City present a stunning contrast to the jungle of reproduction which was old Shanghai. During the first six months of 1973 there were ninety-two births and ninety deaths in the neighborhood. In recent years the birthrate has been a tiny 0.4 percent. Are there no big families now in Windy City? "Certain couples have six children," the doctor replies. "These all married either before Liberation or rather soon after. A few even have more than six children — these marriages all date from the old society."

I meet a kitchenful of old cooks at one of Windy City's canteens. Looking into their faces I wonder (rudely, but to myself) whether any of them were once singsong girls in Yellow Banks district. Do any of them remember the brothel-hotels, where girls arrived from the countryside like merchandise, and each floor specialized in the beauties of a certain province? Or the days when the Bund building of the *Shanghai Post & Mercury* was a singsong house, with cubicles laid out on the top floor for clients (later the newspaper used the cubicles to store its back files; today, I am told, the cubicles again have beds — for staff of company offices beneath). Was one of these leathery cooks, perhaps, among the thirty thousand girls of the night who were set to work after Liberation, making artificial flowers and labels for matchboxes?

Sometimes in China the disapproval of even the mildest flirtation seems very prim. But view it against the bitter story of how girls were once used in Shanghai. In an idle moment I remark on the beauty of a Shanghai air hostess. The response is that external appearances are "unimportant"; it is "the inner thoughts" which count. Rather stuffy and unreal.

But look at it from the point of view of Chinese emotional memory. The case is not of one Chinese passing comment on the prettiness of another citizen of new China. Because a Westerner makes the remark, what seems a simple human sentiment apparently comes over, to a Chinese who knows Shanghai's past, as a political observation. The visitor cannot go to Shanghai as an objective recorder of a new social experiment. *Who he is* is part of what he concludes; who he is is part of the impact he makes.

❈ ❈ ❈

There are more surface signs of militant leftism in Shanghai than in most Chinese cities. The lady doctor at Windy City's clinic wears a Mao badge (a rare trapping in China of 1973). An overzealous Public Security officer asks a foreigner to go back to his hotel, breaking up a casual street conversation which was furthering the friendship of the peoples. In Shanghai theaters alone do actors still bawl out the political song "Sailing the Seas Depends upon the Helmsman" at the end of a show (though without the waving of the Red Book which was de rigueur in 1971).

The newspapers bend over backward to praise the Cultural Revolution, and all the "new socialist things" to which it gave birth. Even after the Tenth CCP Congress, *Literary Currents* still chooses to urge implementation of the line of the *Ninth* Congress (which was a little more left-wing than the tenth).

Yet beneath the surface the extreme Left seems to have suffered a setback in Shanghai as in the rest of China. The passing of its day of glory is clear in the decline of the Red Guards, and the parallel resurgence of the Communist Youth League (CYL) and the trade unions. Both the CYL and the unions were strong before 1966. But the CYL fell victim, as a junior partner of the Party bureaucracy, to Cultural Revolution attacks. The rather moderate and economically minded trade unions were accused of rightism in 1967.

87

A morning with Mr. Ch'ien and Mr. Ko of the Shanghai CYL makes clear that in Shanghai youth politics, a socialism of order has replaced the late-1960s' socialism of rebellion. These two men are tough and practical, without intellectual pretensions. They cannot hide their satisfaction that the turn of the wheel has landed the Red Guards in the countryside and themselves in the front rank of Shanghai's youth affairs.

The Red Guards now exist only as a club in the middle schools. Once they fired shots at the Party bureaucracy with Chairman Mao's blessing; now their every move is "under the leadership of the Party." In the onrush of their movement the CYL more or less died. When the CYL reemerged with a big congress in 1973 (Shanghai's was the first branch to resurface) Red Guards were invited as observers — not delegates.

Toward those 300 observers the congress of 1,503 delegates made a gesture full of bitter irony. Just one Red Guard was elected to the new CYL committee of 103; a young man who had gone to a village after the Cultural Revolution. He is still in the village. He was not at the congress. He was graciously named *in absentia* to the CYL committee!

Mr. Ch'ien, who is head of the CYL's Organization Section, explains with cozy frankness that a key aim of the CYL these days is to constrain youth to unite with the workers. "When young people come out of middle school, their ideas are not always oriented to work." Even the sons and daughters of workers, Mr. Ch'ien says, can go wrong during the years of education, by getting out of touch with the world of production. He salutes the virtues of youth. They are the most vigorous, most active, most hungry for knowledge, least conservative group in society. "But they also lack political and social experience — for this they must look to the workers."

A session with trade-union cadres leaves me with a similar impression, that earthy regularity has eclipsed spontaneous flights of militancy. Mrs. Ho and Mr. Mou are modest workers. They apologize that their Mandarin is not accurate. Only when the trade-union organization regained its feet with a congress in April 1973 did these two leave a workbench and become cadres.

88

Mrs. Ho relates how the revived union movement in Shanghai sprang from a group called the General Headquarters of Revolutionary Rebel Workers (GHRRW). It is an interesting birth. The GHRRW was a rebel group, pitted against the pre-1966 Shanghai establishment. But it was not the most rip-roaring rebel group. To the left of the GHRRW was the fiery Second Regiment, led by a militant called Keng Chin-chang.

To the fore in the GHRRW was Wang Hung-wen, a cotton-mill worker who in 1973 became number three man in China. Keng fell from favor, after the power of the moderate Left was consolidated in the spring of 1967.

It seems fitting that Wang, organizational star of GHRRW, gave a keynote speech at the Trade Union Congress of 1973. He is considered a fine flower of the Cultural Revolution at its best: a man of orderly leftism rather than of open-ended militancy.

Mr. Mou stresses that the unions are now under the firm leadership of the Party. The 1,598 delegates at the congress elected a committee of 158; 54 percent of them are CCP members. Five of the six vice-chairman are CCP members (chairman is Wang Hung-wen).

Mrs. Ho hits at several excesses of the Cultural Revolution. "Some people said the works of Marx and Lenin and Chairman Mao are too difficult for ordinary workers." Mr. Mou chips in to say that the source of this idea was Lin Piao. "So these works were neglected — while people read only the fragmentary *Quotations* of Chairman Mao." I inquire if a Red Guard can become a trade-union member. "Red Guard organizations exist only at middle schools. If a Red Guard goes to a factory and becomes a working person, he or she may then become a union member."

If the voice of Shanghai rings militant, then, its social profile reflects practical labor politics. Is it a case of the swing of the pendulum? A time lag before form and content align themselves?

Recall that Shanghai has lunged in and out of many hard and soft periods since Liberation. The initial drive for CCP control gave way to a time of relaxation in 1954. After private business was largely taken over in 1956, there was a trough of calm before the Great Leap Forward galvanized the city in 1958. And the Cultural Revolution was both preceded and followed by an easy spell (during which, it is now said, revisionists had a field day).

I do not think it is possible to survey these swings and make a consistent pattern of the struggles and issues *on their face.* A victor so often appears to strut in the policy garments of his vanquished foe. A "left" idea comes from a quarter that is not "left" in its objective interests. Is there an inner secret to Shanghai's moods, a consistency beyond the inconsistency of words and lineups?

I see a rational secret at the heart of Shanghai's socialist construction. Set to one side two clear-cut kinds of militancy, fairly much agreed upon in Shanghai. The city's opinion makers are left-wing on the major issues of foreign policy. They favor a hard line against imperialism. They have a keen eye for class struggle in any part of the world. They want China to keep up a measure of support for overseas Chinese. They warn against an uncritical attitude to foreign technology, criticizing Chinese who think "the moon is rounder abroad."

The political elite and youth of Shanghai (if not the elderly man in the street) are also left-wing in rejecting every aspect of the city's *taipan,* comprador, and Kuomintang past. It would be a blunder to think that any faction pines for foreign capital; views the Kuomintang as anything but a corpse; favors capitalism as understood in the West.

It is Shanghai as a bastion of the working class that is crucial and ambiguous. This city has China's biggest concentration of urban workers. Since the proletariat is said to be the spearhead of Chinese socialism, Shanghai would seem to be China's political vanguard, and its fount of left-wing theory.

Yet I do not think there is a neat correspondence between Shanghai's sociology and Shanghai's ideology. First, the city's frequent talk of itself as a bastion of the working class is not abstract theory but tough political bargaining. Like any major province in China, Shanghai wants a big say in national affairs. It seeks maximum resources, has strong views on what China's future should be, likes to be praised as a model for other cities. A trump card in the city's bargaining hand — given the CCP's value system — is its proletarian character.

In Shanghai's rhetoric, it is not, therefore, the pure nectar of left-wing militancy alone that we sniff, but the homely aroma of local chauvinism. Wang Hung-wen is the only top leader in China who has recently sprung from the urban proletariat. Shanghai saw his rise at the Tenth CCP Congress in these terms. Its radio said it was a sign of the faith "Chairman Mao and the whole Party have in the working class." But no other province made a similar interpretation of Mr. Wang's inclusion in China's high trinity of power.

Marx's rules notwithstanding, not everyone in China believes that whatever the urban workers do and say defines, as by the stroke of a wand, the proper line of the Left. Not long ago *Literary Currents* urged Shanghai workers to be more tolerant of young student revolutionaries. "We should have profound proletarian feelings toward them," the paper said with a touch of complacency. Yet these battered young veterans, many now working on farms, feel no need of lessons in the meaning of left-wing militancy. They believed they were on history's upward path in 1966–1967, when they pressed for a Shanghai Commune. Is the key to political truth beyond their grasp simply because they are not factory workers?

In fact the Left is a diamond which flashes three different colors according to the angle from which it is viewed. There is the solid red of Shanghai labor; the deep crimson of a "pure Chinese" spirit in the inland and rural provinces; the leaping vermilion of students who jump at communism by an act of sheer will. Sometimes Shanghai labor is found on the left in a policy debate. Other times it stands by its interests, against notions which may well be more left-wing than its own.

There is a second reason why Shanghai's ideology and its sociology do not always line up together as symmetrically as two chopsticks. It has to do with the varying needs and tempos of successive stages of socialist construction.

Here are a half-dozen hotel staff members in a lounge watching evening TV. A documentary from Inner Mongolia; performances of martial arts; a film of Little Red Guards visiting Yenan; an account of new steps ahead in mechanization at Shanghai's cotton mills; storytelling on the theme of army heroism by a PLA officer to a studio audience of patient children.

Every program is woven through with quotations from Chairman

Mao. Success or failure in any undertaking, it is asserted, hinges on the correct political line. My first reaction as a Westerner is that every program has been turned into a political program. Yet the young hotel staff people do not, to judge from conversations with them, feel much political reverberation from the shows. Nothing they remark upon as they watch is about politics.

I do not mean that these youths lack admiration for Chairman Mao, or have a "wrong" political line. On the contrary, all signs are that young Chinese respect the Party and esteem Mao to a starry-eyed degree. But these people seem to take so much for granted the political thread of the TV programs that it does not intrude for them as it does for me.

Three other attractions hold these fresh-faced youths to the TV set. The technical wonder of the television itself (how they fiddle with the knobs!). The sense of excitement at seeing far-flung parts of their own country — which they have not visited — brought before their eyes. The pride and pleasure at the economic achievements depicted.

Socialist construction is a thrilling thing to these post-Liberation sons and daughters. They also take completely for granted that the CCP should lead the way. Yet the rhetoric cannot mean the same thing to them as it does to older folk, who came to socialist construction from a fight against capitalism and imperialism.

This new generation has hit the scene the morning after the political battle has been won. Real to them is the socialism of building, not the socialism of bringing down an old order. There is no angry memory of the past to push them on. For them, opium and VD are as difficult to imagine as witchcraft. They are pulled on by the inherent fascination of constructive tasks.

One of these moderns was a Red Guard in 1966–1967, and he tells me stories of daring acts. What was the coin of his rebellion? Nothing so backward as throwing spears or marching with knapsacks; rather it was flicking switches to try to turn off Shanghai's water and electricity supply!

Shanghai's politics have to be seen in the light of this onward march of new China. The actual tasks of socialist construction are not at all the same in all parts of China — however monotonous the rhetoric.

Shanghai is further down the path of modernization than the army, the city of Hangchow, the countryside of Hupei.

And the issues do not remain the same as new steps are taken down this path of modernization. The angle of vision of the middle-aged members of Shanghai's revolutionary committee is not the same as that of the 25 percent of its members who are under twenty-five, or as that of the *one-third* of Shanghai's workers born in or since 1949.

Around the time of my last visit to Shanghai a CBS team headed by the talented Irv Drasnin spent many weeks in the city filming a documentary which tried to be fair-minded. When the result was shown on U.S. TV in 1974, Chinese officials who saw the program had serious objections to it.

Huang Hua, member of the Central Committee of the CCP, and China's envoy to the UN, explained to me the Chinese point of view. Too many shots of bicycles and masses of people; too few of machines and new development. "It is not only the soul of Shanghai that has changed since 1949," the ambassador insisted, "the material face of Shanghai has changed just as much."

Huang Hua had a point, but what is also interesting is the emotion which underlay his offense at the film. Revealed was the acute sensitivity of Chinese leaders on the issue of how much progress China is making toward modernity.

The CCP has made a revolution which was anticapitalist and anti-imperialist. But the positive point of it was to make China a modern nation. Chinese are irritated when a foreigner appears to romanticize the quaint past, and understate the signs of an emerging modern future. They do not like a film maker to depict a handicraftsman when he might depict a factory worker.

It is true that Shanghai's modernity is a unique kind, dictated by the special social values of the CCP. The heart of it is not technique, nor growth for its own sake, but a new order of relationships among people. At the same time I agree with Huang Hua that the face of Shanghai is changing almost as much as its soul.

The CBS film, informative as it was, did not capture the atmosphere of those young hotel staff members watching TV. It did not adequately convey that Shanghai's character as a center of urban workers, and

93

the logic of its industrial modernization, is the key to the city's political style.

Yet this very point throws the ball back into the CCP court. Since a quest for modernity is the key to Shanghai politics, the politicians of this extraordinary city have to walk the treadmill of change without respite. To make a Shanghai with a new face is to produce citizens with new ways of thinking and fresh expectations.

Of course the worker's son, as Mr. Ch'ien of the CYL says, does not think as his father does, if he gets an education which his father did not have. The urban working class has no eternal traits which stay frozen as society moves on. Success at one stage of modernization is the mother of surprising problems at the next stage. Shanghai is a city to watch, for the sake of China, Asia, indeed the world.

DAIREN

大连

IN THE AIRY LIVING ROOM of a house in downtown Dairen, I play with my tea and chat with the Tan family about life in Manchuria. The Tans have the flat, oval faces of people from this corner of China. Mrs. Tan is dumpy, but dainty in her roly-poly way. Though her face has known its cares, there is still a girlish grace about the mouth. Mr. Tan is tall and bony, like many in the Northeast. He is the nervous host, diffident when it comes to words. His eyes, which seem wide apart, dart around to check that the visitor has everything he wants.

Mr. Tan earns seventy-five yuan a month in Dairen's big rolling-stock plant. He is a member of the Communist Party, which means he is an up-front citizen. Mrs. Tan does not go out to work or belong to the Party, but keeps busy with community work. She also sews for neighbors and this brings in five yuan here and ten yuan there.

The Tans' house forms one-quarter of a two-storied, twenty-six-year-old brick dwelling. From the street it looks like a Western villa. Unlike a home in old Peking it does not have a courtyard, with rooms ranged on all sides and a small door to the street through a gray wall. Unlike the big newer apartment blocks — similar in many Chinese cities — it does not sit sheer upon the street but is set back in a small garden. In front is a typical Dairen stone fence, with the householders' names written in white characters on small red boards.

Being a four-roomed apartment it has its own kitchen and toilet (the crouching kind; a Western sitting toilet is virtually unknown in Chinese private homes). Not being a recent construction, the dwelling has no gas or central heating. A stove using briquettes cooks the food and warms the rooms in Dairen's severe winter. Electricity provides good lighting and the power for a radio which the Tans are planning to buy (a fan as well, later on, says Mr. Tan).

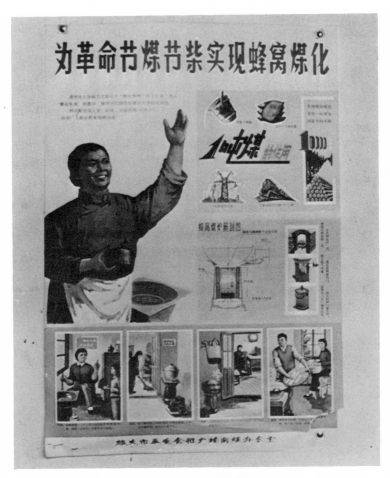

SAVING ENERGY

A poster on the kitchen wall at the Tans, issued by the Office for Promotion of Beehive Coal of the revolutionary committee of Luta municipality. The large characters say: "For the Sake of the Revolution Economize on Coal and Wood, Extend the Use of Beehive Coal." Briquettes in the shape of beehives are apparently a more economical, sanitary, and secure fuel than wood or chunks of coal. The scenes below are of various household uses of this energy saver. Those above suggest how saving on timber and coal can benefit China's industry and agriculture. The diagram at center right is an anatomy of the special kind of stove needed for burning the beehive coal.

The beds are covered simply with matting; shelves above hold heavy padded bedding for winter use. To one side of the poky kitchen is an open balcony with a view of the street, its asphalt shaded by trees planted about ten years ago. Rent is eight yuan a month, including utilities.

A married son lives with Mr. and Mrs. Tan. The young couple are both members of the CCP's grooming organization, the Communist Youth League, which revived again in 1972 after a loss of spirit and almost of body during the Cultural Revolution. His work as a bus conductor and hers at Dairen port bring in a monthly total of 102 yuan. The Tans' daughter of fourteen attends middle school, belongs to the Red Guards. A son, four years younger, is a primary-school pupil and a Little Red Guard; a keen family, the Tans.

Yun-guo, the son, tells me about his school, which has three thousand pupils. His own class of sixty-two contains forty-two who belong to the Little Red Guards, a pep group not unlike a politicized Boy Scouts. Math is Yun-guo's preferred subject, the cinema his favorite outing, and a trip to Peking (1,450 kilometers by train) his big wish for the near future.

The household (a three-year-old child completes a total of seven persons) has no radio, which is a bit unusual, but there is a bicycle and a sewing machine. This last, Mrs. Tan's pride, cost 160 yuan in 1956 and would go for the same or slightly less today. The apartment is shabby yet well ordered. Beyond the screenless window frames the cool green hills of Dairen are visible. Hoots from the port waft across the clear summer air.

Dairen is mainland China's best match for the splendid natural setting of Hong Kong. The city perches at the tip of the Liao-tung ("east of the Liao River") peninsula, between glistening blue waters and round green hills. A central commercial and residential area blends brick and stone buildings in styles influenced by the West and Japan. It has none of Hong Kong's clean white high-rise towers and boxes. I ask for a view from the tallest structure; it turns out to be the eight-story port administration building.

Dairen, like Shenyang (Mukden), a few hours north of Dairen, has buildings in pale cream brick, reminiscent of government offices in Tokyo dating from the 1930s. Also many European mansions with wrought-iron gates and balconies, bay windows, and halfhearted efforts at the gargoyles of houses in 1860s Paris. Inside these mansions you see faded, aging relics of a Victorian past: velvet curtains, soda decanters, giant marble lampstands.

Like Shenyang, too, Dairen has the scattering of Christian church buildings found in all Chinese cities where Westerners took root. None now functions as a church. The former Italian church near Sun Yat-sen Square is a library; a Russian church behind my guesthouse appears disused. All in all, Dairen's buildings in a variety of styles, shapes, and materials would hardly be attractive aside from their setting.

Only parts of Peking are as impressive, however, when it comes to spacious squares, well-paved streets, stylish streetlamps and curbsides. Beyond Dairen city lies a belt of industrial plants, interspersed with large new brick apartment blocks of five or six stories. There is no former city wall or "old town," nor any notable temple or pagoda. Even less than Shanghai does the face of Dairen evoke ancient China.

Life in Dairen has come a long, not altogether smooth way since Japan captured this key Manchurian port in 1894. The Tans are among the 1.1 million people of Dairen, which is part of a larger metropolitan complex, called Luta. The name "Luta" combines part of the term for nearby Port Arthur (Lüshun-kou) and part of the term for Dairen (Talien).

The complex embraces 4.2 million people. It stands about seventh in China's list of most populous cities. Although Luta covers an area thirty times larger than Dairen itself, the whole city is often called Dairen.

Dairen port ranks with Shanghai and Tientsin as one of China's top three. It mounts trade with 130 countries, employs 13,000 workers, is able to handle ships up to 45,000 tons. Luta's scattered plants turn out ships, machines, metallurgical goods, rolling stock (including diesel engines), chemicals, textiles, processed foods.

The value of the city's industrial output was in 1972 eighteen times that on the eve of Liberation. The pace of this great advance is being kept up. The value of industrial output in 1973 was about 8 percent up on that of 1972.

Dairen is a gateway and key component of the small but important province of Liaoning ("Distant Tranquillity"), which is the heart of what foreigners remember as Manchuria and Chinese know as *dong bei* (Northeast). This region differs sharply from all of China's other half-dozen regions.

Its climate is a far cry from the heat and wetness of south and east China. Temperatures of eighteen degrees centigrade below zero grip even south Liaoning during winter. It is common for rivers to be frozen six months of the year. Summers are brief and fairly hot, though in early August I do not find it too hot for comfort. Most of Liaoning receives no more than sixty or seventy centimeters of rain each year.

The Northeast is China's paramount industrial region. Here are deposits of oil shale, coal, iron ore, and various ferroalloys. The area was the only part of China where hydroelectric power was well developed before 1949.

Dong bei is knitted together by China's best transport subsystem. The excellent railways total 12,800 kilometers, or one-third of all China's railways (they would need to be good, for Dairen says goodbye to only two planes a week, one to Peking and one to Shenyang, Liaoning's capital). There are also 24,000 kilometers of fine highways. Fair-sized boats (for moving timber and crops) ply major arteries like Pine Flower River, which serves the pocket of land enclosed by Russia to the north and Korea to the east.

Oil is the talk of the town in Dairen these days. An oil boom is shaping up in China; *dong bei* is its seat. While much of the world felt an "oil shock" in 1973, Dairen basked in the glow of vastly increased oil production. During 1972, Liaoning province refined 71 percent more crude oil than in 1970. In 1971, the Number Seven Refinery in Dairen produced 1.2 million tons; in 1972 it gave China 3.5 million tons. During 1973, crude oil output in Liaoning was running about 50 percent above the 1972 level.

In the face of the energy crisis, Dairen is a "have" city. China has become an exporter of oil; in a couple of decades its exports will be massive. Oil has been sold to Japan in rising quantities; some five million tons in 1974. By 1980 Japan may be buying 10 percent of China's expected three-to-four-hundred-million-ton oil output.* Oil ships leave Dairen every week for Hong Kong, which now takes about 300,000 tons of Chinese oil per year, and often for Thailand and the Philippines as well.

Dong bei has a low ratio of people to resources. It accounts for some 35 percent of China's electric power, 65 percent of its crude oil, 40 percent of its crude steel, and three-quarters of its truck and freight-car production. Yet the three provinces of *dong bei* — Liaoning, Kirin ("Lucky Forest"), and Heilungkiang ("River of the Black Dragon") — contain only seventy million people. Liaoning itself counts thirty-four million in an area a little smaller than Sweden.

The Northeast is also unique in its relative lack of deep roots in Chinese, or Han, tradition. It was a frontier area, home of the Manchus who reached Peking to found their own and China's last dynasty (the Ch'ing) in the 1640s. Only in the very late Ch'ing was much of the region settled by Han people, and developed as a regular part of China. The Manchu dynasty at first prohibited Han immigration to Manchuria. As late as 1900 the region's population was only some eleven million. In these circumstances, Russian and Japanese influence was at times quite deep.

Today the people of *dong bei* like to boast what they can of a Han past — true only for the southern sector which knew Chinese civilization as early as the Warring States period (403–221 B.C.). They are understandably sensitive about the rather absurd Russian idea that China belongs only inside the Great Wall, whose eastern extremity reaches the sea at Liaoning's southwest tip. It is a favorite trick of Liaoning archaeologists, in fact, to unearth in the Northeast relics of Han life which disprove Moscow's notion. Liaoning people have a sense of being a part of China redeemed from the near-thing of Russian and Japanese appropriation.

* China already produces as much oil per year as Algeria (about seventy million tons).

A typical *dong bei* diesel train near Dairen, beside an
older steam train on which is written "Serve the People"

No foreign policy fear is greater for Peking than that of Moscow
nibbling at China's frontier areas. Chinese vigilance was recently
expressed in a redrawing of the internal boundaries of Inner Mongolia. Called an "autonomous region" of China, this southern part of
Mongolia is ruled more or less as a province. Peking resliced it in
1970 in order to hasten the integration of Mongolians with the Chinese from neighboring provinces. A good slab of the 450,000 square
kilometers and some of the five million people which Inner Mongolia
lost in this border change went to Liaoning (other bits went to Kansu
and Heilungkiang).

☼ ☼ ☼

All these traits of Liaoning spring to life before the eyes of a
traveler by rail, by car, or on foot. Fine green diesel trains are common, a big improvement over the jumpy, grime-making steam trains
in more backward provinces of China. The one I take overnight from
Tientsin has a placard on the nose of its sleek engine: "Drive the
Train for the Revolution." As we approach Shenyang I look out on
the flat and tidy landscape of the Manchurian plain.

At 6:00 A.M. peasants are bent in the healthy-looking corn, kaoliang (sorghum), and soybean fields. Clusters of poplars and birches and cypresses dot the scene. Newly planted trees answer the call you find in newspapers: "To cover the province with trees is everyone's responsibility."

There are many wells — equipped with power pumps — that are a major weapon against drought. You see stone houses and dumpy bins for "food shelter" (liang hu). Concrete fortifications with gun holes remain from the Japanese war. Striking above all is the frequency of chimney pots, communications wiring, and sturdy stone-built railway towns.

Rattling tramways (the basic fare is four fen; the drivers are mostly women) give the towns of Liaoning a "developed" air. Railway gates, cool temperatures, and a smoky atmosphere suggest Europe rather than still-peasant China. It is rare, too, to see here the dismal hand-carts with a tray of goods laboriously hauled by a human being which are a commonplace in Wuhan.

Anshan, China's great steel town, a little north of Dairen, is quite like Sheffield, England. Giant blast furnaces; thin chimneys, noble spires of industry's kingdom; drab work clothing; rows of functional housing blocks. The chief difference is the presence in virtually every street of four or six rows of handsome trees.

The foreigner can seldom pick a man of Manchu origin from a Han Chinese. Maybe his features are a shade sharper; he might cultivate a mini-beard; his carriage may be a bit stiff. He will sometimes say nin, a more formal word for "you" than the ordinary ni, and maintain a certain ceremoniousness in the privacy of his household. But none of these traits is marked or widespread.

The Chinese government still lists Manchus among the fifty-five million minority, or non-Han, peoples of China. A distinctive Manchu is more likely, though, than a Peking official to refer to Manchus as a separate race. There is only one pocket of Liaoning — a county which is called by the Manchu organizational name "banner" — where Manchu customs and language really flourish.

I am told Liaoning has as many as thirty-six minorities, Koreans in the eastern villages chief among them, but none is very obvious in the cities. *Dong bei* people strike me as a quietly solid, less stylish, more angular variant of ordinary northern Chinese. They have a kind of slow seriousness of spirit, a manner that is stern but only on the surface. The Dairen man is maybe a little quicker and more polished than his fellow Liaoning provincial to the north.

In Shenyang — its old name, Mukden, is a Manchu word — I visit the Imperial Palace (*gu gong*). The Manchus built it between the founding of their Ch'ing dynasty (1623) and their decision to make Peking the dynastic capital (1644). It is a strangely inauthentic, if lavish, array of pavilions and courtyards. There are treasures in its musty depths, to be sure, including tapestries in gold thread and nimble carvings in camel bone. But it seems incongruous to find this ambitious palace amid the chimneys of dour industrial Shenyang.

The veins of the Mukden palace no longer throb with links to state power, as do those of Peking's *gu gong,* with the homes of Chairman Mao and Premier Chou on its western fringe and the Great Hall of the People, palace of socialist China, outside its southern gate. The Manchu palace has fallen outside political history and become a mere toy for an industrial city.

Most striking is the lack of originality in these pyramids of Manchu polity. You enter their portals to look for high points of Manchu culture, but find at every point imitations of the palace in Peking. The architecture and the musical instruments are no different from those of the Han. The painting, porcelain, and carving lack any Manchu spirit.

Distinctive alone is the organization of the palace interior by the principle of the Eight Banners. These banners were military units, each known by its flag, of the conquering Manchu nation-in-arms. In fading memory of military organizational detail, you have eight reception chambers and ceilings with eight corners.

❊ ❊ ❊

Dairen has an air of spaciousness, even sparseness, rare in large Chinese cities. Luta as a whole covers twelve thousand square kilometers; few of its broad streets lack a vista of sea or hills. Pedestrians do not have to weave deftly among each other as do those of down-town Shanghai. The trams are not as desperately crammed as the buses of Canton. There is no section of terribly overcrowded hovels (unpaved and without running water) as in parts of Wuhan.

One cannot miss a certain social buoyancy that goes with the tang of Dairen's sea air. In part it stems from the relative prosperity which wages averaging sixty or seventy yuan a month bestow; only in Shanghai are wages generally higher than in *dong bei* cities. Yet a comparison with Anshan, 270 kilometers to the north, points us beyond prosperity. The very high wages (seventy-six yuan average, including living allowance*) given for heavy work at Anshan Steelworks give Anshan none of Dairen's sparkle.

Frocks seem brighter and pants less baggy in Dairen. One Sunday morning I watch hundreds of tots gathering to go off in trucks to the seaside; rarely in China do you see such varied and attractive children's clothing. Homes are kept and decorated with pride. Some have screens of colored bead strings hanging as partitions between rooms. Many interior walls are bright with family photos, and with posters which are only sometimes political.

In the streets the foreigner is taken somewhat for granted, gaped at less than in many Chinese cities. During the evening couples and groups promenade smartly. Card games are a magnet for bystanders. Physical recreations unfold quite boisterously. The general air is businesslike by day and relaxed by night.

More than once I find Dairen citizens not so cowed by requirements of politeness toward foreigners that they blush to let a foreigner witness a small fight in the street. One evening two bicycles collide at Sun Yat-sen Square, just as I stroll there from Stalin Avenue. The two riders pick themselves up, eye each other with annoyance, begin recriminations. Within a minute they are hoeing into each other, fists flying, the two bent bicycles forgotten to one side. I watch this altercation for some two minutes, until a standoff stage is reached and fists give way to a new effort at verbal combat.

Another incident occurs when I am driving back to Luta Guest-

* I go into the nature of this living allowance on page 375.

house after an afternoon at a glassblowing factory. While we are at bay like a sitting duck, before a traffic light, a small boy tosses a light stone at our 1940s De Soto. The kid and his companions laugh and flee. The two Chinese officials with me in the car, one a local China Travel Service guide and one from Peking, take it very calmly. "Mischievous" (*tiao-pi*), the Dairen cadre remarks, but no one, to my relief, feels any need to get stern or chase after the stone thrower.

Relics of Japanese and Russian presence crop up in Dairen, as British relics do in Shanghai. Officials in 1973 do not draw a visitor's attention to sites of Japanese atrocities, as they might do (and as Polish officials draw attention to sites of German atrocities). How long-standing is this reticence? Certainly Peking's view of Japan has altered since my last visit to China in 1971.

In July 1971 I found Premier Chou En-lai very agitated indeed about Japan. He complained of the fat size of Japan's Fourth Defense Plan (announced not long before), referred sarcastically to "Japan's so-called defensive activities," and said "the U.S. and Japanese reactionaries together are reviving Japanese militarism." He lambasted the Sato-Nixon communiqué of November 1969, in which Japan referred to its defense responsibilities for South Korea. He pointed out that Japan was expanding economically and flatly declared that "what will follow will be military protection."

Since early 1972 this agitation has given way to politeness on the surface and a wait-and-see attitude in private. Japan is said to be at the "crossroads"; an apt if vague diagnosis. It might be expected that this switch from snarls to smiles in Japan policy would be harder to swallow in *dong bei* than in southern China, which never felt the Japanese heel. If so, this is not evident among Dairen residents I am able to talk with.

If Dairen officials do not attack Japan, neither do they point out that quite a bit of *dong bei*'s industrial base was laid by Japanese. Not in Dairen — but in Tokyo — I hear that Dairen had the first dial phone service on the Asian continent, introduced by the Japanese in the 1920s. The great Anshan Steelworks was established by the Japanese in 1916. At Dairen in the 1920s and 1930s, Tokyo tried to show the world that it could do more to "modernize" China than even the British were doing at Shanghai.

It is not, though, as if Dairen rests on yesterday's Japan-sponsored laurels. As of 1974, no less than 85 percent of Liaoning's engineers and technicians have been trained since 1949.

Rarely do you see a Japanese face on the streets of Dairen, but the city contains a few thousand Japanese residents who chose to stay after Liberation. Many have intermarried with Chinese; quite a few are citizens of China. Culturally the Japanese had curiously little impact on Dairen. Architecturally, they did not leave much cause for Chinese gratitude. Most Japanese structures are oblongs in small fawn bricks, bleak as a hospital, or ugly efforts at the imitation of a heavier German style.

Japan's language, though, echoes on. More students study Japanese in Dairen than in south China cities. And in the nearby hills is located China's crack college exclusively devoted to high-level training in the Japanese language.

Of course there are historical sites that recall Japan's heyday of "coprosperity." One is the rambling villa near Anshan where Tokyo installed P'u Yi — who had ascended the throne in 1909 at the age of three as the last, short-lived Ch'ing emperor — to rest for a time before putting him back on a throne at Shenyang in 1932 as Emperor K'ang-te of Manchukuo ("Land of the Manchus"). Chinese officials show you the haunts of P'u Yi — who later wrote his story, *From Emperor to Citizen,* and died only a few years ago in Peking — with the air of relaxed amusement they often reserve for talk about their nation's feudal past.

Russian relics are both more ancient and more recent than Japanese. Here and there is a Russian Orthodox church, its onion-shaped spires, meant to express the leap of faith, now forlorn against an assertive industrial skyline. Chinese versions of Russian names (e.g., Tolstoy) are used for some streets. A central point in Dairen is a big square in memory of Stalin.

Stalin Square is not well cared for by Dairen standards, nor would it be distinguished if it were. A larger than life statue of a soldier of the Soviet Red Army dominates it. With an inscription in Russian and Chinese, it celebrates the Soviet role in the liberation of Dairen. To one side is a modern building with a Russian flavor where the People's Court does its minimal work. Opposite stares an ugly monolith which houses both the city's Communist Party committee and its revolutionary committee.

Of Soviet persons there is no sign at all. This rich northeast corner of China — long coveted by Russia and sometimes controlled by Russia; whose city of Dairen was handed to Moscow on a plate at the Yalta Conference; where the presence of Soviet troops as late as 1954 marked an astonishing exception to post-1949 China's strict policy of running its own household; whose major factories during the 1950s all had Soviet advisers and modeled themselves on Soviet industry — no longer welcomes brothers from across the border.

There are no Soviet technicians, no visiting groups, not one consular official throughout *dong bei*. Nor does the foreigner in Dairen meet Chinese in the street who address him in Russian, as he still may in Harbin (capital of Heilungkiang), where more White Russians lived before Liberation than lived in Dairen.

A paradox hangs over the explanation given in *dong bei* factories about the role of the Soviet technicians. On one hand their contribution is played down, for emotional reasons which one can understand. Factory after factory tells me that Soviet help was marginal: "only six Russians in our factory of twelve hundred workers" . . . "yes, the equipment is Soviet made, but only in outline — the machines have mostly Chinese parts" . . . "the Soviet personnel made many mistakes; especially they said, 'the more gigantic a factory is, the better it is.' "

On the other hand, the withdrawal of the Soviet personnel in 1960 is on all sides described as a great blow for *dong bei* industry, from which it took years to recover. Output at one machine tools plant dropped 80 percent in 1961 as compared with 1960. "There were two reasons," a senior spokesman tells me: "the Soviet withdrawal of aid and technicians, and the natural climatic disasters of that year."

At Anshan the second of three reasons why there was *no increase in output at all* from 1960 until 1966 is said, by a vice-chairman of

Anshan Revolutionary Committee, to be the "perfidious" Soviet withdrawal. "So suddenly did the hundred-odd Soviet personnel here abandon us, they insisted on a special plane to take them from Anshan to Shenyang the very night of the final break."

Grotesquely enough, the most tangible presence of the Soviet Union in Dairen is a breathtaking network of underground defense tunnels, built for the most part during 1970 and 1971. By the central railway station, doors lead down to caverns which officials claim can hold almost the entire 4.2 million people of Luta.

The shelters consist of ten networks in five parts, which correspond to the city's five districts and are named City Zoo, East Mountain, Victory Bridge, "March 8,"* and Sun Yat-sen (you can enter this one from the basement of Luta Guesthouse).

The tunnels all issue in the East Mountains outside Dairen. They are short-term shelters only, providing instant protection and a way of fleeing to the countryside. They have a psychological function which may be as important as their physical function. Premier Chou says frankly that the shelters must be seen in the context of civilian morale: "Shelters are dug so that the masses may feel that they are secure."

As to where an attack might come from, one incident throws a little light. Not long ago a group of Peking-based ambassadors was given a tour of *dong bei*. As plans went ahead for the trip, a West European envoy asked the Chinese Foreign Ministry if the group, which was to include the Soviet ambassador, could see the defense shelters in Dairen. His insistent request was persistently refused.

At the last moment the Soviet envoy for some extraneous reason withdrew from the tour party. As the group set out from Peking the West European ambassador was told by the Chinese that, happily enough and after much thought, a visit to the shelters had been added to the program for Dairen.

❉ ❉ ❉

Three long walks give me a glimpse of life on the streets of Dairen city. Morning activity in an industrial quarter begins no later than

* International Women's Day.

110

6:00 A.M., when radios start blaring and a clock tower chimes out the political song "The East is Red." The green and blue trams are frequent; you rarely wait more than two minutes for one. But, as all over Liaoning, trams are now frowned on because they cut up the streets, and Dairen plans to phase out its trams.

If half Dairen seems to be squeezed into trams, the other half seems to be riding bicycles. At 6:30 it is hard to cross a street against the swarm of wheels and steel and blue overalls. Happily there are traffic policemen in boxes to direct the flow. Watch this tide, imagine the traffic if each bicycle were an automobile, and you realize that privately owned autos in China would be environmentally absurd, as well as economically impossible.

Fruit and vegetables are laid out at intervals on the sidewalk. Equipped only with a pair of scales, farmers from outlying communes sell their produce to Dairen-ers, who come with big bags and often buy large quantities. Prices of such perishables fluctuate with season and supply, I am told by one shopper; the wise housewife (just as frequently the wise husband) varies her choice of items as value goes up and down.

Most people going off to work carry a small dark bag of the type common in Japan. Quite a few stop for a quick breakfast of pancakes and porridge at a "small eating station" (*xiao-chi bu*). In parks a sprinkling of less hurried citizens read books — not newspapers — and there is a bit of *tai-ji-quan,* the rhythmic physical exercise, though far less than in Shanghai.

In a residential street, householders relax or get themselves in order after the exodus of early workers. Children sit on doorsteps crouched over their breakfast bowls. A middle-school girl languidly combs her long black hair in the small garden of an old housing cluster. The glass windows of an apartment block are pushed back for airing. Inside one row of metal window bars a grandmother shakes and folds bedding.

An evening stroll from Sun Yat-sen Square offers a different world. Here is a smart part of downtown Dairen. Summer crowds are enjoying its liveliness; their eyes give off the glint of good times. The acrobatic theater and two cinemas are thronged with patrons and ticket

III

buyers. It is one index of rising purchasing power in China that places of entertainment are fuller than they were two or three years ago.

Facing the chaste rows of geraniums at the square's center is the Bureau of Culture, a gray stucco equivalent of a Swiss villa. Nearby is the Cultural Palace, from which pour waves of PLA men who distribute themselves, while chatting about the films they have just seen, into a line of waiting trucks. (A disagreeable term, "cultural palace"; is culture a contrived show, or the daily creativity of a whole people?)

Altogether Sun Yat-sen Square is bright and attractive — more so than the square of the same name in Shenyang, which harbors not gardens but a five-times-life-size statue of Chairman Mao, and which could easily be a square in the USSR except for Chinese writing on the buildings.

The smaller side streets are not so well lit. You must pick your path carefully through card-playing clusters, couples sitting on tiny stools in quiet conversation, children scurrying about at games.

A landmark on hexagonal Sun Yat-sen Square is Red Star Inn. It is a quite different kind of hotel from Luta Guesthouse where I stay. The guesthouse is a palatial brick structure with richly ornamented windows, a marbled lobby, a handsome wrought-iron portico. Inside are soft carpets, big bathrooms with ponderous fittings that do not always work, mosquito nets over the beds, furnishings in pleasant dark Liaoning wood, nicely set off by white plaster walls. Guests passing through the revolving glass doors are Chinese cadres plus a few overseas Chinese and foreign visitors. The impression is of space, restrained conversation in twos and threes, and good service.

Red Star is an inn with dormitory-type conditions for Chinese citizens only. It is a post-Liberation building which could be mistaken for a bank in any continent. Its six or eight floors are apportioned to categories of guest: separate floors for men, for boys, for women, for girls. I watch guests lounge about, reading on their beds, playing cards, or gossiping in groups. The beds are close together but the place is clean and well run. Cost of accommodation and meals is fifteen to twenty times cheaper than at Luta Guesthouse.

The Chinese gift for friendship is well expressed around the front door of Red Star Inn. Staff and guests alike are ordinary Chinese, who feel neither inferior nor superior to any person on earth. They are ready to exchange opinions with all comers. If they were "responsible" types, maybe they would feel the need to educate me. But they are average Chinese whose impulse is to be open about themselves and curious about me.

Leading off Sun Yat-sen Square are streets on which apartment houses alternate with offices. Bureaus of the city; units under the authority of the district named Sun Yat-sen; an occasional branch of the People's Bank; a Public Security station. Here and there a food shop or restaurant is still open at 8:30 P.M. From time to time I pass a policeman, or a PLA man standing at the door of a city bureau, but none of them shows the slightest concern at the sight of a foreigner wandering alone on the city streets at night.

Once I exchange a few remarks with a PLA guard. He talks with me as one human to another; not taut like a military man who must put on an appearance of authority in the presence of an unknown alien on an unexplained tour of his area.

If it is true that most urban Chinese wear either blue or white garments to work — blue above and below the waist for a manual worker, white above the waist for an office worker — no generalization is possible about the color of leisure-time clothing in urban China. In the streets of Dairen on a summer night, garments seem just as varied in color as those in a comparable city anywhere.

❁ ❁ ❁

A Sunday walk at 7:00 A.M. in Dairen hits upon a half-holiday and half-work atmosphere not found on a Sunday in most countries. Trams and buses are fairly full, and many of the passengers are going to work. Under China's staggered-rest-day system, not a great many more people rest on Sunday (except those in education and administration) than on any other day of the week.

A brilliant sun lights up harbor and hills as residents emerge to flex their muscles for another day. Men sit on doorsteps and survey the scene; girls go by on errands. Children with nets grope and leap to catch dragonflies and cry with joy when one is ensnared. By 9:00 A.M.

113

there are games in progress in the parks. Lots of people are evidently dressed for a leisure outing.

It is quite different from, say, Canton at a similar hour — everything is so clean and spacious. You do not see a steady stream of people going in and out of public toilets, as in Canton, no doubt because housing is better in Dairen and apartments or groups of apartments have their own facilities.

A long line of citizens stretches from the door of the office which licenses bicycles. Young and old are paying two yuan for the certificate which all bicycle owners must obtain once a year. The rare automobile parked at the curb is an object of extraordinary fascination. Boys will gaze for minutes at an ordinary dashboard; girls will pat a chassis as a foreigner might pat a panda.

An auto driver can toot recklessly — often does — and pedestrians and cyclists scatter as if they had no rights at all. Some drivers grow arrogant — though they do not own the car — in a nation where there is one auto for every eight thousand people.

In the environs of Stalin Street hundreds of children are assembling. Once gathered, they sit down in rows on the pavement, near waiting trucks. They are going to the beach, each with swimming clothes and a packet of lunch. The outing is being organized by two neighborhood committees within Sun Yat-sen district. The children mobilize efficiently yet without shedding the relaxed air of any Chinese crowd. A small band of teachers smile and chat and do not seem harassed by the task of supervising such a group movement.

Later in the day I go to the same beach myself. By midday the sunshine has turned to rain and the truckloads of children begin a premature return to town. My De Soto passes them — not an easy thing to do on the winding dirt road which leads to Dairen's most popular seaside resort — soon after they have left the beach. Their hair has been flattened and their colored clothes made even brighter by the soaking rain.

The beach itself is pleasant though almost without waves, a lack which Chinese bathers seldom complain of. Many holiday makers remain despite continuing drizzle. Some splash in the serene, silvery water; a lot sip tea in the pavilion at water's edge. A few leap at volleyball; more sit at the gentler game of *bai-fen* (a sort of bridge).

Near Stalin Street hundreds of children are assembling
to go off in trucks to the seaside

I am required to base myself in a smaller pavilion for
restricted use

There are changing rooms, beach towels, umbrellas, floating boards and balloons, and other accouterments of a beach picnic. The majority of bathers appear to be in school, work, or organizational groups, rather than *en famille*.

Beside the public pavilion is a smaller pavilion for restricted use. I am required to base myself here. It turns out that I share it with one other party, headed by a portly older man with a damaged eye and close-cropped hair. As I arrive on the balcony from my changing box he climbs up from the sand and we fall into conversation. Though he wears only his bathing costume it is plain from the dress of his five or six young companions that these are PLA men.

Comrade Ho (as he introduces himself) works in the army and is sixty-two years old. He is very interested in why I have come to China and on precisely what basis. No less so in my impressions so far, and how they compare with those of my 1971 visit. Since my answers include reference to an apparent reduction, since 1971, in the role of the PLA in nonmilitary life, our conversation is at once keen and delicate. I know that Ho must be a senior officer, to be still active in the PLA at the age of sixty-two.

At one point we discuss industry in Dairen and I ask him if he lives in the area. No, he lives in Shenyang, is down for a short break. Shenyang is not only the capital of Liaoning province but the seat of the important military district which embraces all of *dong bei*. Its commander, just now, is also number one Party man in Liaoning, a Politbureau member, and one of China's top dozen figures. I inquire about him.

"Do you know Ch'en Hsi-lien?" Comrade Ho shoots me a sharp glance, then hides his surprise by gazing far out to sea as he quietly replies: "Yes, certainly; we work together." Now he knows that I know he is a senior officer. He adds one remark before the talk spirals down to banalities: "Ch'en Hsi-lien is above me" (*shang ji*).

It is hardly necessary to talk with Ho to find out that his position in the PLA is not a lowly one. As he comes up from the sand one of the young PLA men puts a towel over his round and chubby shoulders. Before we settle into cane armchairs another lad approaches Ho with a shirt and puts it on him. During the conversation Ho calls out "socks"; a bright-eyed soldier hands over a pale blue silk pair. Soon the whole uniform is on, though Ho looks no more authoritative in it than out of it, for Chinese military officers (since 1965) wear no insignia of rank.

At one point Ho spots a floating log not far from the shore and expresses curiosity at it. One attentive assistant is soon stripped to his bathing suit, into the water, and out again carrying the unremarkable piece of wood, for our inspection.

I reflect that, if style echoes substance, the military in *dong bei,* where the top army and political people seem fused into a single elite, may not have suffered the eclipse since 1971 that the central military apparatus of Lin Piao suffered.

❊ ❊ ❊

Returning to Dairen my De Soto gets caught in a traffic jam such as you rarely see in China. Toward the city, buses, trams, and the usual swarm of bicycles are joined by the string of khaki trucks full of picnickers pouring back from the beach. So although automobiles are few, it takes us ninety minutes to cover a stretch that only took thirty minutes on the way seaward.

One landmark by the roadside catches our attention: a large signboard at a fork in the way some eight kilometers from Dairen. As we pass the signboard four workmen are painting over a quotation from Mao in white characters on a red background. Of course it is possible that the white characters will be restored later. On the other hand, all over Dairen there are plain red signboards where there used to run political exhortations.

By all measures available, Dairen in 1973 does not seem a very politicized town; certainly it is less so than Shanghai, Wuhan, or Peking.

Hardly a building has a slogan atop it. Billboards with a word from Chairman Mao are rare. Fences, trees, and trams do not carry political messages. Former Christian churches are not adorned with posters about class struggle. I do not see a single Dairen citizen wearing a badge with Mao's face or a slogan.

The ear receives the same impression as the eye. Factory workers and supervisors do not dress up every point in political garments. The wrong line of Liu Shao-ch'i and Lin Piao is scarcely mentioned unless I raise it myself. The Cultural Revolution as a whole does not bulk large in accounts given of life and work in Dairen, except in the sphere of education. Fewer works of Marx, Lenin, and Mao have been distributed in Liaoning than in most provinces (six million items during 1972 sounds a hell of a lot; but at one item for every six people the ratio is comparatively low).

To be sure, the heart of Dairen beats according to well-established political choices. Society is run on socialist principles: equality, dominance by the working class through the Communist Party, service to the people. But in the city's 1973 mood, politics is generally implicit, built into daily choices and priorities, rather than an emblem added to each thing said or done.

After I left Dairen, this mood changed a bit. In the glow of the Tenth Congress of the CCP, there was a rise in political temperature. By late 1973, it was apparent in cultural affairs; to a lesser degree also in industry and in general political line.

At one construction engineering company, an intriguing issue arose near the end of 1973. Is "wining and dining" of clients and colleagues just an exchange of courtesies, or something more sinister? Most of the company's leading people felt it was quite harmless. But dissenters — younger men and women, with grievances against the top leadership — murmured from the wings.

They took a cue from the Tenth Congress of the CCP, at which "going against the tide" was a keynote phrase. They "dared to go against the tide" of the company's Party elite. Wining and dining, they said, expresses the "decadent style of the bourgeoisie." The question, they contended, is one of struggle between two class lines.

Within a couple of months their insurgency had won out and won fame. A report was published in *Liaoning Daily* which summed up: "Going against the tide is a Marxist-Leninist principle."

Going against the tide became a bandwagon. The target was stuffy Party (and other established) authority. A big shift, this, from the time of my visit in July 1973, when Party authority was riding high. By autumn it became fine, at least for a season, to do things which could be explained by flourishing the phrase, "It is right to rebel."

It was fashionable, suddenly, to assert that no criticism of the Cultural Revolution was tolerable. By October 1973, there was even a call to "let a hundred flowers bloom, let a hundred schools contend" — shorthand for speaking your mind, standing up against tin gods who possess office but not wisdom.

The struggle of a schoolgirl against "the tide" hit Liaoning as a big news story in January 1974. Thirteen-year-old Yang Yin faced a fifth-grade exam in social studies. "To go from Peking to Canton by train," one question inquired, "what major cities must you pass through?"

Little Yang Yin wrestled with the question, felt it a mindless burden. She took her courage in her hands. From her pen crept an apt, if pert, poem which began:

> *Every railway leads to Canton,*
> *Our teacher's question is wanton.*

The poem claimed that the distance from Peking to Canton is not so far that a roundabout trip can be ruled out. It snorted about "questions without qualification" that are "worrisome to pupils."

Teacher Ma said Yang Yin's poem was counterrevolutionary. He ordered her to cut grass as punishment. Classmates were mobilized to bother her. She was excluded from classes. Her father — a middle-school teacher — was pestered with questions from the leadership of Yang Yin's school, until he burst out to Yang Yin one day: "Maybe you can go on, but I cannot stand it any longer. You have to go to school there; I have to work here."

Yang Yin decided that enough was enough; she sent a complaint to the CCP committee of the city. The city authorities supported Yang Yin. Her climb back to dignity began. But teacher Ma still made difficulties for her, if more cautiously. She took the matter higher; the poet's pen turned out a letter to the Liaoning CCP.

This time Yang Yin hit the headlines. Her letter struck the right note for the times. It splashed the front page of *Liaoning Daily*, evoked an editorial. The paper praised Yang Yin for refusing to be "as obedient as a little sheep." Ma was flayed for caring too much about his prestige. "Is this not to inflate the arrogance of the bourgeoisie and display the power of Confucius?" Little Yang Yin found herself a model rebel, symbol of a healthy challenge to arbitrary authority.

Especially in culture, "going against the tide" became a motif of Dairen life during early 1974. There was also a sharpening of line in some other spheres. "Special privilege" was hit: securing easy entry to schools, using high office to get a fancy apartment. Certain individuals were lauded for putting "principle" above the smooth benefits of Party membership. Everyone was warned against backsliding from the concert pitch of the Cultural Revolution. The countryside was insistently hailed as the true frontier. The exam system was sniped at. The People's Militia was trumpeted. All signs of a breeze from the left.

But it was not a hurricane like 1966. A tightening of the existing policies, not an injection of brand new concepts. A shaking up of stragglers, not a drive to remove top officeholders.

Two slogans were bandied about in Dairen during 1974: "support the newly emerging things of socialism," as well as "dare to go against the tide." The first was relatively moderate; the second was radical. "Newly emerging things" refers to policies and organs which emerged after the dust of the Cultural Revolution had settled. "Going against the tide" is the pure milk of Cultural Revolutionary principle. No one opposed either slogan. But some favored one, some favored the other. Neither slogan triumphed, neither went under. Dairen walked on two legs. The push of consolidation; the pull of a fresh sally.

❁ ❁ ❁

Coming into Dairen by train you enter a forest of new housing blocks. In *dong bei* (as in much of China) it is not the growth of production that is spectacular, but the improved facilities of daily life. You see it in the free and easy access to culture of quality (if laundered for controversial content). In the stirring advances made in health, education, and welfare. In the position of women and other previously disadvantaged groups.

You see it in the range of consumer goods available to the average Chinese purse, which for a still-backward nation is quite good. Take three items which Dairen people like to save up for. Sales of wrist-watches in Liaoning in the first half of 1973 were up 33 percent as compared with the first half of 1972. Sales of sewing machines were up 26 percent; bicycles, up 11 percent. These are figures of a society that is raising its standard of living rapidly.

But it is statistics on new housing supplied to me in Dairen which really make the point. Dairen itself (with its core 1.1 million of Luta's 4.2 million people) has built, since Liberation in 1949, 2,330,000 square meters of new housing space. The pace of increase in new homes accelerates. Nineteen seventy-two saw 106,000 square meters added, compared with 34,000 square meters the previous year. The expectation in August 1973 is that by December the figure for new space completed in 1973 would rise to 450,000 square meters. This is a high rate of new housing construction for an Asian city.

I visit a number of homes in two quite different parts of Dairen. One is the Eternally Red (Yong hong) neighborhood, in a downtown district called Mouth of the Sandy River (Sha-he kou). It is here that Mr. and Mrs. Tan live.

By Dairen standards the area is pretty dense with people; 5,320 within 1.5 square kilometers. But the beat is measured, not teeming; the appearance ordered, not cluttered. The streets are broad and well paved, the skyline punctuated with telegraph poles and chimney pots. The homes are one or two stories, in brown brick or fawn stucco. It is a modern scene in its total impact. Narrow your eyes until the Chinese faces are blurred, and you could easily imagine yourself in the *banlieue* of Marseilles or the hilly fringe of Stuttgart.

A number of the homes in Eternally Red roughly resemble the Tans', but there is no standard model and they date from various periods. Quite a few houses are single storied, with two, three, or four families within the one building. The only touch of uniformity present up and down the community is that the wooden window frames are painted sky blue.

Move out beyond the central districts to those in the suburbs and the housing picture differs. I visit one new neighborhood called Facing

Late afternoon amid the apartment blocks of Facing the
Sun neighborhood

the Sun (Xiang yang), within Sweet Well (Gan jing) district. Its 857
households (3,720 people) occupy multistoried blocks put up since
Liberation. They are flat-roofed and built on four levels, the first in
local stone, the higher ones in brick. Concrete balustrades run the
length of each floor, some softened by mini-gardens in pots. In several
new blocks a modern supermarket occupies the first floor. People lean
from windowsills, gazing down with wide grins, as I inspect the blocks
from among rows of young trees.

Facing the Sun was planned around a few big plants. Five hundred
sixty of the 857 households have at least one member working at a
nearby chemical complex; another 140 have a member at Dairen Iron
and Steel Mill. The slightly higher wages as compared with Eternally
Red (highest wages are paid in big plants) are now and then reflected
in the contents of the homes — more sophisticated toys, a higher in-
cidence of transistor radios, two bicycles in the family rather than one.

In this new housing area the ratio of toilets and kitchens to apartments is higher than in Eternally Red, though still less than one to one.
Central heating is fairly general — the roofs of the blocks look odd

for Dairen since there are no chimneys — and so is gas in the kitchen. Residents talk of how gas is more convenient and less polluting than the briquette stoves they previously used. On several public walls I see a red poster: "To Use Electricity Sparingly Is Everyone's Responsibility!"

Rents are more uniform and a little higher than in the older housing areas. Dairen now has a standard rent charge of thirteen fen per square meter for recent and new apartments. It is a reasonable price by Chinese standards (the figure in Shenyang is twenty fen per square meter) and comically cheap by American standards.

Mr. Wang and his family welcome me to their home of four rooms, which is about the size of the downtown home of the Tans. Its third-floor view is well exploited by balconies on each side. From the outside one we see Dairen port as a pale blue pencil line on the horizon. Down in the block's leisure yard two Ping-Pong games are going on. The surface of the table is concrete; the improvised net is a row of bricks. The skill of the child-players startles a Western visitor.

Mr. Wang works as a technician at the chemical plant. He is a member of the Facing the Sun management body (revolutionary committee). I wonder if this helped him acquire the third-floor location — preferable to those at the top because there are fewer stairs to climb, preferable to those at the bottom because of its view — but he laughs and says absolutely not.

The Wang household of eight has five breadwinners and a high total monthly income of 290 yuan. Out of this, 12 yuan goes for rent including utilities — half as much again as the Tans pay. Miss Wang, who is a schoolteacher, observes that although rents have not risen in Dairen over the years, utilities have recently gone up slightly.

The Wangs are better off than the Tans, possessing two bicycles and both an ordinary and a transistor radio. But even in this advanced apartment with its gas and central heating there is no question of a bath, a telephone, a TV, or a refrigerator. A public bathhouse is just down the street; a public phone is downstairs; TV is available at work and recreation centers. The only place in the neighborhood with a refrigerator is the medical clinic.

✸ ✸ ✸

Each of Dairen's five districts has within it a number of communes, and within these are the neighborhoods.* Thus Eternally Red neighborhood is part of Sun Yat-sen Park commune, which is part of Mouth of the Sandy River district. The purpose behind dividing districts up into communes and neighborhoods is to mobilize and control people at their place of residence.

Mr. Shih and Mrs. Yang do not seem fazed to have me come quite early on a Sunday morning and ask how Eternally Red works. (I cannot help noticing that Mrs. Yang has three vivid pink lovebites on her neck, but our topic of conversation lies elsewhere.)

As a local government unit, the neighborhood revolutionary committee gets its power by delegation from the district and is responsible to the commune and the district for good performance. There is a Communist Party branch within Eternally Red. Its members are found among the leading members of the revolutionary committee, which acknowledges that it works under the guidance of the Party.

There is more activity at the neighborhood level than there used to be, because the Cultural Revolution stimulated local initiative. Mrs. Yang, a plain, forthright woman who takes great pride in Eternally Red, explains the stepped-up program in political education.

There are seventeen groups studying Marxism. They meet after 4:00 P.M., three times a week, seeking to understand Marxism and apply it to local, national, and international issues. Most of the groups are now concentrating on three works: excerpts from Lenin's *State and Revolution,* Mao's simple yet brilliant essay "On Practice," and his piece about the relation of ideas to material forces, "Where Do Correct Ideas Come From?"

With Mrs. Yang trailing behind, I wander to a group of apartments not far from the neighborhood committee office. A knock on one door disturbs a young man who is resting and reading. Mr. Liu is twenty-eight and single; he works in a metallurgical plant. He used to be a pilot — flying a plane similar to the Soviet MIG 17 — and concedes that life in the air was more fun than life in the factory. But his wage

* Concerning the Chinese term translated here as "neighborhood" see note on page 78.

124

of sixty-five yuan a month is more than he got in the PLA (the term People's Liberation Army covers all three military services).

Mr. Liu is spending his day off around the house. With him for the afternoon is a former school friend, now a functionary (*zhi-gong*) in far-off Kiangsi province. Visiting Dairen on business, he has a few hours off and relaxes at Liu's place. Both men have been browsing in recent issues of *Scientific Experimentation* (*Ke-xue shi-yan*), a monthly of text and pictures started in 1971.

What arrests me in Liu's neat room is a framed montage of several dozen Mao badges. "They look colorful on the wall," I remark, "but why don't you wear one?" Liu seems a bit shy on this matter. "They are too big. It is not so convenient to wear them; better to frame them."

This exchange throws light on the Marxism study groups, and on the general approach to politics in 1973. During the Cultural Revolution a man felt naked without a Mao badge. Seldom was there not within reach the little red book, *Quotations from Chairman Mao*. But in the last couple of years ritual has faded and study has surged. Although Mr. Liu tries the answer about the badges being too big to wear, a moment later he acknowledges a change of political atmosphere since the time of badge wearing and the vogue of *Quotations*.

Today it is not enough to cite a sentence from Mao, used like a biblical text in an emergency. Study of longer slabs of Marxist writing is required, as well as their application to concrete problems. Mr. Liu is a member of one of the seventeen study groups in Eternally Red. During 1973 he read *State and Revolution,* and we discuss this high-flying essay.

Liu cannot quickly name a case of how he has applied Lenin's analysis to a current issue. "There are certainly people within the neighborhood," Mrs. Yang observes from behind my shoulder, "who find the Marxism study difficult." Some (I later learn) sigh at the piles of pamphlets to be read: "Our minds get as full of studying things as the heavens are vast and the earth broad" (*tian ye da le, di ye kuan le, nao-zi li xiang de shi-qing ye duo le*). Others complain that "old books" and "foreign books" have no use for China today.

At any rate Mr. Liu is making an earnest effort to tap any lessons

Lenin may have for Dairen. Meanwhile his badges, bereft of their political meaning as weapon and shield, have become museum pieces, decorating a wall, humbled beside photos of airplanes and the family.

The neighborhood exercises social functions of a cradle-to-grave kind. Primary schools, kindergartens, and a clinic with paramedical personnel ("barefoot doctors") are administered by Mrs. Yang and other busy bees on the committee. The 170 retired folk in Eternally Red are helped with the painful logistics of life by special service teams. And they are drawn into study groups where they testify to others about the bitter days before Liberation, and try to learn the strange new things of Marxism.

Eternally Red trains and mounts its own teams in basketball, badminton, table tennis, volleyball, and football (soccer). It does not, though, possess its own gym or playing field. Mouth of the Sandy River district organizes matches in these sports between its component neighborhoods. Eternally Red also gets its people out for informal recreation. A favorite excursion is to the broad beaches of Pohai Bay, sheltered by the Liao-tung peninsula.

The neighborhood committee carries on a kind of moral-political supervision. Typical is the mechanism for dealing with marital squabbles, which Mrs. Yang explains to me. The neighborhood appoints a "reconciliation committee" (*tiao-jie wei-yuan-hui*) of wise and reliable folk, to try to put the pair back together again. Thus the problem is quickly made a thing of neighborhood concern. In the course of its work the reconciliation committee gathers evidence at the workplaces of the sparring couple. I do not know how troubled partners view this approach; none were within reach for interview.

The reconciliation committee can only wield the power of reason. But it also has on its side the nibbling social pressure which is a fact of life in a Chinese city. Socialist China does not like to see too high a rate of failed marriages. Women are well to the fore on the neighborhood committee, and so on the reconciliation committee as well. The pressure on the couple to patch up their marriage, therefore, is very strong. If the committee fails to smooth the partners' feathers, one of them (or both) may go to the district and ask for a divorce. Then it is a matter for a law court to decide. If a divorce is granted, it doesn't cost a fen.

When it comes to social morals — politics in China is an octopus; morals is one of its tentacles — the neighborhood committee supervises life in the community partly through the subunit of a residents' committee (*ju-min wei-yuan-hui*). In Dairen, and *dong bei* in general, the residents' committee is less important than in most Chinese cities. This is because the neighborhoods are themselves, by national standards, very small, there being in *dong bei* cities a commune level between that of neighborhood and that of district. The need for subdivision of a neighborhood is less pressing.

Eternally Red is made up of four residents' areas. A residents' committee has no complex financial structure like a neighborhood committee; its budget is small and self-generating. It does not have full-time administrators. Nor do residents' committees of Eternally Red run economic enterprises — "production teams" — though residents' committees in many Chinese cities do.

But the residents' committee is a shepherd to its flock in numerous ways. It maintains a service station with a telephone and message facilities, a breakfast shop, and a mending and repair service. Especially through the feminine eye, which counts for even more at the residents' committee level than at the neighborhood level, the residents' committee looks to household sanitation. Are there rats? Lay DDT. Do the Wangs leave garbage about? Fine them. Is Mrs. Tao pregnant again? More sessions on family planning.

Eternally Red does not keep its own figures on birthrate and population increase, as do neighborhoods in some Chinese cities. But the municipality supplies an overall statistic. During 1972 the population increase in Dairen proper was at the rate of 17.4 per thousand (officials expect the 1973 birthrate to be 0.25 percent lower than that of 1972). It is a moderate rate by national norms; higher than Shanghai and Peking but lower than some cities; much lower than the rate in most of the countryside.

Being sparsely populated — even Liaoning province, the densest of the region's three provinces, has only about eighty people to the square kilometer — *dong bei* has not felt population pressure to the same degree as a crowded city short of housing like Canton. Still, education about family planning is accelerating in the city and the immediate aim is to bring the annual rate of population increase down to fifteen per thousand.

❀ ❀ ❀

I am introduced to the economic life of Eternally Red by a cheerful, leathery cadre called Shih. What he has to say, Shih can put briefly. We talk about wages and output, but I never feel I'm dealing with an organization man. Over and above the facts and figures, there is the sense between us of two human beings groping with a will to meet each other.

The citizens of Eternally Red work at some two hundred different factories and offices. But 330, all but 20 of them women, work at several enterprises run by the neighborhood itself. These enterprises are rather profitable. Output was worth 500,000 yuan in 1972, and the profit, after paying wages, raw material costs, and taxes to the district, was a healthy 100,000 yuan. Mr. Shih — who until recently was a cadre in another district of Dairen — says this level of profit is quite common in Dairen's neighborhood factories.

I visit two of Eternally Red's factories. Eighty women, plus a few boys, sit in pleasant rooms lit with fluorescent lights, sewing by machine. This factory turns out a range of colored leather shoes. Blackboards are chalked with details of work schedules and target quotas. The atmosphere is one of brisk industry, though workers chat quietly with each other as they stitch.

Posters urging birth control stare down from the walls. They depict a beaming, sturdy, almost extravagantly healthy-looking family of four persons. Mother and father each carry a work tool; she looks as tall and robust as he. The four family members loom large on the poster. In the background are sketches of scenes of production, leisure, and family life, which hint at the advantages of families' having only two children. At the foot of the poster five characters say, "Family Planning Is Good."

The leather for the shoes comes, already cut out, from a leather concern in Mouth of the Sandy River district. Other raw materials are purchased directly from various sources by the neighborhood. A shoe is almost but not totally finished at this factory; it goes off to the district plant to be steamed. The marketing is done through Luta's Bureau of Light Industry.

The eighty cheerful ladies, like medical personnel in their crisp white caps and starched aprons, make 570 pairs of shoes each day. Their factory is paid, by the district enterprise, thirty-five fen per pair for the processing it performs. I watch workers arriving with raw materials, departing with shoes ready for steaming. Everything is carried on tricycles with a tray fixed to the back; the factory does not have a motor vehicle.

Mr. Shih walks with me through some placid lanes to a second factory run by Eternally Red. This one makes large metal boxes, used for drying purposes by a nearby biological sciences research institute. These workers, too, are nearly all women. All whom I chat with were until the Cultural Revolution simple housewives.

The factory is within two or three minutes' walk from the houses of these women. They go home for lunch, keep in close touch with their children. Toddlers are cared for either at the neighborhood nursery or by a grandparent living in the household. Conditions at the box factory are clean, spacious, and airy, as at the shoe factory, though there is not the same buzz of conversation. Like the shoes, the gray boxes are being processed under an arrangement with a district enterprise.

Wages in the factories of Eternally Red average thirty yuan a month (the highest is ninety yuan and the lowest is twenty-four yuan). Much lower, then, than wages of workers in the larger enterprises run by district or municipality. Eternally Red can give me no figures for the average wage among all its employed residents. But at Facing the Sun (where many residents work at a large new chemical complex) this figure is just on seventy yuan. Twice as much, in other words, as the thirty-five yuan averaged by workers in Facing the Sun's own factories.

In Shenyang I meet two remarkable women, leaders of a group that founded a neighborhood committee factory out of nothing, making steel products from waste materials. They earn but thirty-four yuan and twenty-nine yuan, while their husbands, who could hardly be working harder than these indefatigable women, make eighty-five and eighty-seven yuan in a big plant outside the neighborhood. (I will return to these ladies in a moment.)

Of course most neighborhood committee factory workers were not long ago housewives earning nothing. Quite a few, too, are retired folk who just wish to keep busy. The work is also light, the pressures are mild, compared with larger industry. Fewer workers in neighborhood committee factories are CCP members than is the case in industry at large. Of the 330 who work in Eternally Red's factories, only 15 are Party members, and a further 10 are CYL members.

Occasionally the founding of a local factory is a story of amazing grass-roots initiative and persistence. Mrs. Ma and Mrs. Wu (the two steel women) are worth a short detour to Shenyang for an illustration.

West of the Railroad district in Liaoning's capital is made up of communes, normally a rural unit in China. An unusual arrangement, a *dong bei* specialty, it is a leftover from an experiment in urban communes which began in 1959 but in general did not come to much. Citizens in West of the Railroad, even so, do not refer to themselves as "commune members" — as country dwellers do — but as "neighborhood committee residents."

Heavy Industry commune — place-names do not soar in Shenyang — contains ten neighborhood committees (forty residents' committees within these ten). Each neighborhood runs one factory. Smelting Powdered Metal factory in Number Seven neighborhood gives me as fascinating a glimpse as I have ever had of Chinese industry.

Mrs. Wu and Mrs. Ma are both characters, of quite different types. Mrs. Wu is lean and nimble, her face a bit horsey; she fronts the world with her teeth. Her wiry frame seems emphasized by loose blue overalls and a shirt that is too big for her. She talks in gruff tones, her features screwed up together in one total smile. She leans against a wall, one hand cupping the chin, weighing me up as she chats with me.

Mrs. Ma is a burly woman, made to seem even more so by monstrous overalls and a green shirt like the sail of a galleon. Easy to imagine her captaining a ship or driving a truck. She is the key leader in the story of Smelting Powdered Metal. You can see it in her stance

Mrs. Ma is a burly woman in monstrous overalls. . . . Easy to imagine her captaining a ship. Mrs. Wu is lean and nimble, her face a bit horsy

The slogan "Learn from Ta Ch'ing" is found in many Chinese factories. The smaller banner in this Dairen plant reads: "China Ought to Make a Greater Contribution to Mankind"

and face. The hands do not fidget, but hang down by the blue denim as if they own their air space. The mouth spreads out in a line of authority; the cloth headgear sits on a face that has no illusions. But the features are still attractive when the big smooth face breaks into a smile. Her complexion has stood up well to eight years of steel dust.

Mrs. Ma, Mrs. Wu, and seven other housewives started the factory in 1966. They said to themselves, "We women also have two hands," sought a way to push up Liaoning's industrial output. They dropped in on factories to ask advice. Especially did their ears prick up at the suggestion of turning waste iron oxide into steel products.

Veterans laughed at them. One even said: "You will have terrible difficulties, and shed tears. The tears will be like noodles running down your faces. Better for you girls, after all, to make noodles than to try to make metals."

But the gritty nine persisted, grabbing like a lifeline at Mao's teaching, "women hold up half the sky." Eventually Heavy Industry commune tossed them without enthusiasm a strip of waste land. A flicker of a smile replaces Mrs. Ma's austere expression as she recalls this first triumph.

To get started the housewives needed ten thousand yuan, as well as fifty tons of fire bricks to build a kiln. Waste half bricks they scrounged from a fire-brick factory. For the outside (less vital) parts of the kiln, they used ordinary red bricks. They found old tar drums and rolled them back through the streets to make a chimney. Their husbands began to help them on Sundays.

West of the Railroad district was now convinced the ladies meant business and gave them small but rising grants of cash. After months of work the pioneers received for the first time a token wage. Entirely by the hands of the nine a patchwork plant eventually went up. One sifting machine that I see, still in its original form, is a creaking miracle of waste tin and 186 separate pieces of wood. Raw materials for the brave new factory were wheedled from a workshop which makes cables at Shenyang Rolling Mill.

Seven years later the factory turns out eighty kinds of simple tools. In 1972, after paying 55 percent of its profit to Heavy Industry commune, it had thirty thousand yuan left over to "expand production."

In the meantime the 9 persons have grown to 167. Thirty of these are men, but Mrs. Wu points out briskly that the revolutionary committee and the Party committee are "entirely female." The number of cadres has been held down to nine.

The raw iron, which used to come free from the Shenyang Rolling Mill, now costs fifteen yuan a ton. But as always the steel girls waste nothing: surplus heat from a contraption which heats the iron oxide is used to cook lunch.

At the dawn of things, picking out the iron ore from other materials, by hand magnet, used to take twenty women two weeks to prepare one kiln load. Today an electric-powered magnetized belt — developed entirely within the factory — enables three people in one day to muster one kiln load. The ladies began with will alone; they have added technique. (The ore is packed in cylinders, mixed with layers of newspaper and charcoal. It is heated at one thousand degrees centigrade, then fashioned into tools.)

Both Mrs. Ma and Mrs. Wu have visited Great Celebration (Tach'ing), the oil field in Black Dragon River province which is China's leading model industry. Their factory has notices hanging up which say, "Learn from Great Celebration." Housewives at the almost overpraised oil field have banded together, rather as the Shenyang nine have done. Whether it is Great Celebration that keeps these tough but gracious women going, or the inspiration of female creativity, or the simple human drive to be useful, they have made of mud and waste a temple of socialist self-reliance.

You could not say their life looks attractive, or their plant impressive. They work from 7:30 until 4:30 with an hour for lunch, six days a week, and have seven days off each year. The average wage is thirty yuan (highest is thirty-six, lowest is twenty-four). The factory lacks a trade union branch, pays only 70 percent of its workers' medical expenses, has no cafeteria or clubroom. There being nowhere for Mrs. Ma and Mrs. Wu to receive me — the first foreigner, they say, to come to the factory — we perch on logs of wood in the yard.

The workers are mostly simple, narrow women. They do not speak very good Mandarin. A chat here and there leaves me feeling that they inhabit an awfully circumscribed world. Political study at the factory seems fairly low-key. There are only 12 CCP members, plus 10 CYL members, among the 167.

And yet this factory with its unforgettable spirit is in a way more important to Liaoning and China than the giant rolling mills of Anshan. Japan laid the basis at Anshan. The nine housewives' feat is cut from the seamless cloth of post-Liberation China.

The Middle Kingdom is proud but also poor. It is too big, as well, to get rich simply by a single spasm of technical advance, or a dose of foreign aid, or even a bold new national economic plan. It must also mobilize month in and month out the hearts and sinew of its people; not instead of capital, but to ensure that limited capital is effectively used.

China must remake the motivations of its 850 million, not because attitudes alone determine history, but because no structural arrangements decreed from Peking will of themselves, today any more than during the dynasties, automatically enhance day-to-day human performance in the far provinces.

The spirit of a whole people, and the sense of responsibility of each person, is not less vital to building up a socialist society than to the original revolutionary seizure of power. These considerations, not high-powered technical advance, make the nine housewives important for Chinese industry.

For women in Liaoning, the feat of Smelting Powdered Metal has been a shot in the arm. But young women of tomorrow will not have it so tough as the nine had it. Mrs. Ma and Mrs. Wu made their own breakthrough only against great odds. The torch they lit is being passed to girls who don't need to start so far behind.

A province-wide congress in August 1973 gave a fillip to the women's movements of Liaoning. It was reported that 36,000 women have joined the CCP in Liaoning since the Cultural Revolution, and 400,000 girls have joined the CYL (43 percent of the CYL's province committee are female). Running through the congress like a refrain were two themes: women will be liberated only when they leave housework for productive labor; women's units will get nowhere save under the "absolute" leadership of the Party.

(In the countryside, women's rights lag as do other things. Many farm women are still chained to domestic routine. Marriage as a business transaction — the phrase is *Liaoning Daily*'s — remains a black cloud over women's hope for true individuality. The press often has to report that educated girls going to the communes get treated without respect.)

❖ ❖ ❖

I visit the Chou family in their apartment near the shoe factory. This leads me to a shell-carving factory, where twenty-five-year-old Miss Chou is a veteran of eight years' experience. Dairen Shell Carving Factory, under the authority of the Light Industry Bureau of Luta, must be among the most pleasant of the two hundred places at which Eternally Red residents work (only a few of them work in Eternally Red's own factories).

Miss Chou cycles ten minutes each morning to the factory, a yellow building with tall windows put up in 1964. She is a senior-middle-school graduate. All of the factory's 350 employees are graduates at least of junior middle school. New recruits seldom have experience of shell carving before joining the factory. How did Miss Chou come to enter this factory? "The state sent me." But first, "I expressed interest in coming here, because in school I was very interested in art."

For her work as a designer — carved shells are encrusted on the outline of the design — Miss Chou earns an excellent sixty-five yuan a month. The average wage (plus living allowance) is fifty yuan, the highest ninety-six yuan, the lowest thirty-one yuan. For a work force whose average age is twenty-seven, this is good pay. The average wage is two-thirds higher than that (thirty yuan) in the factories run by Eternally Red.

Work is eight hours a day, with one hour for lunch, six days a week. The only regular annual holidays are May 1, China's National Day (two days off), New Year, Spring Festival (three days), and March 8 (Women's Day).

But individuals get leave on other occasions. For illness of oneself or a member of one's family there is time off according to need. For the death of a parent, three days. For maternity, fifty-six days, seventy-two for twins.

Sunshine streams in from large windows to light up the
colorful scene of shells, paints, illustrated folios

Sunshine streams in from large windows to light up the colorful scene of shells, paints, illustrated folios, and the jazzy clothing of the workers, masked a little by white work coats. Air coolers keep the sultry day at bay; there are water pipes for winter heating.

At one of the tables with sunken tops, an old teacher (*lao-shi*) is passing on advice and gently making corrections. I watch him show a young girl, her complexion as fine as the smooth shells she is handling, how to use an electric drill to shape a shell. A thousand pieces from shells of twenty different kinds, he tells me, often go into the making of a single work.

Art books lie among glue pots and powdery knives. Miss Chou today culls design ideas from an illustrated copy of *Dream of the Red Chamber,* a famous historical novel still read but not often on sale. Her work group is producing a series of framed montages portraying scenes from this Ch'ing dynasty book. In another workroom, scenes of an elegant old court dance called *chang kong wu* take on the pink romanticism of shell form.

The walls are bare of political exhortation or propaganda. Dairen in general during 1973 is light on the former. Most of the shell carvers are unmarried, too, and thus unsuitable targets for birth control education — the topical line of wall propaganda in town. Copies of *People's Daily* and *Liaoning Daily* hang on hooks in all workrooms.

You feel no tension, sniff no militancy in the atmosphere of this factory. It produces some goods with "feudal" or even "decadent" themes which during the Cultural Revolution were quite out of bounds in many Chinese craft factories.

I do see a few works like "People's Communes Are Fine" and "Raise High the Red Banner of Mao Tse-tung's Thought." But there are more whose theme is from novels of the past, or from legends, such as "Monkey Subdues the Demon" and "Chang-O Flies to the Moon." Workers I chat with are not able to give examples of how the themes chosen for carvings are now more class-conscious than before 1966.

Neither Red Guards nor great turbulence hit this place in the overheated days of 1966–1967. Some PLA people joined the factory's revolutionary committee for a while, but all had gone by early 1971. The proportion of CCP members in the factory is low (25 of 350).

But that of Communist Youth League members is high (103 of 350).

Miss Chou is not a member of the nine-person revolutionary committee which runs the factory, but Mrs. Chang, one of its five women members and its vice-chairman, meets me and answers questions. Mrs. Chang is a woman of drive. Quality and quantity of production seem to be the gods before whom she kneels. She explains the way things work with frankness and patience.

The factory began in 1958 as a producer of "plaster products" and "wax fruits." Only later did it begin the more exacting craft of shell carving, and acquire some *lao-shi* who were specialists at it. Twenty percent of the shells and other raw materials come from the Dairen area, the rest from Kwangtung and Kwangsi provinces, including Kwangtung's lush Hainan Island just by Vietnam.

Before the Cultural Revolution carving was two-dimensional. Shells were arranged into montages, to make a screen or to be framed and hung on a wall. But since the Cultural Revolution three-dimensional work is taken in stride. I see a Dragon Boat, shimmering, pristine, made from shells of twenty colors, in the showroom's glass case.

It comes as no surprise, after seeing the price tags, to learn that most of the goods are for export. Sometimes you see a shell montage in the corridor of the first-class section of a train, or a shell ornament in a public building. The prices are well beyond a private Chinese purse.

Mrs. Chang was trained as a tailor and cannot carve shells. When this factory was established — amid the Communist Party's zeal during the 1950s to revitalize crafts — she left her needle and thread and came here as an administrator. The Party secretary, the factory's number one figure, does not know anything about shell carving either; he arrived from another trade only last year. However, all eighteen cadres, including the Party secretary, spend one or two days a week at hand labor.

The shell-carving factory works to three plans — yearly, seasonal, monthly — which are set, after consultation with all members of the factory, by the Bureau of Light Industry. In 1972 the value of output was 480,000 yuan. The plan for 1973 set a target of 700,000 yuan. I ask how such a leap is possible and Mrs. Chang replies: "Because a particularly large number of apprentices have recently completed their two years of learning and taken their proud places as full producers."

❀ ❀ ❀

One young resident of Eternally Red, twenty-two-year-old Mr. Kuo, works as a furnace operator at Dairen Glass Products Factory. Kuo is a handsome man, with a rather flat face and fine features, born in Shantung province (source of much of the original immigration from the heart of China to Manchuria).

His household setup would be unusual, were there not in Chinese homes so many variations from a straight father-mother-children pattern. He is single but dwells with the wife of his brother. The brother has a job in Anshan and "we do not know when he may come back." It is not apparent that the wife is yearning daily for his return.

Living in the small apartment are two little children of the marriage and also the mother of the wife. Kuo is younger than his brother, seems respectful of his sister-in-law and her babies. I meet him at home on his rest day. He is rather vacantly nursing the younger child, while the grandmother copes methodically with household matters.

Later I drive to Kuo's factory, just before boarding the afternoon express for Peking. The Dairen Glass Products Factory is old but its present plant, established in 1958, is ten times as large as the one on a previous site. Into the factory go truckloads of feldspar, lodestone, and other stones. Out flow three thousand kinds of bright, cunning, amusing glass goods, 60 percent of them for export.

A worker twisting a molten ball into an elegant, gleaming fish or panda is a dramatic sight. A pull here; the eyes appear. A flourish there; the tail has formed as if by magic. A nip with the pliers; the fish's lips curl into a grin. All before you could count to twenty.

Liaoning province has three other such factories; China has fifty-odd. This one employs fifteen hundred workers, 40 percent of them women, and is considered a medium-size factory.

Working conditions are good except for excessive heat in the area of the furnaces (it is fifteen hundred degrees centigrade inside these monsters with orange eyes). The glass-people seem relaxed as they pad back and forth in cotton slippers (*bu xie*). Electric air blowers reduce the heat from stupefying to roasting. Tall, earnest workers, wearing a variety of caps, have the grave, angular faces of the Northeast. They wield pliers and hooks in hands protected by thick white mittens. Everyone has some kind of stick in his hand, as if the room is full of people ready to go fishing.

Wages here are fairly high as all over *dong bei,* in both state and local factories. A technician who is a college graduate tops the wage list with ninety-nine yuan a month. The lowest wage is forty yuan. The average is sixty yuan (plus a living allowance which approximates five and a half yuan). All workers are middle-school graduates, all have been trained in glasswork entirely within the factory.

The factory has its own kindergarten, a clinic with four doctors and five nurses, a full range of sporting and cultural activities. At the rather bare factory canteen almost everyone eats lunch (ten to twenty fen), and some two to three hundred eat dinner as well. Few eat breakfast there but it is possible to do so.

Like the shell-carving factory, the glass factory operates under the Light Industry Bureau of the city. Its revolutionary committee, functioning of course under the guidance of the factory's Party committee, is made up of five cadres, six rank-and-file workers, and two PLA persons (four until 1972). Thirteen percent of the fifteen hundred workers are cadres. These "white shirt" types must put in at least forty days per year at physical labor.

The factory has its own Party branch, and the figure for Party members is a very high four hundred out of fifteen hundred. Another one hundred younger workers try their fortune in the resuscitated CYL. But as elsewhere in Dairen, one has no impression of red-hot political consciousness. The Cultural Revolution did scorch the glass factory more than it scraped the shell-carving factory; the continuing presence of PLA cadres testifies to it. Red Guards lived among the furnaces for two months, blowing much hot air but no glass.

Those days seem far away. Mr. Kuo remembers them with a detached, even irresponsible amusement. He let his hair down for a time, and later, as if it were neither good nor bad, but inevitable, he stepped back from the spontaneities of free-for-all politics and resumed the routine of production.

Tall, earnest glassblowers have the grave, angular faces
of the Northeast

A word from the sponsor stands guard over Dairen port

Today the trade union branch, felled by the huff and puff of the Red Guard period, is back in place. Since May 1973 it has its own office at the factory. Everyone belongs to the union. Its main current task is to cut down the heat in the workshops during summertime.

Three technical advances have been made since the Cultural Revolution. Risk of lung trouble from stone grinding has been reduced by a special rinsing process. The furiously hot furnaces are operated from a greater distance. Three colors can now be blended in a single piece of glass, instead of one as before.

There has been no attempt, though, to fulfill the Cultural Revolutionary call for handicraftsmen to stop fashioning "emperors, nobles, and beauties" and start knocking out "workers, peasants, and soldiers." Here they make eye-popping toys, amusing fish, figures from China's dynastic past. But no images of toilers, no statues of Mao Tse-tung, nothing that could speak a political message to a hungry heart.

The chairman of the revolutionary committee seeks to reassure me: "We may try some products depicting socialist construction at a later date." But he does not try to squeeze out from the principles of class struggle a direct application to the transformation of lodestone into glass fish. If these glassblowers were once tugged by tension between "red" and "expert" they seem now to have found a stable balance between the two, which does not require them to wear their politics like a garland of gaudy beads.

✿ ✿ ✿

Inevitably a few at least of those residing in Eternally Red are found among the thirteen thousand workers at the vast port which stretches out like the forehead of Dairen. The married daughter of Mr. Tan, whose home we have visited, is one of fifteen hundred women in this army of thirteen thousand. As an invoice clerk Ai-mei counts as part of the thousand office personnel (*guan-li ren-yuan*) who process papers which help keep the ships of forty lands gliding in and out.

Dairen port is a splendid sight on a summer morning. It has a wide ocean setting, which Shanghai's and Tientsin's do not have. It is more expansively laid out, and its air less polluted, than either of these.

Neatly cultivated gardens run beside the railways which lead onto each of twelve docks. Dozens of ships, most of them twenty-five thousand tons or more, are lined up like ducks feeding at the edge of a pond.

A large tablet with a poem in Mao's own handwriting stands in a central spot, alongside two banner phrases in red letters on a white fence: "Ten Thousand Years to the Great Leader Chairman Mao"; "Ten Thousand Years to the Communist Party of China."

A passenger terminal throbs with the bustle of travelers who find a boat cheaper than a train. Third class to Shanghai costs fourteen yuan and second class is eighteen yuan; the cheapest train seat sets you back thirty yuan.

The docks themselves present as international an array of faces as you will see in China, with African, Arab, and Asian seamen to the fore. Armed police stand impassive outside blue wooden boxes at intervals along each dock. From the top of the port administration tower I may freely photograph the dock area, but not the opposite perspective of Dairen city.

Spokesmen of the port's large revolutionary committee seem proud of the progress made, and with some reason. They talk in concrete terms. No mention is made throughout an entire morning of Liu Shao-ch'i, Lin Piao, or "struggle between two lines."

The facility, begun in 1899 and completed in 1930, was planned to handle twelve million tons of cargo each year, but this figure was never reached under Japanese rule. On the eve of the Cultural Revolution the full capacity of tons was topped for the first time. In 1972 no less than twenty million tons of cargo was shipped or received. In the first half of 1974, 21 percent more traffic was handled than in the first half of 1973.

Mechanized work has now reached 80 percent of the whole, compared with 60 percent on the eve of the Cultural Revolution. Fifty ships of up to forty-six thousand tons weight can be handled at the same time, aided by conveyor belts introduced during the last five years, and specialized docks for timber, coal, charcoal, and petrol.

I ask the vice-chairman when the remaining PLA cadres (9 percent of the revolutionary committee) will leave the port and return to their military duties. He replies with spirit: "When the port has finished re-establishing the rules and regulations necessary to efficient work."

Ai-mei says she likes the cosmopolitan atmosphere of a workplace which deals with ships of forty nations and seamen of seventy-odd nations. She values, too, the chance to assist China "make a greater contribution to the world" through trade. She points out with pleasure that a number of the ships — including one that I see unloading wheat from Canada — were built in Dairen within the past three years.

Ai-mei has picked up a few phrases of Japanese and English at the port. Apparently because of circumstances in the Cultural Revolution, she did not complete junior middle school. Her wage is nevertheless fifty-four yuan a month, slightly more than that of her bus conductor husband.

The average monthly pay packet at the port is a fat sixty-nine yuan (plus five yuan living allowance). The lowest is fifty yuan. The highest, earned by technical personnel among whom are graduates from colleges all over China, is eighty yuan. This range of wages — it was wider before the Cultural Revolution — is perhaps the narrowest I have encountered in a large enterprise in China. Can there be a smaller wage differential in any enterprise of thirteen thousand persons anywhere in the world?

Still a long way off for Ai-mei, retirement at the port comes five years earlier than in all but heavy industries. At fifty for women, at fifty-five for men; at sixty and sixty-five for office personnel including cadres. As is fairly standard in China, the retired worker receives 70 percent of the wages he was taking home at the time he stopped work.

Ai-mei and her husband live with her father, so she does not benefit from the port's housing development of fifty thousand apartments at a rent of three yuan a month. But she enjoys the free facilities of the port's own hospital, with its 260 medical staff including 50 doctors. Cultural activities go on at the port — Ai-mei belongs to a dance troupe — but foreign sailors have their own recreation center. It is sealed off entirely from the social activities of the Chinese dockers.

❁ ❁ ❁

In Eternally Red every family seems to have a foot in the world of education. The Tan family includes one primary- and one secondary-school pupil. Miss Chou of the shell-carving factory has two brothers at middle school. The sister of Liu, the metallurgical worker, is a chemistry student at college. Study books can be seen in all living rooms and many bedrooms. There is great keenness for what is summed up as "learning for the sake of revolution." Among the 5,320 people of Eternally Red, the number of pupils and students is an astonishing 1,860.

Even in Luta as a whole — semiagricultural outskirts and all — the percentage at books is not much lower. Of the 4.2 million population, 1.1 million are pupils or students. This means full-time learners, not counting those at spare-time (ye-yu) schools, or the political study groups that meet perhaps three times a week.

The Chinese are making up for past lost educational time. The slogan is "popularization of education." This includes universalization of school attendance by children of primary-school age in backward pockets of the nation where a substantial minority were until recently absent from schools. Luta long ago achieved that basic goal (it boasts 1,750 primary schools).

The slogan also refers to a big effort to hoist the percentage of youth going through to the end of junior middle school toward the 100 percent mark, at least to the 80 or 90 percent mark. Luta, with 280 middle schools, is also a leading urban area in this regard.

Education beyond middle school has been and remains a more problematic realm. I peep into it by inquiring after Miss Liu, the chemistry student, who attends the Dairen Polytechnic (gong-ye xue-yuan). There are nine colleges: Liaoning Teachers' College, Dairen Polytechnic, Dairen University, Japanese Language College (outside the city), Light Industry College, Medical College, Railway Institute, Shipbuilding Institute, Finance and Economics Institute.

I spend an afternoon with five faculty of Liaoning Teachers' College and two faculty of Dairen Polytechnic. It is a warm day and I have come in a hurry from the seaside, wearing sandals and casual clothes. To my relief, the teachers are dressed about the same, except that their sport shirts are hanging out while mine is tucked in, and they wear socks under their plastic sandals. The conversation is as informal as the attire, though it leaves me with mixed impressions.

Both Liaoning Teachers' College (LTC) and Dairen Polytechnic (DP) were founded after Liberation and faced in the Cultural Revolution their first great crisis. They are still emerging from it. Ten percent of the revolutionary committee in each college are still PLA personnel, a legacy from the time when the military arrived to create order from the chaos of factionalism. The Party secretary — top man — in each college is still a PLA officer.

LTC trains teachers in seven fields: Chinese literature, foreign languages (Russian, English, and Japanese; Russian was formerly the largest class but now English is), physics, chemistry, mathematics, geology and biology. Since the Cultural Revolution a new field of political history edges into operation. DP has the same list of departments it has had for many years: mechanics, chemistry, shipbuilding, hydraulics, radio, mathematics-physics.

I come across no unit in Dairen as much affected by the Cultural Revolution as these two colleges. After several years during which political struggle replaced usual classes, LTC took in nine hundred teachers for a refresher course of one year in 1972. Only in September 1973 did it take in a batch of eight hundred regular students. In earlier years the standard enrollment was twenty-five hundred students.

The story at DP is similar. Nineteen seventy-one saw the first batch of post–Cultural Revolution students (twelve hundred), though in 1969 the college accepted some veteran workers for a short special course. Enrollment in previous years had stood at seven thousand.

The colleges were hit in the late 1960s by four demands:

- a cry for new and more informal recruitment policies, so that an ordinary Chinese boy or girl would have a better chance of higher education;
- a call to make of the learning process not just a thing of the classrooms but an equal blend of "theory" and "practical execution";
- a demand for politicization of the curriculum (more political study sessions; use of the Marxist method of class analysis as a framework for every piece of knowledge);

146

- a demand for graduates who would be more immediately useful to the concrete needs of the Chinese nation.

None of these demands proved unambiguous in meaning, free of controversy, or easy to implement. I find LTC and DP still grappling with them, trying to put flesh on the angular bones of principle.

Entrance exams were swept away in the storm of the Cultural Revolution. New students were recruited through consultation by bodies mainly outside the college. No one could come to college direct from middle school, but only after two years in a factory or a commune. Workers and peasants could be considered for college even if they were not middle-school graduates.

Enrollments after the Cultural Revolution dropped. A gap of two years between school and college made it hard for science and language students (in particular) to pick up the threads of learning. Miss Liu, the chemistry student, forgot most of what she had learned about chemistry at school, she says, while cultivating soybeans in central Liaoning. Workers and peasants arrived at the foothills of higher learning without having negotiated the plains of lower learning. Special preparatory sessions had to be set up; standards sagged at times.

The principle has been kept but the mode is less pristine. It is still true that a student almost never moves directly from middle school to college. A kind of entrance exam, however, has crept back in 1973. It goes under the name "investigatory examination" (*kao-cha*), more acceptable to purists than the ordinary word for examination (*kao-shi*). This test weeds out those — however strong their recommendation by bodies outside the college — whose preparation seems weak.

Mixing classroom instruction with practical work outside the college has often been fruitful. The guiding principle is a "three-in-one combination" of teaching, labor, and research. It seems bound to become an enduring feature of Chinese higher education. Logic textbooks are now compiled from contracts, notices, regulations, observed in communes and factories.

LTC and DP have, though, retreated somewhat from the original conception of a fifty-fifty time division between class and field or bench. Pressures arose in 1971, especially from science and foreign language circles, for stepping up the percentage of time spent in the classroom. At LTC during 1973–1974, the division of time averaged two-thirds in class and one-third at labor. The principle remains but it is being bent.

At DP the ratio has tipped even further. Almost 90 percent of the student's time is spent in instruction, some 10 percent in factories. A polytechnic finds itself in a special position, it is explained to me, compared with a university or a teachers' college. The courses are by their nature practically oriented. Quite a few of the students are twenty-five years of age or older, and have already worked in industry.

Politicization of the college — a third consequence of the Cultural Revolution — is like a ride on a tiger, in that it is hard to see how or where the process ends. More study sessions on the thought of Mao is a clear enough step. DP now requires its technical students to spend 20 percent of the school week on politics.

A big increase has also occurred in the proportion of students who belong to the CCP. At DP four hundred of the twelve hundred students are Party members; a further five hundred are CYL members. The percentages are similar at LTC and in both cases the rise since the Cultural Revolution has been steep. Another step of politicization is LTC's new department of political history.

As for intensifying the use of class analysis in tackling subject matter, it has been a simpler matter in some subjects (e.g., philosophy) than in others (e.g., Japanese). Even in philosophy there is the problem of finding time to teach students about philosophies other than Marxism — if you know the enemy you can vanquish him — when so many hours are devoted to Marxist texts.

The five courses taught in the philosophy department are Marxian philosophy, scientific socialism, political economy, history of the CCP, and social development of humanity. In all five the readings seem almost entirely from Marx, Engels, Lenin, Stalin, and Mao. The well-meaning idea of introducing "bourgeois" thinkers for negative example has just about succumbed to time pressure.

Pressure of time has become a central issue in the fourth challenge to colleges, to turn out graduates who are an immediate economic asset to China. One response to this imperative has been to cut the length of courses, from five years to three years at DP, from four years to three years at LTC. Of course controversy swirls over what to leave out of the plan of study.

LTC professors have since the Cultural Revolution made a massive effort to be of more immediate service to Liaoning's middle schools. They go out in teams to give courses to middle-school teachers in a given locality; three thousand teachers have been trained in this way since 1969. They offer correspondence courses for teachers. They have taken in more than two thousand teachers for one-year refresher courses. "Mobile lectures" have been given, far from Dairen, to some forty-five thousand teachers.

DP professors, too, have reached out beyond the campus to the community. They have organized more than twenty "spare-time universities," with a total of two thousand students, in Dairen factories.

The five faculty members from LTC and DP seem in a slightly chastened mood. For years they've had crises on hand. One teacher of CCP history at LTC, a graduate of the Chinese People's University in Peking, asks me as we walk alone about my impressions of educational life in China. I reply that the popularization of middle-school education is a fine achievement, but that colleges seem gripped by uncertainties. He rejoins with only a brief remark: "Your viewpoint and ours are similar in a number of respects."

The *structures* of college life have not shaken down after the Cultural Revolution. The *general atmosphere* of the campuses, however, has stabilized to some extent. Spontaneity and militancy have, by mid-1973, lost ground to regulation and studiousness, compared with the heady days of 1967. No Red Guard organizations exist in these two colleges today. There is once again a student union (*xue-sheng-hui*), as before the Cultural Revolution, but it is a bland association embracing the entire student body.

Our talk about college life in Dairen dies down. It is my turn to "share experiences." I present a summary of conditions at Harvard University and questions follow. How many American students study China? What attitudes do they have to the topic?

It is not easy to explain to these teachers, whose society knows a high degree of mental unity, that American students have an enormous variety of opinions about China. But the Dairen teachers are gratified to learn that a large number of students study China and its tongue.

What really arrests the Chinese professors is my report on the materials available to U.S. students for the study of China. It comes as a surprise to them, I think, that *People's Daily* (China's leading newspaper) and *Red Flag* (the CCP's political monthly) are taken by many of our university libraries. A buzz goes around the room as I tell them my students read the writings of Mao.

Can it be, they seem to be wondering, that Americans are at last prepared to look with an open mind at "Communist China," and listen to what Peking has to say for itself?

❁ ❁ ❁

Around the time of the Tenth CCP Congress, a breeze from the left blew upon Liaoning education. Typical was the case of Chang T'ieh-sheng. He is one of the one million graduates of Liaoning's middle schools who have, since the Cultural Revolution, left the towns to take up peasant life (130,000 from Dairen alone).

By 1973, Chang's thoughts turned to college. He sat for the province college-entrance exam. But five years of farm work in Hsingcheng county had taken a toll of his knowledge of chemistry and physics. He could scarcely scratch out a single answer. Instead he penned a few acerbic thoughts on the back of his exam paper.

He had forgotten all his book learning — that was true. "During the busy hoeing period, I just could not abandon the tasks of production and hide myself in a small room to study. That would have been very selfish." What is the purpose of education anyway, Chang was bold enough to ponder. Is it not to serve others by helping to build socialism?

Elements in the Liaoning CCP backed Chang. *Liaoning Daily,* reprinting what he wrote during the exam, declared that exams should test ability to understand things and solve problems, not how many books the candidate studied at middle school.

Chang became such a hero in Liaoning that a few months later he was the keynote speaker at the entry ceremony of Liaoning Agricultural College! He spoke as representative of the entire freshman class.

He said he was determined to keep daring to go against the tide. He hit out at those who would try and stop the education revolution halfway. In January 1975 he was elected to the presidium of China's parliament, the National People's Congress.

Like a grenade thrown in the packed trenches of orthodoxy, Ch'ai Ch'un-tse's case also burst on Liaoning at the end of 1973. Ch'ai had been a Red Guard in a town called Chihfeng ("Bare Peak"). Graduating from middle school in 1971, he was the first in his class to volunteer to go and live in a remote area. Ch'ai chose a God-forsaken place, cursed with sandstorms: Wengniute banner (being a Manchu zone, within Liaoning, it has banners rather than communes). He did very well as a peasant and became a leader of his brigade.

Came a disturbing letter from his father. Old Ch'ai said there were vacancies for coal miners, in the mine where he himself worked, and Ch'un-tse must come back to town and be a miner. "Any coal mine should give first consideration to the sons and daughters of its workers and staff members, when more manpower is needed." In fact, Father Ch'ai was also trying to use parental authority to kill the idea of his son's spending a lifetime in Wengniute.

Father Ch'ai had picked up a stone only to drop it on his own feet. Ch'un-tse was not a submissive son of days gone past, but a red-hot Marxist. In between sandstorms, he had read the *Communist Manifesto* (four times), the writings of Chairman Mao, and Engels's essay "The Origin of the Family, Private Property, and the State." He had written 280,000 words of notes on how these works relate to the struggle for a new socialist agriculture. Ch'ai Ch'un-tse sent back to his father a scorching letter — with a copy to the Party branch in Wengniute.

Ch'un-tse said his father had lost the spirit of revolution. "You fought heroically against the enemies. In those days you never thought of family, not even of your own life. . . . We younger ones must inherit the task from you revolutionary predecessors." Wengniute had been a place of heroic fighting against Chiang Kai-shek forces. The same revolutionary zeal must now transform its aridity into socialist prosperity.

Ch'un-tse argued that his own feelings must be aligned with the glorious march of China. "Our concept of the family," Ch'un-tse announced, "cannot be separated from the emancipation of all mankind." He made an appeal to his father: "Make a lofty wish, vow to break with the old concepts for the sake of spreading communism throughout the world."

Father Ch'ai had said his son would not get on, in his job or in the Party, if he stayed in the boondocks. Ch'un-tse retorted: "You have been a CCP member for twenty-seven years. I suggest you check your views to see if they jibe with the Party's interests." He said — here he really went against the tide — "it is wrong to abandon principle in order to become a Party member." A fascinating battle was joined; new China on trial before the pull of old China.

It must have been a shock to Father Ch'ai when *Liaoning Daily* published his son's letter. A few days later, the paper also published the father's original letter to Ch'un-tse, with an editorial. The new young peasant was praised for scorning the "six relationships" of Confucianism — they require filial deference — and so became a figure in the Anti-Confucius Campaign. His "rebellion and sedition" was termed "a very good thing."

Eventually Father Ch'ai made a self-criticism. "I have been a Party member longer than my son has lived. In the old society I looked after buffalo, did odd chores for landlords. I now give my blessing to my son who wants to be a peasant. After all, we must not forget our beginnings. . . ."

In February 1974, the *People's Daily* of Peking reprinted the two letters, added its own investigative report, editorialized on the values at stake. Liaoning had raised up a model for the whole nation.

❀ ❀ ❀

In June 1952 *People's China* of Peking wrote: "Today *dong bei* offers a preview of all China in a few years' time." It has turned out that way. *Dong bei* is not so "special" in relation to the rest of China as before. In 1943 it produced 93 percent of all China's steel, 78 percent of China's electric power. Old Manchuria now produces just 40 percent of China's steel, 35 percent of China's electric power. The industrial gap between *dong bei* and the rest has narrowed. Dairen is today one Chinese industrial city among many.

In 1951 Dean Rusk, while assistant secretary of state, referred to the fate of Manchuria (along with Mongolia and Turkestan): "China is losing its great northern areas," he mourned, "to the European empire which has stretched out its greedy hands for them for at least a century." The greedy hands may still lie close but Manchuria is today securely part of China.

The region of *dong bei* has come home after much wandering. Mountains made it until the late nineteenth century an outpost, rather than a full part of Chinese civilization. The Manchu dynasty, fearing the racial dilution of its homeland, kept it separate from the court's new base at Peking. Despite these barriers, *dong bei* began to grow as a branch of the China tree in the early twentieth century.

But this was just the epoch when foreign powers, fearful of each other and hungry for resources, took *dong bei* by the throat. Caught between Japan and Russia, the Chinese regime was too weak to protect its own branch. The world talked of Manchuria going its own way (just as some now talk of Taiwan going its own way). Meanwhile Manchuria's economy was forced to go Japan's way; to buy from Japan, to make what Japan wanted it to make.

Today's *dong bei* is no longer an international football. National planning, better transportation, good organization, a surge in education, pride in China's new place in the world — all these have knitted *dong bei* together with the rest of China. It does not any more hang loose, as a place over which rivalry of nations might lead to war. Gradually it has taken its place within the new China. If there is separatist feeling in the Northeast, it is well hidden.

It is often asked outside China, "Are the Chinese people happy?" I do not see how a non-Chinese can give a clear answer to this question. But after a look at the people of Dairen I say they are not unhappy.

First, spontaneity is apparent in the streets and households. Uninhibited laughter, the vigorous play of youth and children, people engaging with one another in obvious enjoyment of each other's company — are these signs of grace found among a collectively unhappy people?

Second, you do not sense an underlying furtiveness in society. If there are moments when I feel tension, it comes not from outside in, but from my own uncertainty in the face of a culture so self-assured. A foreigner moves along Dairen's lanes; seldom if ever do residents get up-tight and start to play stiff roles (when well-rehearsed children do so it is obvious and proves my point).

The people of Dairen are not wound up like a spring, reserves of conviction stored away, unable to speak their name. If they took the zigzags of politics 100 percent seriously, they might well feel themselves living on a knife-edge. In fact, politics does not seem to reach to the inner core of the average citizen — as the lack of newspaper reading indicates.

Third, the citizens have those basics of material life and security which seem among all peoples to be the essential foundations of happiness. Watch the people eating and you see that the food is good and being enjoyed. Walk the Dairen streets and the people look healthier, sharper, and more impressive in physical form, indeed, than a crowd of people in New York. Complexions are fresh, eyes shine bright, limbs are firm, walk is springy. When these folk are aged forty they look twenty-five, when they reach sixty they could pass for forty.

You cannot find in Dairen a mass of homeless or unemployed people, or people in need of yet without medical care. Children do not arise who are denied entry to the world of knowledge. Parents do not have to fear watching their offspring fall into a physically or mentally stunted condition.

All these things together do not permit me to say the people of Dairen are happy, but I think those who have such things are not, as a city community, in a state of unhappiness.

HANGCHOW

杭州

Hangchow has an agreeable way of looking like a town rather than the city of 900,000 people it is. It nestles easily with the hills and waters on every hand; a vase, as it were, supporting but not dominating its flowers.

When Marco Polo visited Hangchow in the thirteenth century, its population was about one million and the city proper covered about twenty square kilometers. Today the outline of the city is little altered from those Sung dynasty times, though the buildings are largely new.

Hangchow has not eaten up the territory around it, as so many cities do. It has renewed itself upon the old foundations, preserving a fair balance between what nature bestows and what man adds. Man has been kind to nature, too, in Hangchow. Since Liberation more than *thirty million* trees have been planted on the hills around West Lake.

Hangchow is one of the oldest big cities in the world. Once it ranked as the world's largest and richest city (seven hundred years ago). Though today a city with a population greater than that of San Francisco, it is as dreamy and placid as a remote Caribbean isle. There is nothing ugly to see in Hangchow.

Very tall modern buildings do not exist. The wavy hills, dotted with temples and pagodas, have the skyline to themselves. They rise on three sides of famous West Lake. The fourth (eastern) bank of the lake gives on to Hangchow's low-key central district. West Lake is not big — a surface area of twelve hundred acres — which permits an intimacy to this valley of porcelain blue water and boulevards shaded by maples.

A shopkeeper on the western edge of the city district may step out from behind his counter, cross the broad asphalt street which hugs the lake, and sit on a bench to gaze on a scene whose peacefulness few city centers in the world can match. The harmony between town and

157

water must in some ways be even more complete than in ancient times, for the city walls, which used to cut the central districts off from both the lake and a nearby river, have disappeared entirely, thanks to war and decay.

The shopkeeper sees the various banks of the lake quite clearly from his bench. The northern bank snakes along at the foot of Jewel Mountain (Bao shi shan). It is obscured for a stretch by a lofty island called Lonely Hill (Gu shan), one of four islands in West Lake, which I will soon describe. To the west, the lake is broken into two by the Dike of Six Bridges, sometimes known by the name of Su Tung-p'o, a poet-governor of Hangchow who had it built late in the eleventh century. Behind it rises a pile of hills, topped by the Peak Which Flew Here (Fei lai feng).

On the slopes of these hills the shopkeeper may glimpse flecks of the roofs of several treasure houses of Chinese Buddhism. It was a Buddhist monk, arriving from India in the fourth century, who gave the Peak Which Flew Here such an odd name. Finding its texture familiar, he declared that the arresting peak must be a segment of Mount Grdhrakuta, "flown here" from India. Large houses on the lower reaches of the western hills were once owned by rich merchants, who would travel the 190 kilometers from Shanghai for an interval of fun and games. Today they are rest homes and sanatoria for trade unionists, who may apply to go there through their place of work.

From his park bench in the city the shopkeeper confronts to the south a vista just as pleasant and full of history. The high curved hills on this fringe of West Lake are capped by Mount Wu (named after the State of Wu which once lay to its south) and Phoenix Hill, which used to be the quarter of the Imperial Palace, in its Forest of Ten Thousand Pines. West of these two lies Dragon Well (Long jing), a nest of hills secreting two delectable springs, on which is grown Dragon Well tea, China's most esteemed green tea.

Across the smoky blue expanse of the lake the island called Place of Small Abundance breaks the southern shore. Within the island itself are four tiny lakes that are smothered, in this summer season, with flowering lotus amid flat green leaves.

❁ ❁ ❁

The area of the Lower Yangtze River, whose southeastern corner Hangchow adorns, is China's most densely populated region. It is one of the most densely populated parts of the world. Some ninety-five million people eat their breakfast here, 368 to each square kilometer. This density of humanity is six times that of Liaoning, the most crowded northeastern province.

Hangchow is the capital of the province of Chekiang, a small but attractive and rich province tucked into China's east coast. Shaped like a square chunk, the province gathers twenty-nine million people into about 100,000 square kilometers. So Chekiang spreads over 1.1 percent of China's total expanse, and counts just under 4 percent of China's total population.

The land of the Lower Yangtze is a lush, hot, wet land of lakes and canals. Rainfall in Hangchow is double that in most of Liaoning. The summer is long. Even in midwinter the average temperature does not fall below freezing. The land surrounding the city is planted not with corn and sorghum and soybeans, as in *dong bei,* but with rice on the flat areas and tea along the hills.

With its hot and humid clime, its fertile alluvial soil deposited by the sprawling Yangtze, and its silver spider web of some 800,000 kilometers of canals and waterways, this Yangtze delta is China's main rice-producing area. And it is one of China's great fish producers; in Chekiang province there are half a million fishermen. Also abundant are winter wheat, rape, and silkworms. Cotton is a major crop in the saline soil along a coastline which pushes steadily out to sea, by natural silt accumulation, at a rate of some twenty-five meters each year.

If *dong bei* towns often seem like those of Europe, except for the people's faces, the city of Hangchow does not recall anything far from China. And it is mostly unlike Manchuria, except for the Han faces of its people. Old by most standards — if hardly by Chinese — it was already a significant town when it got its name in the sixth century (Sui dynasty). Politically and culturally it ranks as a major jewel in the crown of Han tradition, for it was the gay, prosperous capital of China during the Southern Sung dynasty (twelfth and thirteenth centuries).

Like Dairen it developed a seafaring outlook. But foreign influence touched Hangchow less than Dairen. What there was flowed not from

Russia, but from the West and Japan in the nineteenth and twentieth centuries.

Hangchow ("Boat Place") is to water as lips are to teeth, to adapt a Chinese image. Its setting on West Lake has shaped its life, from the time the court of the Sung dynasty searched for a southern capital after being ejected from the north, and hit on Hangchow, to the 1970s, which finds the town a mecca for holiday makers from all over China.

Some history buffs believe that Ch'in Shih Huang Ti, an emperor of the third century B.C., moored his boat at a spot near today's Hang-chow, and thus gave the town its name. At that time the site was on the coastline, but over the centuries a curious change has come over Hangchow's relationship to the sea.

When Ch'in Shih Huang Ti — a great unifier of China — made his southern trip, the East China Sea probably lapped a line about fifty kilometers inland from its present position. Topographically, China is like a descending staircase from the mountains of the west to the flat-lands of the center and the eastern seaboard. With the years, and the rushing of the Yangtze, more steps are added to the bottom of the staircase.

As silt built up and tides changed, a strip of land appeared, which cut off what is now West Lake from the sea. This new piece of land also elongated the course of the Ch'ien-t'ang, the modern name for the Che, Chekiang's longest river (410 kilometers), which empties into Hangchow Bay. Today Hangchow sits between West Lake and the Ch'ien-t'ang. It is now quite a way from the bay. The lake is so named because it lies on the westward, or inland, side of the city.

So Hangchow not only owes its glory to water but it actually ap-peared from the depths of the water. Water also turns the city's looms and lights its houses. Since the nearby Hsinan River project was re-cently completed, Hangchow has made big strides in hydroelectric power, and greatly reduced its reliance upon coal.

Looking west from Hangchow to the top of the "staircase," a magic eye could spot Lhasa. The Tibetan city shares with Hangchow a lati-tude of 30° north. On the north-south axis, Hangchow Bay lies just over halfway down the fourteen-thousand-kilometer coast of China, midway between the mouth of the Yalu River on the Korea border, and the mouth of the Peilun River on the Vietnam border.

Hangchow Bay is a dividing point between two quite different sections of this massive coastline. To the north the coast is sandy, mainly silt-mud, and the beaches are smooth and good for creating salt fields. South of Hangchow Bay the coast gets rocky. Mountains run close by this sea line, and the thumping of waves against them has sculptured many a rocky cliff. Thus occurs the hilly, indented coastline of southern China, punctuated by deep harbors and hung about with offshore isles.

In few cities as far south as Hangchow do people speak an accent as close to Mandarin (northern) Chinese as in Hangchow. This is a legacy, some people think, of the two centuries when the city glittered as capital of the Sung court. The resulting speech is a mixture of Court Speech (Mandarin) and what are called the Wu dialects (from south Kiangsu province and north Chekiang).

Yet in other ways Hangchow is very much a city of southern China. Its people, though not as small as Cantonese, are not as big as northerners. When the court moved south to Hangchow the image of an ideal lady changed. During the T'ang dynasty in northern China, she was tall, with hair piled up to make her even taller, and altogether rather stiff and formal. The Sung ideal came to be a slender, petite, and dainty creature.*

Hangchow folk also do things which only Chinese south of the Yangtze do and which northerners generally dislike: eat dog flesh; take cold-water showers; wear sandals without socks and short pants in summer (the men). Rice, not noodles, is the backbone of Hangchow meals.

The surrounding countryside, too, has all the marks of southern China. Two rice crops can be grown each year, as well as one of winter wheat or rape. Oranges are abundant and tropical fruits can be found. The *kang,* a combination stove and bed built in brick which heats

---

* For details of Sung times I have drawn on J. Gernet's excellent *La Vie quotidienne en Chine à la veille de l'invasion Mongole 1250–1276* (Hachette, 1959), translated as *Daily Life in China on the Eve of the Mongol Invasion* (Allen and Unwin, 1962).

peasant homes in northern China, is generally obviated by the mildness of the winter.

One also finds among Chekiang people the quick sharp temperament of the south, rather than the slow grave temperament of the north. These folk seem outstanding among the Chinese for intelligence, frankness, good sense, and humor. They have acute features and responsive eyes; their movements are quick and neat. Locals say that Chekiangese are supposed to be good at money matters and shrewd and persistent in argument.*

Two of the Chinese revolution's greatest figures, Chou En-lai and the writer Lu Hsün, sprang from Chekiang and bear out some of these traits. Lu Hsün, who died in 1936, I know only from pictures, his writings, and accounts of his life. These show a quick, fine-featured, ironic, nervously energetic man. As for Premier Chou, impressions from a 1971 meeting flash into my mind throughout a stay in Hangchow: fastidious mouth and darting eyes, a busy walk, a certain intensity of manner.

Hangchow's location has always inclined it to be a window on the world. When the city was China's capital, the court took an unusually keen interest in the seafaring activities of Chinese merchants. Links have long existed to the South Seas (as the Chinese used to call Southeast Asia). In modern times the traffic back and forth to Japan has been more than incidental. The Shimonoseki Treaty of 1895, imposed by Tokyo on a vanquished China, opened Hangchow to Japanese trade. Some of the sophistication and mental cosmopolitanism found in Hangchow may have derived from such intercourse.

The foreigner in this city is met at every turn with a ready smile. People constantly cross his path who are interested in the place "across the seas" from which he comes. He finds humor near the surface and poised for expression in many a situation.

As for frankness, one exchange with a young Hangchow professional suffices. I tell him I have just eaten a "mandarin fish" from

* The traits I mention are strictly speaking those of east Chekiang, rather than of the Tai hu delta, Hangchow, and the hilly western regions of the province; however Hangchow, as the province capital, has come to reflect these strong Chekiang characteristics.

West Lake and judge it delicious. "Yes," he replies, "the mandarin fish is tasty and it has few bones." Then he smiles and his eyes twinkle: "Above all, when it is served to foreigners the mandarin fish has *very* few bones."

※ ※ ※

I come in toward West Lake by air from Canton, and find Hangchow's serenity soothing after the shabby, distracted southern city. It is always, too, a slight relief to disembark from a plane of Civil Aviation Administration of China (CAAC) because most of them roar and shake so. The Chinese have some British Trident jets, and now also ten Boeings, but on most routes within China the passenger finds himself in a Russian propeller Ilyushin 18, or the small grasshopper of an Ilyushin 14.

From Canton to Hangchow the flight takes two hours and the larger Ilyushin is used. Unlike the "14," it has seatbelts and a public address system. From a big kitchen-type "Moscow" brand refrigerator, a hostess brings around watermelons. She offers chewing gum in wrappers which proclaim the comprehensive motto of CAAC: "Safety, Speed, Comfort, Convenience." A distinctive smell arises from the bamboo fans and the fragrant tea which is constantly served.

New for me on this first flight of my 1973 trip is the marking of the aircraft's exterior. In 1971 all planes I boarded or saw had blazened on them in red characters — overshadowing the black marking of the airline's name — the exclamation "Ten Thousand Years to Chairman Mao." But now the red slogans are painted out against the silver fuselage and there remain only the smaller black characters indicating the carrier. Nor do the hostesses this time — as they did in 1971 — begin their briefing to passengers with an appeal to the teachings of Chairman Mao.

Although the name of the airline company is Civil Aviation Administration of China, *zhong-guo min yong hang-kong,* which appears on the tickets, the planes have on them the more usual China Airlines, *zhong-guo hang-kong.* This latter phrase is used by the company's Hong Kong office, and it creates a risk of ideological confusion for the Chinese customer. For the Taiwan airline, which also has a Hong

163

Kong office, gives itself a name almost identical to that of the Peking carrier: *zhong-hua hang-kong* (also China Airlines; the *hua* and the *guo* are interchangeable so far as the meaning in English goes).

But let the Chinese step aboard a Peking plane and he will soon know he is not on a Chiang Kai-shek plane. The hostess begins her announcement with a crisp separation of the sheep from the goats: "Comrades and passengers . . ."

One more curiosity about CAAC before my Ilyushin 18 lands at Hangchow. After gazing down for a hundred miles at the Warlike Barbarian Mountains, which interweave the provinces of Fukien and Chekiang, I inspect my airline ticket. On the inside of a cover which depicts Tien-an men Square are listed (in Chinese) ten points "necessary for the traveler to know." Foreigners in China do not need to know most of these points, since China Travel Service arranges all their travel, but Chinese do.

To read the ten points is to feel that American airline companies treat passengers leniently. Any reservation will be canceled unless the ticket is purchased a "specified" period (not, in fact, specified on the ticket) before the day of travel. When you buy the ticket, the rules continue, your work document must be presented at the airline office.

Tickets are valid for ninety days only and they come in three varieties: full fare, to be paid by those twelve years or older; half fare, for children between two years and twelve years; a 10 percent fare for tots under two, provided that an adult escorts him, that he does not occupy a seat, and that no adult has more than one tot with him. Free luggage allowance is one-quarter less than in most countries — fifteen kilos per person, plus five kilos for hand luggage (the tots under two, paying 10 percent, are allowed only the five kilos). You may not carry "rotten goods" on board, nor take photos from the air.

The rules about cancellation and "no-show" would make a U.S. airline executive rub his hands with glee. If you cancel more than two hours before your flight, you may return the ticket but must pay a "procedure fee" of two yuan (or 10 percent of the ticket's cost, if it was under twenty yuan). If you cancel within two hours of your flight, the procedure fee climbs to 20 percent of the face value of the ticket. But no procedure fee is charged when a small-child ticket is canceled.

The no-show passenger is addressed generously as one who "misses his flight." But he gets back only 60 percent of the cost of the ticket, and that only if he reports in less than twelve hours after his flight's departure. Forty percent of the ticket cost is paid to the airline as a "missed the plane" fee. If he does not appear within twelve hours, his ticket is void and there is no refund at all.

The tenth point "necessary to know" is that the Chinese airline does not pay for meals eaten in airports during transit, nor for overnight accommodation during a long and complex trip. There are many such trips in China, for flights are few — ten in and out of Canton per day, four or five at Hangchow per day — and they proceed in short hops. CAAC pays for accommodation only when an overnight delay is "due to the airline."

The descent into Hangchow gives no sense of drawing near a city. As the Ilyushin 18 hangs and sways toward the earth, you see only an audience of hills and a mirror of waters. A few white specks among the trees betray the new housing blocks which are Hangchow's discreet nod to the high-rise era. The traveler finds a smart new airport terminal, for which he may thank the United States. The cream brick and glass building was rushed to life between the time Richard Nixon decided to visit Hangchow, late in 1971, and his arrival at the city in February 1972.

❁ ❁ ❁

A walk through the cicada-shattered stillness of a summer morning takes me high onto Lonely Hill. Largest of West Lake's islands, it is joined to the mainland on the east by an ancient dike and Interrupting Bridge. From the west, the town is reached across a stone bridge called Western Trickling. Alongside it is the quaint tomb of a passionate beauty of the fifth century, Su Hsiao-hsiao, who threw the idea of free love against the repressive walls of feudalism. Wu Sung, the tiger-killing hero of *All Men Are Brothers,* was also buried here — according to fond legend.

An anatomy of intestinelike paths leads from the smoky blue water's edge to the wooded slopes and peak above. Of the spectacle from these twisting paths the poet Su Tung-p'o wrote: "Pavilions, now seen, now

165

unseen; the distant hills indistinct. Every pebble and fish clearly seen in the limpid waters." Two old buildings recall Manchu emperors. Emperor K'ang Hsi (1662–1722) liked to sit and watch the moon reflected in the lake during the fall. He had erected at the eastern corner of Lonely Hill a pavilion which is still called Pavilion of the Autumn Moon on the Calm Lake.

I watch old men fan themselves in the pavilion as they gaze out over the glassy lake. Children climb on its well-kept wooden balustrades. A youth sits in a corner strumming the three-stringed Chinese banjo (*san-hsien*).

Nearby is a sumptuous library which Emperor Ch'ien Lung set up in 1773 for special manuscripts. It was nicely called Hall of Flourishing Literature (Wen-lan ko). Now the vaulted chambers provide the kernel of Chekiang Library. Cheek by jowl with it is the former mansion of Yang Hu, one of Chiang Kai-shek's generals, who built the place for himself as a pleasant retreat in the 1940s. When Chiang heard about this pretty house he went to Yang and asked: "Who did you build that for?" Yang Hu knew his boss well enough to reply: "Why, I built it for you!"

It turned out to be of little use to either of them; it, too, is now one wing of Chekiang Library. The library has about one million books and seems a scholar's delight, amid such green peacefulness. But it is still being "rearranged" after the ructions of the Cultural Revolution and is not open to a visitor without prior request.

Next to the peak of Lonely Hill you come upon another shaded mansion which is the home of Hangchow Seal Society. The entire isle is a treasure house of stones covered with the handwriting of men of passion or power. This attracted a group of scholars who liked fine calligraphy, seal-engraving, and rubbings, to settle here at the turn of the twentieth century. They founded the Seal Society which has continued ever since, even through the buffetings of the Cultural Revolution.

Over the top of the peak is a structure with a curved roof and a fantastic past. It is called the Pavilion Where the Crane was Sent Out. A recluse poet and painter, Lin Ho-ching, built himself a hut here during the Sung dynasty. He loved to watch the lake, grow plum trees, and care for a splendid crane. Legend says Lin took the plum tree as his wife, the crane as his son. When guests came to drink and listen to Lin's poems, the crane would fly out from the pavilion, flapping its wings in excitement. When the poet died in 1028, three hundred plum trees withered and the crane expired of heartbreak. It was during the Mongol dynasty that the pavilion was built to honor Lin's art and love of nature.

Along the ridge of the peak is the Sun Yat-sen Garden where people come to rest and play. An area paved with stones in crazy shapes is surrounded by cypresses so gnarled and eccentric that the whole park has the twisted, almost surrealistic quality of a scene viewed through wet glass. A tea shop in a converted pavilion offers snacks which are listed in chalked characters on boards attached to a drunken tree. There are stone benches, and tables for a game of chess or cards. There are deep cane armchairs, in which a man may feel a king, supine, set about with beauty, halfway between the water and the clouds.

It is going to be a hot day. Early birds have shrewdly occupied the best grottoes, grassy mounds, and tables well shielded by generous plum trees. Two middle-school boys in blue T-shirts are playing chess on stones that are still nice and cool. A group of girls, silk spinners on their day off, they tell me, take one another's picture beside a tall needlelike pagoda which soars atop some camphor trees.

Veteran workers, comfortable in floppy shorts and dirty white shirts, are hunched in collective gossip, their wrists leaning against the inside of their knees. A few wear long trousers which are rolled up to the knee for coolness. Faces crease with a relaxed smile when I approach with a camera. One man prefers to roll his trouser legs down before I press the button. Another deigns to glance up from the battered book which engrosses him.

The whole atmosphere in this park is one of human beings taking their place quietly and gratefully within nature's pattern. Their manner almost seems to draw something from the suppleness of the willows and the equanimity of the blue-silver lake.

Returning from Lonely Hill toward Hangchow Hotel I come across two Chinese holiday makers bent over a map of the city at Western

On Lonely Hill human beings take their place quietly
and gratefully within nature's pattern

Trickling Bridge. One of them looks up and addresses me in halting English. He is a square, solid man with a broad face and rough grin. Clearly he is not a Chekiang man, and I am not surprised when he says he is from Szechwan. He and his companion (a smaller man from Yunnan) have knapsacks on their backs.

Both travelers "accepted the call" to work outside their own province and now teach engineering in China's far west region of Sinkiang. We sit on the bridge and chat until the roasting heat of an unfolding summer day drives us on. On Hangchow's places of interest we exchange opinions, and then conversation turns to Sinkiang, where foreigners almost never go.

These engineering teachers find Sinkiang a bit remote, but also a challenge. They tell me its population, only some two million at Liberation, has now grown to eight million. One of their themes is the need to develop this border region of China in the light of the "arrogant attitude of social imperialists" (the Russians).

The Szechwanese says he learned his English "partly in school" and "partly somewhere else." It turns out that he worked in Chungking, Szechwan's largest city and China's wartime capital, during the 1940s. Maybe he worked for Americans or British? He does not care to specify.

❁ ❁ ❁

The layout of Hangchow is a mirror to the city's functions. Down its eastern flank runs the railway. Nearby is the Grand Canal, with Peking fourteen hundred kilometers at its other end. Not far beyond both flows the Ch'ien-t'ang River. All three arteries, dating from different epochs, have made Hangchow a pivot for Chekiang and the Lower Yangtze delta.

The Grand Canal was built under Emperor Yang of the Sui dynasty in the seventh century, to link the Yangtze with the basin of the Huai River. Before the railway came into Hangchow in the nineteenth century, this canal was a vital means of transportation to the Chekiang capital. Goods and travelers approaching from the north would use it as a matter of course.

As the provincial capital, Hangchow is scattered with offices of

Chekiang CCP Committee and Chekiang Revolutionary Committee. Two of the largest bureaus, not surprisingly, are those for silk and tea. Striking are the white walls, with black tiles along the top, which surround large compounds and the courtyards of old villas. They are starker and fresher to the eye than Peking's rusty-red walls topped with green tiles.

Hangchow has long been one of China's cultural centers, known for poets, scholars of the classics, and Buddhism. The hills around the town are still studded with Buddhist shrines. A mosque that is much known to history — since Arab traders who frequented it wrote descriptions of China — is prominent on the city's main boulevard.

Six of Chekiang's seven higher education institutes are in Hangchow. The leading general schools are Chekiang University, in a handsome garden setting northwest of the lake, and Hangchow University, which is an enlargement (dating from 1958) of Chekiang Teachers' College. There are several bookstores which are large and well-stocked in science and politics.

Although the economy which centers upon Hangchow features silk, tea, rice, and fish, industry is moving ahead. Hangchow used to be nicknamed "West Lake plus scissors." Handicrafts, among which scissors were famous, were all that the city produced. But "West Lake plus scissors" has become a phrase in history. Province officials say that Chekiang's industrial output value in 1972 was almost double that of 1965.

Quite a bit of this progress — from an admittedly tiny base — has occurred in Hangchow city. An area north of the central district, and a strip northwest of the center, toward the Ch'ien-t'ang River, are its main sites. There are medium-sized machine-tool plants; tractor, excavator, and chemical works; a steel plant and a big truck plant. Here, too, stand Hangchow's relatively few new housing blocks in modern boxlike style.

Happily, all this has wrought remarkably little change in Hangchow's personality as a lakeside town. Trees have been zealously preserved. The factories are cradled in foliage which not only masks them but — locals say — absorbs some of the polluting fumes.

Hangchow's supreme function, today as long ago, is as a holiday resort for tired frames and sagging spirits. A few foreigners come here, as the Arab traders and Marco Polo once did, but the vast majority of the tourists are ordinary Chinese from other parts of the country.

You watch them arrive at Hangchow Station, clambering with their bundles past the rhododendron pots and enamel goldfish tubs which brighten this railroad terminal. You see them checking in to simple inns (*lü-guan*) all over the city. You notice them on winding paths in the wooded hills around the lake, map in hand, asking directions from time to time. Many come for a weekend trip on double-decker trains that run the 190 kilometers between Shanghai and Hangchow.

Others, I find, are on an extended journey from another province, visiting relatives who live in the Lower Yangtze area. They take the opportunity of what may be a first trip in East China to see the lake which is a legend to every Chinese from childhood. You see them stuffing their shopping bags with the specialties of Hangchow. Fans and embroidered silk pictures; pears and peaches; souvenir plaques of West Lake; the famous and not inexpensive wine from nearby Shao-hsing (hometown of Chou En-lai's family).

Marco Polo considered Hangchow "the greatest city which may be found in the world" and so pleasurable that "one fancies oneself to be in Paradise." What strikes me about the city now is that it has sur-passing beauty but no apparent opulence. Once a paradise of con-spicuous consumption for China's rich, Hangchow is today an aston-ishingly bland paradise. It is a paradise without paupers, a resort that has no rich.

The trilogy sounds a cliché because of its political usage, but it is nonetheless a fact that Hangchow's tourists are mostly workers, peas-ants, and soldiers. Apart from the prodigal luxuries of nature, there are no luxuries to be had in Hangchow (unless they be in the govern-ment villas at the foot of Jewel Mountain). Certainly there are no more brothels, finery, or retinues of servants and private guards. The only way to spend a vast amount of money in Hangchow would be to go to the post office and send a cable, at the high rates China charges for international cables, to a distant friend, telling him at length of the loveliness of the hills and waters. Hangchow, you might say, is like a ravishing maiden who has never heard of cosmetics.

171

❀ ❀ ❀

Even within the single season of summer, West Lake offers a variety of moods and aspects, and the best way to explore them is by water. The boats are either owned by organizations or else they are pleasure boats for rent. I hire a graceful old craft with hand-carved sides. It has a canvas shade overhead, lace-covered seats for four people, and a table for the never-absent teacups. The oars have stamped on them in red paint the two characters for West Lake. We set off toward the tiny Island at the Heart of the Lake.

When the sky is overcast West Lake turns glass green. But this morning a fierce sun burns down and the water is Dresden blue. A slight haze turns the usually sharp greens of the surrounding hills to a smoky teal. There are gaudily painted boats full of tourists with bags and cameras at the start of a day's outing.

There are also battered brown fishing boats equipped with nets. Some fishermen still follow the ancient method of suddenly knocking the hull with a pole to frighten fish into a deployed net. The lake became more fertile in fish after being dredged in the 1950s — its first dredging in three hundred years.

Watching this banquet of boats one recalls Marco Polo's report from these very waters some seven hundred years ago:

> On the lake of which we have spoken there are numbers of boats and barges of all sizes for parties of pleasure. . . . Anyone who desires to go a-pleasuring with the women, or with a party of his own sex, hires one of these barges, which are always to be found completely furnished with tables, and chairs and all the other apparatus for a feast. . . .
>
> And truly a trip on this Lake is a much more charming recreation than can be enjoyed on land. For on the one side lies the city in its entire length, so that the spectators in the barges, from the distance at which they stand, take in the whole prospect in its full beauty and grandeur, with its numberless palaces, temples, monasteries, and gardens, full of lofty trees, sloping to the shore. And the Lake is never without a number of other such boats, laden with pleasure parties; for it is the great delight of the citizens here after they have disposed of the day's business, to pass the afternoon in enjoyment with the ladies of their families, or perhaps with others less reputable. . . .

We hire a graceful old craft with hand-carved sides

Seven hundred years later it is much the same, but with a change in the attitude toward women.

At one point strains of music glide across the water. Drawing closer to the island we see in silhouette a long thin boat with four boys squatting in a row from bow to stern. Their reflections seem to tremble in near perfection underneath their boat. One of them is playing the flute with more than average skill, and no instrument could be more apt in this dreamy natural amphitheater.

When we land I chat with these boys. They have moored their slim craft and are stretched out on the grass beside brilliant red fuchsias. They seem typical Chekiang youths, of medium size, with bright eyes, quick movements, and a somewhat impish manner. They wear white T-shirts, cotton shorts, and plastic sandals, with a wristwatch on every left arm.

It is rest day from the Hangchow Hemp Factory, where they have been working since graduation from junior middle school. Music is only a hobby for all of them, but the flutist plays with a music group at the factory. The teasing tune he played does not seem to come from

173

the standard "revolutionary" works of Chinese stage and screen. I inquire of the flutist. It turns out to be an indolent Chekiang love song.

The island itself is like a green rug dropped by Heaven on the blue carpet of the lake. The grassy lawns extend to within inches of the water, lapped by the faintest of ripples caused by an occasional boat. Leaves have dropped from paternalistic willows to lie lazily — cool while everything else is hot — on the gently swaying surface of the lake.

Chief attraction on the island is a stately Ming pavilion, named, with fine Chinese naturalism, Pavilion in the Center of the Lake. From the water's edge you approach it through an ornamental stone arch. The walls carry carvings of fantastic animals and the three Chinese characters of the pavilion's name (lake-middle-pavilion). The airy chamber itself, topped by tiles of flaming orange, is now a public retreat, ideal for contemplating the lake on which the tranquil little island seems to float.

Our boat moves on to the garden most celebrated among Chinese who visit Hangchow, the Park for Watching Fish in Huakang Pool. It is full of the mounds and rockeries and gnarled pines which the Japanese copied from this part of China during the T'ang dynasty, and which foreigners now consider to be traits of a Japanese garden. Even the pitiless July sun has not subdued the brilliant greens of foliage and grass.

Ornamental walls break the curvaceous flow of the gardens. They seem at first to be buildings, rising mysteriously among the dancing verdure, but turn out to be handsome screens. Their style is unique to the Lower Yangtze Valley. The main body is white plaster, the top is nicely contrasting gray tile with curved edges, and under the eaves a strip of frescoes in colored tile depict Chekiang landscapes. The walls are broken by "windows" of a bizarre kind. Each window is almost oval, but the sides bulge, so the effect is of four curved arcs, the vertical ones flatter than the horizontal, placed end to end to form the window frame. Within the frame there is no glass, but carved reliefs of birds and rocks and branches.

The fringes of the lake and of various inland pools are dotted with green wooden benches. Vast willows lean deep down to the water of secluded inlets, as if their green leaves were seeking out the green of the water. Two gardeners are at work, in loose blue hemp suits and straw hats, pulling out weeds from the orange soil of a path which winds along the water's edge. Squatting with hands between knees stretched far apart, they put the weeds into straw baskets carried at the waist.

The chief attraction at Huakang Pool is a cruising mass of fat orange fish. Tourists, leaning from concrete bridges, endlessly feed the fish with crumbs and rolls. It is hot as well as sticky, and quite a few adults carry a black umbrella against the sun. The visitors are mainly younger people; maybe it is too hot today for older folk. A scattering of army uniforms breaks the sea of white shirts on the men and floral blouses or skirts on the women. It is a rare group or couple that lacks a camera (all made in Shanghai).

To one side a mixed band of youths is poking around with sticks in the weeds, picking something from the water and putting it in straw bags which look like upturned hats. Watching them laugh and jump around together you are struck by how easy seem the social relations of girls and young men.

Children, as so often in China, are the center of indulgent attention. It is these youngsters, with bright T-shirts and supple brown limbs, who lead the assault on the already bloated stomachs of the goldfish, crying out with pleasure when they get a heavy fish to heave itself up for yet one more morsel.

With one young woman, a bus conductor for Hangchow Transport, I fall into conversation and she introduces me to her shy but smiling little son. Her accent is hard to follow so I stick to very simple questions. Is her boy in kindergarten? It is an embarrassing mistake. The mother replies that her son is nine years old, has long been at school, and is keen on mathematics.

West Lake is hardly less seductive after sundown than before, its fringes thronged with city folk stepping out for a change of pace. Cicadas pound the ear, but there is a sweet fragrance from lotus flowers, and the eye is soothed at every turn. Sitting in a small wooden pavilion at the northwest corner of the lake, I watch a marvelous change from dusk to darkness.

The water turns from gray to iridescent silver, the cherry trees grow black against this silver stage, and the hills behind lose their greenness and become hulks of midnight blue. There is a stunning tranquillity about Hangchow's lakeside by night: unruffled by auto horns, unclouded by pollution, virtually unlit by any man-made light.

I notice groups of students, an old man with an old book, family ensembles, a band of girls who break now and then into song. After darkness has fallen there is scarcely a park bench without an embracing couple (no curfew these days, as there was after the Mongols took Hangchow from the Sung in 1276).

In the pavilion I am joined by two students from Chekiang University who talk with me about the Cultural Revolution (I record their comments on pages 178 to 179) and current world affairs. In the relaxed atmosphere of these magic gardens, I find it unnecessary to approach people for a conversation (and thus risk putting them on the defensive). People come up to me without apparent embarrassment at addressing a foreigner from they know not where. The two Chekiang University students move on, and others make friendly remarks, including two physics majors from Hangchow University.

These two girls chat about current affairs as if there were nothing more exciting in the world. One asks me: "Have you heard the news of Chairman Mao's meeting with Yang Chen-ning?" Dr. Yang is an American-Chinese physicist and Nobel laureate at present on a visit to scientific circles in China. I had read of the meeting in *People's Daily* during a flight from Canton to Hangchow. They had heard of it on the radio and read of it in *Chekiang Daily* (*People's Daily* they rarely read). I remark that the talk between Chairman Mao and Dr. Yang might augur well for United States–China relations. The girls see another side of it. As Chinese students of science, they find it exciting that the Chairman should honor an overseas Chinese man of science.

The Chekiang temperament, an advanced school system, and a scholarly tradition, made the province a vanguard of the radical activity that built up in China after 1900. Students went to study in Japan and were stirred and often radicalized by the experience. Around Hangchow a new kind of "modern" school mushroomed. It broached politics and Western knowledge, rather than merely rehearsing the conservative canon of Confucianism. Pressure from secret societies (like the Dare to Die Corps) and radical clubs (such as the Restoration Society) was one reason why Hangchow fell easily, like a ripe plum, to the revolutionary winds of 1911 that toppled the Ch'ing dynasty.

Again when the May Fourth Movement burst out in 1919, Hang-chow became a leading arena of this radical upsurge triggered by China's first wave of modernized students. At the time of the Chinese Communist Party's founding meeting in 1921, Chekiang provided hospitality to the CCP's early small band of visionaries. Mao Tse-tung at that time began, on an uncertain note, his long-continuing love affair with West Lake. The infant CCP was in council at Shanghai, sleeping in a girls' school and holding sessions in a house lent by a friend (see page 33). But the secret police of the French Concession tracked the conspirators down. A move became necessary and Che-kiang friends came to the rescue.

Mao reported to his friend Siao-yu: "One of the delegates has a girl friend from Chiahsing . . . and on the way from Shanghai to West Lake you pass through Chiahsing. Just outside that city is another lake called Nan hu [South Lake] and we are going to visit it as if we were tourists and have our meeting on the boat. We shall try to avoid the police, but to make doubly sure, we shall buy train tickets to Hang-chow as if we were going to West Lake." The plan worked and the Communists resumed their meeting on South Lake. On board a six-teen-meter tourist boat they proclaimed the founding of the Chinese Communist Party.

Mao said to Siao-yu: "After the meeting we'll go and visit West Lake. Since I was a very small boy I have been told about the beauti-ful scenery there and now, thanks to the Shanghai secret police, I'll see it." The two of them took the train ninety-five kilometers southwest to Hangchow and found the lake at its brilliant best.

But Mao was morose at the contrast between the splendor of the holiday scene and the sad deprivation of the Chinese masses. He re-fused to share Siao-yu's admiration for the hills and villas and gardens:

"This is a criminal production. Many people use their money for criminal purposes." Siao-yu rejoined with a smile: "Well, we shall be two temporary little criminals today." Mao was still unmoved and he declared: "Tomorrow we must get away from here quickly."

But he went back many times, finding the charm of West Lake more acceptable after Hangchow was liberated on May 3, 1949, than he had before. He maintains a cottage at the foot of Jewel Mountain, its porch lapped by the northern waters of West Lake. There he repaired for several months in the winter of 1965–1966 to set the stage and write the opening lines for the Cultural Revolution.

The Cultural Revolution knew some fierce moments in Hangchow (and smaller towns in Chekiang province south of Hangchow). Splintered extreme left-wing forces, as well as some pure adventurers, came up against a PLA which had been ordered to move out of its barracks and restore order. Mid-1967 was the most hectic period, several residents tell me.

One recalls fighting with spears in Hangchow streets; another speaks of hearing gunshots by night; a third of a takeover of the railways in midsummer by a gang of adventurers. There followed public trials, which ended in execution for a few citizens who opposed the PLA or profited by the chaos to commit crimes.

In these distracted days some damage was done to ancient monuments, as I see for myself. Yet few cities put behind them the strident and excessive ways of the Cultural Revolution as completely as Hangchow did in the early 1970s. The mood I sense in 1973 is conveyed by a conversation with an engineering student from Chekiang University.

When we meet by chance one night on the northern fringe of West Lake, he tells me of two stages in his life. The first was the Red Guard period, when he was a senior at middle school. He denounced everyone in sight, tripped to Peking for the frenetic rallies of August 1966, and joined in a certain amount of destruction at the ancient Ling-yin temple nearby. "An exciting time," he sums up.

The second period he speaks of is his present career as a student of civil engineering. A second-year student, he entered Chekiang University in 1971 after a cooling-off period on a tea commune. In the future he would like to work on a great construction project in one of China's frontier regions. I ask him which of the two periods he values more. After a moment of reflection he replies: "My study of engineering has more significance after all."

This student does not speak negatively about his Red Guard days. But when he stops to compare them with his present life, it is as if he becomes aware for the first time of how far he has drifted away from Red Guard conceptions. In a number of ways the judgment he catches himself making fits in with the priorities I observe in Hangchow in 1973: routine above impulse, study above slogans, socialist production above socialist posturing.

The CCP makes good use of the talent of the Chinese people for organization and ingenious teamwork. In 1954 the National People's Congress (China's occasional parliament) enacted a law "for the organization of City Street Offices." This applied to all towns with more than 100,000 people, and many with 50,000 or more people. Hangchow was among the first Chinese cities to put the law into effect. The street offices were a predecessor of what became, after the Cultural Revolution, the more ambitious "street committees," or *neighborhood committees,* as I prefer to translate their Chinese name (see note on page 78). Today Hangchow is honeycombed with these local government and civic organs.

Hangchow municipality with its 900,000 people is carved into six districts. The district on the east wing of downtown Hangchow, which I visit, is broken into seven neighborhoods. The neighborhood committee on which I focus especially — Establish Virtue Neighborhood Revolutionary Committee — has under it twelve smaller residents' committees.

The Chinese have long tended to rely on informal bonds and sanctions, rather than formal government structures, and the residents' committee carries forward this tradition. Though instigated by the state, the residents' committee is not part of the state administrative ladder, but a formation of the citizenry.

It has been claimed in the West that the neighborhood level, too, is separate from the formal state structure. However, it is made clear to me in several Chinese cities during 1973 that this is not the case. The Chinese press in 1974 confirms this finding in stating that the neighborhood committee (*jie-dao wei-yuan-hui*) is "the basic-level organ of people's political power, *the lowest level of government administration in the city.*"

The tentacles of state administration, then, do extend down as far as the neighborhood, but not so far as the residents' area. The residents' committee remains outside the formal government process, though by no means beyond the control of the Party. It is described by Chinese officials as "a self-governing people's organization, not a unit of government."

In the neighborhood, government and Party have their last chance to shape the conduct of citizens. At this level the life of a citizen meets the socialist priorities of Chinese society as a whole. The urban man and woman are wrapped in a blanket of care and control.

In Hangchow, neighborhood areas are much larger than in Dairen, though not more so than in other large cities outside *dong bei*. Several tens of thousands of citizens live in each of the neighborhoods on Hangchow's eastern side. Within Establish Virtue there are forty thousand people.

A revolutionary committee of fourteen persons, six of them women, runs Establish Virtue along lines laid down by a Party committee of seven persons. Those whom I meet among this core of cadres seem canny and experienced organizers. No doubt they must be, to care for and control a population equal to that of a sizable town.

Because the neighborhood areas of Hangchow are larger than those of Dairen, the subunit of residents' area takes on more important functions in Hangchow than in the northeastern city. I go to one of the twelve residents' areas under the umbrella of Establish Virtue. It contains seven hundred households and some three thousand people. From a three-story building you can see just about the entire residents' area, which occupies less than one square kilometer.

This part of Hangchow was once more densely settled than it is now. Sung dynasty records speak of poor folk crowded six or seven into a tiny room. You cannot see that in Hangchow of the 1970s.

Over the centuries the multistoried houses of the Sung era all got burned, and houses built later were seldom more than one or two stories high.

These inner-city streets contain no flat-roofed new apartment blocks, virtually no housing at all that dates from after Liberation. The homes are of myriad shapes and designs. Rents also, though always cheap, are not standardized at so many fen for each square meter as are those for new apartments.

Many buildings are of white plaster with unpainted Chekiang oak windows and doors. They stand on a concrete base ten inches high, to keep away dampness and the waters which wash through the lanes in the wet season. Some homes erected in the past thirty years are in brick, now judged the best material for residential construction.

An attractive feature is the typical front door, closing off a household from the rhythm of life in the narrow street outside. The doorway is equipped with two doors, one for summer and one for winter. During the hot days of my visit there is in use an outer door, only a little over half-height to allow the air to circulate. It is a double door of natural Chekiang wood, with a curved top like that in an old-fashioned barbershop. A heavy full-sized inner door to serve winter need remains swung back throughout the warm months.

Some families are housed in larger buildings dating from the 1920s or 1930s, originally used for commerce, but now subdivided into housing units. The ceilings on both levels are pleasantly high. Clothes are strung up across the rooms, photos decorate the upper reaches of the walls. There are even electric fans, some of which function. Beside the ground-floor entrances are public toilets, labeled in bold red characters, which suggests that the toilet facilities inside the apartments are limited.

The windows on the second level consist of a latticework of green painted beams, with no glass or paper filling. The upper half of the window space is filled with vertical beams only, giving the rooms a grandstand view of the street below and the hills beyond. The ground-level windows are of close latticework in cast concrete, of the type seen in Hispanic lands. Such windows give an agreeable sense of communality and openness toward nature.

181

✦ ✦ ✦

I stop at one sixty-year-old dwelling of a different kind. Opposite it are several houses made of brick at the ground level and unpainted vertical boards above, the second level protruding some fifty centimeters further into the narrow alley than the first. The old dwelling itself is in white plaster, decorated with fawn-painted cornices, ornate windowsills, and mock archways like raised eyebrows against the stark white walls.

A small wooden front gate leads from the street into an oblong courtyard. From this courtyard, one apartment gives off to each side, and two give off to the rear. It differs from many Peking courtyards — around which rooms are spread on all four sides — for one side of the courtyard is simply a wall against the alley outside.

The courtyard is of handsome cobbles, shiny with wear and age. Several white tiles are inset into the middle of it, each bearing an inlaid black Chinese character. The total message exhorts householders down the generations: "Get Rid of the Four Pests: Rats, Mosquitoes, Flies, Bedbugs."

There are eighteen people living in the complex, grouped in four families unrelated to each other. The scene resembles an old extended-family setup, in its physical form, while being, in its living content, a new nuclear-family setup of socialist China. Each family has essentially two rooms at its disposal and there is one kitchen between two families. As I read the warning about the Four Pests, some people emerge from the various doors and we begin to chat about things in Hangchow.

Chinese workers are not reticent to tell you how much money they earn — or how old they are — and here I find wages a little lower than those for comparable work in Dairen. One shy couple in their late thirties are both middle-school teachers and their combined monthly pay is ninety yuan. They have two children, living not here but with a grandparent in Shaohsing, eighty kilometers from Hangchow. The family gets together twice a month.

In the second of the four households the wife and husband also have the same job. This young pair earn eighty yuan between them at a large factory (five thousand workers) in southern Hangchow which makes hemp bags for carrying rice and other grains. Living with them is the girl's mother, a short brown nutmeg of a woman, who proves to be a lively character.

She has lived in this house all of her fifty-eight years. How much worse the Four Pests used to be than they are now, she tells me, and what havoc fire used to cause among the wooden homes, now mostly burned and replaced by brick or plaster ones. A recent recruit to the CCP, this energetic old stick gathers medical herbs during her walks in the Hangchow hills, which she turns over to the clinic in Establish Virtue.

A third couple earn a total of 101 yuan. He is a forty-eight-year-old engineer; she is a forty-four-year-old worker at one of the city's many silk-weaving factories. The engineer's room has three shelves of well-thumbed political books. There are key works of Marx and Engels, which one sees everywhere in China, including the *Communist Manifesto* and *The Class Struggles in France*. As well, I notice rarer documents from CCP meetings going back twenty-odd years, and texts of speeches by Premier Chou and other Chinese leaders on a variety of topics. The engineer is proud and pleased when I take an interest in these books. He is forthcoming about their context and content.

There are also many volumes of materials published by the Soviet Communist Party — all the foreign items are in Chinese translation — but our conversation about these works quickly gets stiff. I try to focus on *Proceedings of the Twenty-first Congress of the Communist Party of the USSR*. Yes, the gentle engineer has read portions of this book. But no, he cannot say if it contains any wrong points. He gives me a slightly pained look and I leave the subject.

Books are to the fore in other households of Establish Virtue neighborhood. Wandering at will into one home, in a narrow, well-paved alley, I find a young man reading a book on his bed (which is covered with rush matting and toweling, just as beds were in Hangchow under the Sung). It is a Chinese translation of Tolstoy's *Anna Karenina*, published in Shanghai twelve years ago.

The youth is much engrossed in the novel and I hate to disturb him. He explains that he is a middle-school student and that this is vacation time. In answer to a question he replies with a smile: "No, *Anna*

Karenina is not a text for schoolwork. It was lent to me by a friend, whose father passed it on to him."

In one large household the attention given to a tattered book seems a tribute to its quality. The reader is a chemical worker in his twenties. The children of his elder brother, who is head of the house, swirl around at games, and the brother's wife is chopping up pork and vegetables in the elaborate Chinese manner. All this in a tiny apartment of three rooms.

Yet the chemical worker has already read much of the book today, his rest day. Entitled *Pictures of the Grassy Country*, it is a collection of stories set in Inner Mongolia. He says the tales are rather gripping and that north China, being apparently so different from the Yangtze Valley, is a place he would like to visit one day.

The only books in a foreign language which I notice in a home of Establish Virtue are on the shelves of a technical worker at a silk embroidery factory. He must be a senior man for his wage is eighty-two yuan. When I arrive he is at work, but his wife shows me his library of some hundreds of books. They are mainly on technical subjects, and a scattering are in Russian.

In none of these four homes which have a larger or smaller quantity of books do I see a single newspaper. None of them, I learn, subscribe to a newspaper. Those household members who go out to work say they look at a paper in the factory or the office. This means a local (*di-fang*) newspaper only. Outside the ranks of cadres and intellectuals, one does not come across people in Hangchow who see every day the *People's Daily* of Peking. In the homes of Hangchow, anyway, you see many books before you see a newspaper or magazine.

❁ ❁ ❁

Establish Virtue neighborhood runs seven light-industry and handicrafts factories of its own, with a total of 1,005 workers on the payroll. Most of this economic activity started only recently; all of it since the Cultural Revolution. The cadres from the revolutionary committee who supervise the factories are obviously pleased at the work's profitability. In 1972 the efforts of these mainly female workers brought in a profit of no less than 660,000 yuan. Three hundred thousand of it, the cadres report with pride but no great cheerfulness, went up to the district in taxes.

Most of the residents' committees within Establish Virtue have small "production teams" of their own. Here housewives keep busy for rather low wages. I come upon one task force of a production team. They are tinting embroidered silk pictures, on a piecework basis for a large silk firm within the district.

Lacking a workshop of their own, they sometimes do this meticulous work in their own homes, and sometimes (as today) they make use of the residents' area canteen. Lunch being over, the wooden benches and tables are unoccupied for a few hours until suppertime, and they make a good place for silk work.

The canteen is a large airy rotunda with a pointed roof. Its cooks are already at work on supper and they chat with me as they chop up seaweed. The dish they are preparing is called "pork and seaweed," said to be as popular as any they serve. Fish is the specialty of the Hangchow area. Pork is also abundant. Beef is not regularly offered. The kitchen is big, and clean as kitchens go, but it has no refrigeration at all.

These grinning men and women cooks serve meals at a cost of fifteen or twenty fen to an average of fifty or sixty folk, who for one reason or another prefer to eat here rather than at home. Of the residents' areas within Establish Virtue, some have canteens while others do not, but people from one residents' area may eat at the canteen of a nearby residents' area (they still remain within Establish Virtue neighborhood).

Only a fraction of the wage earners in Establish Virtue are employed at the neighborhood's own factories. A lot of them work in the city's silk industry. Two residents of a four-apartment block, Mr. and Mrs. Kuo, both work in the Hangchow Silk Embroidery Factory. When I call, Mr. Kuo is at work but Mrs. Kuo, on her rest day, is at home with her parents who also live in the household.

Mrs. Kuo is a small, sharp-featured, resourceful woman, with fine hands and a perpetual smile. She guides me around her house, while hissing an occasional aside to her mother, and tending to an aromatic pot cooking in the kitchen. There are four rooms altogether (forty-five square meters). The young couple and the old have consolidated their housing-space allowance and thus got one large place instead of two small places.

Mr. and Mrs. Kuo earn a monthly total of 101 yuan. They have managed to put away several hundred yuan, which earns 3.3 percent interest in a local branch of the Bank of China. Mrs. Kuo's two young children spend the day at the factory's kindergarten, at a charge of 2.8 yuan per month. Occasionally Mrs. Kuo also makes use of the kindergarten's dormitory, where babies may sleep, six to a room, for one or several nights. She seems to care well for the children but she is not sentimental about them.

Later I go to Mrs. Kuo's factory. It is a state enterprise under the municipal Bureau of Silk. Seventeen hundred workers (40 percent of them women) are putting out satins, velvet, and silk pictures. It is a place where work is done with pride and apparent absorption.

Chekiang has only a modest industrial capacity (1 percent of the nation's), but it is among China's leading provinces for silk. Hangchow has eighteen big silk mills. The city's output of raw silk is eight times that of 1949, its output of silk and satin goods nine times that of 1949.

Traditions go all the way back to Ko Hung, a Taoist alchemist of the fourth century, who experimented with dyes in Hangchow and came up with hues which are still admired by the city's silk people.

Founded in 1921, the factory underwent an enormous expansion after Liberation. From 10 rooms to 330 rooms, from 42 kinds of products to 1,000 kinds, from purely black-and-white embroidery to the use of sixteen colors. The average wage is sixty-three yuan (highest is ninety-two and apprentices get thirty). Women retire at fifty, men at sixty. The factory is run by a revolutionary committee made up of seven cadres, eight workers, and two PLA representatives.

The facilities include hairdressing salons, a kindergarten, and a clinic with nine doctors. On a large board in the factory yard are notices about swimming, basketball, track and field, and table tennis events. One sports notice catches my eye. It is an excited report about the visit of several Chinese sporting teams to the United States.

Though Mrs. Kuo is reticent on the subject, the most interesting

186

topic of my talks at the factory is the Cultural Revolution. Mr. Liu of the revolutionary committee mentions the struggles of 1966–1968 perfunctorily. When I ask in what *way* the "political consciousness of the workers has been raised," and the "revisionists led by Liu Shao-ch'i beaten back," his answers remain vague. The "enemies" of those contentious days seem to become phantoms when you try to track them down.

Concrete conditions at the factory, however, have changed since the Cultural Revolution. Although two of the PLA men who arrived in 1967 are still here, a net result of the upheaval was a reduced administrative superstructure in the factory. There are now seventy-eight full-time cadres as compared with ninety before 1966. Several workers express praise for this "necessary cutback."

There have also been technical innovations, which a number of people attribute to the stimulus toward better work that Cultural Revolutionary criticism provided. Since 1969 there are two new machines which save a lot of time. One automatically mends a broken thread; another automatically changes a shuttle.

A third change affects the worker most. Gone are the bonuses (*jiang-jin*) in their pre-1966 form. The bonus used to add ten or even twenty yuan to the monthly earnings of a keen worker, who might mind two machines instead of one, or overproduce his target. Now the take-home pay of the seventeen hundred workers is somewhat more equally distributed than before, though ways are still found to reward extra effort (see pages 289, 293 to 294, 375).

※ ※ ※

If economic enterprise at Establish Virtue is above average in scope, activity in politics and social mediation is not. The revolutionary committee feels that most citizens are drawn into political study groups at work, and that a major effort in this sphere within the neighborhood is not necessary. Similarly, the numbers involved in Party and CYL branches are not high — some thirty or forty CYL members in a residents' area of seven hundred households — again because it is assumed that factory, school, and office branches are doing the job.

When a crime is committed — fights are the most common — the matter goes straight to the police; maybe then to the district law court. Attempts at mediation by authorities of the neighborhood or residents' area are not frequent. This pattern also holds true for budding divorce cases. The partners make direct application to the district. The issue is rarely even discussed in the neighborhood or residents' committee.

Light is thrown on this fairly bureaucratic style of work, I think, by the organization of the police network in this neighborhood. Often in Chinese cities the small police offices — as a rule one office for each residents' area — are responsible only to the Public Security Bureau of the district. Cadres of Establish Virtue tell me, however, that the nine full-time police working in the seven residents' areas of their neighborhood operate under the "dual control" of Public Security *and* Establish Virtue's revolutionary committee.

The streets in Establish Virtue do not look or sound like those of an American inner city, especially when it comes to the role of the machine. Technologically, these Hangchow lanes are hardly distinguishable from a village. No glint of steel or toot of horns breaks in on them. A lady in black pants and a blue blouse walks with her string bag down the middle of the street on the way to market. She shops as a rural housewife shops, because she lacks the refrigeration facilities that would permit her to shop like a Western urban woman. The products she buys are fresh and unpackaged like those in a rural market.

One must also say that Establish Virtue lacks what we in the West call sophistication. A woman does not blush to breast-feed her baby on a front doorstep. Nor a father to feed his twin daughters with a bottle in a crowded park. Old men with shorts and portly stomachs, hands clasped behind their backs, watch the scene impassively. Men of all ages walk by hand in hand with small children. People seem to pop in and out of each other's homes in a breezy way. There is no daring place of distraction for restless citizens to go to; the signs and posters are all either factual labels or political maxims. The tonal light and shade of the area comes only from the personality of its lively people.

There is a socially undifferentiated quality, amounting perhaps to dullness, in the steamy air. No stylistic surprises confront you (aside from a dressed-up group of children, envoys of the residents' committee, coached to sing and dance for a visiting foreigner). Women ordinarily wear dark pants and light blouses, not very distinct from the trousers and shirts of the grown men. For a leisure outing, though, the younger women will don a skirt and the older ones a colored pants-suit. Nearly all the girls have braids. Boys lean to T-shirts with a colored stripe. Everyone wears sandals without socks. The toys of the children are not smart or complex; nor are they dangerous.

Establish Virtue boasts tiny parks which, like oases, dot the neighborhood. No one's house is far from one of them. Only twenty or thirty meters across, they are softened by maples. For a quiet rest there are chairs made of cane — which is cool — with an adjustable back and arms that consist simply of three beams hooked up to the front legs. There are bushes with brilliant flowers, and rockeries that Westerners might call a "Japanese garden."

Women back from shopping pause at these spots with their bulging straw baskets and knobbly string bags. Street sweepers under the supervision of the residents' committee take their break here. They sit beside their box-on-wheels which holds the rubbish, and their scrawny, almost medieval-style brush brooms. This city neighborhood has not let itself become a concrete jungle.

It is interesting to recall Hangchow's heyday as capital of the Sung dynasty, and to see how the physical shape of the city and the ways of its citizens have changed over seven hundred years. Of the city ramparts and the imperial palaces in the southern district nothing at all remains (though travelers in the nineteenth century spoke of seeing parts of them).

In Sung times a street sixty meters wide ran five kilometers north and south from the gate of the imperial palaces to the far city wall. Marco Polo said this Imperial Way was paved in stone and brick. The street survives as Hangchow's main boulevard, Sun Yat-sen Avenue. It is less wide than it was, but still handsomely paved, and nicely shaded by maples with bright green leaves.

"The city," Marco Polo recorded, "is situated in such a way that it has on the one side a lake of fresh water which is very clear, and on

189

the other an enormous river. The water [of the lake] feeds a number of canals of all sizes which run through the various districts of the city. . . . One can go everywhere about the city by means of these canals."

It is surprising that one who has seen the Yangtze and Yellow rivers would call the Ch'ien-t'ang "enormous." Whether the water of West Lake is clear, too, depends somewhat on the weather. As for the canals, quite a few have by now been filled in, and it is no longer possible to go about Hangchow by canal.

Some waterways remain, mostly running parallel to Sun Yat-sen Avenue on its eastward side. It is one of Hangchow's delights to abruptly come upon a canal when strolling down a side street. But Chinese-made buses, painted blue and white and lumbering in movement, have replaced boats as the city's staple transport.

Charming stone bridges also link the present with the Sung dynasty. They span canals, dikes, and streams in the hills. Polo put on the wings of exaggeration when he wrote of "twelve thousand bridges of stone, for the most part so lofty that a great fleet could pass beneath them." There are no bridges so lofty in Hangchow today, nor do pictures or documents confirm that any ever did exist. Yet Hangchow does strike the visitor as a city of little bridges, if less spectacularly so than Soochow, a companion city in beauty, 110 kilometers to the north in Kiangsu province.

It is the careful attention Chinese people pay to nature which above all provides continuity between past and present. All sorts of places in Hangchow are named by reference to natural features. Island at the Heart of the Lake; Road Around the Lake; Northern Mountain Street; Purple Cloud Cave.

This deep sense of place makes of the Chinese a fixed and naturalistic and history-conscious people. The more abstract and mobile ways of the West made a sharp, tragic contrast, when in the nineteenth-century a rooted China met a roving Europe.

Prince Kung, an official of the Ch'ing court who negotiated with thrusting foreigners in the 1850s and 1860s, once told Lord Elgin how puzzled the Chinese were that the British should have mounted such a navy and strayed so far from their own land. It had long been

Tiny parks dot the neighborhood like oases

Boys use a bucket on
a string to draw up
water from wells in
the lanes

Peking's theory that the reason must be Britain's small territory and large population, which meant "the greater half of the people were compelled to reside afloat."

When the Restoration Society was founded to seek a solution to China's miseries in the early twentieth century, its members swore to "restore the Chinese race and recover our mountains and rivers." Saving the Chinese nation included saving the tie between the Chinese people and China's portion of nature.

The point about naturalistic place-names is that they are just as vivid and apt for a Hangchow resident of the 1970s as they were during the Sui or the Sung. The North High Peak is still north of the Ling-yin temple. The West Lake still flanks the western edge of the city.

To be sure, the sense of place had superstitious overtones during the dynasties which mean nothing for urban Chinese today. The wrong location for a grave, it was once believed, could prove disastrous for the life after death of a departed one, as well as for his descendants. Today's Chinese have left behind the old cosmic philosophy. Yet they have retained the naturalism which went with it. A sense of the hills and waters among which he lives permits the Hangchow resident a secular bond with his ancestors.

He sees around him, at the same time, some totally new place-names which abandon a sense of place in favor of didactic abstraction: "Liberation Street"; "Red Guard Square"; "August 1 Street" (in memory of the founding date of the PLA). So Hangchow's place-names are a mixture of many which are very old, local, and naturalistic, and some which are very new, abstract, and political.

A typical Chinese case of change in substance yet continuity in natural form may be observed at the Altar of the Southern Suburbs. Here the Sung emperors performed rites at the start of spring, the winter solstice, and when rain was needed to break a drought. The place was called Field of the Eight Trigrams; the Altar of Heaven in the center was surrounded by eight fields making up an irregular octagon. To keep nature in good humor, sacrifices were made to the planets, the 360 stars, and the legendary emperors of the Five Colors.

With the centuries the altar has crumbled and only a raised mound remains. But the eight fields are here in the same shape as through time immemorial, now tilled in all nonchalance by the cheerful, matter-of-fact members of a people's commune.

So frequently has Hangchow been razed by fire that few ordinary houses from the Sung period remain. Basic building materials were then wood and bamboo from nearby areas, together with tiles and bricks made in the city. Homes were open to the street, in the southern way, rather than walled off as in the north. It was common in the central district to find shops and workrooms on the ground floor, with the living quarters above, the two levels connected by a small internal ladder.

In the crowded inner city the scene is not all that different today. Most dwellings blend wood with brick or white plaster — bamboo is rarer — and the alleys are still well paved with vast square slabs. Wells have been sunk here and there beneath the paving stones. Boys use a bucket on a string to draw up water through the well's earthenware mouth.

The streets are probably tidier than they have ever been before, helped by the presence of rubbish bins that look like miniature furnaces. There are virtually none of the "boat people" who were once so numerous. These dwellers on canal craft have been resettled in functional housing provided since Liberation.

Ancient Hangchow had no public street lighting and even today there is not much. A dreamy gloom engulfs the wider streets during the evening. This pleasantly enhances the glow of moon and stars, luminescent through the pattern of maple leaves overhead. The narrow lanes which have no trees become a chessboard of shadows by night; paving stones reflect the shape of poles with hanging clothing, and the zany angles of roofing patched many times.

In Sung days Hangchow people were early risers. About 4:00 or 5:00 A.M. the bells of the monasteries rang and monks walked the streets, beating an object in the shape of a fish, announcing a fresh day. They called out information about the weather: "It is cloudy"; "The sky is clear"; "It is raining." They gave details of official functions due that day. Along the Imperial Way a lively trade began in breakfast dishes: hot pancakes, soups, bits of goose and mutton, fried tripe. Peddlers offered hot water for washing the face, pills to restore the *qi* (breath or life-force), potions from rhinoceros horn or snake-skin to boost the ailing.

The people still rise early but the chime they hear is the political song "The East Is Red," not a monastery bell. The day's briefing on weather and the world comes not from a big-throated monk but from Chekiang People's Radio. The three meals are still taken around dawn, noon, and sunset, as they were on the old schedule.

"Breakfast stations" run by residents' committees make the morning action on Sun Yat-sen Avenue resemble what it once was on the Imperial Way, except that there are no peddlers and no vociferous sales cries. I do not see goose or tripe, but plenty of fried and steamed pancakes, various soups, and a kind of soybean porridge (*dou-jiang*) with spices sprinkled on top. There are still one or two Moslem (or Hui) eating shops where Islamic dietary norms are respected.

As for exotic and ingenious potions to cure ailments, they have by no means disappeared from modern China. Two young Hangchow acquaintances tender me the earnest advice that an extract from snakes is excellent for arthritis, and the bone of the tiger a fine general tonic.

Marco Polo would today recognize only residual aspects of the amusements and festivals which made Hangchow seven hundred years ago the very definition of excitement and dissoluteness. Especially at New Year people used to indulge their boundless zeal for festivals. A porridge of red haricot beans was offered to the guardian spirits of the house (there was even a god of the bed to be propitiated). At dawn on New Year's Day the emperor burned incense and asked Heaven for an abundant harvest.

Toward the close of the New Year period came the gay Feast of Lanterns, when Hangchow was ablaze with light. There were round glass lanterns from Soochow, white jade ones from Foochow, others in the shape of boats and sedan chairs. There were lanterns which a descending trickle of water caused to rotate and reveal a panorama of landscapes and birds.

194

During the Festival for Sacrifices to the God of the Soil people did extraordinary things in the hope that their fortune and happiness might be enhanced. Pigs and chickens were slaughtered with abandon, there was clowning and juggling, and special dishes were eaten and strong cups tossed down.

Even when no festival could be greeted, Hangchow residents might find an excuse for distraction in hearty wedding celebrations. Or they would take time out to visit "pleasure grounds" where one could laugh or marvel at puppeteers, acrobats, snake charmers, storytellers — even shellfish hypnotized by a Taoist hermit.

There are echoes in today's Hangchow of this delight in a show, yet the framework for it all is now an egalitarian people's culture. Residents speak with a certain excitement about Spring Festival, and — in a different way — about the two great socialist festivals of May 1 (Labor Day) and October 1 (National Day). There is at least one day off from work for all these (three days for Spring Festival, which is Chinese New Year, and two days for October 1).

People dress up a bit, special dishes are prepared, and there are colorful public rallies. At New Year and Spring Festival the accent falls on family gatherings. Labor Day and National Day are serious political occasions. The undoubted fun of the marches and glamour of the decorations is supposed to be incidental to a message of memory and hope, proclaimed from the city rostrum and reinforced by an editorial in *Chekiang Daily*.

These celebrations deserve their official label of "people's" occasions because the social distinctions of old Hangchow have sunk almost without a trace. There was more of a common culture under the Sung than in many periods of Chinese history. Hangchow during the Sung was nevertheless a drastically unequal society. Just as curved roofs were reserved for official buildings or houses of people of high rank, so did garments provide an instant guide to a man's status and income. The elite wore a ground-length robe of embroidered silk. Common folk wore trousers and a blouse of hempen cloth.

Today garments leave a man exactly where they find him. The vice-chairman of the Hangchow revolutionary committee greets you in the same kind of shirt, pants, and sandals worn by a shop assistant or a student in class. All crowds in China, even at the opera, are as undifferentiated in badges of status as a battalion of soldiers.

There are limits to the possibilities of any Chinese "showing off" during a season of celebration. He is unlikely to have anything very special to parade before others. And he is frowned on if he tries such a display. This accounts, I believe, for the relaxed ambience of today's China. So far as possessions and customs go, the strain of trying to impress or manipulate other people by a show of ostentation or fancy manners has been largely removed (not entirely in Shanghai) by the equalizing of wealth.

This does not mean the Chinese people do not have a good time during festive hours. Weddings are certainly still a great event. Three days off from work are granted the partners. I meet women who spent two or even three months' wages on their wedding dress.

For the most part, however, the holiday sights around West Lake and in the hills are those of people taking simple pleasures — outings which are spontaneous rather than prepared; play which is subdued rather than boisterous; pleasures which rely on nature and companions rather than on spending or elaborate equipment.

At the amusement parks one finds the nearest equivalent to the gay and goalless promenading which used to go on in old Hangchow. During the Sung the term for them was "pleasure grounds"; today it is "cultural parks." In the evening these places offer a banquet of activities. On an open-air stage local songs and sketches are performed by students from surrounding schools. A storyteller, equipped only with a microphone covered by a red scarf, presents extracts from the novel *Taking Tiger Mountain by Strategy,* while hundreds listen on the edge of their chairs. A game of chess is played by skillful volunteers from the crowd, each move announced by a boy at a microphone, while another boy uses a long pole to hoist cards on a massive billboard made out as a chessboard, each card representing to the crowd a piece in the actual game below.

There is a basketball match between a team from an electrical firm and one from a metal-making firm. All the players are women, though 90 percent of the spectators are men. There is also a skating rink, where the atmosphere is more unrestrained than anywhere else in the park, and table tennis in a small brick pavilion with benches for a silent, head-swiveling audience. At an air-gun gallery, youths fire shots at moving targets, arranged to look like bandits maneuvering through a south China landscape. Groups in quiet clusters play *bai-fen,* while the occasional couple is busy at sweet nothings in a shadowy corner.

The greatest difference between the pleasure ground of the Sung and the cultural park of Mao's China is suggested by the name of the latter. The ordinary man in China today is allowed to be, and hardly allowed not to be, a participant in the politics and culture of the socialist society he lives in.

The Cultural Park has notice boards with photos and text about CCP meetings, anniversaries of the founding of the CCP and the PLA, and exhortations to greater feats of socialist construction. The ordinary man can read the Chinese characters, which his ancestor from the Sung could not. And he feels obligated — some feel enthusiastically drawn — to know about and affirm a fixed consensus about where China is going, as his brother under the Sung did not.

You do not find the love of alcohol which used to require a tavern every few yards in Hangchow streets, and made drunkenness a point of honor on all great occasions. Nor are there any more of those "singing girls" and "flowers" who were available by the tens of thousands at the bridges and markets of Hangchow in Marco Polo's time. Organized and open prostitution has simply vanished. Nor yet do you come across carousing bands of merrymakers, or goings-on which border on the riotous.

All this reminds us that Hangchow is a work-oriented city. This was hardly true of twelfth-century Hangchow, a town that consumed more than it produced and was a parasite on the countryside around it. A contemporary Chinese crowd at leisure does not seem far from the workbenches from which it has just come and to which it will soon return.

The clothes being worn are seldom much different from work clothes. Girls and women do not walk like playthings. At recreation as at work they do mostly the same things as men. People in the parks

197

during the evening are often, with bag in hand, on the way home from the office or factory. While sitting under a willow a citizen may well hear a broadcast proposing 10 percent more effort in order to produce an extra thousand yards of silk.

The pleasures of Hangchow, in a word, are not the professional pleasures of the brothel or the ski slope, but the low-key pleasures of a respite from work in the company of fellow-workers.

❀ ❀ ❀

In the parks of Hangchow games are played with an earnestness that recalls ancient Chinese game playing. In Hangchow under the Sung, the rage was "double six," a dice game not unlike backgammon. Upon this folly, one observer of the twelfth century said, the rich would stake their slaves and horses and the poor would wager the next round of drinks. Dominoes, chess, and *mahjong* were popular, as well as a formidable game called "jug," which required throwing darts into a vase with a narrow neck, by making them first bounce off a drumskin placed halfway between thrower and target.

In Hangchow of the 1970s, the games are simpler and there is virtually no playing for money, yet not all has changed. Of "jug" there is no trace, and "double six" is seen mainly in museums, where lifelike figures in clay or stone bend at the game. Chess and dominoes you see quite a bit. Neither can match, though, the surge in popularity since the Cultural Revolution of the card game *bai-fen.*

Mahjong is not common, though it has made a timid comeback since the Cultural Revolution. I ask one official when he last played *mahjong* and whether it was for money. His most recent game was in 1965, he replies after a moment of thought. The last game for money was "some years before that."

It is still true, as of old, that the Chinese play games far into the night, and games still throw down a bridge between young and old. Nor has the CCP broken continuity with the past by injecting politics into games. I do not see games where a visage of Confucius stands for the villain, or where a likeness of Liu Shao-ch'i represents the "capitalist enemy."

A game which I notice a lot among Hangchow workers is "army

game" (*lu-zhan qi*), more popularly called "military game" (*jun qi*). Boys play it with zeal and concentration in a park or on a broad sidewalk. There is often a crowd of onlookers, whispering suggestions to each other as to what the strategists ought to do. To study the game at leisure I go to the New China (Hsinhua) Bookstore and ask for a set. It is handed over with an amused giggle by a young girl assistant.

A map depicts a terrain of mountains, camps, railroads. There is a home base at each end for the two contending armies. Twenty-five playing pieces are available to each side to deploy over the terrain. Headed by "commander in chief," the ranks run down through "army commander," "division commander," "brigade commander," "regiment commander," "battalion commander," "company commander," "platoon commander," to the rank-and-file "engineer." Each side also has two "bombs" and two "land mines." Mines cannot be moved around like the soldiers and officers. But to move onto a position occupied by a mine is to be blown up and leave the board, except that an engineer can overcome a mine.

The game depends on secrecy in the deployment of one's forces. This is achieved by standing the playing pieces — which are oblong blocks with the name of the piece written in two characters on one side — so that the enemy cannot see the names of your pieces. (Nor of course can you see the names of his.)

As the game begins each strategist arranges his pieces as he wishes on his side of the board. Skill is here called for. The formation chosen determines how successfully the enemy will be able to weave into your territory, and how readily you will be able to get across the mountains and make inroads into his areas.

The aim is to penetrate the enemy's home base and grab his "flag." This means victory, though it is only half a victory if, in the course of the enterprise, your commander in chief happens to get killed.

As well as the two strategists there is a "judge" or "arbiter" (*gong-zheng ren*). He decides which moves are legitimate, and declares the outcome of any encounter between two pieces. Only he knows which pieces meet each other in a given encounter. If my platoon commander falls, I do not know — but the judge does — whether it is your company commander, battalion commander, or some even higher piece which has done it. The rules lay down that the judge "is not permitted to involve himself in the military planning of either side."

"Army game" gives rein to the Chinese passion for strategy. No doubt it owes part of its attraction to the fact that China made its revolution by armed force. Yet nothing about the game has an explicitly contemporary ring. There are no political overtones in the names of the pieces, on the board, or in the detailed list of instructions. The style of it all is professional-military, without any effort to make points for socialism. Indeed I am struck that "army game" has eight officer levels, whereas China's PLA has (since 1965) no ranks whatsoever.

The number one collective entertainment in China is the movies. Some four billion cinema tickets are bought each year. Some residents of Establish Virtue tell me of a cinema called "Pacific" which they sometimes go to. There is a good film showing there just now called *Five One,* they say. I set off to see it, by Number Seven bus from Hangchow Hotel north of the lake, to Sun Yat-sen Avenue in the central district. I go alone because my two companions are not keen to come. My local guide has already seen the film. Mr. Liu wants to look up a friend at Chekiang University.

Everywhere in China during 1973 I find the cinemas crowded and tickets not easy to come by (unless the foreigner uses the special channels available to him). Tonight in Hangchow is no exception. I arrive an hour early for the 8:00 P.M. show and manage to buy one of the last remaining seats.

It is quite shadowy as we line up on the sidewalk and few people notice that I am not Chinese. But on reaching the head of the line I accidentally become the center of attention, for I hand over a ten-yuan note to buy the seventy-fen ticket. There are one or two gasps from people near me in line; some boys whisper and point. But the girl behind the grille is impassive and gives me a fistful of change without comment.

When the time comes to enter the cinema I quickly take a place not far from the back. As people flock in, however, it turns out that the seats and tickets are numbered. The person duly arrives who has the seat I am sitting in. Happily, an usher is nearby and she leads me to my proper seat, as I mumble that I am new and don't understand the procedures.

The air-conditioned if rather shabby auditorium holds some fifteen hundred people. As the lights go down not one of the hard, varnished-wood seats seems vacant. The audience is informally clad — many men have singlets without shirts, shorts are more common than trousers — and smelly with sweat and work clothes. But above all it is a lively tiger of an audience. Before the show begins the babble of gossip is almost raucous. As the film gets under way there is still a lot of noise. Whispering here, a ripple of laughter there, a wave of positive or negative reaction from all reaches of the cinema.

Five One turns out to be a documentary of the celebration in Peking of May Day, 1973. There are sustained close-ups of many Chinese leaders, festive scenes, and segments of the entertainments offered during parties for this key date in China's calendar. In general there is little audience response to the political side of the film: clips from speeches, revolutionary songs, the appearance of leaders (Mao is not present). The audience responds most warmly to the rousing artistic spectacles, especially some swashbuckling sword fights between small boys and girls.

Yet there is one political appearance during the evening which stirs immense reaction. The second biggest target of the Cultural Revolution, after Liu Shao-ch'i, was the head of the Communist Party organization, Teng Hsiao-p'ing. The Maoists lambasted him as the "number two man in power walking the capitalist road." In the course of 1973, however, this skilled administrator gradually resumed a public role.

Tonight his cheerful face flashes twice onto the screen. In a short newsreel film which precedes *Five One*, he is seen welcoming a Chinese delegation on its return to Peking after a trip to Japan. During the May Day festivities he clumps toward the camera, beaming cautiously, a chunky and inelegant figure in his blue-gray tunic.

On both occasions the Pacific Cinema erupts with excitement. The "oohs" and "ahs" are sharp and immediate. There are some loud cries of "Oh, oh." Uncertain laughter flutters here and there. Altogether a shock wave seems to sweep through the auditorium.

Of course many people must have read that Mr. Teng had made a timid comeback in Peking. But not for years has the public seen the former secretary-general in the cinema or on TV. The audience does not cheer Teng. Yet it does not fall silent with embarrassment at his appearance. The reaction is like that to the sudden appearance on the screen of a favorite villain. A character very familiar to all, known to have been in great trouble, but widely thought to be not all bad.

After the show I hurry down Sun Yat-sen Avenue to catch the 9:30 bus, which is the last for the evening. Unsure of where the bus stop is, I ask a young man who also happens to be waiting for the Number Seven. We travel together in the dark bus. We chat about our jobs — he is an insecticides specialist in a bureau of Hangchow municipality — and later about the scenic spots around West Lake. Like almost all Chinese with whom I fall into casual conversation, he asks about my family. How many children do I have, is my wife in Australia or in the United States? I was to remain on the bus until the terminus, which is just near Hangchow Hotel. The insecticide worker rises to alight a little before this. As I thank him for his kindness, he shyly pops one more question on the topic of jobs. "How much do you earn a month?" he inquires quietly. I hardly have time to answer before he is off into the sweet evening air.

Leaving Establish Virtue neighborhood one afternoon, I head westward to savor on foot the transition to central Hangchow. The change is gradual, the differences not so great. It is the ebb of the afternoon. Counters are busy with last-minute buyers, before closing time which for many shops is 7:00 P.M. Broad leafy sidewalks are thronged with young and old. Shiny asphalt roads shoulder bicycles and the intermittent bus. But there are no noises more shattering than a bicycle bell. The ambience is far from frenetic.

Nothing is either very ancient or ultramodern in downtown Hangchow. Few commercial buildings predate the destructive years of the Taiping Rebellion (1850s). Many of the larger (two- and three-story) structures are not more than thirty or forty years old. There are verandas, but the sidewalks are not totally covered like the semi-enclosed sidewalks of Canton, where the weather is more tempestuous.

Although the shops are virtually all state-owned, supervised by various bureaus of Hangchow municipality, they do not lack individuality. The buyer has no stronger impression than in Manhattan or Chicago stores of uniformity, mass-produced styles, chains, or other signs of centralized organization. No two of the innumerable restaurants and eating stations seem alike. And there are still large numbers of small and specialty shops.

The price of some items in specialty stores would require careful saving up, or a dash of recklessness, on the part of most Hangchow purses. Here in Liberation Street is a shop selling only silk shirts, and few are offered at less than fifteen yuan. One-third of the monthly wage of a worker is a lot for a shirt.

Around the corner on the handsome concourse of Sun Yat-sen Avenue, a fur shop's prices raise the same question. Two gentle old men emerge from the shadows of a mellow chamber fitted with wooden shelves and cabinets. They know their furs inside out. They have been selling them in this same store since well before Liberation, formerly for themselves and now for the state. The cheapest fur coat is seventy yuan and some are twice that. One of the old salesmen avows that customers are not as infrequent as I might guess: "The people are not a few who will save two months' wages or more to buy a winter coat."

I drift into Hangchow's premier department store. It is smaller and less fancily got up than the best in Shanghai and Peking. The counters stocked with appliances and technical items are busy. Transistor radios sell for 70 to 90 yuan, cameras for 80 to 100 yuan, sewing machines for 150 yuan, bicycles for 140 yuan. Cosmetics are on display, though of far simpler character than the eyebrow black, false hair, and exotic perfumes once considered necessary by upper-class women in Hangchow.

There is a section with birth control devices, where qualified shoppers may stock up on their requirements. The pill, increasingly popular in China, is not available at this store, but only through a clinic at places of work. Here married men may buy sheaths. "Women of child-bearing age" (unmarried women are not considered part of this category) may buy the ring.

Food is often sold at specialty shops: one for meat, another for sweets and pastry, a third for vegetables. Prices for most items are not only reasonable but virtually unchanged from those I noted during visits to China in 1964 and 1971. The housewife's major food expense is meat. Various cuts of pork and ham start at seventy fen per half kilo, and rise to more than one yuan.

You see shoppers pulling coupons from their bags. All grain products are rationed at present, on a complicated schedule based on work done and family situation. Cotton cloth is also rationed, at five meters per person per year.

One shop that brings an intriguing surprise is a silk embroidery parlor. It is standard practice for shops to offer paintings, postcards, embroidered portraits, and other likenesses of Chairman Mao, Marx, Engels, Stalin, and Lenin. Now and then a contemporary foreign figure, most likely Ho Chi Minh, joins these fabled ranks. But in my past experience the likeness of no CCP leader other than Mao has ever been on sale.

Yet here in the silk parlor I find a dashing, even-eyed, embroidered portrait of Chou En-lai. Purchasing one, I ask the shop assistant about it, but she limits herself to a reminder that Chou is "our country's prime minister." Of course it is also true that Chou's roots are in Chekiang province.

In a bookstore the foreigner who can read Chinese always finds a warm, even awestruck welcome. In the New China Bookstore I browse among the fiction cases as a group of assistants stand by with shy glances. "Do you think he can read Chinese?" one quietly murmurs to her colleague.

The China Travel Service official accompanying me says this foreigner does indeed read Chinese. A young man assistant then briskly announces: "I would like to *hear him speak* Chinese." Though it is closing time the bookstore staff all forget the hour. They spend thirty minutes trying to tickle my fancy with the latest publications.

Aside from the usual flood of technical books and pamphlets — in response to the keenest preference of young Chinese today — there is a broadening trickle of stories and social studies. Translations of Maxim Gorky's work have just appeared. Lu Hsün's stories and essays

周 恩 来 同 志

中国杭州东方红丝织厂 95×146公分

Yet here in the silk parlor I find a dashing, even-eyed
embroidered portrait of Chou En-lai

are offered in a "Self-study Series for Youth." There are recent short stories on the theme of fertilizers and petrochemicals, said to be written by ordinary workers and peasants.

Two regular publications on international affairs sell well, according to the young man assistant. *International Events (Guo-ji shi-shi)* carries mainly documentary matter, at fifteen fen for an issue of seventy pages. *International Knowledge (Guo-ji zhi-shi)* offers fairly objective background pieces in a similar format for twelve fen.

I also pick up a couple of interesting new dictionaries. *Workers, Peasants, and Soldiers Dictionary* (1973, seventy fen) makes an admirable effort to give a word's meaning, Chinese to Chinese, in a clear and simple way. *A Small Dictionary of Chinese Proverbs (Han-yü cheng-yü xiao-ci-dian)* would surprise anyone who believes that the Communists have got rid of rich, colorful sayings and phrases from the past (1972, seventy fen). These items are very cheap indeed. But it is possible to spend twenty yuan on a handsome color volume which reproduces relics of dynastic China unearthed during the Cultural Revolution.

This Hangchow bookstore is just the tip of an iceberg. Chekiang has been having a book boom on a scale to turn the whole province into a classroom among the hills. To meet the mental needs of peasants and educated youth who have been rusticated (these young folk are described on pages 216 to 218), New China Bookstore has established thirty-one hundred book supply centers in Chekiang's rural areas. Through these centers no fewer than thirty million books were sold in the Chekiang countryside during 1972. The topics of these books — many of which we would call booklets — were mostly the science of farming and political knowledge.

✿ ✿ ✿

Among the hills on the western outskirts of Hangchow is Dragon Well (Long jing) brigade. It specializes in cultivating the much-liked Dragon Well tea. This is a semirural locality, organized as part of a commune, like all of China's countryside.

Dragon Well brigade contains 1,356 of West Lake commune's 11,000 people. The brigade, in turn, is made up of fifteen production

Blending Dragon Well tea in heated vats

teams, thirteen of which grow tea. Brigade headquarters stands in a valley of orange soil, with teal-blue hills rising above. The cottages gleam with whitewash, capped by gray- or brown-tiled roofs.

Brigade members I talk with display an easygoing but authoritative spirit. For twelve hundred years their ancestors have been producing tea on these very slopes! The loam soil is rich in acids which account for Dragon Well tea's special flavor, and its capacity for cooling the blood in hot weather. Hills rising at thirty degrees and more guarantee fine drainage and plenty of sunshine for the fields.

You see at Dragon Well signs of prosperity and progress not present at truly remote rural communes. Average annual income for the brigade's 255 households is high by countryside standards: 950 yuan (compared with 150 yuan at Liberation). The brigade has just bought a new truck (price 10,000 yuan) and a new two-wheel tractor (3,000 yuan). It has an electric cable hoist to transport baskets up and down the sharp slopes. Films are shown once a week in the brigade's cultural center, which is equipped also with a TV set.

All children who are of school age attend primary school. The brigade also has its own junior middle school. Four or five young people from the brigade get to enroll each year at university. There is virtually no one in the brigade, a spokesman claims, who cannot read and write at all. At the clinic I ask one of the two barefoot doctors what are the most common diseases. Her answer speaks volumes about the people's health at Dragon Well: "Colds are easily the main problem."

The story of birth control here is more like an urban than a usual rural tale. During 1972 the birthrate in the brigade was 1.7 percent. The target is to lower it still further to 1.4 percent. (Interestingly, the rate had gone down to an extremely low 1.2 percent a few years ago, but as in many parts of China, the coming of the Cultural Revolution brought a neglect of birth control work and a rise in the birthrate.)

The revolutionary committee of the brigade stresses three methods in pursuing a lower birthrate target. Late marriage is encouraged by a rule of thumb which frowns on a union of any couple whose combined age is less than fifty years. Various birth prevention materials are distributed, among which the pill is not the main one but may soon become so. The third method is sterilization of either the man or the woman; it is done only when an individual or family requests it.

In one respect the birth control picture is representative of rural China. There is still, according to the brigade spokesman, a marked preference among the peasants for baby boys over baby girls. This stems in part from feudal attitudes which have no rationale in today's society, where old folk are guaranteed a livelihood. But brigade leaders frankly mention a continuing economic reason for the peasants' preference. Boys generally earn more work points than girls. This boosts family income. Boys are also more useful at household tasks like chopping wood than are girls.

In many aspects of daily living, Dragon Well, though within reach of a rest-day's outing to Hangchow, is far removed from the ways of Hangchow city. The peasant's political knowledge and consciousness is noticeably below that of the urban worker. He is less interested in the daily news and in the world beyond China than is his brother in the city. His attachment to Chinese social traditions is greater. He is more likely to visit his ancestors' graves; to spend lavishly on weddings; to object to cremation; to want to marry before he is twenty-five and rear more than two children.

Robert Fortune, a Briton who visited the tea-growing areas of

Chekiang in the nineteenth century, wrote in *Journey to the Tea Countries of China*: "The people of Hangchow dress gaily, and are remarkable among the Chinese for their dandyism." It is still true of Hangchow, yet the remark about gay dress seems even truer of the rural areas outside Hangchow. The peasants of Dragon Well really go overboard in experimenting with clothes of bright hues and bold patterns.

Wages and housing both sharply mark the peasant off from the worker. Earnings are lower in the countryside, and they are calculated in a cruder way. "Work points" determine wages. These accrue strictly according to a peasant's productivity and hours on the job. Compared with this the wage of the city worker is more or less a salary.

When it comes to housing, the peasant often seems better off than the urban worker. Almost all Chinese peasants own their own houses. Practically no urban workers do. Partly for this reason, peasant homes vary in style and size. Those at Dragon Well are more spacious than the houses of Hangchow city workers.

I go into one Dragon Well home in which eight people live. It is two-storied, with four bedrooms upstairs, a kitchen about five meters by three, and two downstairs rooms, one of which measures ten meters by six. Equipment within the home does not seem far behind that of the norm in Hangchow. There is a sewing machine, a radio, two bicycles. In addition the family, like virtually all rural families, has its own little strip of productive property, the private plot. On it, vegetables are grown and pigs raised that augment the household income by 10 or 20 percent. Produce from the private plots is sold at a daily market organized on an adjacent commune.

When educated youth from Hangchow are sent to live at a brigade like Dragon Well they face the need for big adjustments. This becomes clear from inquiries about three educated youths who came down here a couple of years ago. "They worked quite well," a brigade spokesman says uncertainly. I find out that after a short stay they left and now work in a city factory.

It is clear from a reference to these young folk as "foreign students" (*yang xue-sheng*) that the peasants viewed the three as alien elements. The girl among them, I gather, was particularly unable to be accepted as an equal by ordinary brigade members. None of the students found it easy — on the brigade spokesman's admission — to pile up enough work points to earn a decent wage.

All of them, I suspect, were taken aback at the heavy sense of soil and hearth that marks peasant life. They must have been disappointed with the different beat of social life as compared with downtown Hangchow, where they had attended middle school. As for the Dragon Well peasants, one is left with the impression that none of them would weep if educated youth never came again.

The sending down of educated youths to Dragon Well had several aims, which have met varied degrees of success. One aim was to achieve the reeducation of the youth at the hands of the peasant masses. This was probably a mixture of success and failure. It was also hoped that the educated youth would contribute to rural development by applying the knowledge they had acquired from the classroom. The impact of this at Dragon Well was negligible. A third aim was simply to remove the pressure in Hangchow city on university places, and on job openings suitable for middle-school graduates. That aim was at least temporarily fulfilled.

Since the Cultural Revolution, policy for higher education has been a lively subject in Chekiang, as talks with teachers and students of Hangchow University and other schools make plain. Hangchow has an exceptionally large student population (befitting its traditions) and it experienced wounding struggle between "leftist" students and those resisting them in 1966–1968.

The city's top politician, T'an Ch'ih-lung, first secretary of the Chekiang Party committee, has long been zealous for the proper education of youth. Even during the unmilitant days of 1963, T'an was sounding tough warnings about the danger of "peaceful surroundings" filling the mind of youth with "hankerings for ease and comfort." Himself an old peasant guerrilla fighter, the first secretary observed tartly: "Some people can stand the test of war but cannot stand the test of a peaceful surrounding. Cases like this are many. . . ."

A decade later, this recurring problem is still acute amid the peaceful surroundings of West Lake. Two issues bob up. In what ways can the vision of a new education-for-everyman which soared during the Cultural Revolution be pinned down in day-by-day practice? And how can educated youth relate to rural life? The countryside is China's backbone, but most students are as removed from it as elegant fingers.

At the city's two leading universities, practical pressures and a slight backlash mentality chipped away at Cultural Revolutionary principles during 1972 and 1973. It was not too hard to maintain these high-flying principles in the pilot scheme days of 1969 and 1970, when student numbers were tiny (and 80 percent or more of the students were members of the CCP or CYL). Chekiang University in 1969 took in sixty-one carefully selected worker-peasant students of mature age for a course in engineering. They were groomed with enormous care along the new lines. Politics was intensively taught in a tutorial manner, and these sturdy young pines of engineering alternated between the classroom and Hangchow Machine Tools Plant.

After three years they graduated and the Chekiang CCP was very pleased with them, on three counts. They went back to their previous posts with enhanced technical knowledge that proved immediately useful. They have never missed a chance to impart to fellow workers what they learned at school. And a spell at university did not turn their minds; "they still maintain the essential political qualities of working people." Small classes of worker-peasant-soldier students also graduated in 1972 and 1973 from Chekiang Fine Arts College and Chekiang Agricultural University.

A gradual return of student numbers to pre–Cultural Revolution levels has made it hard to sustain this pristine pattern. The viewpoint of a young teacher at Hangchow University (let me call him Chu, a teacher of Russian) brings into focus issues that have arisen during the past two or three years.

Chu graduated from this school a decade ago and now works as an assistant professor (*zhu jiao-shou*). He is a good-looking, elegant young man with a sharp-featured Chekiang face and a wit that does not lack irony. His intelligence and ability at languages are formidable. His calm realism about shortcomings in China goes along with a strong belief in socialist ideals. He lives with his young wife, two babies, and his mother in university housing on the campus of Hangchow University.

Hangchow University resumed its educational life with a substantial intake of one thousand students in the fall of 1971. The new student body was only a quarter of the usual pre–Cultural Revolution enrollment. Its arrival, however, signaled an effort to clothe the new educational vision in everyday garments.

Excellent was the spirit of the new recruits. They were relatively young, but fresh from a stint in farm or factory. Many of the reforms have won universal praise, such as the open-book exam (*kai-juan kao-shi*). Students now take reference works and dictionaries to the exam room, instead of being "ambushed" naked by questions which tax their memory to a crazy degree. Also popular has been the abolition of the elaborate, elitist "five-grade" marking system copied from Moscow in the sunny days of Sino-Soviet harmony.

But one problem for Chu, as a language teacher, has been how to fit his material into two or two and a half years instead of four as previously. He says flatly: "We cut out the study of literature." He feels — and believes that teachers in the four subdepartments of Russian, English, German, and Japanese all agree on this — that three and a half years are necessary if the foreign language student is to truly grasp his subject and effectively serve the revolution.

Endless discussions have ensued on this point. For the second batch of post–Cultural Revolution students, a class of three hundred enrolled in the fall of 1972, it has been decided to compromise on a course length of three years. So on this question the university has gone partway back to the 1965 setup.

Another problem for Chu and his colleagues on the faculty of the foreign languages department has been the time gap, under the new arrangements, between a student's graduation from middle school and his arrival at the college door. Ninety percent or more of the students who entered Chekiang universities in 1973 and 1974 had spent at least the previous two years at manual labor.

Chu has mixed feelings about the effect of this interregnum on the tough task of learning a foreign language. "Generally speaking, the younger the student the better for studying another language. On the other hand these new, more experienced students grasp the illustrative texts better." Clearly, on this issue the eleven departments of Hangchow University cannot easily have identical views.

Nor are they a nest of singing birds when it comes to agreeing on how much time is to be spent in the classroom, and how much outside it. For majors in foreign tongues, a scheme has been evolved which fulfills the principles of 1967–1968 in letter but maybe not in spirit. The spell "outside the classroom" for these students consists not of manual work but of experience in another classroom. They go out to middle schools for, teaching practice (many of them will later become middle-school teachers).

Throughout the university, the period spent at commune or plant has dropped to about one month each academic year. It is more than the two weeks which obtained before 1966, yet it is well short of the fifty-fifty model broached in 1967–1968.

In vocational institutes such as Chekiang Agricultural College, it is less difficult than at Hangchow University to arrive at a proper blend of theory and practice. The tea department of this college saw in the new revolutionary line of the Cultural Revolution an opportunity to bring the science of tea down to earth. Some members said it is unreasonable for an agricultural college to be located in a city. They called for "a new type of socialist agricultural college."

The result was a substantial shift of the department's activities from the Hangchow campus to the tea hills of rural Chekiang. *Chekiang Daily* admired the tea people's efforts as a radiant flower from the garden of the Cultural Revolution. Were there critics who murmured about sagging standards and disruptions? The newspaper brushed them aside as people "with their eyes blocked by a single leaf."

Discussion often springs up about how much time students should spend in political study. Mr. Chu says that at Hangchow University foreign language students spend two afternoons a week on politics. Faculty from the politics or history department come in to teach these lessons. But since the Cultural Revolution there has also been stationed on the campus a Workers' Mao Tse-tung Thought Propaganda Team.

The team members are workers who have not graduated from a

college. They believe it is Chairman Mao's wish that "the working class occupy the cultural and educational sphere." They say straight out that the universities are the places "where revisionism is most likely to grow." They seem especially fond of the following teaching of Chairman Mao: "In the problem of transforming education it is the teachers who are the main problem." The team really becomes a pressure group pushing faculty and students toward a more resounding, measurable political militancy.

During the summer of 1973 pressure accelerated in Hangchow University against backsliding from the task of political study. With the arrival of the documents from the Tenth CCP Congress, the stage was set for the propaganda team to try to raise the political temperature. When term began in the fall, students of all departments were required as their first order of business to begin study of the Tenth Congress documents.

The case of the politics department shows how urgent the spirit of militancy became during the fall. The department was set to teach the history of "ten struggles between the two lines" in the history of the CCP from 1921 to the present. But instead of beginning with the 1920s and Ch'en Tu-hsiu, the first of the ten renegades, the politics classes leaped across the decades and started with the crisis of 1971, "in order to give prominence to criticizing Lin Piao throughout the course."

There are other spheres in which the college is being hustled to embrace Cultural Revolutionary ways, described as "the new emerging things of socialism." Workers and peasants who have proved their mettle at practical tasks are brought in as lecturers, though some faculty feel this can harm standards. Bands of roving teachers are sent to communes, factories, even to offshore islands, to bring knowledge to those who cannot come and get it. Since 1969 more than six hundred teachers from Hangchow University have joined in this teaching on the hoof. In the course of it, the teachers are also supposed to learn politics and practical things from working folk.

One new emerging thing which is taking a great deal of time is the preparation of new textbooks. These became necessary following the denunciation of many pre–Cultural Revolution teaching materials.

Faculty of the seven Chekiang colleges have since 1969 produced no less than sixty-seven million words of new (mostly mimeographed) texts to replace "old poison."

In an English department it is especially hard to avoid "poison" in selecting texts. Hangchow University students of English sometimes read articles from the *New York Times* in the classroom (the university library gets the paper each day by sea mail). I find they have been reading a series of articles by John Service on the *Times* Op-Ed page about his visit to China in 1971. There was no opportunity to ask anyone from the propaganda team whether the English teachers were wise in this choice of material.

All in all the education policies in Hangchow's schools seem far from settled. The new educational vision of the Cultural Revolution hovers in the balance at several points. Mr. Chu does not hide his feeling that the Cultural Revolution went to excess at times. He mentions that in August 1966 he made a trip to Peking and saw Chairman Mao at one of the big Red Guard rallies. Was he, then, a Red Guard in those ardent days? No. Were any of the younger Hangchow teachers Red Guards? "Some became self-appointed Red Guards."

Chu thinks opportunism raised its ugly head during 1966–1968. He does not regret a certain modification of education policy between the Ninth Party Congress of 1969 and the Tenth Party Congress of 1973.

On the other hand some members of Hangchow's universities — military men and nongraduate administrators rather than teachers — feel that the bright light of Cultural Revolutionary innovation has dimmed too much. Future discussions on policy issues could easily swing now one way, now the other. It would not be too surprising if T'an Ch'ih-lung should decide that "peaceful surroundings" are once more corroding the revolutionary sharpness of Chekiang educated youth. He might crack the whip for a fresh gallop toward the idyll of "everyman an intellectual."

If the key political issue in college circles is what to think about the line of the Cultural Revolution, the key practical issue is how students should relate to peasant China. During the summer of 1973 the Che-kiang CCP held a "Forum for Intellectuals" at which two key points were rammed home. The question of "for whom" college people carry on their work is basic. Teaching and research alike must be for the broad masses of the people. How can intellectuals guard against the wrong political line? By "integrating with the broad masses."

In the concrete conditions of China today, the main way for a student to integrate himself with the masses is to get involved in rural life. A staggering number of graduates of middle school and above have since the Cultural Revolution gone to the countryside to be "re-educated" by the peasants. From Hangchow alone, since 1969, over 100,000 have packed their bag and taken on the rural life. The Hang-chow revolutionary committee now has a special department to organize this program, the Office for Settling Educated Youth in the Countryside.

The enterprise is nothing less than a Promethean effort by Mao to tear down the wall between town and country, which hinders China's growth, and to bridge the chasm between the intellectual and the simple man that disfigured Confucian China. Future fruits from the policy may be rich. Present opinions about it are mixed.

Many educated Chekiang youths are sent to communes within their own province. Some are lucky enough to go to a brigade as close to Hangchow as Dragon Well. But a substantial minority find themselves in distant parts, including Sinkiang, Inner Mongolia, and other border regions. That they do not always like their new jobs is clear from the newspapers.

Some students behave like a "willing ox"; others like an "arrogant dragon." Cool and tough attitudes to the students on the part of commune folk are so frequent that when a brigade leader shows kindness or respect to students the newspapers write him up in heroic terms. Students living on communes within Chekiang are sometimes allowed to come to Hangchow to see relatives or go to the doctor. Neighbor-hood committees are asked by the city to arrange "healthy entertainments" to humor the young visitors.

Students at times find the more backward rural areas crude and dull. They generally lack the strength and experience to pile up as many work points as the peasants around them. A youth from a family with a middle-class background does not find it easy to approach a peasant girl, or to substitute peasant entertainments for the Hangchow cinema and the books in his father's home.

Small wonder, then, that neighborhood committees and factories in Hangchow need to send "comforting letters" to the rusticated students at New Year. Or that the Chekiang CCP committee dispatches "comfort teams," which include some parents of the students, to buoy the fifteen thousand Chekiang educated youth who are holed up in the far border areas of Sinkiang, Ninghsia, and Inner Mongolia.

Hangchow CCP chiefs also send "checking teams" of cadres to try to smooth out problems that arise. These emissaries explain to brigade leaders that city youth have been used to different ways and need time to adjust. They also remind the youths of the Party's decision that going to the countryside is not temporary but for good, that there is no alternative but to buckle down and get used to pigs and mosquitoes and food with less variety.

The checking teams visit units and neighborhoods back in Hangchow to tell the city not to wash its hands of the students once they leave, but to plan follow-up activities and take responsibility for any zigs and zags in the rustication program. They carry around propaganda pamphlets with relentless titles like "Show Warm Concern for the Maturing of Educated Young People Settling in the Countryside," and "Our Countryside is Vast and Has Plenty of Room for Fully Developing Talents."

Cadres in Hangchow recall a rally sponsored by the municipal CCP committee in the spring of 1973, to discuss and popularize the sending of youths to the countryside. Five thousand people attended this rally and heard T'an Ch'ih-lung and other Chekiang leaders congratulate youth who had resettled, and call upon leading citizens of Hangchow to persuade their children to volunteer for the countryside.

Hangchow newspapers hammer away at arguments in favor of the program. One article in *Chekiang Daily* during the summer of 1973 is typical in the appeal it makes to reluctant parents. It boldly aspires to analyze the nature of true parental love:

The view that farming is such laborious work that people cannot bear to see their sons and daughters doing it is [quite] unacceptable. Love has a class character. Regarding sons and daughters as private property to be kept in a comfortable place within easy reach, or regarding them as fruit or flowers to be nourished in a greenhouse, is not proletarian paternal love, but blind love which will eventually harm the children. . . . We must regard our children as assets of the Party and the state. . . . During the revolutionary wars we sent them to the fighting front. Today we should send them to the countryside, where they will be tempered in the stormy weather of the three great revolutionary movements and trained as successors to the revolutionary cause of the proletariat.

It is not surprising that these policies are controversial among the people, if we recall what a sharp departure they are from Chinese traditions. The intellectual used to enjoy very high prestige in China. Competitive public service exams were *the* great gateway to high status and even power. In Hangchow under the Sung, leading households in search of a husband for a ripe daughter would try by all means to get their hands on a scholar. When candidates for the exams came to Hangchow for the grueling tests, these top families might arrange to kidnap a candidate who came near the top of the exam list. They would then spirit him back as a prize husband for the trembling maiden.

In a threefold sense socialist China is standing on its head past traditions about education and youth. Whereas mental work once enjoyed the highest stature and physical work the lowest, the CCP says it is a splendid thing for children of intellectuals to become workers and peasants.

Whereas city life was rated more desirable than rural life — especially for the educated man — the CCP tells students the countryside is where glory is to be won and where they must go, without any expectation of return to city life.

Whereas a youth's future was planned by his family and for the family's interests, the CCP asserts that since "love has a class character," the Party and the state can best guide a family about the future of its young (hence the notion of "proletarian paternal love").

The paradox is that while Chairman Mao bids for such a breathtaking break with the past, the past remains stubbornly present. Three small incidents with Mr. Chu and other Hangchow professionals suggest the continued existence of a gulf between intellectuals and workers which America has never known.

One morning we hire a boat to explore West Lake, and it is painfully rowed by a lady about sixty years old. This makes me, a professor from a bourgeois land, quite uncomfortable. Yet it does not make Mr. Chu uncomfortable, though he is a professor in a socialist society where intellectuals are told they have less worth than workers and peasants.

Another afternoon, Chu talks with spirit about the relative position of workers and professors at Hangchow University. Chu earns about sixty yuan each month, not much more than manual workers around the campus earn. As a teacher, his rent is set at four yuan per month, while a worker's family is charged one yuan for a similar apartment. The ratio of pay as between teacher and worker is about the same as on an American campus (where an assistant professor earns about $10,500, a little more than the wage of a janitor, a little less than that of a campus policeman). The rent discrimination, though, is not paralleled in the United States.

Now Mr. Chu is as much exercised by the equality of this pay scale as he is little exercised by the inequality in the boat on West Lake. "Teachers have to work harder than workingmen," he observes. "They cannot simply stop work at 5:00 P.M., but must read at night in preparation for next day." When I agree he adds: "Working people do not always understand this." As he enumerates other hardships for intellectuals, I venture to point out that conditions of work are often much worse for the working class, such as the physical danger in coal mines. He demurs slightly: "You must remember that conditions in the mines are very much better than they used to be."

On a third occasion, the topic of military training comes up during a conversation in a bamboo grove with two intellectuals. When I reminisce about serving in the infantry of the Australian Army, both companions confess they have never done military training. It is their attitude which is striking. The army is viewed as rather sordid. They count it almost a point of pride that they have never been in it.

219

To be sure, these men are already in their thirties. Distaste for military service would be harder to find among intellectuals ten years younger. Nevertheless, one feels during this talk in the bamboo grove an echo of Chinese tradition, which put the scholar at the top of the prestige pole and the warrior at the bottom.

To send intellectuals like these "down to the countryside" or to live with a PLA unit, as happened during the Cultural Revolution, is not really an extreme measure. It gives the Chinese intellectual the taste of a slice of life which he may need more than do most American intellectuals.

The situation of the intellectual in China is opposite to that of his colleague in the United States. The mental freedom of expression of the Chinese is bounded by the presence of an official ideology, which exalts toilers and suspects intellectuals of hankering for the bourgeois past. On the other hand there is sometimes a social elitism about the demeanor of the Chinese intellectual which recalls the tenacious feudal past of a society five thousand years old.

The mental freedom of expression of the American intellectual is virtually boundless. His problem is rather that within the pressures of a competitive society ideas are seldom a match for hard realities. On the other hand, the American intellectual meets any person in his society on a remarkably give-and-take basis. The views he utters may seem "decadent" in the light of China's ideology; yet his conduct can often seem more socially progressive than that of many a Chinese intellectual. He is more likely than Mr. Chu to chat with the worker who rows his boat, less likely than Mr. Chu to disdain army life.

It is time, before we leave Hangchow, to wander in the hills which rise above West Lake.

When Marco Polo saw Hangchow, his Christian pen noted that on the hills around West Lake there sprouted "many abbeys and churches of the idolaters." The Chinese people are doubly faithless today. Even Buddhism, the major religion of China's past, has shriveled into the ritual of a tiny minority. Yet despite evaporation of faith and physical ravage by fire and war, Hangchow's hills are still studded with the abbeys and churches of the idolaters.

It is one of the great religious tours the world can offer to climb the maze of paths within these wooded slopes. Here are temples, grottoes, carved inscriptions, and monasteries, which tangibly tie socialist Hangchow to its more superstitious past.

The largest and grandest Buddhist edifice in Hangchow is the Temple of the Retreat of the Soul (Ling-yin si). The sixteen-century-old structure nestles·high among larch, fir, and bamboo trees, north of the Peak Which Flew Here. It was built by a monk from India. He arrived with his monkey, found that the monkey liked the mountain, so decided to stay and set up a monastery.

Fine use has been made of differentiated levels, to make the lofty wooden temple fit unobtrusively into the hillside. The main shrine hall is approached across a sunken courtyard of multicolored pebbles. This expanse breaks into a shallow stone staircase, over which a gleaming brass incense burner stands imperious sentry.

Across the front portico is a panel of gold bearing four big black characters that say: "Hall of the Great Hero." Inside the hall gleams a golden Buddha the size of a small mountain. On each side of it are disciples of the Master, depictions of Kuan Yin, Mistress of the Waters, and weird beasts and fish that seem to be beating drums and cracking whips.

The vaulted chamber with its myriad woods and musty smell lends an immediate peace. Through brown latticework you look out on foliage made luminescent by an afternoon sun. Lofty verandas mediate between the shadowy interior and nature's blaze of green. On a nearby rock face are sculptured galloping horses, on whose shapely backs the sacred Buddhist books are borne. No wonder it was said of this temple: "One Foot Below the Western Heaven."

The twenty-meter-high Buddha in lacquered camphor wood was added by the Communist government during the 1950s. At Liberation there were three figures in the center of the shrine hall, but they were in a state of collapse. A Hangchow professor was asked to design a single new statue. The resident monks did not like the professor's design, commissioned to "reflect the spirit of the new society." There ensued a controversy and Premier Chou En-lai himself took a hand in it.

Chou looked at the design and resolved matters in favor of the monks: "The feet should show more," he laid down, "the legs should be spread wider, the hair should be in whorls, and everything must be in accordance with Buddhist tradition." The incident is interesting in light of what took place at the temple during the Cultural Revolution.

During 1966, the militant tide against the "four olds" lapped against the temple. A great confrontation took place in the pebbled courtyard. Red Guards of all stripes agreed that the temple should be "struggled against." Slogans such as "Smash the Old World" were pasted up inside and out. But should the old world be smashed only with words or also with hammers?

One group of Red Guards, for the most part university students, felt that the struggle against the temple should be rigorous but not in the form of physical assault. A second group, who were middle-school students, disagreed and wished to deface and even tear down the temple. The university Red Guards built a high wall in front of the main shrine hall to protect it from the wrath of their younger confreres. This wall they manned against "the foe."

With the bold presumption which often marked Red Guard campaigns, they also cabled Premier Chou to seek his views. And with the judicious attention to detail which makes the premier a master of big situations and small, Chou cabled back substantially on the side of physical restraint. The temple gained yet one more extension of its curious life.

Much of this is related to me by a professor who had hovered on the fringes of the 1966 struggle. What about the monks, I ask; did the Red Guards confront the monks as well as their temple? "They were too busy confronting each other," he replies. "Anyway, the monks were hardly a force that needed to be confronted." My request to visit the remaining monks, who live in a monastery sheathed in bamboo just by the temple, cannot be met. A temple official of tender years says cheerfully: "The monks are few and very old." At any rate the temple during 1973 displays no posters, no pictures of Mao, not a single political slogan or caption.

Within the crowd on this Sunday afternoon I detect no clear sign of religious reverence. The main function of the temple seems to be as a tranquil place for rest, and a backdrop for photography of almost Japanese incessancy. The visitors are of all ages, and those not clicking cameras are mostly reading. Occasionally an older or scholarly person gazes at the inscriptions or images with more than vacant curiosity.

At one point I see a young man in workingman's garb bow deeply before one of the holy figures in the main shrine hall. Intrigued by this isolated act of possible piety, I gaze at the young man until I notice my own companions smiling at me. Looking back at the young worker, I see him suddenly draw up from his "devotions." He and his friends laugh heartily at what has been a little charade. As for the Peking official who accompanies me, I ask him later about the temple's name. Can the soul really retreat into a temple? He replies squarely: "I like to retreat into my home."

Another ancient and popular Buddhist site in Hangchow is the sixty-meter-high Pagoda of Six Harmonies. Its octagonal bulk overlooks the city from the banks of the Ch'ien-t'ang River. Like Marco Polo before him, Wells Williams of Yale University found a little painful the idolatrous state of the Chinese people. "No town is considered complete without a pagoda," he haughtily wrote a century ago, "and the ruinous condition of most of them indicates the weakness of the faith which erected them."

It is true that Chinese buildings were less often designed for the ages than were medieval cathedrals in Europe. But even Wells Williams conceded that the Pagoda of Six Harmonies had done pretty well, the alleged weak faith of its erectors notwithstanding. It was built a thousand years ago during the Five Dynasties period, when Hangchow was gathering momentum as a town. The purposes of this hefty octagonal tower were three: to house some bones of the Buddha; to serve as a lighthouse for boats; to keep back threatening tides by its benign influence.

The pagoda is peculiar in that it has seven floors in its stone inside

223

but thirteen floors on its wooden exterior. From a distance the ocher-red balconies blend richly with a spectrum of greens which the sun refracts through surrounding trees. Each balcony is roofed with glazed tiles that curve up pertly at the edges. From these spiky hooks hang cast bells which are supposed to jingle in the breeze.

Crowds flock to sip tea in the pagoda grounds, and to front the wind and survey the city from the thirteenth balcony. They contribute a great deal of innocent graffiti, which ease the boredom of the long climb up the spiral staircase. The summit affords one of Hangchow's best views. Ch'ien-t'ang River stretches wide and muddy toward Hangchow Bay. A wavy golden pencil line of sand demarcates its dusty tones from the leaping greens of wooded hills.

Looking northeast toward the city, you see scattered industry cradled in foliage. The roofs are mostly rust-colored, unlike the gray roofs of older parts of central Hangchow. Prominent is that of the former Hangchow Christian College, erected by American missionaries — with strong faith, it would so far seem — and now an outlying campus of Chekiang University. The first double-decker bridge ever built in China, finished in 1936, lies like a black snake across the muddy waters.

A look at Hangchow provides no support for the notion that the People's Republic of China has neglected the physical care of its national heritage. In fact the money spent on the upkeep of monuments and gardens could well seem staggering for the budget of a poor country.

All around West Lake, gardeners meticulously prune and conserve. Maples along the boulevards are sprayed with various insecticides. Any tree with a problem is treated as doctors might tend a sick child.

Hundreds of small bridges on the dikes or over canals and streams have been repaired or rebuilt since Liberation. Among the hills it is rare to find a pavilion whose red wooden pillars have not recently been painted, or whose gray tiles have a broken patch still unmended.

Hangchow's downtown mosque, the Phoenix Temple, founded during the T'ang dynasty, was renovated from paving stone to gargoyle in the 1950s. Some Buddhist temples whose roofs were shaky have been restructured at great expense of time and money. On the repairs at the Temple of the Retreat of the Soul, and the installation of its new Buddha image, the government spent some U.S. $200,000 between 1953 and 1958.

It is not that the government of Mao is uncritical toward the long Chinese past. Indeed, the tool of class analysis, like a sharp plow on settled soil, is wielded daily against the world of Buddha and Confucius. The point is that the Chinese Communists, despite and through all such criticism, show enormous *attention* to and betray a massive *regard* for the past.

❁ ❁ ❁

Other beauty spots and remnants of history abound among the slopes and valleys around Hangchow. Wells Williams liked the bamboo groves, and found the hills "still more interesting to the mind" by virtue of "several thousand repositories of the dead" on their lower reaches. Not many of these are still visible (cremation is almost universal in Hangchow today).

The bamboo groves remain to offer an aura of fragile peace. The slender, sensual trunks seem frail but reach high into the sky. According to farmers the bamboo grows during spring at the astonishing rate of one meter per day. At one cool grotto which is popular with Hangchow residents on a hot day, the Yellow Dragon Cave, I come upon a very weird bamboo. It is absolutely square in its trunk, said to be the only square bamboo in the world.

As well as being a symbol of nobility in Chinese literature, the bamboo is used to make all kinds of utensils and instruments. And its shoots form part of many a Chekiang dish. The locals say that, though the shoots can be picked and eaten all year round, they are most piquant in winter.

The Tiger Spring is less pretty than Yellow Dragon Cave, and does not offer the same view of Hangchow filtered through thin bamboos. But it is an agreeable playground and it has a nice legend behind it. During the T'ang dynasty a monk arrived at this hill south of Hangchow. He lacked water and approached Buddha with this problem.

225

The Temple of the Clawing Tigers has been turned into
a tearoom, where families and groups of friends while
away a day

Buddha sent two tigers from Hunan province to claw open a spring
for the thirsty monk. Hence the full name of the spot, "Spring Clawed
by Tigers" (Hu p'ao ch'üan).

Legend also has it that the water from the spring is the best possible
for making Dragon Well tea, and this at least is believed by Hangchow
people of the 1970s. The Temple of the Clawing Tigers has been
turned into a tearoom, where families and groups of friends while
away an entire day. These folk are relaxed about the appearance of
a foreigner. A smile here, a wave there, frequently no reaction at all.
I ask for information or directions several times, and one lady even
asks directions from me.

Sipping tea in a cool pavilion, I notice a middle-aged man reading
a book printed in large characters with a border around each page.
It is certainly not a contemporary book. I ask my companion from
Peking what kind of books are printed in that style. "Probably a very
old book," Mr. Liu replies.

We go over to find out, and start to chat with the reader. He is a
worker from Shanghai, down for the day to get away from big-city

bustle. The T'ang dynasty is present at Tiger Spring today in more than legend. The Shanghai worker's book is called *Three Hundred Poems of the T'ang Dynasty*. It includes verse by Li Po and Tu Fu, two of China's most famous poets.

Like most of the male tea drinkers, readers, and chess players around him, the poetry reader has rolled up his T-shirt to keep his torso cool, exposing eight inches of smooth yellow flesh. Beside his chair lies a straw hat of the type favored around Hangchow. Not the cone-shaped hat of the southern peasant, nor the round-topped and broad-brimmed hat you see in the north, but a straw version of the ordinary Western hat.

Suddenly a pretty girl who works in the tea shop comes up, draws a table close, and places upon it a china teapot and bowl. At first it seems she is going to serve us refreshments. But a small crowd gathers and she begins an odd demonstration.

From the teapot she pours water into the bowl until it is full. She gently keeps pouring, but the water does not overflow the bowl. Children gasp with admiration. The waitress is not finished. With a look of potential triumph, she begins to drop coins on the surface of the surcharged bowl. One by one the coins fall down. I myself drop a five-fen piece from a height of half a meter.

Yet the coins float on top of the water. The level of the water is now, in the waitress's estimation, four millimeters above the level of the edge of the bowl. Even the old men are beaming; the kids are agog. It is true that Chinese coins are very light, but the water of Tiger Spring clearly has what it takes — not only to make good tea, but to make a moment of more or less scientific magic for Chinese holiday makers.

Jade Spring is a Hangchow landmark, at which you see again how easy to please are the Chinese. It is a pool-and-pavilion where children of all ages delight in feeding already overfed black carp and goldfish which cruise lethargically in murky water. Jade Spring used to be part of the Monastery of Limpid Waves, first put up in the fifth century. As late as the 1950s the monastery still functioned, but there is not a monk in sight today.

The pavilion is elegant but it has been allowed to become shabby.

There are wooden tables with glass tops, around which people sit in curved cane armchairs and sip tea from porcelain mugs of grandfatherly size. The floor is stone worn shiny with the decades, cool even on a sweltering afternoon.

If the tea drinkers do not wish to watch the gluttonous fish they are offered a fine spectacle in the opposite direction. The whitewashed wall is broken by windows that are glassless, but pretty with latticework in hand-carved wood. Beyond the lattice are bamboos, grotesque rocks, magnolia trees whose branches race to all sides in a zigzag shape.

I talk for a while with three Hangchow factory workers, dressed in navy blue singlets and smoking one cigarette after another. They are more shy than many folk I casually meet. Two of them jig their legs in nervousness while trying to think of something to say. The third discusses with me the question of how Hangchow people differ from Shanghai people. "They are bigger than we are," he ventures, "and they speak fast — that's why nobody can understand them."

Preferring to copy rather than feed the fish, I suggest that we go swimming. Adjacent to the slimy Jade Pool for carp, there is a smart new pool for humans. Today the swimming pool has been taken over by a Hangchow middle school, but I am allowed to have a dip nevertheless. The students are in training, they tell me, for an upcoming swimming competition among middle schools in the metropolitan area.

The pool is of Olympic standard, though changing rooms are ramshackle huts. About thirty girls and boys are working out in a relaxed way under the instruction of two coaches, one of whom appears to be Eurasian. The swimmers' bodies are brown and lithe, firm but not muscular. At the end of the pool is a large billboard lit by electric lights. It is painted over in red paint, but one swimmer tells me that it used to have a political message on it.

A boy is resting between tryouts, and I sit beside him to watch the others streak up and down through the blue expanse. He is in his last year at middle school; what does he plan to do next? "It depends on the state," he says. "They will send me somewhere to work." It seems a shade more low-key than an answer I often hear: "Serve the Revolution!"

Girls and boys, seminaked though they are, mix so easily that they

228

do not seem very conscious of sexual difference. There is no segregation by sex as they stand around in groups waiting for the next race. No self-consciousness is apparent on the part of one boy and girl who sit close together on the grass in quiet conversation. Indeed the girls — with their one-piece costumes, long legs, thin small hips, square-faced handsomeness — can hardly be marked off from the boys.

Wandering back to Jade Pool, I mentally finger the term "balance" which pops to mind often during a stay in Hangchow. In a list of Chinese traits I would put balance near the top. Hangchow is sprouting factories, yet there is no Faustian limitlessness about the city's attitude to industrial growth. Production is for use rather than for wealth. The environment is considered a setting, not a hunk of raw material. Agriculture is not generally looked down upon as an ugly sister.

People work hard at their jobs, but they know when to stop and overtime is rare in industry. When the Chinese sit down to eat they focus on the business at hand no less earnestly than when they sit down to work. The face of Hangchow and its ethereal lake is etched with the past, yet there is nothing stagnant about the city's modes. Trying to mold a new kind of socialism, Hangchow is neither unmindful of history nor bemused by it.

Students struggle against each other with bloodcurdling phrases, but after lunch the same antagonists go boating on West Lake and sing gentle songs, as if the whole world were as dreamily harmonious as Hangchow's exquisite portion of nature. (Maybe Hangchow's colleges will even find a balance between the intoxication of Cultural Revolutionary ways and the sobriety of ordinary students' impulses.)

The most famous saying about Hangchow claims a kinship with my theme. "Above there is heavenly paradise," someone remarked in the tenth century, "below there is Soochow and Hangchow." Even Heaven must concede a balance between itself and the charms of Hangchow.

WUHAN

武汉

THE GREAT POINT OF REFERENCE in China is usually nature, and Wuhan is no exception. North China's features fade away as you fly south from Peking. Furry-looking hills begin to break the flat expanse. Pale hues give way to stronger ones. Terracing lends the fields a busy look. Water glistens from the surface of what is one of China's main lake areas. When you swoop down upon Wuhan, it is as companion to the River Yangtze that the city presents itself.

Few inland cities anywhere are as splendid to approach by air as this central China bastion. From the windows of a bobbing aircraft, the Yangtze seems a yellow sea. Can it really be a river still one thousand kilometers from its mouth? As the plane sinks lower, the river's glitter turns a deep mud color with a reddish tinge. A lesser stream flows into it from the northwest. This is the Han, chief tributary of the chief of China's rivers.

Dotted here and there, as if in respectful attendance on the confluence of these two life-giving streams, are a score of lakes. Their satin blue faces smile up at the midday sun. The scene is fringed by lofty hills. Greenish blue, they make a sensual contrast with the golden Yangtze.

Wuhan took its place as by-product and trustee of this rich patch of nature's handiwork. Modern as it has become, the city remains the child of its location. No Chinese industrial city other than Shanghai is better placed for transport links than Wuhan. Here is the only port in the world which is a thousand kilometers inland yet can receive large oceangoing ships. This is its link with the products and markets of Shanghai, with the intervening provinces of Anhwei and Kiangsi, and with the world beyond Shanghai.

But Wuhan is by no means the end of the line for the Yangtze. Through gathering mountains to the west, medium-sized boats ply twelve hundred fifty kilometers to Chungking. Lesser trading boats go still further up, into Tibet. Wuhan is thus a natural point of entry for the rich mineral supplies of Szechwan province and the crops of Kweichow province, as well as a natural point of departure for manufactured goods going west (two hundred million Chinese people live west and southwest of Wuhan).

Tributaries of the Yangtze also give Wuhan access by water to key economic areas to both south and north. Steamboats go northwest up the Han, itself no mean stream of 2,450 kilometers (and the site of a fantastic recent water harnessing project — with six generators of 150,000 kilowatts, and a 150-ton elevator that picks ships up from one section of the river and sets them down at another). This permits easy delivery of wheat, sesame and cotton from Shensi and Honan provinces. Small rivers and lakes to the south bring to Wuhan's doorstep the tea and rice which are the middle Yangtze's biggest crops.

As the fifty-eight-hundred-kilometer Yangtze is China's horizontal axis, so the nineteen-hundred-kilometer Peking-Canton railroad forms a vertical axis. Wuhan stands at the intersection of this cross of communication. It is more or less equidistant from the four great urban guardians of China's compass: Peking to the north, Canton to the south, Chungking to the west, Shanghai to the east.

Wuhan is the belly button of China in substance as well as in form. It is the focus of a vast area of crop production and rising consumer demand. The waters offer fish; the hills contain coal and iron; the fertile fields yield two crops a year (growing period is three hundred days a year). And the men and women of the middle Yangtze Valley are gaining a buying power that the *taipan* and missionary only dreamed and prayed might exist.

Wuhan unites rich resources with modernizing people. It is a trading post with ready outlets; a manufacturing metropolis with plenty of nearby customers; a great industrial center whose raw materials are within efficient reach.

Such a pivot gathers to itself military importance. Wuhan (particularly the Hanyang part of it) has been a seesaw in a number of China's historical battles. It was a major crucible of the revolutionary struggle

234

which put an end to the Ch'ing dynasty, and eventually gave Mao victory over Chiang. And in very recent times (as we shall see) Wuhan has rattled the saber of regional military defiance.

❈ ❈ ❈

The name "Wuhan" is the label of a mixed package. The city is a set of triplets. Wuchang ("Military Glory")* lies on the south bank of the Yangtze. Hankow ("Mouth of the Han") is a crescent shape resting against the Yangtze and the Han. Hanyang ("Bright Han") is a wedge tucked west of the confluence of the two rivers.

During the Ch'ing dynasty, Wuhan became the nickname of these three neighboring towns. In 1927 the short-lived government of the left wing of the Kuomintang proclaimed — as its capital — the united city of Wuhan. Today Wuhan is run as a fully integrated city. With 2.7 million people it is the fifth largest in China.

From the air you sense how the three parts fit together and serve each other. Wuchang retains the shape of a walled administrative city which it was for many centuries. The square town is cut in two by lovely Snake Hill, its long back turquoise colored from on high. The modern buildings with their red tile roofs (a feature of Wuhan) are cushioned by foliage still lettuce green despite the summer heat.

Wuchang's outskirts are met by the meandering East Lake. On the slopes of the lake's protecting hills you catch sight of dark green tiles, and brown roofs in the old style with turned-up corners. Wuchang has most of what Wuhan still offers in the way of temples, pagodas, and imperial mansions, some in fine red sandstone. Beyond East Lake the air is smoky and chimneys crowd the skyline. Underneath that blur is the second largest steelworks in China.

Across the river you look down upon the gray commercial flatness of Hankow. "Mart of Nine Provinces" was once its caption. The close-packed streets still bespeak trading bustle. Hankow does not have the broad roofs of institutions, spaced well apart, as Wuchang does, but the zigzag gables of narrow tenement strips. Part of the skyline is clipped, Shanghai-like, with Western spires, domes, and porticos. It is

---

* The two characters for Wuchang are a short form for a longer phrase, "Becoming Glorious Through the Military" (yi wu er chang).

235

obvious from the air that Hankow contains the biggest population among the triplets.

You reflect that the Yangtze enabled Hankow and Wuchang to keep their distance from each other, as they also used each other. Wuchang had the style and power; Hankow the substance and money. Hankow's proud brow is the Bund along the Yangtze. Ships in a line seem to be nibbling at the row of wharves and warehouses.

Less than most things in Wuhan has this trading activity changed since Liberation. But as with Wuchang, the old in Hankow is flecked with the new. North of the belly of its crescent-shaped area, the city has burst the old bounds with housing blocks, and concrete boulevards bordered by flower beds.

Hanyang is a compact city gathered at the foot of another turquoise landmark, Tortoise Hill. Like Wuchang, Hanyang had city walls, but today you see only their outline. The walls, and much else, were ruined during the Taiping Rebellion.

Hanyang's meager acres are neatly demarcated as to function. Tortoise Hill used to be called — with apt and typical naturalism — Great Hill of Division. It is indeed arbiter of the town's parts. To the east and south are porcelain lakes around which many Hanyang legends cling. From the large one, Moon Lake, Hanyang took one of its nicest nicknames: City of Moonbeams.

North of the mountain lie an arsenal and part of Hanyang's old iron and steel works (the first in China). A famous governor-general, Chang Chih-tung, in office at Wuchang from 1889 to 1907, built these and made of Hanyang the industrial triplet of Wuhan. South of Tortoise Hill, within the crumbled outline of the old town walls, are the red tile roofs and tree-lined streets of Hanyang's residential heart.

Sight of the mountain — it does resemble a lumpy tortoise — makes plain why Hanyang was the strategic prize of Wuhan, in days when the triplets were more separate than now. All three cities are packed against the confluence of rivers. But Hanyang has Tortoise Hill right by the water, whereas Hankow lacks a hill. Wuchang of course has Snake Hill, yet the Yangtze (1,700 meters wide) was far harder to cross than the Han (150 meters wide). So Wuchang was not

236

in as good a position as Hanyang to command the rather defenseless Hankow.

That calculation has now become a relic of the past. Although the eye surveys three parts — political Wuchang, trading Hankow, industrial Hanyang — there is a dramatic transforming addition. A mighty serpent of steel and concrete has been tossed across the Yangtze; and a lesser belt across the Han. Wuchang is no longer isolated from its sisters. Hanyang is strategic boss no more. The three cities have been scrambled into a smooth totality. The great Wuhan Bridge (finished in 1957) is the city's birth certificate as a major world metropolis.

The bridge is an imposing sight to match the resourcefulness of its engineering. From the air it makes a unified ridge out of Snake Hill and Tortoise Hill. These two provide a marvelous natural anchor for the 1,670-meter-long structure. Highways curve from each hill to the bridge towers. These are thirty-five meters tall, with turned-up corners to their roofs, as if in reminder that this is not Illinois, or Germany, but age-old China. Six lanes of traffic are carried on the top level; trains rumble by on a double track at a lower level.

Eight white piers rise eighteen meters from the yellow smother of the Yangtze. Supporting the approaches are stone pillars which relax at the top into graceful arches. These look ecclesiastical at close range; indeed, the whole achievement is a kind of cathedral. It roots in a daily landmark the spirit of long, tough struggle by the Chinese people against the disabling gash of the Yangtze River.

A glance across Snake and Tortoise hills shows the converting power of Wuhan Bridge. On the Wuchang side traffic from the bridge unravels into two strands. The railroad hugs the northern side of Snake Hill's back; the road follows its southern ridge. From Wuchang the railroad goes on to Changsha, and, since 1936, to Canton. On the Hanyang side, the line which winds north (first crossing the Han) was famous after its completion in 1906 as the Peking-Hankow railway.

The lines were separate in name; equally separate in fact. It took two hours to ferry a cargo train across the river; longer still when the Yangtze was in fury. Today the trains move across in two minutes.

237

Supporting the approaches of Wuhan Bridge are stone
pillars which relax at the top into graceful arches. . . .
the whole achievement is a kind of cathedral

They scoff at storm and rising water levels; they do not even slow
down. A true Canton-to-Peking (and Harbin) railroad at last exists.
Wuhan Bridge links south and north by wheel for the first time in
Chinese history.

I take an elevator in the bridge tower on the Wuchang side. Two
of the bridge's two hundred staff members receive me for a chat. Mr.
Wang is an engineer, proud of his bridge. His big cashew-brown hand
is never without a cigarette; his wiry head of hair is like a stiff brush.
A flicker of amusement plays at the corner of his mouth as he weighs
up this foreigner who has come to see Wuhan Bridge but knows nothing about bridges.

Mr. Ch'en is a political officer, handsome, with square cheeks and
a smooth high forehead. The two pockets on his white shirt bulge
with pens, cigarettes, notes on scraps of paper. He mops his brow
with a white handkerchief, as he urges me to smoke and drink.

We go into a lounge high above the river, where the noise of an occasional train is just a faint rumble beneath the carpet. We sip tea among an outcrop of potted plants, cooled by quiet electric fans made in Wuhan, bathed in the pink glow of a neon sign that urges "Ten Thousand Years to Chairman Mao."

My mind mulls over a comparison with Nanking Bridge, which I saw a couple of years ago. It is one of two great Yangtze bridges — there is another at Chungking — which have followed in the footsteps of Wuhan Bridge. Nanking Bridge, Mr. Wang explains, is different from this one in two ways. At Nanking the technical problems were greater. There were no Snake and Tortoise hills to give the bridge a flying start. And Nanking Bridge was a 100-percent-Chinese effort, whereas Wuhan Bridge used Soviet materials and twenty-five Soviet technicians.

This second point has to be somewhat dragged from Wang and Ch'en. They stress the technical superiority of the job at Nanking. They leave the puzzling impression that Soviet help at Wuhan was either not very good or not necessary. A few years ago, though, visitors to Wuhan were told in detail of important Russian help, especially techniques for operating underwater, enabling the Wuhan workers to do without caissons (airtight boxes), which were of dubious value here because the river is silty and up to forty meters deep.

Mr. Ch'en is happier when tracing the long sad story of abortive efforts in Kuomintang days to put up a bridge. "They brought in an American expert who declared a bridge impossible because the river bed was too unstable." The Kuomintang at one point, according to Ch'en, collected taxes specially to finance the bridge, but never went ahead. "So the Wuhan people made a play on words and called the Kuomintang the *Gua*mintang" (*kuo,* or *guo,* is "national" but *gua* is "fleece"; the nickname meant "Fleece-the-people Party"). "What the Kuomintang chattered about idly for years," Ch'en rounded off, "we accomplished in two years."

There is a touch of the Promethean spirit in Wang's talk of how the bridge has drawn the teeth of nature. An old saying in Wuchang expressed the accepted hopelessness of creating a path over the Yangtze: "To get a bridge across the Yangtze, the sun would have to shine 360 days in a row."

239

I am shown with triumph a text emblazoned on one of the bridge towers. "A bridge can never be built," it translates, "the river can never be crossed." The quote is ancient, but the handwriting is Chairman Mao's. Then comes Mao's proud answer to the conventional fatalism: "A bridge flies across the river from north to south; a deep chasm becomes a thoroughfare."

Just over Tortoise Hill you come to the smaller new bridge over the Han River. It is a sad commentary on the state of China in the decades before Liberation that this bridge was not built long ago. An American visiting Hanyang in 1921 remarked on the slow and ponderous crossing of the river. "And the Han could so easily be spanned by a bridge, with probably a small proportion of the money which is now being expended at the arsenal through the petty jealousies of China's generals." In 1954 the job was done; the Han and the Yangtze no longer make fragments of Wuhan.

One turns to a passage in a Chinese classic, *The Book of Odes,* written well before the time of Christ:

> *Grandly flow the Kiang [Yangtze] and Han,*
> *Regulators of the Southern States*

The two rivers flow no less grandly than they did twenty-five hundred years ago. But now they are servants rather than regulators of the provinces they feed.

❀ ❀ ❀

As Wuhan is a city in the middle, so the character of its people is more a blend than a clear-cut extreme. The central panel of China which Wuhan dominates was in Ming dynasty times called Broad Lakes (Hu kuang). Wuchang was the capital of this province. The largest of China's many great lakes, Lake Grotto Hall (Tung-t'ing hu), was its glistening landmark.

There was an old saying about the rich fertility of Broad Lakes. "Kiangsi province can give China its breakfast, but only Hu kuang can maintain China altogether." During the Ch'ing dynasty Broad Lakes was divided into two provinces which exist today: South of the Lake

(Hunan) with its capital at Changsha; North of the Lake (Hupei) with Wuhan as its capital. From Wuhan the lake is a half-day's journey by rail or water.

Sitting in the middle of China, Hupei is also of middling size and population (thirty-eight million) among China's provinces. A Chinese saying runs: "When northerners enter a train, the flies fall down dead from the ceiling." Wuhan's remaining flies are not threatened when a Hupei man steps into a train. Hupei folk are of solid, medium build, shorter and more sensuous than northerners, taller and less soft-looking than southerners. Wuhan youths have firm and muscular bodies; the women are often square and sturdy.

As to temperament, the people of Hupei are considered skillful at handling people and things. Not so bold and inflexible as their neighbors to the south, but less measured than Peking or *dong bei* folk. Without the elegance and wit of Hangchow types, and less facile and socially adept than the Shanghai man, with all his experience of foreigners.

The Wuhan man seems to be an all-round type. If not a city sophisticate, he has an urban quickness to his manner. Hardly a born businessman, he is not a vulnerable romantic either. He is heir to the tough, independent, intrigue-minded traditions of the Broad Lakes region.

Coming down to Wuhan from the north, you sense a gutsy, fluent spirit in the city. It is as if the gush and bounty of the Yangtze washes off on the people. There is a spring in the step, a gleam in the eye; altogether, a vitality which is lacking in the dry and stony regions of the north.

Wuhan has been socially progressive, as in women's rights. When the Communist Youth League got itself together again after the Cultural Revolution, and held a congress in 1973, 49 percent of the delegates were women (and 42 percent of those at the Hupei province CYL congress a little later). Yet Wuhan's style is not pretentious. When a national political campaign sweeps down from Peking, Hupei joins in as it must, but with few flights of fancy.

In February 1973 the *Hupei Daily,* Wuhan's leading paper, ran an editorial on criticizing Lin Piao (though not by name) which was then de rigueur. Like voices from other provinces, it declared that the campaign "has been developing in our province in a deep-going way." But after "deep-going" the *Hupei Daily* threw in an adverb you see less often: "and *down-to-earth* way."

When assailing Confucius became a preoccupation some months later, a Wuhan politician gave a speech opening a series of national soccer events at Wuhan. He denounced Confucius and Lin Piao root and branch. Only by struggling against these two, he said, will sportsmen be doing the right thing. Then he set that theme aside, like an athlete shedding his track suit. More important than anything else, he resumed, soccer players must play soccer *well*. Wuhan is not a city where the practicality of a matter gets lost while theory soars; not a place where purity elbows out effectiveness.

In the way of life of its people Wuhan is a pivot between north and south. They speak Mandarin — with Hupei variations — and have no separate spoken tongue as the Cantonese do. Summer dress, on the other hand, is casual and flimsy as in the south. Few men bother with long pants; brief shorts and singlets are enough. The girls are nearly all in dresses; slacks are rare.

Aside from its own striking dishes, the Hupei kitchen leans to southern tastes. Rice is the favored vehicle for a meal, not noodles. Very spicy items are put away with no trouble at all. Dog is a welcome addition in winter (said to enhance virility). But there is not much bamboo. Nor does the Wuhan area grow bananas — key item of a southern fruit market.

Hupei's tastes are "southern" enough to have scandalized northerners at least since the Sung dynasty. A book written nine hundred years ago tells a story about how people from Hu Hsiang (an area around Broad Lakes) liked to eat large frogs. Folk in the north (then called the middle region, *chung-chou*) often laughed at this funny habit. A distinguished northerner decided to test his own folk's pretensions on the question of frogs. This official, after being transferred to a post in the south, one day served his household frog, but under the label of quail. After everyone declared the dish delicious, he told them they had eaten frog. Since that day, the historian claimed, patricians from the north have been less inclined than before to laugh at the kitchen habits of southerners.

Hupei for the most part plants two crops a year. This compares with a pattern in north China of one crop a year above the Great Wall, and three-crops-in-two-years within the belt bounded by the wall and the Huai River (which flows about 320 kilometers north of Wuhan). On the other hand, Hupei is less fertile than the three-crops-a-year valleys of Kwangtung province.

Wuhan gets a bit of snow, which Kwangtung never does. My hotel has a good heating system in readiness for midwinter. There is a saying here which reminds us that the Wuhan district is not a cornucopia of twelve-month food supply: "When snowflakes fill the air, up goes the price of vegetables."

The banks of the middle Yangtze are rich and hot and wet. Different from north China's plains, so flat and sparse, with a light that is steady and even. Yet Hupei countryside is not the southern kind which inspires most Chinese landscape painters. The mountains do not rise at giddy angles; their peaks are seldom lost in mist. The Hupei heavens do not play at lights with the magic touch that gives Kwangtung its ever-present rainbows. Less common, too, are the bamboo groves which seduce painters and poets to the world of south China.

The hills of Wuhan are modest and undulating. Nature's contrasts are held within reason. The five elements have come to a fair agreement among themselves. It seems a proper order of things for a pivot city. Wuhan's door is open to the tastes and traffic of all four points of the compass. Extreme tendencies are cut down by a moderating current from one direction or another.

All over Wuhan you come upon institutions whose name begins *Hua-zhong,* an abbreviation for Central China. Central China Agricultural College; Central China Cinema; Central China Teacher Training School. More than any city in China is Wuhan entitled to throw about this prefix *Hua-zhong.* If middle China can be represented by a metropolis — any more than middle America can be — then Wuhan is the gate of middle China.

The first British officials to sail from Shanghai to Hankow marveled at how deep into China they had penetrated. One of them, aide to the chief of mission, Lord Elgin, recorded in his diary for 1858 the hoisting of the flag on arrival (over their leading ship, the *Furious*): "It was not possible to help feeling a thrill of exultation as we watched the British ensign fluttering for the first time *in the very heart of the empire*." Even trains and a few planes a day have not removed the sense you have in Wuhan of being in a real hinterland.

Wuhan is not remote by China's standards, yet one can share a bit of Lord Elgin's awe. It is a surprise to find this oasis which is so much a world of its own. The city has its own natural mold. It serves itself and does not look elsewhere for basic things. It has its own style and

Wuhan may be the Chicago of China but its airport is not like O'Hare

ways, for which it feels no inclination to apologize. As a badge of China's continental depth, Wuhan is a kind of Chicago. Just as one has a distinct feeling, walking up Chicago's Michigan Avenue, of the East Coast on the right and the West Coast on the left, so in Wuhan one senses Shanghai far to the east behind Wuchang, and the western mountains beyond the banks of the Han.

The Yangtze alone is enough to justify this city's cool self-possession. By the time a ship has come as far inland as Hankow, the river's yellow stains seem part of it, like a baptismal mark. The middle Yangtze takes the ship in its charge. The vessel's alien, oceangoing face puts on the calm smile of the hinterland.

244

In Elgin's day, Wuhan expressed its middle Chinese character in ways that did not always please the strutting foreigner. Antiforeign feeling was stronger here than on the coast. Christian missionaries found the going even tougher here than in blasé Shanghai.

The Yangtze had something to do with this. European steamships worked a bad effect on river navigation, to which the lives of millions in Hupei and Szechwan were tuned. On one hand the new vessels took away freight traffic from the junks and sampans. On the other hand they constantly ran down and sank these Chinese craft.

Consider an incident which an American geologist watched with his own eyes in 1863:

> A steamer which had just been repaired made a trial trip with many of the most distinguished foreigners of Shanghai who, like myself, had been invited for a pleasure excursion. . . . As we steamed along at full speed, we saw at some distance from us a sampan so heavily loaded with bricks that four Chinamen could only with difficulty manage to row it. They saw us coming and, well aware how narrow was the canal, worked with all their might to give the steamer room to pass. As we stood watching the slow motion of the sampan during our approach I listened for the signal to stop our engine. The awkward vessel was still in the middle of the stream, while the coolies strained every muscle to hurry the slow motion of the sampan and at the same time shouted imploringly for a few moments' grace. There was still time to avoid the collision when the pilot asked: "Shall I stop, sir?" "No," shouted the captain, "go ahead!" There was now no help for them. Terrified at hearing this cold-blooded order, I waited, breathless, for the shock, which soon followed. A shout, a crash, a swaying motion throughout our boat; then we steamed on up the canal. I went to the stern but could see there only one of the coolies, and he was lying motionless in the water. Of the many foreigners on deck very few gave expression to the feelings every newcomer must experience on witnessing such a scene. The captain and the mate of the steamer glanced quite calmly over the railing to see whether the bow and paddle-wheels had been hurt, and the remarks they made had no reference to their victims.

No surprise that foreign steamships took to covering their sides with steel plates, as protection against furious assaults from Chinese farm-

245

ers on the riverbank. Nor that Lord Elgin found, on arrival in Hankow, proclamations posted in the streets, assuring people that the foreigners' visit would be brief and not commercial.

For whatever different reasons, the foreigner in Wuhan may even today feel a little less at ease than in Hangchow or Shanghai. Residents of this city — with who knows what inner feelings — express more sheer amazement at the foreigner than do those in most parts of China.

If Wuhan has often been a city with its own mind, it could never be a city-state with its own separate body. As a regional bastion it was able — and still is — to speak to the center with a strong voice. But geography, which gives Wuhan influence, has always forbidden Wuhan the option of secession. As soon carve the stomach from the body, as set Wuhan free from China.

Wuhan in this respect is in quite a different position from Dairen, which was cut off from China for half a century. Or from Shanghai, where foreigners could readily set up an important enclave. Or Canton, from which separatist governments have sometimes given the north a run for its money.

The short-lived Wuhan regime of the left-wing Kuomintang in 1927 collapsed in part because of the city's middle location. Pressure from warlords to south, north, and west — and Chiang Kai-shek's threats from the east — cut across the precarious ties between the left Kuomintang and the CCP which the regime reflected. The hard reality of guns and generals in neighboring provinces made academic the verbal struggles and paper policies at Wuhan.

The city's link with Shanghai, moreover, was no advantage in circumstances where the left-wing government at Wuhan was at odds politically with Shanghai. The Wuhan economy suffered when hostile forces further down the Yangtze put pressure on it (such as discounting Wuhan money, when changing it for Shanghai money).

It is not only in location and manners that Wuhan is a piece of middle China. In basic measurements, and in the rhythm of its days, Wuhan is an all-round city.

Here is China's second biggest steel center and a key military base.

246

Yet much of it looks like a resort town, with lakes, hills, pleasure boats. Machines hum away in a city that is set within a great primary produce area of China. The "province of a thousand lakes," as Hupei is sometimes called, has as its capital one of China's four or five hearths of heavy industry. Wuhan is able, Janus-like, to turn the face of iron or the face of silk.

The city boasts a bridge that cost forty million U.S. dollars, and a plant that employs sixty thousand workers and uses some techniques of world standards. But these efforts can seem like a show of advanced streaking in a very traditional backyard garden. It is jolting to see so much painful — and painfully slow — pulling of freight by hand. An old lady heaves on a rope that pulls a tray of soy-sauce urns up the incline toward the Han River bridge. A group of old men strain to the utmost with a cartload of building bricks that rebels against a small rise in the road. Wuhan's modern sector is set within an overall municipal economy that is not yet very modernized. All this makes Wuhan a typical city of China in the 1970s.

Especially since it is an amalgam of three towns that were once dissimilar, Wuhan has gathered to itself most of the strands that compose China's rich experience. Through Wuchang it has a background in the administration and scholarship of the dynasties. In Hankow the trade, and in Hanyang the manufacturing, developments of the nineteenth century were represented. And when the revolution went forward, Wuhan proved to be one of its major spearheads. All the while, the city continued to be the focus of farming and traffic in the middle Yangtze region.

Wuhan knew less Western impact than Shanghai; yet Hankow was a major treaty port and felt the fist of imperialism. Wuhan cannot match the almost perfect scenic harmony of Hangchow; yet it is one of the prettiest of China's very big cities. Wuhan is a port and industrial center to match Dairen; but it has a pedigree from two thousand years which Dairen lacks — as well as backward aspects from which the new-cut Dairen is free.

Wuhan's summer heat is so fierce that Hankow has been known as the Gates of Hell. Officials in Wuhan greet a visitor with the cheerful admission that of the "Three Furnaces of China" (Chungking, Nanking, Wuhan) Wuhan is perhaps the hottest. The temperature often gets to forty-two degrees centigrade (107.6 degrees Fahrenheit).

A blanket of somnolence falls over the city after lunchtime. A 2:00 P.M. street scene belies Hankow's nature as a commercial hub. The only business activity is the buying of fruit drinks at innumerable "cold drink shops." The siesta claims the afternoon, man's minimum reply to heaven's extremes. After work and on holidays the banks of East Lake are thick with swimmers. Several times I join them, but the water is dismayingly warm. The same problem exists at the many fine swimming pools that have been built across the city since Liberation.

Back at the hotel in Hankow, I also find that my great weapon against China's summer heat is blunt in Wuhan. The cold bath is by no means cold. I had grown used to the delight of a cold bath in the middle of a searing Peking day. But the water in Wuhan, unlike that in Peking, does not come from natural wells. In midsummer it is a few degrees cooler than a hot cup of tea — and a few degrees warmer than East Lake.

The special summer problem of Wuhan (it has the same latitude as New Orleans) is that the evenings don't get much cooler than the days. You wake up feeling melted to the straw matting of your bed. You reach for the cold water flask and find it as warm as a dog's tummy. Many city residents, I discover during long walks, decline to be baked all night in their houses. By midnight the narrow streets of Hankow are so crowded that you might think a mass exodus was under way. The sidewalks look like a city-wide pajama party. Young and old are settling down to sleep on knee-high cane beds, hoping to intercept whatever feather of a breeze the night might offer.

❁ ❁ ❁

In Wuhan you sense a diverse past; no one layer smothers the others. Already in the period of the Warring States (403 B.C. to 221 B.C.) Wuchang emerged as a government town. The southern state of Ch'u embraced the area at that time. Hanyang residents still speak of two nearby hills as "Large Army Hill" and "Small Army Hill."

They were so named because on them camped the rival forces of Wu and Wei in the third century B.C.

Under the general umbrella of the later Han dynasty (which began around the time of Christ's birth) the state of Wu made Wuchang its capital for a time, from the third century. Wu was one of three kingdoms which cropped up toward the end of the Han. Hanyang and Hankow did not in these epochs amount to much. You see few relics of Ch'u and Wu in Wuchang, but the city likes to refer to its ancient roots.

The modern history of Wuhan is a duet of rebellion and the rise of trade and manufactures. A catalyst for both forces was the Western presence which followed the "opening" of Hankow as a new treaty port in 1861.

Early Western travelers had marveled at the size of this inland metropolis. A French priest who saw Wuhan in the 1720s judged Wuchang alone to be the equal of Paris; he called Hanyang another Lyons. "Should one from an Eminence view this Vast Extent of Ground, covered with Houses," Father Du Halde recorded, after a climb up Tortoise Hill, "he would either not believe his Eyes, or own that he saw the finest Prospect of the Kind in the World."

Abbé Huc, another French visitor in the 1840s, even guessed the population of the three cities at eight million. Said this visitor — who wore a yellow cap and red girdle that startled the people of Wuhan: "I hardly think there is another port in the world so frequented as this." But Huc must have been swept up by giddy thoughts of myriad new souls for Christianity. Lord Elgin's (Protestant) secretary, noting crisply that "the Jesuit missionary [Huc] is not always scrupulously accurate in his statements," put the population at one million. In fact the British estimate was itself too high. Only in the early twentieth century did the tri-cities reach the one million mark.

Yet Lord Elgin permitted himself a lively excitement at Wuhan's commercial possibilities. Here was water thirteen fathoms deep yet one thousand kilometers from the sea; products from all over central China; a vast market and an industrious populace; streets "superior to any I had seen in any other city of the empire" (he referred to Wuchang).

249

Elgin strode among the amazed people of Hankow, shouting the phrase *"Bu-pa, bu-pa"* ("Don't be afraid, don't be afraid"), which he had been advised to utter with dignity when confronted by China's millions. His secretary's diary conveys the cocky mood behind British efforts to pull Wuhan by the neck into the civilized world:

> Many years hence, when there are steamers plowing the waters of the Yang-tse as freely as they do now those of the Mississippi, old men will tell their wondering progeny, who are probably stokers, that they remember the day when foreign ships, then supposed to be under demonical influence, suddenly appeared for the first time among the now obsolete craft, formerly known as junks, at Han-kow, and, after remaining a week, as suddenly vanished; and how, for some time afterward, until barbarians again reached Han-kow and built a magnificent city upon its river-banks, it was popularly supposed that the apparition had been supernatural.

A little pressure, to be sure, was needed to bring this magnificent city to birth. The Ch'ing dynasty had insisted, during every bout with the British, that foreigners stay out of China's "inland waters." But the British were able to bypass this little hurdle. They forced down China's throat the view that Hankow was a "seaport," and thus by definition not "inland waters."

While at Hankow, Elgin brushed aside the governor-general of Broad Lake's refusal to receive the foreign party personally. "The petty mandarin Wang," Elgin's aide recorded, "who had yesterday expressed the hope that Lord Elgin would not visit the governor general in Wu-chang, was this morning dispatched to that city with a note to his excellency, informing him of Lord Elgin's intention to visit him tomorrow" (which Elgin did, with forty marines and thirty bluejackets as his guard of honor, and a gun salute such as had "never before resounded through the crowded streets of Han-kow, or shaken the frame-works of its wooden houses").

Elgin used his four ships as levers to try and make the viceroy cooperate with the British vision of Hankow's future. When the head of Broad Lakes dragged his feet, Elgin moved his cruiser across the Yangtze to face Wuchang's main gate. "This demonstration produced the desired effect," says the British record. The mandarins' "tone" picked up at once.

The British did not discover Wuhan at its best. The city had just been a major battleground in the Taiping uprising of the mid-1850s, China's first ideological revolutionary movement. The Taiping leader, Wuhan folk like to point out, had his state seal cast here in 1852.

Wuhan has never seen fiercer days than those of the Taiping battles. As the rebels sailed toward Hanyang from the upper Yangtze, the Manchu commander at Wuchang took rash steps. All houses within ten yards of Wuchang's walls were ordered burned, the better to defend Wuchang. One man from each household had to remain on vigil all night.

The Taipings dug tunnels and mounted ladders, to propel themselves into Wuchang and Hanyang. They used poisonous smoke; they aimed fire-tipped arrows over the walls to start a conflagration.

Terrible was the destruction — much of it by fire — as parts of Wuhan changed hands half a dozen times. Tens of thousands were killed or committed suicide. "So grim was the carnage," one Chinese memoir avows, "that the sun itself went dim." It was made worse by ineptness and poor morale on the Manchu side. Many of the steps taken against the passionate and feared Taipings were unpopular. When the Manchu commander ordered the burning of thousands of houses, crowds wept and hundreds of people jumped into the river in suicides of despair.

The Manchu armies were full of out-of-town soldiers. Greedy Wuchang merchants would fleece these men by high prices and sharp practices. Troops actually started to rebel against merchants on the very eve of a Taiping attack! In the fighting, the out-of-town soldiers fared far worse than local soldiers — who could flee to their houses at crucial moments — and 80 percent of them died, as against 25 percent of the local soldiers.

As in previous battles over Wuhan, Hanyang's Tortoise Hill proved crucial. It was the first citadel captured by the Taipings; installed there, they commanded both the Han and the Yangtze; from it they lunged successfully at Wuchang's north gate. To cross the Yangtze, the Taipings stretched two lines of boats end to end, and marched over them to Wuchang. Vantage Hill (Heng shan), a picturesque area by East Lake, was also a vital launching pad for the rebels.

In their brief span of control, the Taipings gave Wuhan its first taste of ideological politics. The people were indoctrinated with the half-Christian teaching of the rebels. Some joined a tight cell of ten people (*guan*) to train as Taiping soldiers. Others were allowed to go on with their usual occupations so long as they bestowed gifts on the rebel authorities. Wuhan residents were asked to adopt the clothing style of the newcomers, including cloth wrapped around the head rather than a hat. Many people who were not judged reliable had to leave the city and live in camps beyond the city walls.

One day in Wuchang, after a swim in East Lake, I walk in the green hills of its northern bank. Here stands one of the few Wuhan structures with echoes of the Taipings. It is a pointed cairn of stones, covering the bodies of nine women. Their names are not known; they were members of the Taiping army. They were killed when they refused to surrender as Manchu forces countermoved against the rebels. Along a gravel path, bordered with long grass and pretty flowers, swimmers from the lake sometimes come up to read the stark, sad tablet stone. Nine girl fighters, who fought and died before the time when girls were supposed to fight. Nine among several hundred thousand Wuhan people who struggled for the Taiping cause.

Over the next fifty years Wuhan recovered from the Taiping civil war, and by 1914 Hankow stood third among the treaty ports in volume of trade. Foreigners never took hold of Hankow's body and spirit, though, to the degree they did of Shanghai's. Chinese politics were a more serious complication in this inland pivot than on the coast. Chinese business was also a more powerful contender with Western business here than in semiforeign Shanghai.

Wuhan traders had long been at the job and well organized in groups: guilds of various provinces, each with a headquarters club (*hui-guan*); business associations (*bang*); associated business offices (*gong-suo*) of towns and regions all over China. There was a grouping called a *hang* which tied together all the shops which sold a particular product; the tea *hang,* salt *hang,* medicine *hang,* and some 350 others. A foreign firm in Hankow was merely a branch of a Shanghai house. But its Chinese rival in Hankow was a headquarters firm with a branch in Shanghai.

And it was true in Hankow as elsewhere that foreign hopes for trade with a backward China were simply too high. The bluster of the Europeans came up against two hard realities. The Manchu dynasty was having a hard time keeping order, navigating a future for itself between the Scylla of internal revolt and the Charybdis of foreign assault. The Chinese people did not have much taste for the gewgaws of Europe's overproduction.

Disappointment had to be the result for those eager merchants (the English in those days still had a sharp business edge) who hoped to put a Manchester shirt on every Hupei back; for optimists who sought to edge chopsticks off the Chinese table in favor of knives and forks from Sheffield.

The merchants were in no mood for the degree of caution that even a study of Elgin's first foray into the mart of Hankow might have induced. Elgin's secretary described an encounter which many a China-trader could look back on with a rueful pang of recognition. The British had gone on board some junks moored on the Han River, in search of facts about the Wuhan trade:

> It was hopeless to expect them to comprehend any inquiry which presupposed any premises whatever [runs the British report]. You could not begin by asking where silk was grown. The introduction necessary to arrive at this result is the incontrovertible statement, "There is such a thing as silk."
>
> Chinaman repeats eagerly, "There is such a thing as silk; oh yes; ah! there is such a thing as silk."
>
> "Silk grows in some provinces; in some it does not."
>
> Chinaman repeats, thoughtfully, "Yes, silk grows in some provinces; in some it does not."
>
> By-standers, who have taken up the idea with greater rapidity, remark to one another, "Ah! true; in some provinces silk does not grow."
>
> "Does this province produce silk?"
>
> "Yes."

"Does Szechwan produce silk?"

"No."

"Then do you carry silk to Szechwan?"

"No."

"What do you carry to Szechwan?"

Chinaman repeats, puzzled, "What do I carry to Szechwan?"

By-standers all repeat, vivaciously, "What do you carry to Szechwan?"

Chinaman: "Sometimes I carry silk to Szechwan, and sometimes I carry cotton."

"Does cotton grow in Szechwan?"

"Yes."

"And yet you carry cotton to Szechwan?"

"Oh! sometimes I bring cotton here from Szechwan."

By-standers, unanimously: "Sometimes he brings cotton here from Szechwan." And so on until one's patience is fairly exhausted, and one wonders wherein the indisputable intelligence of a Chinaman consists. . . .

Yet the quest for profit — and adventure — went on.

⚙ ⚙ ⚙

Spurred by the Taiping attacks, Hankow built around itself a stone wall seven kilometers long and four meters high. A Bund took shape, with arches, parapets, and iron fences, to serve as the foreign seat. From its hulks and godowns steamboats left for Europe; by 1877 a tea clipper made the trip in six weeks. Other exports were vegetable oil, sesame, cotton, silk, beans and bean cakes, hemp, cowhides; major imports were cotton, kerosene, sugar.

The British had the best site and the noblest buildings. North of the British Concession was the Russian, dating from 1896, where the specialty was compressing tea bricks. Next was the French Concession, also won in 1896, which had fine restaurants and the best hotel, the Terminus. The German area was the largest of all (104 acres), but in 1918 it reverted back to the Chinese (without ceasing in practice to be a foreign enclave).

The northern fringe of foreign Hankow went to the latecomer.

Japan got its concession only in 1898. By the end of World War One, though, the Japanese population of Hankow had risen to thirteen hundred (equal to the total European population). As well as its centerpiece of commercial houses, each concession had banks, post office, consul; umbilical cords to a world across the seas which few foreigners left in spirit.

Like a Great Wall of social demarcation, a busy street called New Life Road ran between the British Concession and the "Chinese City" to its south.

Here in Hankow's heart were unpaved streets as narrow as corridors, full of smells and noises, mats spread across them to deflect the summer heat. Here were hawkers; coolies with crushing loads; barbers at work in the open air. Workshops were open to the street — as Chinese workshops always are. Beggars vied with mangy dogs and scavenging pigs. There were fortune tellers, with a colorful tambourine, a brass disk, or a live bird, to give an air of mystery to their use of simple psychology.

Set apart from all this, on Hankow's western outskirts, were two oases that made life worthwhile for many a foreigner: a racecourse and a golf club. There was a separate racecourse for Chinese.

Hankow had a stir and bustle fitting to a carrefour of the provinces. Turbans and Tartár features marked off traders from Tibet. There were square faces from Szechwan, round faces from Kwangtung, fine features and small bones from the border of Annam (Vietnam). Elgin's secretary had his own brand of comment on this Chinese cosmopolitanism: "Flat noses and oblique eyes are universal, yet it is scarcely conceivable how many distinct varieties of flat noses and oblique eyes there may be."

Wuhan soon had a roster of Christian mission groups as long as a list of the books of the New Testament. With what they called "sanctified common sense," the missionaries fixed on Wuhan as an ideal base from which to redeem central China. An early titan was Griffith John of the London Missionary Society. "Among the congregation are many aged men and women," a colleague wrote of John's Gospel Hall in Hankow, "old pilgrims to Zion who will soon see the King in His beauty. There are bright boys with hymn books and Bibles tied up in their handkerchiefs . . . girls with gay attire, hair tightly braided."

Next came the China Inland Mission, whose guiding star, Hudson Taylor, had declared China to be "a Niagara of souls, crashing down to perdition." The Italians put up a convent the size of a palace. The Lutheran compound near Three-Eye Bridge was a kind of fortress. The Episcopal Mission to Wuchang taught Chinese boys in white surplices to sing "God Save Our Emperor" to the tune of "America."

A partial division of the field of central China was agreed upon by the Protestant — but not the Catholic — mission societies. "They wisely follow the principle," observed one clergyman, "that while the supply of heathen holds out, competition for the same converts should be avoided."

The people of Wuhan did not rush to the new faith. Griffith John confessed that "two or three hundred *cash* a week have a greater attraction for the average Chinaman than the salvation of his soul." Would the Chinese, then, all end up in hell? The Reverend John liked to rephrase this logical question. "Do you suppose that they are all going to heaven?" He gave a reply that was grim but with a sting of inspiration in its tail: "One thing I am perfectly sure of is that they are not fit to go to heaven; and if I could tell you tonight that all the Chinese were launched into heaven just as they leave this world, I venture to say, my friends, that very few of you would care to go there at all unless you went as missionaries."

Hankow's true Holy Wafer was the humble tea leaf. Its de facto priests were the tea merchants. Its supporting flock were the tea drinkers who raised their morning cup around the globe. Tea had made Hankow, and the tea season brought a Lenten concentration to the Bund.

Once it had been necessary to carry the tea of central China on men's backs over the Meiling Pass to Canton. But the opening of the Yangtze made Hankow (by World War One) the loading point for 75 percent of China's black tea, and the manufacturing place of 90 percent of China's brick tea.

Hankow seemed to reach over to Hanyang across a bed of junks,

their masts lined up like the teeth of a comb. These ingenious craft —
some twenty-five thousand were registered at Wuhan in 1923 — were
the sinews of the city's tie with the middle Yangtze.

There were narrow, dainty boats, with bows turned up like a
Turkish slipper; vast, flat sailboats with a lofty cabin at the stern;
sampans as simple in design as their name suggests ("three boards").
There were Kiangsi junks, wide in the middle with pointed ends,
bringing in pottery and rice and bales of paper; Szechwan junks,
larger than most, and smartly varnished; square-fronted junks from
Hunan, groaning with charcoal, tea, and barrels of vegetable oil. And
there were local junks, nipping back and forth between the triple
cities, like minnows among sharks.

Some of the junks' sails were inky blue; some a delicate faded
orange; others like patchwork bedspreads. Many boats lay flat on the
yellow ripples; others rose as tall as they were long; a few had masts
that reached for the clouds.

Central China in the late nineteenth century was a choppy sea on
which diverse forces maneuvered at cross-purposes. Foreigners modernized Hankow, in an uneven way, for their own purposes, keeping
their distance from Chinese society. Meanwhile, Chinese-sponsored
industry and education arose in Hanyang and Wuchang.

Chang Chih-tung, governor-general at Wuchang, wanted to keep
the West at bay by copying some of its methods. He made Wuhan a
leader in the fitful industrialization that marked the sinking decades
of the Manchu dynasty. The Peking-Hankow railroad was his first
great project (it met great opposition from people who objected that
couriers would be put out of work and that villagers would riot). In
Hanyang he set up China's first big iron and steel works. Under
his patronage Wuchang sprouted technical, language, and military
schools.

These monuments to Chang's energy you still see in today's Wuhan.
His railroad tracks and chimneys have done good service to a new
era. But Chang would be staggered by the anti-Confucianism now
taught within the walls of the colleges he built.

Chang was a shrewd traditionalist. He thought the Confucian way
— decorous, hierarchial, snobbish — could be kept alive by an infu-

sion of new techniques. He gave no thought to mobilizing the people. He refused to join the rising tide against the Ch'ing dynasty. His division of knowledge into substance (which should be Chinese) and function (which could be Western) was rigid and wrong. The efforts of men like Chang, moreover, were spread far too thin to remake a China starting to shake at the roots.

Above all, Chang had no solution to the problem of power, in particular the power of imperialism in China. Even his pet railroad project turned out to be an advertisement for the gap between China's aspirations and its way of going at them. Lack of capital and disorganization led to the railroad's being a Belgian concession, financed by French francs, protected by Russians.

CCP officials seldom allude to this isolated giant of a dying order. (Some of his deeds have been swept from mind. Officials at Hupei Museum tell me that no museum existed at Wuhan before Liberation; yet Chang established two museums at Wuchang — one for Western methods, one for Chinese substance.) This is not surprising, though Chang was a local hero in his day. The mandarin of Wuhan tried to ward off the foreigners in order to save Confucian China. The Communists of Wuhan, when their hour came, used resistance to the foreign world as a springboard for making a new people's China.

Yet Chang and the CCP share one basic value: technique should take second place to a moral social order.

At the foot of Snake Hill in Wuchang, a fatal blow was struck against the Manchu dynasty in 1911. The Manchu ship of state had been springing leaks for years. Up in arms were most intellectuals, part of the army, a fringe of the gentry. Nationalism was the sentiment of the day. Sun Yat-sen's alliance of progressives was on the rise.

A branch of Sun's movement was strong in Hankow. A government move against these dissenters — made possible by an accidental bomb explosion in their lair — led three thousand fellow-dissenters in the army at Wuchang to stage a grass-roots coup. The governor-general and his military chief fled. Within two days the rebels controlled the tri-cities. The uprising spread to other cities. Two thousand years of feudal dynastic rule came to an end in China.

The future leader of the CCP spent his formative years on the fringes of this revolt against feudalism. In his native Hunan province, 320 kilometers to the south, Mao Tse-tung read of the Wuchang events in a newspaper. He set off at once for Wuhan to join the revolutionary army. But revolt was becoming a rosy rash all over China's body politic. Not long after reaching Wuchang, Mao heard that the provincial government had been overthrown in Hunan. He quickly went back to Changsha and the scene of fresh action.

The house in the Russian Concession of Hankow where the bomb exploded is no more to be found. The fires of revolution were very literal in Hankow that fall; much of the city, including the nest of revolt, caught fire and was destroyed. But you may still visit the site of the Wuchang coup, along a street now called First Uprising.

The scene is a trinity of red walls, green leaves, and white paving. A red-brick mansion rises against Snake Hill. Before its high iron gates a concrete square extends. Trees with pale green leaves and clean white branches soften the large open space.

In Street of First Uprising stands the (rebuilt) garrison where troops of the New Model Army raised the banner of revolt on that famous October 10 (the anniversary is always referred to as Double Ten). On a nearby terrace the rebel leader Huang Hsing, who had founded the Society for the Revival of China, was appointed military chief of the post-Manchu regime.

I wander further through the historic square. Here is the unmistakable figure of Sun Yat-sen, viewing with a bronze eye the flagstones where his movement reached its climax. The gown comes down to the ankles; a Western hat is clutched in the right hand; there is the look of antique dignity which Dr. Sun had even in life.

Behind Sun's statue is the mansion itself, in which the new government found its feet on October 11, 1911. It looks like a sprawling monastery, or a luxurious school in imperial Singapore. Red tiles; imposing verandas on each level; brick walls punctuated by white concrete pillars with cornices. On the roof is a flagpole — without a

259

flag: the success of the new order no longer has to be declaimed —
and in the ample grounds an army of cicadas has possession of the
trees.

In the driveway to the mansion a wooden signboard admonishes:
"Serve the People." But two large concrete billboards by the front
gates have been scrubbed clean; with glum faces they await a fresh
command. A plaque on the high brick wall, erected in 1961 by Hupei
province, under the authority of the State Council at Peking, has
an inscription that spears memory with a pen: "Former Seat of the
Military Government of Wuchang Uprising."

I look back at the square but not a soul fronts the afternoon heat.
The cicadas are lone guardians of this spot where history stops still, at
least in the mind of one who sees it for the first time.

The revolution of 1911 put an end to an old order, but it did not
secure a new order. For sixteen years, until Chiang Kai-shek set up a
more-or-less national regime at Nanking, left, right, and center battled
for the future. Wuhan was a key stage during these seesaw years of
hope and defeat.

There had been no radical intent behind the industry which foreigners and Chang Chih-tung spurred in Wuhan. But the workshops
proved a two-edged sword. They had an unforeseen political effect.
Planned as a conservative step, they fed the Left by providing an
urban working class. This was especially true of the railways. (Railways are still a two-edged sword in China. Proud badge of socialist
construction, they have also been seedbeds of "revisionism." During
the Cultural Revolution, some railwaymen made a bid for the political
authority they judged fitting for workers of an advanced industry. At
home with machines, accustomed to precise schedules, in touch with
people coming and going all over China, they did not always lie
down like lambs before loud and abstract extremists.)

An angry mass of thirty thousand Peking-Hankow railroad workers
began a strike in February 1923 — following other strikes against
British firms in Hankow — and within a few days the warlords who
ruled the area massacred the strikers. The affair momentarily triggered new rounds of labor militance in many provinces.

"Two Seven" (from the February 7 date of the assault on the

260

strikers) is a famous phrase in Wuhan. The visitor meets many echoes of this event which was a tragedy but is distant enough to be called glorious. Hankow has three railway stations: East Han, Hankow Central, and River Shore (Kiangan). The River Shore district covers part of the former Japanese Concession. It was here that Hupei authorities murdered the strikers on "Two Seven."

You can visit the River Shore Rolling Stock Plant, whose workers blew the whistle that signaled the start of the "Two Seven" strike. South along the bank of the Yangtze you find the former British consulate. Here on the night of February 6, foreign diplomats and heads of foreign firms met with the police and army of the warlords to plan the bloody attack of the morrow.

Near the station is a monument to the martyrs of this first urban workers' battle in Chinese history. The simple obelisk is close to the old European racecourse; a piquant juxtaposition. There were the British: sure of themselves and of the future, enjoying the horses while business ticked ahead on the Bund. And the Chinese workers: setting a first, unsteady step down a path which, though rocky, eventually led them to be masters of Wuhan.

There are old folk in River Shore district (I spend a day here with neighborhood officials) who remember "Two Seven." They relate a scene on the platform of River Shore station on that fateful morning. The branch secretary of the union based at this station, Lin Hsiang-ch'ien, was being held by troops. He was told to order what remained of his men to go back to work. He refused. The militarists beheaded him then and there in front of the crowd.

These veterans can look back on the setback of "Two Seven" — at the time so chilling to the Chinese labor movement — as "just one twist in the Yangtze River." The accelerating stream reached the sea, after all, in the Liberation of 1949. And the Wuhan trade unions today? They are a toothless tiger. But there are no capitalists to lord it over workers, these days. Nor foreigners who carve out enclaves of privilege and make the Chinese pariahs in their own land.

There is a shady old part of Wuchang, north of Snake Hill and close to the banks of the Yangtze, where two handsome buildings recall the past. One is a gray brick villa; the other is a comfortable high school. Mao Tse-tung and some of his circle lived in the villa from the winter of 1926 until the fall of 1927. Within the salons of the school, over a similar period, Mao and others ran the Central Institute of the Peasant Movement.

These were epic months in Wuhan, which once again took center stage in the Chinese revolution. Left-wing forces, which had formed a government at Canton in 1923, moved north in the summer of 1926, to try and wrest territory from warlords. The CCP and the (much larger) Kuomintang were at this time linked in uneasy harness. The Kuomintang was deeply split on how to deal with the CCP. Chiang Kai-shek was already anticommunist to the core, and he set up a government of that ilk in east China. Increasingly he sank to the level of a semifascist warlord.

The left wing of the Kuomintang, however, joined forces with the CCP in a regime of hope and pathos at Wuhan, 1926–1927. The Central Executive Committee of the Kuomintang moved to Wuhan from Canton. The Central Committee of the CCP moved from the French Concession in Shanghai to Hankow. Thus did Wuhan become a halfway house, in every sense, for the march of the revolution. Thus, too, did Mao Tse-tung enter, for the first time, the political whirlpool of the tri-cities.

You cannot but salute Mao's taste in bourgeois villas. A merchant's domain, the house's high ceilings and dark vertical boards give its chambers a mellow look. There is a sense of retreat from the hubbub of the street outside and the nearby rows of humble houses. Successive archways lead to courtyards paved with diagonal stones. Interior windows are wood lattice; the furniture is dark and square and solid.

As I admire the place its curator points out that such a house was not Mao's natural level. "Nineteen twenty-seven was a time of Kuomintang-CCP united front; it was the Nationalists who obtained this house for Chairman Mao." As he had done previously at Changsha, Mao managed to secure a working base of peace and comfort.

The bedrooms are set up just as they were when Mao came north half a century ago. Cool stone floors; small washstands; no clutter of

You cannot but salute Mao's taste in bourgeois villas.
The inscription identifies "Comrade Mao Tse-tung's"
house of 1926–1927 days

ornaments or knickknacks. The beds are like open boxes, with chests underneath and a roof above, from which nets hang down to keep out Wuhan's militant mosquitoes. In one room Mao slept with his (second) wife. Mao's mother and his two children shared a neighboring room. A third belonged to P'eng P'ai, a CCP colleague from Canton who had also come north.

Like the rural organizer P'eng P'ai, Mao kept a keen eye on the peasantry. It was a major difference of approach between him and the left-wing Kuomintang. It marked him off even from many of his CCP coworkers. Soviet influence was deep at Wuhan in 1927, and Moscow said that urban workers, not peasants, were the cutting edge of the revolution. In these circumstances, Mao could by no means work his will on CCP policy. At the Fifth Congress of the Party, held at Wuhan during the spring, he failed even to be elected a full member of the Central Committee.

One room in this merchant's villa is a shrine to Mao's independence from the line of Moscow, a baptismal font of Mao's turn inward to the heart of rural China.

It is a small brown writing room. Wooden shutters swing outward to one of the house's whitewashed courtyards. A lean kitchen chair is drawn up to a desk which has on it a kerosine lamp and a jar of writing brushes. Beside the lamp is a copy of the first edition of a famous pamphlet: *Report on an Investigation of the Peasant Movement in Hunan*. Mao wrote it at this desk.

The *Report* put the peasants at the center of the Left's thinking. It gave the theory of the Chinese revolution a stamp of originality from Russian canon. (Though the CCP, at the time, declined to publish the *Report* in its journal.)

A girl who works as a guide at the villa sits with me in a courtyard. We dig into history's hamper. Miss Tu explains that the Cultural Revolution changed the CCP's view of Wuhan's past. This occurred when people were encouraged to speak their minds. Some veterans recalled important things which turned out to be at variance with orthodox views. Two changes at the villa are interesting, if a bit paradoxical on their face.

The caption in Mao's writing room used to refer to the Hunan

Report as a "classic work of Marxism-Leninism." Discussions during the Cultural Revolution led to the conclusion that this was wrong. "The praise was really too high," says Miss Tu briskly. "The *Report* is not necessarily apt for lands other than China, so the word 'classic' is probably not the right one."

Nonetheless, before the Cultural Revolution the villa was little noticed or visited. "The house was only properly restored and put in order in 1967," relates its custodian. "Some people had underplayed the role of Chairman Mao in Wuhan's revolutionary history." This seems surprising, but reference to Chinese maps and handbooks underlines Miss Tu's point.

A 1950 tourist map of Wuhan does not show the villa. But on my 1973 map it is vividly marked in red characters (an honor given only one other site: the Hupei Party and government offices). A 1958 introduction to Wuhan does not mention Mao's name in referring to 1927 events. A 1973 account of Wuhan, on the other hand, touches on both the Hunan *Report* and Mao's teaching at the institute. The same two publications vary also in that only the later one refers to Mao's many swims in the Yangtze.

No less interesting, a 1965 article on Wuhan, in the course of recounting the city's socialist glories, includes this sentence: "Here Comrade Liu Shao-ch'i led the trade union struggle from 1926 to 1927." Not the slightest bow is made since the Cultural Revolution to Liu's role in Wuhan. Was it Liu's hand, maybe, that previously underplayed Mao's own work at Wuhan?

These days, at any rate, Mao's house and the institute are valued props for political education in Wuhan. Just before my 1973 visit, the Wuhan CYL held its first congress since the Cultural Revolution. One day the delegates walked across the bridge en masse from Hankow to see the two sites and be briefed on their significance.

I walk down a somnolent street of low stone houses and spreading maples to the former Peasant Institute. Middle-school pupils must have sighed to leave this place in 1959, when Hupei turned it into a museum. It is typical of the best premises in Wuchang. The verandas and airy archways speak of the south; but the garden growth does not quite have Canton's lushness.

Lawns lead up to the red wood pillars and gray bricks of a handsome building. Double doors with red frames open out from the salons to grassy courtyards. The garden is full of shrubs in porcelain tubs. Old men scrape at the red pillars, preparing to repaint them. Each pillar is an actual rounded tree log, one workman tells me, and has to be painted every three years.

Inside are heavy black-wood conference tables, dotted with tea mugs. There are cane armchairs here and there, and lecterns like music stands. The medicines in the institute's first-aid room are almost entirely Western; in 1927 the CCP had not yet begun to smile on Chinese traditional medicine.

From many provinces, especially Hupei, Hunan, and Kiangsi, came peasants (and some workers and students) to study within these unlikely portals during 1927. On paper the institute was a joint Kuomintang-CCP affair. In reality the CCP dominated it, although outnumbered two to one on the school's standing committee.

With fascination I gaze at the ragbag of teaching materials used. There are Chinese translations of pamphlets by European Marxists — some who are now famous, others who never caught history's eye. There are early works of Mao in roughly printed or mimeographed form. Their contents were still, in 1927, live ideas hardly pinned down. Simple dress for them was appropriate; Mao's writing did not yet possess authority beyond the power of its aptness for a task at hand.

The walls are decked with slogans which are exact replicas of those which hung on these walls during 1927. One salon has a black and red strip poster which cries: "Workers, Peasants, Soldiers, Rise Up with Arms." All three elements studied here, though the slogan is an even better reflection of today's Wuhan, now that these three are China's chosen social trinity.

Another banner crosses the decades with a contemporary tinkle: "Down with Chiang Kai-shek." Although the united front in Wuhan collapsed only in July 1927, the CCP had given up nearly all hope for Chiang well before that date. The institute was veering more to the left than the Kuomintang could stomach. Mao had already chosen the path of peasant revolution.

In the garden stands a speaker's platform of black boards which looks like an old-fashioned bus shelter. A banner still hangs there from March 1927: "Congress of Honan Province Armed Peasants." A notice explains that Mao addressed this meeting on the situation in Hunan; Honan had come to the institute to learn from Hunan's experience. The notice also says that funerals were held here when, after the fall of the united front, the Kuomintang started to massacre Communists.

Before the Kuomintang-CCP break in July 1927, China's revolution knew at Wuhan nine months of winsome adolescence. Glimpses of the future broke in, though the realities of the present were often intractable. It was as if some hidden projectionist of the revolution had mixed up the order of his reels. A foretaste of socialist society was screened at the tri-cities.

But it came too soon and it was ill prepared; it was out of relation with the wider context. The flowers of socialism bloomed for one lovely season, but with little soil beneath them.

Wuhan had been taken from warlord hands by revolutionary troops of the Northern Expedition in September 1926. City workers welcomed the left-wing government with drums, firecrackers, and posters — some showing a Chinese shaking hands with a Russian — in December 1926. A few days later the government declared Wuchang, Hanyang, and Hankow united, for the first time in history, as the single city of Wuhan.

At the site of the 1911 uprising in Wuchang, 300,000 people flocked to a rally. The square was divided into four parts, with one platform each for workers, soldiers, students, and merchants. (No platform for peasants, the key to China's future; symbol of why the new government was soon knocked from its perch.)

Russian dancers and singers began to appear on Wuhan stages. The government proclaimed holidays never heard of before in China: Death of Lenin, Birth of Marx, Proclamation of the Paris Commune. International Women's Day was celebrated on March 8, with a parade of twenty thousand liberated girls in Hankow; one of their struggles was against the cruel custom of foot-binding.

The All-China Congress of Trade Unions came to hospitable Wuhan for its fourth congress. Tom Mann arrived from London as head of an international workers' delegation which came to offer a handshake of encouragement. The British Communist addressed a May Day demonstration of 300,000 workers *at the racecourse,* thus neatly turning imperialism on its head.

Along the Bund the foreigners took a beating in body and spirit. A left-wing government at the heart of the Yangtze Valley was an especially black cloud in imperialism's sky. Britain was top dog in China; the Yangtze Valley was Britain's "sphere" (as the southwest was France's, Shantung once Germany's). So a Wuhan government with Communists in it seemed a dagger at the heart of a foreign privilege.

A surging crowd advanced from the "Chinese City" and captured the British Concession in January 1927. British marines were manhandled; many Britons fled to ships moored on the Yangtze. Communists in Hankow set up a mock "funeral of British imperialism." John Bull was borne through laughing crowds in a vast coffin. Wreaths were labeled with the names of warlords and Kuomintang rightists. Mourners, dressed to portray these two groups, walked as a cortege in plumed hats and paper coats, weeping tears of grief and fear.

There was a new mood of defiance by workers toward the foreigner. If a ricksha man was not paid the proper fare, he would no longer accept the loss, but call a crowd and make a scene. Notices on the benches of the Bund which said "Only for Foreigners" were pulled down. The arm of the trade unions was newly nerved. A weekly day of rest was secured for the first time in China's history. Strikes broke out against foreign firms.

When workers at the English-language *Hankow Herald* walked off the job, the management put a notice in the window of the office: "Why isn't the paper coming out? Don't ask us, we don't know. Ask Borodin, he knows."

Borodin was the resident Soviet adviser, trying to keep the unruly horses of the Wuhan coalition on what Moscow considered the correct road. He was lodged in a Hankow mansion with damask wallpaper and period furniture. What a shock for dignitaries of the treaty port to have this Bolshevik calling the shots from their own back garden! And how astonishing (given all that has happened since) that CCP and left-Kuomintang politician alike were ready to lap up the Russian's every word!

Many newly arrived Soviet civil and military advisers lived in the two-storied brick houses of Lockwood Gardens, a square owned by Jardine-Matheson, chief of all the British *taipan* firms. Ministers of the government moved into other European villas. You can still see these gray, shabbily elegant houses in Hankow today, serving as schools, offices, and dormitories for single workers.

The widow of Sun Yat-sen, who leaned toward the Communists (she still holds office in Peking today), took over the top floor of the Central Bank. With her for a while lived Anna Louise Strong, an American idealist who got wrapped up in the Chinese revolution.

Miss Strong had sailed up the Yangtze to sniff the flavor of "Red Hankow" and report it to the world. On board the steamer from Shanghai, a German who had long resided in Hankow warned her: "There is no place to go in Hankow except the race-course. No theaters and only two 'kinos.' Dull, deadly dull." But for many scribblers of the international Left — another American idealist, Agnes Smedley, was among them — Wuhan was at that moment very nearly the hope of the world.

It was a springtime of hope, but winter was around the corner. The Wuhan government lacked deep roots; part of it was wavering and timid. Militarists were pressing it on all sides. The Nanking regime of Chiang glowered at it from lower down the Yangtze.

"Did you ever see a rabbit before an anaconda," said Borodin one day to Anna Louise Strong, "trembling, knowing it is going to be devoured, yet fascinated? That's the civic power before the military in Wuhan."

Borodin came to realize by the early summer of 1927 that the Wuhan excitement was but an hors d'oeuvre, not the full banquet of revolution. Soon he shut up shop and went back to Moscow. Just before leaving he mused to Miss Strong: "You thought we did a big thing when we made the Revolution in Russia? Well, this Revolution is many times bigger. It is one fourth of all earth's people. It will take long. It will kill more than one Borodin before it is through."

Lean years ensued for Mao, the CCP, and Wuhan. Chinese memoirs tell vivid tales of the dark terror which met Wuhan's left wing from August 1927. The unions were suspended or broken up. Many Communists were shot; some fled the city or the cause. The Party organization went underground, mainly in the French and Japanese concessions.

By mid-September there were only about thirteen hundred members of the CCP in all of Wuhan. A half-cocked insurrection was mounted at the end of the year, but it failed. Success in the city seemed impossible until the peasants were organized for revolution in the surrounding countryside.

Youth in particular kept the Left alive in the days of terror. At Wuhan University Communist students battled against high odds to reorganize. Political activity was forbidden. Spies were omnipresent. Examinations were turned into political interrogations. One exam question at Wuhan University in 1928 read: "Is there, or is there not a conflict between giving in to world tides, and appropriate national feelings?" It was cleverly designed to catch leftists in the net of patriotic sentiment; "world tides" meant Bolshevism.

Anyone who raised a voice against imperialism, in Wuhan during 1928, was stamped on as a subversive and simply liquidated. The militarist authorities proved eloquently that the struggle against imperialism and the struggle for socialism were indeed (as Mao believed) two sides of the same coin.

Schools took on the functions of a police station. All students who were socialists were at one point required to "declare themselves" as such to the authorities by "next Friday." It was an invitation to suicide. A group of Communist students posted this reply: "When Friday passes, there is still Saturday. But only we shall achieve the victory of tomorrow. They [the authorities] have no tomorrow."

It was a courageous response; but also that of a weak group, resigned to a long winter of defiance. The revolutionaries were for the time being a tiny bunch in Wuhan. Inextinguishable hope was about all they had.

The secretary of the Peasant Institute, Hsia Ming-han, fell to a raid on the Left in 1928. Ready for execution, he was asked if he had any final words. He scribbled four lines:

> *What does it matter if you kill me?*
> *Communism is Truth*
> *When you've done with Hsia Ming-han,*
> *There will still be successors.*

One more time before Liberation, Wuhan briefly became the center of the action in China. As the Japanese ate deeper into China, the Nationalist (Kuomintang) government shifted its capital west from Nanking to Hankow. From January until October of 1938, the official government of China ran its pathetic defense against Japan from the tri-cities. Those nine months were another poignant, but also hopeless, moment in the life of Wuhan.

The city at least proved once more its geographic importance. The rivers and railways crisscrossing it were the main pathways by which Nationalist China retreated from Japan's invasion. The bureaus and the files sailed upstream from east China. Chiang Kai-shek took up residence in Wuchang, shifting from house to house when the bombing began, to evade Japanese efforts to blow him up.

So much did the Japanese threat pervade all that the Kuomintang and the CCP were back in tepid association. The Left was aboveground again, in the grim circumstances of war. Chou En-lai lived in Hankow as a liaison man. He wore a Kuomintang uniform and was a leading figure in Chiang's National Military Council.

Chou graced Hankow dinner tables — not excluding those of missionaries — and took a patient, modest line on all issues. "This slender, refined, cultured man," one European correspondent wrote, "with a brilliant mind and a kindly understanding soul, gave us the outlines of China's Communist program for the next fifty years. I can still see his

271

pale, ardent face . . . telling us in his mellow, earnest voice that the first and foremost task was to rid the country of the invader."

At the bar of the Terminus Hotel in Hankow, even the drink list fell in line with the policy of United Front. One day a U.S. military officer, Evans Carlson, returned to the hotel after a talk with General and Mrs. Chiang Kai-shek. He had found them in a state of "icy indifference" about China's real condition. He needed a drink to recover, and asked a lady friend to join him.

Old-fashioneds were ordered. The barman had never heard of this drink — Americans were relative newcomers to Wuhan — so Carlson taught him how to mix it. The cocktail was judged delicious on all sides. Inquired the barman: "Please what name say again?" The lady chipped in to reply evenly: "United Front Cocktail." The barman took note; a new drink was born in wartime Wuhan.

A fatalism hung over the city, which the cheery, optimistic posters on Hankow's walls could not disperse. The government was a shrunken elite, serving special interests rather than China. There were virtually no planes to intercept the Japanese bombers. The concessions in Hankow were the best place to shelter from bombs. But foreign banks, hotels, and firms would not give refuge to natives, only to Europeans. After each raid the city was dotted with mangled Chinese bodies.

Pitiful were the wounded men of the Chinese armies. They staggered in from all over central China, but death was all that awaited most of them. Their situation reminded one eyewitness of that of the Russian wounded in 1812, as Tolstoy gives it in *War and Peace*. Heroic individual Florence Nightingales — including foreigners such as Agnes Smedley — could not change the basic bleakness of the soldiers' fate.

Japanese warships anchored in the Yangtze in October, signal of the end of the resistance. The Italian consul-general greeted the Japanese officers at the Bund and congratulated them on a great victory. As Japanese troops marched through Hankow, beaming White Russian girls gave them cigarettes. For thousands of Chinese, death by execution came as a replacement for death by bombing.

Business at the foreign firms was heavily hit. The racecourse was like a morgue. Japanese occupation put an effective end to Hankow's eight decades as a treaty port.

As for the government of Chiang Kai-shek, it packed its boxes again, and moved yet further upstream to Chungking. But the real political heart of China now throbbed to the north, where the CCP fought Japan and built socialism from its dusty base at Yenan.

A decade later, when Wuhan was liberated in May 1949, it was from north China that the city's new rulers came. A firm new order at last replaced the monarchy that Wuhan had led the way in knocking down in 1911. When the People's Liberation Army entered the streets of Wuchang (ten days before it entered Shanghai), one old man stretched out his hand to a soldier and said: "We have been waiting for you for thirty-eight years."

As for Chiang, it was westward once more, and again to Chungking, that his tubercular regime fled in 1949. Then to Chengtu, then to Canton, then to Hainan Island, finally on December 9 to Taiwan, where he spent twenty-five bitter years until his death in April 1975.

The curiosity at foreigners in Hankow is enormous, yet different from that in Shanghai. Here I am one morning in a cluster of lanes in the old British Concession, near the Central Plain (Zhong-yuan) Cinema. The clock strikes eight and many people are on the way to work.

It is sustained amazement that greets me in these shabby back streets. Hankow folk do not seem to believe that when you have seen one foreigner you have seen them all, or that when you have glanced once at a foreigner you have seen him all.

The curiosity is intense but more distant than at Shanghai. Hankow people are more restrained in a direct relationship, and in that sense more polite. But they are also less relaxed toward the foreigner. Some are so amazed that they fail to smile. People discreetly point you out to one of their friends. A parent and child whisper about the foreigner, and wonder to each other what he is doing in Hankow on a summer morning. The exhortation not to stare at foreigners, to smile instead, and to think of them as "foreign friends," has not yet sunk into the rougher parts of Hankow.

The point, I think, is that Wuhan people are less accustomed to visitors from abroad than are Shanghai people. This lends a bit of distance to their attitude. It explains why they seem more polite (in not jostling or putting their face into yours), yet also a little colder (in not coming straight up to you with a smile) and a shade less discreet (in some of their stunned remarks).

A trace of irritation with foreigners was in the air at Wuhan during 1974. Some German visitors in the spring had a few stones thrown at them. Two Wuhan politicians associated with foreign cultural exchanges, Han Ning-fu and Kung Ching-te, were lambasted in wall posters during the summer. Even Chou En-lai, China's number one host to foreign guests, was obliquely criticized in Wuhan posters. The Wuhan PLA also chose, in May, to mount an exhibition recalling Japanese atrocities — burying people alive, burning houses — in the Wuhan area during 1941.

For my part, not once in Wuhan or anyplace in China has hostility been shown to me. Even when I have probed to the point of intrusion, or obstinately gone off the beaten track, I have never felt a flash of hatred toward me as a white man. No term of abuse, gesture of distaste, angry show of impatience. It is remarkable, given the shadow of the past. Either the Chinese are extremely open-minded, or they are actors who can totally hide their feelings.

I think the first is true. Though China suffered from the West, her people have not stored up grudges. The Westerner in China meets nothing to equal the dislike of Turk for Greek, Jew for Arab, Indian for Pakistani, or a dozen other bitter doses of history's emotional fallout.

If Wuhan people have not been schooled — like those of Peking and Shanghai — to treat the foreigner smoothly as a guest, there are other reasons, too, why you sense a certain raw edge to the Wuhan social scene.

The blunt, loud-swearing Hupei temperament has something to do with it. There is also a current problem of drifting youth. One million Hupei young people (out of a province population of thirty-eight million) have been sent, since 1969, from towns to farms. Quite a number

274

of these — maybe tens of thousands — have slipped back without authorization to Wuhan.

Lacking jobs and correct identity cards, they lead a twilight existence, from the haven of a relative's household. It is not surprising that some of them get into trouble. The Party complains that pornography is raising its head. Young idlers have been found reading "bad books" and singing "bad songs." Underground economic activities — trading in this, sideline production of that — have surfaced, and there have been speculators (called "yellow oxen," *huang niu*). Hard-up youths have approached overseas Chinese visitors with a request for a few yuan. All these deviances bring a ragged note to a society normally tuned to a high pitch.

Wuhan is not Peking, finally, and a distant province is not the center. The events of 1967 proved, to Peking's great shock, that a tide of Wuhan rebelliousness is a potential fact of political life. What happened, in a nutshell, was the following.

The first stage of the Cultural Revolution had been a surge against "capitalist roaders." Chairman Mao's weapon to humble these right-wingers was the Red Guard movement. But in some cities, including Wuhan, the left-wing Red Guards were not as popular as Mao wished or believed. Two forces in Wuhan resisted the young firebrands.

One was made up of military men, headed by the commander of the Wuhan Military Region, Ch'en Tsai-tao. Born and bred a Hupei man, Ch'en had been entrenched as Wuhan's number one soldier for thirteen years. He had no desire to see law and order undermined by a bunch of crusading kids.

The second force was an organization of rank-and-file workers, with the splendid name "One Million Heroic Warriors." These folk from Wuhan Steel and other factories were no more enthusiastic about the Red Guards than was the hard-boiled Commander Ch'en. During the early summer of 1967, Wuhan was tense with struggle between the Left (riding high in Peking), and these two strong, not very leftist forces that reflected local realities.

A great issue all over China at this time was how an intoxicated Left would relate to the solid rock of the military. The Cultural Revolution

Group, Mao's left hand in Peking, was starting to confront this problem. In such an atmosphere, the group sent two emissaries, Wang Li and Hsieh Fu-chih, to iron out the contention in Wuhan.

Wang and Hsieh almost got ironed out themselves. From Peking they brought a message of support for the local Red Guards. These leftists, organized under the apt title "Revolutionary Rebels," had a stronghold in Hankow, at the People's Cultural Park in Sun Yat-sen Road. They felt beleaguered in the face of Ch'en and the "One Million Heroic Warriors." Cried one Red Guard appeal on their behalf: "Wuhan is in critical danger! The Hill of the Tortoise and the Hill of the Snake are roaring. So are the Yangtze and the Han rivers. The tri-city of Wuhan is engulfed in white terror!"

White terror or not, it was enough to put Wang and Hsieh in virtual captivity. Force 8201, a Public Security unit based in Hanyang, arrested Wang, and berated Hsieh to the point where he fled to a college on Vantage Hill. The locals simply would not swallow the pill of "supporting the Left." Chou En-lai himself flew down from Peking to tackle what had become a rebellion by the city of Wuhan.

There was chaos, bloodshed, and alarm in Wuhan. The locals termed it "a disorder of sevens and eights" (*luan qi ba zao*), the Chiese way of saying "at sixes and sevens." So great was the confusion that at one point a mob of "Warriors," seeking to attack Wang at the East Lake Hotel where he was staying, set upon Commander Ch'en by mistake. Ch'en was then observed shouting out: "I am Ch'en Tsai-tao, *not* Wang Li."

On arrival, Premier Chou himself was nearly captured. But he diverted to a second airport when warned, by air force elements loyal to Peking, that Ch'en had sent twenty-eight trucks to nab him at the first. Chou succeeded, as he generally does, but not without the help of five ships of the East Sea Fleet, which steamed up the Yangtze to Wuhan. Wang and Hsieh were prised out of Ch'en's hands, brought back to a warm welcome in Peking. Ch'en himself fell from grace and from power. Wuhan returned for the moment to the fold of national policy.

What did this drama of spears and planes and endless meetings prove? Wuhan showed itself to be a regional power base which Peking cannot trifle with. The city had its own views on the Cultural Revolution. Peking could not snap its fingers and have the tri-cities at its heels. Commander Ch'en had sat astride Snake and Tortoise hills for so long that he imagined he could throw Wuhan's political weight wherever he chose.

The Wuhan incident was the most dramatic of a string of provincial incidents since Liberation which show that China is by no means a tidy chorus. The CCP weighed its words with care, when in 1974 it coined a new phrase about central control. The Party must exercise overall leadership, said the statement issued for the CCP's fifty-third birthday, "whether in the east, west, south, north or center of our country." No one in Wuhan can doubt that this sentence has a special barb of meaning for the tri-cities.

At the same time, the drama of July 1967 proved some rather different things about Wuhan and China. It showed how seriously the Chinese take the matter of what principles the good society should be based on. Not mere power but also issues about the nature of socialism were at stake. And the summer events showed that a pent-up desire for meaningful participation in politics had existed in the breasts of ordinary people. Tens of thousands took to the gallop of factional politics like cats to the pursuit of mice.

The Wuhan incident was also a reminder — if anyone needed it — that Chinese politics works in underground ways as well as through formal channels. How did Peking learn of the mutiny by Commander Ch'en against Wang and Hsieh? No one knows. But word somehow reached the capital almost instantly, which led Chou to speed to the scene.

And the incident, in the end, proved an impressive degree of civilian control over the military in China. Ch'en Tsai-tao did not succeed, for all his guns, in making an independent kingdom out of Wuhan. Nineteen sixty-seven turned out to be, after all, a polar opposite of 1927, when warlordism won the day in Wuhan.

Of damage to property there was little. The pockmarks on the walls cannot compare with the ravage Wuhan knew in its pre-Liberation history. Look around the tri-cities, indeed, and the claim that the CCP has *physically* attacked the past seems odd. The Taiping fighting razed much of Hankow and Hanyang. Fire often took an awful toll. The battles of 1911 did damage in Wuchang. Japanese bombing put paid to many a landmark in all three cities. No physical destruction in Wuhan since Liberation remotely matches these hazards of the century leading up to Liberation.

The CCP, moreover, has restored treasures neglected before 1949. The one, sad casualty I know of since Liberation is the Yellow Crane Tower. This hoary pavilion, first built seventeen hundred years ago, was badly burned early in the present century, but parts of it survived into the 1950s. These were taken down in 1956 to make room for the pillars — on the Snake Hill side — of Wuhan Bridge. A Chinese magazine called *Traveler* noted rather lamely: "The modern age has made the Yellow Crane Tower obsolete. But when people praise the Yangtze Bridge, they will think of Yellow Crane Tower."

Production was interrupted in 1967; senior cadres make no bones about that. Worse, some hundreds of people probably died over the whole period of the struggle.

If the Wuhan incident was a climax, it was also a turning point. In the politics of China, as of all countries, joy in the morning can be followed by bitterness in the evening. In Wuhan, as elsewhere in the nation, the Left crumbled into a factionalism which made Chairman Mao weep in despair. After the summer of 1967, the philosophic lineups of the Cultural Revolution became less clear-cut.

It was not out of character that Wuhan had been the site of a bout of defiance toward Peking. Yet Wuhan made its point, even at its moment of humiliation. It is no accident that, "after Wuhan," the Cultural Revolution came down to earth a bit. Abstract ideas began to count a little less, the sociology of groups a little more.

There were really three successive targets over the whole period of the Cultural Revolution. The "capitalist roaders" were knocked down first. Portions of the Left then became a target for criticism. Though the Red Guards had been a fine spearhead against the "capitalist roaders," some went to excess and had to be curbed. During a visit to China in 1971, I found criticism of "ultraleftism" a major political theme.

But Chairman Mao had for some time been wheeling a third target into place. Though the military did good work in cleaning up excesses

278

of the Left, some soldiers grew too fond of the garments of political power. They went against Mao's iron maxim that "the Party rules the gun, the gun does not rule the Party." Here lay the main point of the Lin Piao affair, which came to a sordid head in the fall of 1971.

The walls of Number Two Cotton Mill are riddled with pockmarks of 1967 rifle shots. Who fired at whom from where? Who was hit and who was unscathed? What motive stirred the finger which closed on the trigger? The passion — and the point — of it all has faded from mind. Events of seven intervening years have rewritten the lines and recast the actors of the 1967 drama.

You do find in Wuhan today a fallout from the Cultural Revolution. But the dust has settled in unexpected ways. The pattern of three successive targets made the outcome complex. Each element won a bit, each element lost a bit. Some "capitalist roaders" were able to slip back into place after a period of reeducation. Even more so, their policies made a modified, discreet return to favor.

The Red Guard Left has not fared very well, but neither has its voice fallen silent. There is a big notice on Tortoise Hill which is jarring in August 1973: "People of the World Unite and Defeat the American Aggressors and All Their Running Dogs." Various left-wing slogans are still around — as are giant statues of Chairman Mao — which in many other cities have been taken down.

In the realm of culture the Tenth Congress of the CCP, in August 1973, led to a small surge of leftism which would have pleased the "Revolutionary Rebels." When meetings are held in Wuhan on art and literature policy, it is lately the leftist Propaganda Department of the Party which convenes them, not the more moderate Culture Department.

As for the military, there is more continuity with the days of Ch'en Tsai-tao than Red Guards of 1967 would find to their taste. Ch'en himself fell from his perch when Premier Chou landed at Wuhan in July 1967. Wuhan has heard many a lecture from Peking on the evil of "independent kingdoms." Yet Ch'en met no fate equal to the gravity of his defiance. After Premier Chou took him up to Peking, Red Guards gave Ch'en a tough grilling. He made a confession. Today he holds a minor post — but not in Hupei.

Wuhan is of course one of China's major military seats. Shanghai, Dairen, and Hangchow lack this status. They are not the headquarters of a "military region" as Wuhan is. There has always been, too, a warrior streak to the view of affairs in Broad Lakes. In this respect the man of Wuhan is poles apart from, say, the more aesthetic Chekiang man. There have been more great battles fought than great poems written at the confluence of the Han and the Yangtze.

Even a casual visitor notices a lot of soldiers and military installations around the tri-cities. Armed PLA men stand at many a gate and door. When a political shot in the arm is called for, it is generally a military group which is sent to the place of need. Are fish ailing in the breeding ponds? The army moves in with special chemicals. Is water short on the plains? Wuhan air force units make artificial rain.

One day at the Central Peasant Institute, I am standing at the gate reading the guideboard when two cars swish to a halt behind me. Out spring a group of PLA personnel. Most of them are in their thirties, and a few are women. They are coming to look over the institute, so far as one can tell, just like the rest of us. But these young professionals hop from their vehicles as if cars were as much an everyday device for them as bicycles are for others. Their step has a zip of authority. They move through the crowd like a knife through butter. The girls — unless my judgment is awry — are highly pleased to be in such company, proud to be seen knocking about in a PLA group. The army seems an "in" job at Wuhan.

When Lord Elgin saw Wuhan for the first time he noted: "Altogether the military display at Wu-chang was more complete and extensive than any thing I had yet seen in China." Were he to return 125 years later he might repeat his remark. A still-strong role for the military in the city's life hints at the persistence of Wuhan in its own ways.

❀ ❀ ❀

If Wuhan University has often known turmoil, no one could blame its location. Few campuses anywhere match this pretty belt of small hills on the banks of East Lake. The upper reaches of the tranquil campus are not unlike the hilly parts of the University of California at Berkeley, but a little less manicured, a little more like a sprawling natural reserve. Wuhan, you realize, does not have the land-space problem of a port city.

Tile roofs peep out from a mass of maples and willows. The new white buildings are tiled in red. The roofs of the older gray ones are sea green. Their shiny tiles sweep down to curved eaves, and are broken at the top by ornamental gables. Seen close up, these baked green tiles are so fat they look like water pipes split in half.

The fortress-shaped library affords an especially fine view of Wuchang (its chief librarian, Huang Tsung-chung, was to visit Harvard a few months after my own visit to his campus). Up a quaint spiral staircase we puff, through reading rooms that hold 1.2 million books, to a lookout on the roof. The octagonal balcony is ringed with totem carvings and huge gargoyles.

From this cool perch, you see Wuchang nestling on a dozen peninsulas, like fingers pushing for respite into the water. East Lake's thirty-five square kilometers lie on three sides, a sapphire rug tossed between the university and the chimneys of Green Mountain to the east. On one bank stands a monument to Ch'ü Yüan, poet and patriot who died in 278 B.C.

Established in 1913 (as Sun Yat-sen University), the school is known for its role in Wuhan's revolutionary dramas. During the May Fourth Movement of 1919, the left-wing honeymoon of 1927, the period of the Anti-Japanese War (when Chou En-lai lectured here) and again in 1947 — when Kuomintang troops shot at student demonstrators, killing three — life at Wuhan University rose and fell with the rhythm of revolution.

Never did the university's life intersect more with that of the city than during the Cultural Revolution. Much of my half-day's talk with three professors hovers as if by magnetic attraction around the events of 1966–1967. An issue lingers to haunt me: who is the class enemy?

There are a lot of fascinating things going on in Wuhan University — one of twenty colleges and tertiary institutes in Wuhan — about which much could be said. The main theme of its work seems to be a quest for high goals that always falls short. This is what three scholars from a certain department convey to me as we walk the grounds

281

and sit in the library sipping tea. Wuhan University keeps on falling short because of "class enemies." This seems a funny idea in a society that smashed all privileged classes years ago. How can it be?

Class enemies have twice since Liberation done major damage to the university's life. In September 1958, Chairman Mao visited the campus and put his stamp of approval on a radical education line. It gave a big role to practical experience. Mao urged that moral and physical growth be given an equal place with intellectual growth. He said students should be shaped into "socialist workingmen." The work of the university ought to be a three-in-one blend of teaching, production, and scientific research.

But this line was not consolidated at Wuhan University during the 1960s. Say the scholars: "The working class did not have leadership in the university for much of that time." Class enemies in the form of "revisionists" ran the place. Education slid back toward bourgeois ways: learning for its own sake; authoritarian teachers; neglect of the world of production; "surprise attack" exams; bias against working-class people in recruitment policy; teaching by the "injection method" instead of the "inspiration method."

It took the Cultural Revolution to rid the campus of revisionism. The Party secretary and the president since 1953 (the famous Li Ta) were hauled down from their perches. Amid the stress the seventy-five-year-old Li Ta died "of twelve diseases," one professor tells me with a smile. But during this storm, anarchism broke out, excesses occurred, and the issues got overlaid. The two real issues were: are the leading cadres good (no); were the 1958 reforms good (yes).

Two factions, Dragon and Tiger, occupied buildings and began physical combat that did no one any good. Few teachers, curiously enough, joined either faction. My informants (who are teachers) say that little of the anarchism was genuine. "These people weren't in favor of no government; they simply wanted government by themselves." Yet few members of either Dragon or Tiger faction were "bad elements."

Class enemies were *using* anarchist disturbance for a right-wing purpose. They "waved the red flag to oppose the red flag." When the university set up its revolutionary committee, in April 1968, the enemies were rolled back, and the campus moved ahead. During the early 1970s, though, backsliding again occurred. Some teachers are alleged to have said: "Tension is needed for exams" and "Exams are to test those who fail to study well on a regular basis." This shows that the class enemies have not laid down their sword once and for all.

It is stressed that nearly all the students meant well. The class enemies have all along been a "small group." But it seems strange, I say, that the Party secretary, President Li Ta, and a few others could have exercised the influence attributed to them. I am wrong in my assumption. These men were not the class enemies. The Party secretary is still to this day on the staff of the university!

Li Ta was no doubt arrogant and a bit conservative. ("In the academic field, I can contend with Chairman Mao," he once boasted. On another occasion he said of one of Mao's famous maxims: "Abstractly speaking, I agree that the east wind prevails over the west wind; concretely speaking, I have my doubts.") For all that, none of my three informants call Li Ta a "class enemy."

Then who were the class enemies? I press for names of people in the university who turned out to be out-and-out followers of Liu Shao-ch'i or of Lin Piao. None are given. One professor volunteers that he himself "carried out the revisionist line" as chairman of his department. He had been required to confess and to mend his ways. But no one judged him a class enemy. He just *carried out* a wrong *line*. Every person who taught in this department before 1966 still teaches there today — except for one man who died.

The class enemies seem to vanish, like a shadow, when you get close to them. My informants finally announce — you could hardly gather it from an account of events — that no class enemies were found in the ranks of the university. All the class enemies came from, or operated from, outside the campus. "Remember that the Cultural Revolution at Wuhan University was part of the Cultural Revolution in the wider society."

What this means, I believe (the three scholars may not agree with me), is that university people fought a battle whose overall logic did not arise from the situation on campus. I am not surprised that no class enemies were uncovered at Wuhan University. Local and campus issues are probably not easy to link up with national and ideological issues.

In the case of Liu Shao-ch'i, and again with Lin Piao, Peking presented the crisis as a class struggle. Wuhan academics thus had no choice but to talk of class enemies. Whether a student who had a novel view of Confucius, or a teacher who favored a greater specialization of studies, were really class enemies is another question. It is indeed not easy to link Lin Piao with Confucius.

The frame of reference is handed down from Peking. Everything has to be fitted into it. This means locals may struggle fiercely over things they do not fully understand. It also means that a decision from the center — changing the frame of reference — can hit the local scene like a thunderclap. Black suddenly becomes white; "left" is overnight turned into "right."

Do the "people rule" in China? They do rule, I think, in many day-to-day ways. But they are like fish in a net when it comes to a major change in line. Maybe Li Ta was not all wrong when he said in 1957: "In Wuhan University a wall and a ditch separate the Party from the masses."

I have exaggerated this rigidity in the Chinese way of politics, yet it is basic in the system. It explains why, when asked for a fact, a local official often replies with a conception; when questioned about an event, he paints ideals. He has to talk in the language of the lofty norm and the larger framework. It is less likely that he will *act* with these big wings of theory clipped to his back.

Of course there have been class enemies in the recent past of the Chinese revolution. Class struggle of a sharpness quite unknown in American experience took place in China. To cast the present as a war against class enemies serves the useful function of keeping alive the lessons of this bitter past, especially for the young.

Time comes to leave the campus and go back into town. The smooth green beauty of the setting helps one step aside, for a while, from Wuhan's daily bustle. It has been for me a worthwhile conversation; also for the three scholars, it seems, for they ask that we meet again tomorrow. Yet as we stroll down a hillside I remain puzzled.

To cast every debate as class struggle creates problems. It takes

284

initiative out of local hands. To declare someone a class enemy is a serious thing; a low-level official cannot presume to do it. It also obscures the fact that local difficulties often arise from structural dilemmas that, in today's socialist China, have little to do with the class cleavages of the past.

A third problem is that willing hands may become weary of campaigns without end; eager minds may grow cynical about convictions that change like the seasons. Chinese leaders, on the other hand, may well feel that to keep the pot of controversy always on the boil is to keep the people always on their toes.

❁ ❁ ❁

It is Wuhan's heavy industry, as well as its middle location and regional spirit, which makes it seem a Chicago of China. The steel plant at Green Mountain east of Wuchang is a city unto itself of 300,000 people. The heavy-machine-tool factory is the largest of its kind in China.

Wuhan as a heavy industry center is a CCP creation. There was less to build upon here than in Dairen, even than in Shanghai. What existed — mainly the Hanyang Iron and Steel Works — was sadly run-down after decades of flux and plunder. Never in its life (since 1907) did the Hanyang plant reach an output of one million tons of steel. And what it did produce — as in the case of nearby Great Smelting (Tayeh) iron ore mines — was mostly exported to Japan.

The decision was reached in the early 1950s to make Wuhan a great steel city. It was based on an assessment of the needs of central China for finished metals and machines. Here was a major step in the CCP's policy of developing the whole of China, not just those coastal fringes which foreigners had developed.

It was not efficient to bring all the steel needed in central China from the Northeast. The nation, too, would soon use far more steel than Anshan alone could make. (China's steel output, it turns out, has risen from well under one million tons in 1949, to more than twenty-five million tons today.) The Wuhan area had the raw materials — iron ore at Great Smelting, coal not far north — to make it a logical extra steel center.

The Korean War had also led China to think hard about the geography of national defense. War mobilization gave a living demonstration of China's vulnerability: heavy industry was bunched in too few spots and these spots were all near China's borders; moving supplies between south and north was slow and costly; the south was weak in the sinews of heavy industry.

So the new leaders in Peking — at once modernizers, nationalists, and shrewd politicians — gave Wuhan a key role in the First Five-year Plan (1953–1957). Among the plan's special projects were the building of Wuhan Bridge, and turning Wuhan into the second steel city of China (Anshan was and is the first; Paotow, in Inner Mongolia, was chosen as the site for a number three steel city).

Today Wuhan is one of the four or five chief pillars of China's industrial power. Back in 1917, an American in Hankow spoke of how the government intended to develop Wuhan:

> There are plans to build a bridge across the Yangtze to Wuchang, and another across the Han to Hanyang; to make roads and boulevards; to fill in low lying swamp lands and provide decent homes for workingmen; to put adequate drainage and wider streets in the native city, burned during the Revolution. A railroad siding is to run through the British Concession, and another through the native city to the wharves. New embankments are to be built, and wharves, and the Government expects to purchase and unify the electric light and water system.

Almost none of these things was done between 1917 and 1949; every single one of them has now been done.

By 1973, Wuhan's total industrial output value is *twenty-seven times* that on the eve of Liberation. Of this output, 55 percent can be considered heavy industry, compared with 5.8 percent before 1949. As well as iron and steel, the triple cities now turn out ships, cars, rolling stock, electrical machinery, machine tools, meters, mining and metallurgical equipment.

Products of which cadres are especially proud — they are tricky, and highly useful to the Wuhan area — include ten-meter vertical lathes, optical curve grinding machines, and 2.8-meter pumps. Cadres also like to stress the care Wuhan gives to meeting the machine needs of agriculture: sprays, double-share plows, hand-guided tractors, diesel engines.

The annual rate of industrial growth can be roughly gauged from figures available at the time of my 1973 visit. During the first five months of 1973, the value of industrial output in Hupei province was 11.2 percent above that for the same period in 1972; by September 1973, it was 16.4 percent above the same nine-month period in 1972.

Green Mountain is no longer that. The grassy surface has given way to brown and gray construction. The hills have simply been moved away. Veteran workers say that the earth scooped up during the building of the steel plant would, if made into a wall one meter wide and one meter high, stretch around the world.

Green Mountain has become an extension of Wuchang. A long road leads out from Snake Hill. After half an hour, you think you have reached the edge of Wuchang. Then all at once the road turns into a new bit of industrial Wuchang, writ large and loud and metallic.

Planning for Green Mountain began in 1952. An agreement with Moscow for technical help was signed in 1953. Twenty thousand men were working at the site by early 1956. The furnaces poured out their first steel in 1958, and Chairman Mao came down from Peking for the occasion. Cooperating with the project were two hundred factories in forty-seven Chinese cities, as well as one hundred factories in Russia. From Anshan alone, two thousand technicians came to help spark China's number two steel center.

All kinds of problems were overcome in the spirit of excitement at a great task. The twenty-five-ton double-bell blast furnace top, made in Shenyang, proved too wide to pass through railway tunnels. The Railways Ministry produced a special wagon to take the monster as far as Dairen. A ship made a specially fast trip — time was of the essence, in the mood of the Great Leap Forward — to carry the furnace top from Dairen to Shanghai. Up the Yangtze it then went to Wuhan as farmers cheered it on its way from the riverbank.

A saying in Wuhan has it that national support for the city came from "four fronts and eight directions" (*si mian ba fang*). The international support is little spoken of now, but it was officially called "selfless" and "crucial" at the time. During his 1958 visit, Chairman Mao remarked to A. I. Podurov, chief Russian technician at the plant: "It is a victory of the cooperation between the Soviet Union and China."

Foreign comment on the enterprise during the mid-1950s was rather skeptical. Yet the results have matched Chinese forecasts, despite more than a few difficulties. And despite a dip in output during what is called in Wuhan the "rip-roaring" climax of the Cultural Revolution.

Wuhan Steel today consists of six mines, four blast furnaces, seven open-hearth furnaces, rolling mills, a sintering plant, coking plants, and a vast factory which makes refractory materials. The company has its own machine-building network, which puts out items like steel rolling machines and monospar cranes (135 tons). Sixty thousand workers are on Wuhan Steel's payroll, 10 percent of them women.

The first blast furnace (1,386 cubic meters; fully automatic; lined with alumina and carbon firebricks) had been scheduled to take two years of work. It was completed in fourteen months. A second (1,436 cubic meters) went up in the astonishing time of 140 days.

After the Cultural Revolution had bubbled down — at its height one blast furnace was totally shut down — two much larger furnaces were added. Number three poured out its first red-hot molten iron in April 1969; it had taken only three months to build. The fourth and latest one, built in four and a half months during 1970, has a capacity equal to the first and second furnaces put together. It has brought Wuhan Steel over its maximum planned capacity target mark.

Total steel output figures are not divulged. But by piecing together iron filings of information in the Chinese papers, and taking into account the rates of increase of output supplied to me, a rough idea of output emerges. Before the Cultural Revolution, the plant's steel output was close to two million tons each year. The figure has doubled since 1965. Wuhan Steel today certainly produces quite a lot more than the 3.5 million tons per year which was the plant's ultimate target capacity (the original target was 1.5 million tons; this was revised upward to 3.5 million tons as success arrived and plans swelled).

Wuhan Steel has long since ceased to be merely a receiver of advice

288

from Anshan, other Chinese cities, and Russia. It is now a major reservoir of experience and expertise, offered to new industrial seed-beds all over China. Wuhan workers used to go north to the Steel College at Anshan for study. Now Wuhan Steel has its own Iron and Steel Institute, to which students come from all of central China and beyond. In line with China's policy of building medium-sized steel plants, in towns of about half a million population, technicians fan out from Wuhan Steel to spur steel production in many provinces. Green Mountain has come a long way in fifteen years.

✿ ✿ ✿

Here is a workshop in the heart of industrial Wuchang. Underneath a lofty roof with skylights, a steady clatter announces the making of vertical lathes. Machines slide and turn, like heavy beasts adjusting position in their den. The gray and green equipment is hung, here and there, with slogans in white characters on red. A big one stares down at me: "China Ought to Make a Greater Contribution to Mankind."

Many banners flourish the phrase "September Fifteen" as an inspirational text. It refers to the date of a 1958 visit to the building by Chairman Mao. I ask if "September Fifteen" is a holiday at the plant. No, it is celebrated by making it the target date for special production drives.

Blackboards around the walls are chalked with targets, and tables of performance by individuals, groups, and the whole workshop. Beside a small railroad that runs out into the sunlight, a large cluster of colored notice boards catch the eye. This is the workshop's "Good Men and Good Deeds Corner" (*hao-ren hao-shi zhuan-lan*). Here the achievements of the few are emblazoned as a spur to the many.

Most of the workers wear floppy shorts and colored singlets. The pace of work is not so stern as to prevent conversations, or the licking of ice-sticks (which are made here in the workshop). Large electric fans make the hot areas less oppressive.

These are glimpses of a workshop at Wuhan Heavy Machine Tool Plant. Of the two hundred major machinery plants in Wuhan, this is the biggest. There are nine thousand workers, 26 percent of them women. It is one of those plants which have been built entirely from scratch since Liberation. Quite a bit of the original equipment came from *dong bei* and Shantung province; the north helped plant the seed of heavy industry in the south.

Construction began in 1956 on a site which used to be a swamp. The first tools were turned out in August 1958, one and a half years ahead of schedule. Wuhan, which could not make a single modern machine tool before Liberation, now boasted China's number one heavy machine tool plant.

Wuhan Heavy is a vast estate of hammering, humming, and organized humanity. Many workshops never close down; three shifts keep them alight twenty-four hours a day. The twenty-six workshops turn out thirty-four kinds of machine tools. Among them are gears; planers, some up to four hundred tons in weight, with worktables up to eight meters in diameter; drilling machines; forge hammers; milling machines; lathes (one vertical lathe, weighing two hundred tons, can process an eighty-ton, 6.3-meter-diameter block to a tolerance of less than 0.03 millimeters).

It is a feature of Wuhan that leading cadres have tended to stay longer in the one job than is usual in China. This has bred traces of two things Peking abhors. One is bureaucratic cockiness by cadres of long tenure. The other is an "independent kingdom" outlook on the part of local power holders who think they, not people remote from the action, know how to run affairs in Wuhan. Such traits lay behind the flurry in Peking-Wuhan relations during 1967.

The issue seeps out from a talk with two leading cadres at Wuhan Heavy. Mr. T'an and Mr. Chang head the General Office of the plant's revolutionary committee. T'an is an old-timer who has made an effective transition to the new society. The face is weather-beaten, foxy in off-guard moments, but the eyes dance with a roguish humor when he smiles. Chang is junior to T'an — they are vice-chairman and chairman of the General Office — and he tends to sit on the edge of his chair while T'an lolls back in his.

Both are sons of Wuhan: square features, solid frames, manners that never put their manliness in doubt. Both are dressed like messenger boys. It is not exterior dignity but power that they exude. They could as much be mistaken for U.S. industrial executives as Huckleberry Finn could be for a bishop.

T'an and Chang breezily speak of themselves and their colleagues on the revolutionary committee as "directors" (*zhu-ren*). It is a term which was frowned upon during the Cultural Revolution. These days, "responsible persons" (*fu-ze-ren*) is the more acceptable term for a unit's top people (or "leaders," *zhang*). But T'an and Chang seem to have come to think of themselves as natural leaders at Wuhan Heavy. No doubt the Party secretary has too — he has been in this top spot for fifteen years. All three men were once ordinary workers, but a long time ago.

You get the impression that "To Rebel Is Justified" would not be considered a suitable slogan at Wuhan Heavy. An ultraleftist tide of spontaneity did sweep the plant during the Cultural Revolution. Red Guards came here and "made revolution." Mr. T'an points out gently that the youths made nothing else. "There was some interruption of production," confesses Mr. Chang with a frown, "and quite a lot of influence within the factory." Some members of the plant were stirred up, in turn, to go out into Wuhan and make revolution. They neglected their duties in the process.

These tough, engaging factory "directors" concede that backsliding had occurred before the Cultural Revolution. There was too much managerialism in the plant. Material incentives (*wu-zhi ci-ji*) were getting out of hand. An unhealthy tendency had arisen to copy the design of foreign machine tools.

Chang points out that the plant has done better since 1970 than before 1965. Output in value terms was 20 percent higher in 1971 than in 1970; 10 percent higher in 1972 than in 1971. Yet T'an and Chang dwell as much on the excesses that arose in the effort to correct the pre-1966 backsliding as they do on the backsliding itself.

They are not proud of the production figures between 1966 and 1970. In those four years the value of output went up only 20 percent (a percentage increase equal to that achieved in the *single year* following stabilization — 1970–1971). Mr. T'an is deft in summing up the effect of the Red Guards on the plant: "From the present point of

view" — he is speaking on the eve of the Tenth Congress of the CCP
— "it was a help to production. But in fact we have to say there was
some influence upon production."

It's no surprise that there are still seven PLA men on the forty-eight-
person revolutionary committee of the plant. These soldiers were
brought in to quell the disorder of left-wing factionalism. They sym-
bolize firm command and opposition to red-hot spontaneity.

No surprise, either, that Wuhan Heavy is less than frantic about
the problem of pollution. I raise with Mr. T'an the question of "waste."
But he interprets it simply as a question about what to do with faulty
products, and how to resmelt faulty products that can be salvaged.
The effect on Wuhan's environment of the plant's smoke and gas and
slag does not stir T'an much. The drive for more output is the thing;
everything else is a bagatelle.

All this is in line with the generally practical mood of Wuhan industrial circles. The Hupei CCP committee recently held an interesting
telephone conference on industry. The published conclusions are un-
mistakably in harmony with the output-minded impulses of Mr. T'an
and Mr. Chang.

"We must persist in making revolution in our spare time and thrift-
ily." No doubt about the emphasis there. "We must resolutely stay at
our work posts, and strictly observe labor discipline." That is what
the Red Guards did not do. "We must have a powerful production
command system." A revealing badge, this, of Wuhan's no-nonsense
organizational approach to giving China the steel and machines it
needs.

When the Hupei trade unions revived in 1973, the mood was also
one of noses to the grindstone of production. A keynote speech at the
congress in June was given by Tseng Ssu-yu, at that time top soldier
and politician in Hupei (successor to Ch'en Tsai-tao). Tseng appeared
to bring full circle the change of line since 1965.

He confided to the trade unionists that the "leftism" of types like
Lin Piao — when viewed with the inner eye of true political judgment
— was really "ultrarightism." He brought up the famous Cultural Revolution slogan about rebellion being justified, blithely adjusted it to
read: "It is justified to rebel against the reactionaries."

A "Glory Board" at Wuhan Heavy, honoring those who
have done well in an emulation drive; photos of outstanding performers and names (lower) of meritorious
performers

Thus did Tseng shrivel the idea of rebelling into an establishment
idea that no one, not even Mr. T'an and Mr. Chang, need find risky.
A rebel can quickly be reined in, after all, by showing that those he
assails are really not reactionary.

The free-for-all of the Cultural Revolution did, nevertheless, bring
a notable reform to Wuhan Heavy. Before 1965, workers who did well
got a bonus. This could amount to 12 or 15 yuan, in a factory where
60 yuan per month is the average wage (highest is 108 yuan, lowest
32 yuan). The bonus system was lopped off, like many an outcrop of
privilege and inequality, during the storm of 1966–1968.

In its place is the less money-oriented idea of "emulation." Set up
in early 1973, the emulation scheme is designed to spur workers to
extra effort. The Chinese term for it (*jing-sai*) can mean "competition,"
but Mr. T'an and Mr. Chang put the stress on emulation. The aim is
to match the best ideal, rather than to beat your brother.

The scheme works this way. A blackboard in each workshop records the production record and special feats of every worker and
small group of workers. At intervals of three months the record is

293

reviewed. Star performers are rewarded in ways that border on the material. "It is mainly a political honor," says Mr. Chang, "for a worker to head the emulation list." But he also receives goods, such as pens, technical books, notebooks, and colored shirts.

❀ ❀ ❀

The life of the workers at Wuhan Heavy is secure. By American standards it seems an unpressured life; also an unvaried one. Working hours are slightly longer than in Western factories. There is no paid annual holiday, but leave of absence is possible.

Leave with pay is granted automatically on presentation of a certificate of ill health from the plant's hospital (beyond six months, pay is 80 percent). It is also generally available to a worker who wants to visit sick out-of-town members of his family. In these cases the plant pays the train or bus or boat fare. A much less frequent leave of absence is given for "private affairs" (si-shi). This is without pay and may be for any duration.

The plant has built housing for its nine thousand workers, in the form of 120 apartment blocks which are several stories high and identical in design. Rent is a derisory two yuan or so per family — one yuan per eighteen square meters — furniture is at factory expense. Quarters for single people are available at forty fen per month.

Wuhan is not as advanced as Peking and Shanghai when it comes to facilities in its new apartments. Heating in the kitchens, for instance, is not by gas but by coal. On the other hand, apartments are often a little roomier than in an equivalent Shanghai suburb.

A family has few major expenses between food, on one side, and major luxury items, like a transistor radio, on the other. The plant pays all doctor's bills of its workers, and half those of their family members. Medicines have to be paid for by the individual. But most of them are cheap and all of them are getting cheaper. The plant bears most of the cost of education.

It is striking how many workers have fat savings accounts. Hupei avidly encourages these; Wuhan alone has 120 savings bank branches. Average wage at Wuhan Heavy is sixty yuan. Most wives work and earn nearly as much as their husbands. It is a rare family that does not have several hundred yuan in the bank. Interest just now is 3.3 percent (not long ago it was 3.7 percent). In the province as a whole, savings during 1973 are up 73 percent on savings during 1966 — and there's no inflation in China.

As bank savings grow, the size of families shrinks. A talk about this with T'an and Chang brings the point home vividly. Mr. T'an happens to have six children. He tinges pink with embarrassment as we discuss the importance of reducing the size of the family. "I was married in the old society," he explains, "and could not help being influenced by its customs."

Family planning efforts began in earnest at the end of the 1950s, but they lapsed during the Cultural Revolution. "No one was in charge of birth control work," shrugs Mr. Chang. "There was anarchist influence. Things were left to slide. The birthrate reached fifteen per thousand." Here is one more grievance the directors have against Red Guards.

Today the revolutionary committee has a vice-president whose sole responsibility is family planning work. The pill is the key weapon in the battle against big families; barefoot doctors give it out free to married women. The birthrate in the plant's community has fallen to seven per thousand. Mr. Chang considers this a reasonable rate, and the plant has not so far set a lower target figure.

It is moving to see how reading and writing have advanced over the years. An index is the fate of the illiteracy classes, called "Sweep Away Blindness Classes" (*sao mang ban*). When the plant was founded in 1958, illiteracy was still common. A big educational effort was set in motion. But some years ago the Sweep Away Blindness Classes ceased. Virtually all workers — their average age is thirty-five years — can now read and write. Mr. T'an himself was one of those who were unable to do so at Liberation, but his blindness has been swept away.

Chatting with T'an and Chang, and gazing at the Good Men and Good Deeds Corner, I ponder the ironic twists of the Soviet role at Wuhan.

Russians were heroes to Hankow workers in 1927. Books published in Wuhan as recently as the 1950s are unfailingly respectful to the USSR. Whenever pre-1917 Russian imperialist activity in Wuhan was written about, the word "Tsarist" was always put in brackets after "Russian," to make crystal clear that China considered 1917 a dividing line between night and day.

Yet these days it is with tight-lipped bitterness that Wuhan officials comment on the Soviet role. Absent altogether is the trembling sense of hope with which Wuhan looked up to the Soviet revolution in Borodin's day, and even in the 1950s.

As for the word "imperialism," the wheel has turned full circle. "Tsarist" is no longer put in brackets in texts about old Russia. The Russian past does not seem so different from the Soviet present — at least when it comes to bullying China. Wuhan officials explicitly call the new Russia "more Tsarist than the Tsars." It is even labeled "fascist," which must mildly shock old-timers in Hankow who stood with Russians in a progressive phalanx against the Axis Powers.

The impact at Wuhan Heavy of Russian technical withdrawal in 1960 cannot have been drastic. The forty technicians at the plant left suddenly in October, taking their plans and papers with them. But the work they had come to do was basically completed. Their contract provided only for a stay until December 1960. A mere three months of their professional help was lost.

Mr. Chang digs out from his memory many grievances over money dealings. All equipment and materials which came to Wuhan Heavy from the USSR were paid for. According to Chang, the Chinese side paid 15 to 20 percent above international market prices for what they got.

I cannot check this startling claim, nor obtain an itemized list of what Russian goods the plant bought. Wuhan Heavy paid more than six million yuan for materials from the USSR, not a trifling sum, but no doubt a small fraction of the total cost of the plant.

Those who worked alongside Soviet technicians speak with flashes of warmth about personal ties. One senior man fondly recalls his former colleagues from Moscow and Leningrad. The Soviet people were not to blame, he explains, for letting China down; only Khrushchev and his ruling clique. The same senior figure claims that many Russians who suddenly left Wuhan in 1960 were as unhappy about Moscow's decision as the Chinese were. Some even wept openly at the farewell banquets.

Twenty years later, it seems surprising that Wuhan got as involved as it did with Soviet aid in the 1950s. It is not that the Chinese could easily have done without Russian equipment. But the Chinese took not only machines from Moscow. They also drank deep at the fountain of Moscow's philosophy of socialist construction.

Here is the translation of a poem, entitled "Electric Shovel," written by a Wuhan worker during the 1950s:

> *She comes from the Urals, my electric shovel.*
> *Huge, rough and full of passion,*
> *With a roar like a hundred lions together,*
> *She bites into mountains and spits out ore.*
>
> *When she brandishes her steel-muscled arm,*
> *Mountain peaks slice off like bean curd,*
> *And crumbling rocks from a thousand feet up*
> *Pour down in a swooping cataract.*
>
> *Gnashing her steel teeth against perpendicular cliffs,*
> *She breathes out mouthfuls of sparks.*
> *But when the rust-colored ore is laid bare*
> *She cradles it gently, piece by piece.*
>
> *Into the waiting freight car tips the ore*
> *And is sped far away to the shriek of the whistle.*
> *— Then, with a laugh like the roll of springtime thunder*
> *She lifts her giant arm with renewed vigor and joy.*

Today in Wuhan's industry, the spirit is not the same as in that eager poem. No one salutes the Urals. It is rare for anyone to personify a machine — almost to worship it — like the miner who wrote "Electric Shovel." The tone is less brash now, more sober by far. The crude march of technique has somehow been softened by the high priority put on bonds between people. Slicing hills like bean curd is fine; but by what light are men to live with each other?

If the Chinese awe for Soviet ways in the 1950s seems remarkable, it is because the Chinese have since 1960 departed so enthusiastically from Moscow's heavy-footed, monumentalist way of industrialization.

It is common in Wuhan to hear someone criticized for "thinking too much of machines" and "failing to see that men play the decisive role." The factory's duty to serve the farm is always stressed. Wuhan workers have a feel for this duty, since many of them used to be peasants (80 percent of the original workers at Wuhan Steel were recruited from farms).

Mr. T'an and Mr. Chang may have a gleam in the eye about production, but they are a long way from making the machine an end in itself. They do not equate socialism with mere industrialization. In these and other respects Wuhan has returned to itself after a season of whoring after false gods.

Here is a steel cadre talking about the spirit of a production drive. "We have a plan to involve people in efforts for still bigger victories," he explains. "Our idea is that if the production time for one ingot can be reduced by one second, we will turn out one extra ingot per hour." This plan is put into action in a rolling mill.

It is calculated that over a certain period the workshop has seven thousand man-hours at its disposal. The mill goes into a huddle of small groups. Will is generated. Stratagems are devised. Obstacles are tapped and weighed from every angle. During the specified period, seven thousand minutes are plucked from the clutches of Father Time. More than six thousand extra ingots leave the rolling mill, to be made into plows and harvesters for agriculture.

Such a scheme can be viewed in different ways. It can seem a pathetic effort to make gold out of straw. It can seem a shrewd harnessing of human zeal. At any rate it is the Chinese way.

One evening after my day at Wuhan Heavy two local officials invite me to dinner at a Hankow hotel. Mr. Li is from Peking, but now serves as Hupei's chief foreign affairs officer. He has the silky touch of a Chinese man of ideas. But he is not so much of an intellectual that a political streak is not also evident. At the Foreign Ministry in Peking he had a spot of bother during the Cultural Revolution — maybe that's why he's now in Wuhan.

Mr. Yüan, born and bred in Wuhan, is head of the local office of China Travel Service. He is a beefy man who moves about with the can-do spirit of an administrator. He puts on no airs. If he says something, he has checked it out with a man above him.

We defy the evening heat and tackle a parade of Hupei dishes. There is "Wuchang fish," a tasty kind of bream, and tortoise soup, king of Hupei's many soups. There is the famous but overrated *dou-pi,* a heavy soybean omelet which Wuhan people like. Not to speak of finely sliced chicken's stomach, sugared walnuts, and seaweed in many hues. Nor to forget some vivid eggs which are preserved but taste as if they were not.

In the face of the more intestinal dishes, I feel a bit as Lord Elgin felt at the table of the governor-general in Wuchang: "A great variety of hot dishes made their appearance in rapid succession, generally somewhat greasy in their nature, but occasionally very palatable to persons of a confiding temperament, and who did not care minutely to investigate the materials of which these various entrees were composed."

Faces a little flushed, sleeves rolled up, elbows leaning on the spattered tablecloth, we talk of trends in Wuhan. "You are from the West," begins Mr. Li. "You come to China and find us still on the upward path of development." He is being a bit defensive; there is a basic point he wants to get across. "We know you are very interested in wage levels, and concrete facts about the lives of people in Wuhan." Mr. Yüan is nodding and smiling faintly; he has borne the brunt of my endless probing.

"Without doubt you find the wages very low, the apartments very simple." If there is a slight discomfort in Mr. Li's expression, he does not let it linger. "But remember what it is we are trying to do in China. It is a giant task, and a long-term one." Li and Yüan have both grown earnest.

One an intellectual from the north, one an earthy veteran of the area, they share what seems a moment of pain and pride. They have a foreigner on their hands; they must reflect Wuhan for him as best they can. The two of them seem gripped by an identical and sincere emotion.

"In China we are developing the country in a way that ensures all of the people will advance together." Mr. Li lists a number of short-comings and unresolved points about development policy. The relation between industry and agriculture is not always an easy one. Hupei must do more to develop the Chianghan plain, and the hilly areas in the west of the province. Mr. Yüan chips in to say that, yes, there are more industrial accidents in Wuhan factories than there should be.

But it is fundamental, the two of them insist, that the welfare of the whole Chinese people, not merely of one section, is the basis of all policy-making. "We do not let one sector — say heavy industry — get far ahead of another sector — say agriculture. That would not be wise politically, and it would not be socialist."

Mr. Li says there is a second fundamental point. "We are putting first things first. China has an order of priorities which does not allow frills to squeeze out basics." Both men set out to sum up what things count most for the ordinary family. They speak quietly but with authority. They broach housing, health, education, and the price of daily goods.

"At Liberation Wuhan had twelve million square meters of housing. Since 1965, we have built ten million square meters of new housing — almost as much as existed when we took over." This has taken a lot of capital, materials, and time. Yet it is indispensable to the new deal the people expect under socialism.

"Consider a worker in Wuhan who needs delicate medical care," Mr. Li continues, "for instance, a brain operation. Today a brain operation costs about fifteen yuan — even a difficult one. It is beyond no one's reach. And even the fifteen yuan will almost certainly be paid by some unit. For ninety percent of the people are covered by a scheme of medical payment."

Mr. Yüan warms to the matter of prices. "No anxiety arises from prices which spiral, or change up and down rapidly. Our Chinese

300

currency is as stable as any in the world — and this in a country where money used to become almost worthless overnight." Mr. Li lit yet one more cigarette and gave some examples.

Within a few months after Liberation, rice had settled at a price of eleven fen per catty (one-half kilogram). "Go out into the street tomorrow morning and see — it is eleven fen per catty today." Medicines are 80 percent cheaper now than in 1949. "We bring down the prices of goods that we learn to produce quicker and better. Medicines are basic; a special effort has been made to reduce their price."

"As for education," adds Li, "you have seen from your talks with people in their homes what a big role it plays. It is open to families who never had a chance of education in the old days. In Wuhan today, out of a population of 2.7 million, no less than 700,000 persons are full-time pupils or students. There are two hundred middle schools, and eight hundred primary schools."

The defensive tone has gone from Mr. Li's voice. Both he and Mr. Yüan seem to sense that I am persuaded of their two basic points. Wuhan's policies are planned to meet the welfare of the vast majority of the people. Fundamental tasks are being tackled first; frills will come later.

Over one last cup of tea I look across at the hot, tired faces of the two cadres. They view the present in terms of a past which they know. That past lends to what might be an austere present an almost intoxicating satisfaction. And they view the present as a step toward a planned future.

They have a memory, then, and also a hope. These twin shafts of the mind transform the present from a point in time to a heartfelt struggle. As a man from the West I cannot expect to understand Wuhan today unless — by moments of communication with Chinese at a dinner like this — I feel the power of memory and hope upon their present.

We stroll out into the sultry Hankow night. I am thinking about the ardent stories of Chairman Mao's visit to Wuhan Heavy in 1958. How can the visit mean so much to the plant's workers? Maybe it is this way. Mao Tse-tung has crystallized for the Chinese people a brilliant myth about their recent national experience.

He conquered the past, by analyzing it correctly; then by striking a decisive political blow against it. *He built a bridge to the future,* by achieving an analysis of the past which had within it the shape of future socialism; then by placing the dream of a modern China within the politics of a mobilized people led by the CCP.

Mr. Li and Mr. Yüan smile as they watch me gazing into space. As we say good-night Li says I must come back and see Wuhan again in five years.

☼ ☼ ☼

Two hundred years ago the German sage Leibniz marveled at the "achievement of public tranquility and the establishment of social order" in Cathay. It was less the writ of Peking that caused it, than the ingenious modes of people who had learned to live outside, even despite, the state. All through China's history, in fact, the individual has been shaped as much by informal social webs as by the formal laws of the state.

That the CCP has reined in the lurching anarchy of Chinese society is a striking fact about China today. The elemental force which is the Chinese people has very seldom been so tamed. That a raw edge should be glimpsed now and then in Wuhan is hardly to be wondered at. The leaf on the ground serves only to magnify the massed foliage overhead.

When they became masters of Wuhan in May 1949, the Communists took the city's people on a double dance of seduction and pressure. To secure CCP rule, the cadres adopted organizational methods which have changed little over the intervening twenty-five years. Consider their business policy.

In that ever-moving winter of 1949–1950, the Communist cadres put a noose around the neck of old Wuhan's economy. The long-term aim was the murder of capitalism, though short-term policy bent over backward in its flexibility.

Commerce was taxed much more heavily than industry. This proved to be a first step toward a total transformation of Wuhan's commerce. A newspaper reader was told, in answer to his query, that a tax on property titles (*shui-qi*) was designed "to protect private ownership . . .

and the freedom of buying and selling." He was not told that such an aim was only for a day.

The economic situation was complex in the extreme. Inflation soared. Some Kuomintang elements went in for sabotage. Business uncertainty hung in the air like smog. Few firms had detailed and accurate accounts of their affairs (in nineteen trades which cadres investigated carefully, 77 percent of the firms had falsified accounts). Fighting had damaged the dikes along the Yangtze — a major source of concern.

With its left hand the CCP swiped hard at big capitalists and Kuomintang people. With its right hand it coaxed the smaller fry into a posture of cooperation. The effort to tax hawkers is an interesting case.

Fear gripped the hawkers when the Hawker Tax Law was announced in January 1950. They used a hundred means to escape the new tax. The Tax Bureau decided to hold a meeting with hawkers representing all the main markets and streets of Wuhan.

Cadres explained to the skeptical hawkers that the purpose of the tax was to protect the "regular hawker." Every bit of tax collected was to be used for the benefit of the people of Wuhan. Hawkers whose trade cannot easily be established in a set place (e.g., hot snacks) were to be protected. But hawkers whose trade competes with regular stores (e.g., clothing) were to be cut back. Individual craftsmen (e.g., those who repair boots or grind knives) would face no tax at all. Hawkers at fixed markets would be taxed lightly. Wandering ("floating") hawkers who cause traffic congestion would be taxed less lightly. These were subtle and just policies, based on careful investigation.

The cadres got as many hawkers as possible to tax themselves. Leading hawkers were encouraged to set up small groups, hold meetings, fix on tax rates, and pay the bank voluntarily. It was a shrewd move, though there were problems. Some hawkers delayed out of suspicion. A few vanished in order to think out their position. Many did not know what the word "democracy" meant when they were urged to join in sessions of "democratic discussion."

Yet progress was steady. Of Wuhan's forty-eight thousand hawkers, fifteen thousand had paid some tax by the end of February 1950. Two thousand had qualified for exemption from tax; four thousand had put in an application for exemption. Eight hundred had decided to seek a different job. Another eight hundred had been found eligible to pay a tax other than a hawkers' tax. Some twenty-six thousand foot-dragging hawkers had still avoided the cadres' net at the end of February.

During those early months the Communists were very frank about problems. A lot of cadres were newcomers to Wuhan. Locals did not always take kindly to authority in the form of recent arrivals from other cities. Even months after Liberation there was much stealing, sabotage, and false reporting.

The caretaker staff at the Wuhan branch of the Central China Department Store proved as unreliable as cats among pigeons. They altered the amounts of checks; they stole fabrics and toothpaste; they ate into a large reserve fund that no one knew existed. The value of the resources ripped off by the caretakers would "maintain a hundred cadres for a whole year." The leadership of the company were ticked off for carelessness, "numbness," and failure to properly educate the caretakers.

The CCP used public opinion as a scalpel. A vivid letter to the editor of *Yangtze River Daily* confessed corruption. The writer was a long-time city official. He had taken bribes of pork, flour, oil, wine, and cigarettes from citizens who sought a favor, especially at holiday times. The old society, he explained, still had him under its spell. The humbled official had begun "thought reform" and vowed to turn over a new leaf.

Here is a report of an arsonist in Hankow. Not keen on the new economic policies, he decided to make havoc and at the same time win praise for himself. He started fires at six factories, then tried to put them out, alarming others as he did so in an attempt to gain credit for his bravery. Only evil minds like this, the report suggested, would pit themselves against the new order.

Each trade held a "self-report public-discuss" session. These created a slow tidal wave of cooperation, if only because they made noncooperation hard and embarrassing. To gain support for tax policy, cadres held a meeting in each street. Called an "evaluation committee" (*ping yi wei-yuan-hui*), this session played upon the public like a masseur's fingers on a stiff body.

Officials were not exempt from pain by public exposure. A branch police station in Hanyang was criticized for a passive attitude when initiative was called for. Told about a lost child, the branch adopted the attitude "if we see him we'll give him back," and failed to alert neighboring branch stations to the child's disappearance.

A delinquent policeman left his post without leave; his mind wandered during study groups; he played around with two women — the first one of whom became insane when she found him in the arms of the second. The newspaper, noting that this cop was a former Kuomintang soldier, reported that he had made an apology, but was still some distance off from true reform.

A letter to *Yangtze River Daily* confessed to a burst of anger unfit for the new epoch. The writer is a cart puller. One day he saw a quarrel near the Gate of Great Wisdom. Two cadres were arguing with another cart puller about the just price for rental of the cart. The letter writer took the side of his fellow puller. He strode to the scene and slapped one cadre in the face. The aggressive fellow was brought to face "examination discussion meetings" (*jian-tao-hui*). At the second session he confessed that he had done wrong. He had made the mistake of looking at the two cadres "as if they were Kuomintang officials of the bad old days."

Sometimes cadres had to rein in the impulses of citizens who wanted to snatch an excess of freedom from the days of transition. A man from a college writes to *Yangtze River Daily* about divorce. Many of his colleagues had had an "arranged" marriage in previous years. These marriages seemed out of line with new social policy. A number of the men wanted an immediate divorce. Some even said they refused to join in the revolution until their old wives were taken from them.

The paper had a cautious response to this letter. Every person must join the revolution unconditionally; otherwise he is putting selfish interests above public interests. Backward girls can be transformed by joining in the new society. Meanwhile, their frugal, industrious ways are better in some respects than the ways of male intellectuals.

And the college men ought to recall that PLA soldiers are still fighting in parts of China, and many of them have had to delay getting married at all.

PLA soldiers had taken over a city that was not used to them. Ties between army and people had to be nursed with care. The CCP used the pages of *Yangtze River Daily* to depict the policy of an army that "serves the people."

Here is a fire in Wuhan Match Factory. The fire occurred on the staff's day off; no one saw it break out. But some PLA men rushed to the scene, the article reports, and salvaged a lot of equipment. One soldier had his cap burned off, but even after that he managed to unscrew three light bulbs and carry them off. "Only among class brothers," the article observed, "is this sort of rescue work possible."

Letters to the editor of *Yangtze River Daily* held a mirror to the conduct of the PLA. A truck driver was on the way to Sandy City with a load of goods in a heavy rainstorm. His vehicle broke down, but a PLA man appeared and managed to repair the truck. The driver invited the soldier home for dinner as a gesture of thanks. The latter replied: "This help to you is my duty; I will not accept any gift."

For a show to amuse the people at Chinese New Year in 1950, a soldier borrowed a special colored shawl from a merchant at the Gate of Faithful Piety. There happened to be a gold ring in the pocket of the shawl. The PLA man pointed this out to the merchant when he brought back the shawl. The merchant was struck by this behavior; he wrote a letter marveling that the soldier did not try to make off with the ring.

On New Year's night, workers from the Hanyang Brick and Tile Factory were invited to a soiree at which a Hanyang PLA unit performed skits. There was a dinner for dependents of PLA men, with wine, soybean curds (made by the soldiers), and a three-hundred-catty pig. The next day the army men repaired roads in the neighborhood. Soldiers were taught local Wuhan customs which, as out-of-towners, they might neglect to observe — no borrowing during New Year, remembering at that time to "speak auspicious words" to the people.

Yangtze River Daily suggested ways for Wuhan people to return the kind feelings of the PLA. Soldiers were still battling in other parts of China; why not send donations to them? To express their warm affection, thousands of Wuhan folk sent money, socks, soap, pencils, and (of course) tea mugs and cigarettes. Instant poems were written on the gifts, to make them personal. Here is a translation of four lines on the wrapping of a bar of soap:

> *Square and square this aromatic soap,*
> *Soldiers, wash your face and keep fit!*
> *The more you attend to hygiene,*
> *The harder the Chiang bandits you can hit*

Across a box of "Invincible" tooth powder:

> *A box of tooth powder, for fighters at the front to use,*
> *The gift is small, but our affection is huge*

Twenty-five years later, the CCP's organizational methods are not very different. Long- and short-term aims are still furtively juggled. Great pains are taken, as always, to mobilize public opinion behind every policy. Though many 1970s cadres are out-of-towners, Wuhan's special traits are handled with fair sensitivity.

Yet the changes are also interesting, as I find during a day at Red and Brilliant (Hong yan), a residents' area in Hankow's River Shore district. Its 2,252 people make up one of twenty residents' areas in a neighborhood called Ball Park (Qiu-chang). Most of them are working-class.

Along one side of Red and Brilliant runs Hankow's broadest boulevard. Liberation Road is so wide and empty of motor traffic that you think Hankow must have a transportation strike. But traffic policemen gravely direct a trickle of red buses, green trolleys, and military vehicles. Under white umbrellas they stand on islands marked by curved barriers, like parentheses, on which is written: "Pay Attention to Safety." Low brick fences, each section bearing a giant Chinese character, fringe the boulevard's ten-meter sidewalks.

Within the crowded blocks of Red and Brilliant, you see the post-Liberation growth of Hankow expressed in the varieties of housing. There are one-story homes with red tiles, iron-bar windows, and uneven floors, built sixty to eighty years ago. At Liberation these were virtually the only type of house in Red and Brilliant. But most of today's 585 families live in two other types.

There are four-storied blocks with flat roofs, many of them built during the 1960s. In these gray concrete oblongs, three households share one kitchen and toilet. A third batch of apartments consists of very new high-rises on Liberation Road, some still in the bamboo braces of construction. Having three generations of homes gives a dynamic look to Red and Brilliant.

These newest homes are done in a semi-Chinese style. Balconies and the wide windows are latticed with a traditional touch. The airy apartments command a fine view over the greenery of Liberation Park, once the *taipan*'s golf course. A similar green oasis is seen enclosing the Second Hospital, attached to Wuhan Medical College, once the Hankow racecourse.

At one block of the "middle generation" I go upstairs to visit households at random. The building is more shabby than you would expect after a decade of use. The stairwell is poky, and not very clean. Mrs. Yao welcomes me warmly, but I do not stay long. Mr. Yao is home today, unwell with high blood pressure, and needs quietness.

Knocking on another door, I meet a lady who seems to be mentally disturbed. She does not answer my questions. Grinning too broadly, she says nothing but points to a framed montage of forty-odd Mao badges on her bedroom wall.

In a third apartment, a lady bank clerk is cleaning up in the kitchen. It is Mrs. Chi's rest day from work, where she earns fifty yuan per month. Her husband earns sixty yuan at the docks. The two of them together save two hundred yuan a year. Mrs. Chi's mother lives here too, and she loves to chat with the sweating foreigner.

As we sit fanning ourselves I notice something unusual on the living-room wall: a Catholic church calendar, of the year 1967, with a colored photo of San Salvatore! No one in the household, however, attends a Christian church. I ask Mrs. Chi's mother if her daughter

Having three generations of homes gives a dynamic look
to Red and Brilliant neighborhood

belongs to the Communist Party. Yes, and her husband too. And what about the old lady herself? She gives me an engaging reply: "No, I'm not a Communist, I'm a grandmother" (*po-po*).

Grandmother tells me how different things are today compared with thirty or forty years ago. She rises, turns on a tap, and beams: "Before Liberation, we had to walk one li [about one-half kilometer] from the house to get drinking water." People used to refer in those days, she recalls, to the "three manys" — fire, unemployment, death by infectious disease — and to the "three fears" — rainstorms, taxes, officials.

By now an officer of the seven-person residents' committee has joined me in the Chi household. Mrs. Yeh is plain, dumpy, energetic. She adds a story or two about Red and Brilliant in the bad old days. A single landlord called Liu Wan-shun owned almost the whole area. It was a slum. Those who were lucky enough to work were porters, small street sellers, riksha men. Mrs. Yeh recalls two sayings which summed up the bad physical conditions: "Rain falls — the ground is like an ink pot"; "Winds blow — the air is fouled as if from an incense burner."

Mrs. Chi's daughter bursts in, mouth wide open at the sight of a Western man in her house. She is a middle-school student, one of 330 among Red and Brilliant's population of 2,252. Mrs. Yeh chips in to say that the residents' area also has six college students and four hundred primary-school children. More than one-third, then, of Red and Brilliant people are full-time students.

I ask the daughter about political classes in the residents' area. They are held three evenings a week, in two-hour sessions, but Miss Chi does not go to them. The two hundred people who do attend are, I gather, mostly older folk. Minds with long memories are more likely to be encrusted with the barnacles of capitalist ideas, Mrs. Yeh thinks, than the minds of post-1949 young people. Miss Chi herself likes to spend the evenings reading, sewing, or going to the cinema.

I cannot help thinking that electricity has made a revolution in the lives of Mrs. Chi and her neighbors. She uses it for a dozen things, including a fan. Later that evening, seeing how brightly lit the apartment block is, I recall a famous British account of Hankow at the turn of the century. "Chinese rooms are inconceivably dark," wrote Mrs. Bird Bishop in *The Yangtze Valley and Beyond*, "and smoking, sleeping, and gambling [are] the only possible modes of getting rid of the long winter evenings among the poorer classes. . . ."

I also marvel at the vitality of the children, when Mrs. Yeh takes me to a downstairs kindergarten. Some are doing a job of work, packing small light bulbs in cardboard trays. Others sing and perform sketches for my entertainment.

One tot plays the part of an old lady, as another comes up to help her cross the street. A group falls dramatically into distress, and a PLA unit rescues them. Beneath a photo of Norman Bethune, a little boy sings that the Canadian doctor's heroic example inspired him to clean shoes for his neighbors.

These children, overdrilled as they sometimes seem, have poise and self-assurance. You see in them a foretaste of the great charm and concentration which Chinese people display when they feel like it. I recall, with wonder at the change, a line of Mrs. Bishop's 1900 description of the children of Hankow: "cupidity and depravity written on faces which should be young . . . watching with greedy eyes the bargains of their seniors."

The healthful look of these children is no illusion. One-month-old infants in China today average 3.25 kilograms. In the 1940s they averaged less than three kilograms. In Wuhan of 1973, children ten years old are five centimeters taller than were children of the same age in 1956. Boys of ten years old are today 2.5 kilograms heavier than were boys of ten in 1956.

The drop in the birthrate, of course, has improved child health enormously. In Red and Brilliant, Mrs. Yeh says, the rate is now 26 births per one thousand people. Infant mortality used to run as high as 20 percent in China, but today it is at the level of the world's modern nations.

Red and Brilliant takes great pains over public health work. Everyone is required to be inoculated against typhus, cholera, encephalitis, measles, and smallpox. The revolutionary committee members lay traps for rats. They spray with DDT to combat flies, warning householders to keep babies and animals out of the way when they are coming around with sprayers. A case of cholera is now rare in the district, though encephalitis, malaria, and hepatitis are far from conquered.

This is all light-years away from the state of things in old Wuhan. Consider this eyewitness account by a Russian of a Hankow street scene in 1927.

As I rushed in a stream of rickshas along Hsin Ma Lu, I suddenly saw a figure in a soldier's tunic stretched out on the sidewalk near a wall. The street was alive with its own activity. Rickshas were rushing by, pedestrians were walking and no one was looking in that direction. I stopped my ricksha and jumped down next to the prostrate man. He was a very young soldier, almost a boy — they took men scarcely older than children into the army then. He lay unconscious, his dull pupils stared out from under his half-open lids, his face twitched weakly. Next to him was a big pool of vomit.

Calling a policeman who was standing at his post nearby I asked him how he could allow a man to die on his beat without extending the slightest help. The policeman was surprised and said it was none of his business. When he had come on duty the soldier had already been lying there. Moreover, it was no longer cold.

Passers-by crowded around. Someone who had carefully looked at the soldier suddenly said "ho-luan" (cholera). Suddenly the crowd shuddered and took to its heels. This word was a terrible one at the time. During the siege there had been a cholera epidemic in Wuhan which carried off thousands of victims. It stopped during the winter but it might flare up again in the spring. . . .

I knew only one hospital in Hankow — the German missionary hospital where our comrades were sometimes treated. In the final analysis they admitted everyone there who paid. I went with the policeman to call them up to send over an ambulance. The policeman shouted "wai, wai" (which corresponds to our "hello") into the receiver for a long time, but he could not get through. The connection was very poor. Just then the ricksha man ran up and said it was no longer necessary, the soldier had died.

Almost in tears I continued on my way.

Today, cholera is as much a thing of the past as the ricksha. Wuhan is well off for hospital beds, and there is no sign of the cold unconcern that used to seem inevitable.

Red and Brilliant has become a calm, bland slab of city life. Organizational ways are in principle those introduced in 1949–1950. There was a tremor of uncertainty during the Cultural Revolution, but the residents' committee did not lose its head (as some more elevated bodies did). In recent years, the Party network has built up again to pre-1966 pitch.

Yet Red and Brilliant does not pound with drama as during the winter of 1949–1950. The problems being dealt with have shrunk. No more Kuomintang agents, private business, incorrigible hawkers. Political confrontation has given way to administrative routine.

Fundamentals do not seem to be at stake in the well-ordered life of Red and Brilliant. The establishment of Communist power is taken for granted. The job of the cadres is no longer to gain control of a situation out of hand, like firemen, but to keep neat an established situation, like gardeners.

The wives are working now, in 80 percent of Red and Brilliant's households. Education is a far bigger force in people's lives than it was twenty-five years ago. Ninety-five percent of the households have a savings account. Even physical appearances have changed, since the vast majority of the area's 2,252 people live in homes that did not exist in 1949. If anything of the old turmoil remains, it must lie well within the minds of men.

The face and rhythm of Wuhan — of most cities — are seen best on foot. A walk before breakfast takes me to one of China's great inner-city scenes: downtown Hankow in the early morning. The streets around the main artery of Sun Yat-sen Road are stirring to confront another day.

At 6:30 A.M. quite a few people are still on their cane beds along the sidewalks of the small streets. Lolling in white shorts, draped in strips of thin toweling, they await the will to rise and join the bustle which has begun around them. Some youths are even still asleep, despite all the chatter and the trill of bicycle bells. No doubt they have become used to endless noise.

These calm, curled-up forms remind me of apathetic Chinese holding back from political campaigns that do not turn them on. Apolitical types draw back into themselves — mental loafers, as these folk on the sidewalk are physical loafers — while the bells and whistles of ideology pass them by. The Chinese are very good at inner retreat from an external event they do not want to join.

All except the tiny lanes have more trees than a typical Shanghai street. Each tree has its square gap of earth, set into the curbside of the brick-paved sidewalks. The buildings are a bit lower and less monumental than Shanghai's, but a splendid bank or church rises now and then above the general height of three stories. Europeans made a show with the front of their buildings: pillars, steps, decorative windows. The best Chinese buildings are, by contrast, secluded behind walls. Their finest face is shown not to the street but to a courtyard.

People stop on their way to work for a hasty breakfast at a small eating station. Mostly they eat a greasy fritter or doughnut, with a bowl of rice gruel topped by a pinch of brown spice, though some prefer a mash of noodles. How young people who eat these things grow up as handsome and strong as many of them do is a mystery.

Larger shops with food supplies are opening their doors. Far more canned foods are available than a few years ago; mushrooms, chicken, fish of all kinds. At a fresh fruit counter I ask the price of pears. An assistant is helpful and she also brings other fruits to my attention. But a crowd gathers; the shop is being disrupted. A senior man tells the assistant that I should buy my pears as quickly as possible.

Some shops have hand-penciled posters at the door which are almost advertisements. They announce the special goods of the moment and urge the buyer to consider them. Restaurants list their menu for the passerby on wooden notice boards. The characters for each dish are scrawled on a horizontal slat, pushed into a groove on the board. A strip of blackboard to the right of the slats gives the price of each dish.

A two-line maxim is displayed inside dozens of shops: "No matter how many questions you ask, we will not be put out. No matter how painstakingly you choose, we will not lose patience" (*wen duo bu fan, tiao duo bu ji*).

Here is a typical street that runs north from the river to Sun Yat-sen Road. Old people are out shopping. Cloth bags; smooth brown faces.

314

Ladies in shiny black suits; men in baggy shorts above spindly legs. A meeting is going on in the open-store-front office of the local neighborhood committee. The people attending are also mostly older folk. They fan themselves furiously as a young cadre cries out a message on environmental health.

Out in the street a militia group suddenly marches by. It is a mixed group of young men and girls. All have rifles, and the last two in line carry enormous targets for the rifle practice. They sing as they march beside me and the whole street seems buoyed by their vigor.

On Sun Yat-sen Road I wander past a leather shop, then turn back for a second look since the goods seem solid. The shop is dim and simple; the hearth of a craftsman. It is not yet open for business, but a man in pajamas comes out and says I am welcome nonetheless.

This genial soul runs the shop; his are the children who creep forward to stare at me. I have disturbed the family at breakfast. They live behind the showroom, as is common in small businesses all over Asia. But the family do not own this store. They run it for the city's Bureau of Commerce.

Such a mode of ownership does not reduce at all the personal service which members of the family give me. I select a leather belt. It is of first-rate quality, marred only by an uninspired buckle. For three and a half yuan it is mine, wrapped up with minute care in an old piece of brown paper. The family give me the kind of farewells suitable for an old friend.

A few moments later I enter a similar place, a fur shop, also on Sun Yat-sen Road. Animals from the four corners of China lie silent, cleaned up, tamed in glass cases with redwood frames. The manager does not press a fur on me, but simply shows me his wares.

A wolfskin from Shansi looks fine, in texture and color, and I take it for twenty-five yuan. (Some weeks later a Hong Kong tailor turns it into a vest. He is tickled that the wolf was bought in Wuhan, his own hometown.) The fur man sees me to the door, sends me off with a double handshake into the rays of the morning sun. Come back again in wintertime, he urges, and see even better furs.

Wuhan, I reflect, has not lost its place as a market for the furs of central China. One turns to the diary of Lord Elgin's secretary: "The

315

fur-shops of Hankow were numerous and well-stocked. The winter supply had evidently just come in, and some of the most expensive and rare furs from the province of Shansi and the Tibetan frontier were to be procured here at the usual fabulous prices."

My eye is caught by a funeral shop; I stop to chat with one of its workers. It is a gay place. There are racks and hooks hung with wreaths in bright colored paper. A fancy one can cost ten, fifteen, even twenty yuan, the young worker tells me. In addition a family has to pay a rental fee for the auditorium down the street, to hold a "memorial meeting." At this meeting family members and work colleagues speak of the one who has died. If it is a prominent person, someone from the Party or the state will also make remarks. But the funeral shop does not sell coffins. In Wuhan — though not in the countryside — cremation is usual.

This is all very different from funeral arrangements before Liberation. Coffins of great cost used to be the norm. If the family could afford it, the heavy box would be lacquered with fine Ningpo varnish, and labeled with characters in raised gold. Fine coffins were thought a necessity, for the body might wait months to be buried. Geomancers had first to fix on an auspicious time and place for returning the dead one to the earth. Money had to be paid to professional mourners, who would gush false tears as they followed the coffin in long white robes. It was also deemed essential in old China for the corpse to take with him an array of clothes and possessions for his long encoffined sleep.

I could not say that the smaller streets of Hankow are clean, despite many red trash boxes labeled "Fruit Peelings Box." Already at 9:00 A.M., you step on ice-cream papers, drink cups, fruit peelings. Many people walk down the road, to avoid the clutter of the sidewalk. The only competition is from bicycles and an occasional military truck.

A novel sight is a kind of cage on the back of a tricycle. I watch one being pedaled with some effort by an old man in a straw hat. From inside the grille around the edges of the cage there peep the beaming faces of a dozen children — on their way to kindergarten.

Treaty-port hands once considered the Hankow Bund the finest in

I could not say that the streets of Hankow are clean, despite many red trash boxes labeled "Fruit Peelings Box"

There is a scruffiness and a raw-edged social atmosphere to this backward patch of Hankow

China. But it has slumped and is not today a fine boulevard like the Shanghai Bund. Its name is simply "Street Along the River." The British part of it was once known as "Flowery Mansions" (*hua-lou*), and there is still a Flowery Mansions Street, north of Street Along the River. You can just detect grandeur behind the peeling paint, mounds of earth, and clumps of weeds. Many of these heavy villas are now bureaus of Wuhan city for trade and shipping matters.

But the big white banks and consulates and merchant houses are not as white as they were. The former United States consulate appears disused; Butterfield and Swire's mansion needs a face-lift; even the Hong Kong and Shanghai Bank building has lost its dash. Piles of bricks and pipes on all sides are as dispiriting as dog shit on a carpet.

High banks topped by a brick wall have been built to hold back the swelling Yangtze at flood time. Big comfortable boats are loading for Shanghai. Dumpy little ferries leave for short trips to the southern bank. The wharf at which the ships moor is floating, so that it may rise and fall with Yangtze waters that can vary by eighteen meters.

The Customs House is just the same as Shanghai's. It looks lonely now, without the environment of commercial rush to which its style seems fitted. A large portrait of Chairman Mao stares out across the river from an upper window. He seems to be casting an uneasy glance at the muddy waters in which his most famous swim was made, in July 1966. Above Mao's pink face are the characters: Ten Thousand Years to Our Great Leader Chairman Mao.

Coming back from the Bund I find some mean and crowded spots, near Tientsin and Cooperation streets, where the Russian and British concessions once met. A dirt path is the sidewalk. Water is being carried in buckets from public taps. From this activity — as from the sight of children urinating in the alley — it seems that the hovels lack running water and toilets.

There is also a scruffiness, a raw-edged social atmosphere, to this backward patch of Hankow. People talk about me loudly to their companions, laughing and pointing at me as they do so.

Looking at the bleak contours of a Hankow slum area, I mull over the idea of the "state." Coming to China from the outside, we may shake our heads at the power of the government over the personal life of Chinese citizens. Each man has to take the job that the "state wants." He is even under subtle pressure to think the thoughts that the "Party wants."

But look again at these hovels. The physical face of the district reminds you of what life used to be like in China before the Boy Scouts of the CCP brought strong, paternalistic government. Yet a sweep of the eye is misleading. River Shore area is certainly not the same as before Liberation. To go into homes is to establish that. Health is far better. Incomes are more equal. Every single young person is being educated. Women are chattels no longer.

This double perception of the scene makes you think about the power of Party and state. I have asked children in Chinese schools what they want to do when they grow up. "What the state needs," is a common answer; or "What the Party needs." In this area of Hankow, pulling itself up from the level of a slum, such answers ring sounder to me than ever before.

What degree of opportunity would be self-generated in this slum *without* the wider rule of the CCP which embraces it? In houses like these, how could a child study if the neighborhood committee did not make sure there was a place to study? How could a housewife learn about the world beyond Wuhan, and beyond China, if the state did not lift up her eyes?

The people of River Shore area would be on a treadmill of daily struggle to make evening follow morning, but for the chance to advance provided by broader bonds of the new socialist state. They would stagnate in a blanket of localism, without the lifelines of communication which the CCP has brought to the inner city of Hankow. The state offers a restless man a life in the army; allows a woman to travel to another province to attend a women's congress; plucks a boy from this ghetto to front commune life in the far west.

There is a noble mission for the state, I feel, in this backward part of Hankow. For all its excesses, the state is an agent of modernization in these streets. Its petty strutting notwithstanding, it enlarges the social freedom of people whose world otherwise remains a row of hovels. No wonder the eyes of a child can glow when he says: "I want to do what the state needs me to do."

319

The Bund and the European buildings apart, you see few traces of treaty-port Hankow. The former Station Street used to be a point of uneasy confrontation between the concessions and the native city. An iron gate not far from Hankow Station divided the two worlds. On one side, the dance halls, brothels, and clubs of the foreigners and a comprador elite. On the other, the shacks and sewers and stench of the ordinary Chinese people.

Today the iron gate is no more and Station Street is a single unit. Many of the old night spots are shops. The former Paramount Dance Hall is an embroidery factory run by women. They left the housewife's life to make quilts and pillowcases for export, and give a boost to China's balance of payments. All told there are now fifty small factories in Station Street. Production by day has replaced distraction by night.

A striking change is the disappearance of the ricksha. The ricksha did not exist until the foreigner came. Hankow saw the first of these hand-pulled carriages in the 1880s. By the 1930s Wuhan had nine thousand rickshas, and twenty-seven thousand ricksha pullers (they worked in shifts, renting the vehicle).

A British merchant would not think to budge from his lair on the Bund without a ricksha. The pullers, a number on each shirt as in a prison, would line up outside the Terminus Hotel, waiting for elegant diners to finish a banquet. They would whisk a European visitor to meet a fortune teller or to see the singing canaries at the waterfront. (At sunset Chinese would bring their birds in cages, airing them as a Westerner might walk his dog. Squatting on their heels, they would start competitions as to the singing skill of the assembled canaries.)

Ricksha men knew to which doors in "Dump Street" they should take a young consul who wanted a Chinese lover. The ricksha was as necessary in old Hankow as the bank, the racecourse, the church.

It was also a thing of indignity to the twenty-seven thousand men who lost their human identity in its harness. Beatings with a *taipan*'s cane; underpayment of the fare; death by hunger in a lean week — these were part of the order of things. The ricksha men were too low in the scale to complain.

The stirring of nationalism in 1927 made it possible for a ricksha

320

man to argue back at a foreigner who refused to pay the fare. Ricksha men also banded together at that time to demonstrate against the introduction of buses; so strongly, indeed, that bus service was delayed for years.

With rickshas as with other things, Liberation brought a fruit of which 1927 was the seed. Many pullers were sent to farms, factories, or water conservation projects. The majority made an effective switch, but some drifted back to the streets of Hankow. It was not easy to stamp out a sixty-year-old habit in Wuhan's life. As a transition step, and a tool for socialist education, the CCP began a campaign to single out "model" ricksha men.

As a more basic reform the pedicab was developed to replace the ricksha. Nineteen fifty-six saw the end of rickshas in Wuhan. The three characters for ricksha are "man-strength-cart" (*ren-li-che*). The pedicab — "three-wheel-cart" (*san-lun-che*) — is really a tricycle, with the pedaler in front and the passenger in a chair between the rear wheels. The remaining five thousand pullers became pedicab men, organized in cooperatives.

The final part of the story of Wuhan rickshas came after the Cultural Revolution. Eighty former pullers, now pedicab men, decided that the pedicab, better as it was than the ricksha, was not modern enough for Wuhan's needs. They drew up a plan to produce three-wheeled motorcars!

Unable to read blueprints, they imitated the parts of an actual car. Lacking meters, they tested the finished parts on a generator. Having no hydraulic press, they made a simple press with a screw spindle and crude iron plates. Within six weeks they had turned out a trial three-wheeled car.

Today in Wuhan bus and trolley are the main means of public transport (five hundred kilometers of lines crisscross the city). But you also see blue or fawn three-wheeled "motorized pedicabs" nipping through the streets. At Wuchang railroad station they are lined up at several taxi ranks, ready to whisk away passengers. The factory which makes the new taxis keeps one old ricksha in a corner. The veterans want young workers to realize what a change Wuhan's "taxis" have undergone over the years. Meanwhile, one of the last ricksha pullers has become a part-time lecturer on "class struggle" at Wuhan University.

The Brilliant Palace Hotel is a fine spot for watching the world go by. The Brilliant Palace is hardly that. It is a small hotel on Yangtze River Street Number Two, in the heart of Hankow. It has none of the trappings of a tourist center. No lobby; no post office; no service desk; no hotel notepaper. Overseas Chinese visitors sometimes stay here. At present I am the only Western guest.

From my balcony the scene is like an oriental version of Hitchcock's movie *Rear Window*. More than fifty bedrooms are open to my gaze, in two, three, and four-storied dwellings. It is 8:00 P.M. and families are unwinding from the affairs of a very hot day. Concrete window boxes and little balconies are hung with plants, vegetables, drying clothes. The rooms contain hardly any Mao portraits, political messages, or posters from the revolutionary operas. Walls are dotted, though, with snapshots. The general air is one of people busy with food, gossip, and family affairs.

Opposite my window is a modest inn for domestic Chinese travelers. There is a comradeship of balconies across the few meters which separate our two hotels. Both buildings are European style, with faded plaster walls, and metal window frames that swing outward.

Some guests in the inn seem to be traveling on business. I never find out for sure because, though we greet each other several times a day, the distance is too great for a conversation. Are they cadres from another province? Workers visiting relatives in Wuhan? Is there a commercial or political conference going on in town?

About 6:00 P.M. each day the guests return to their rooms, each of which has two beds. They change into briefer dress, lounge in front of an electric fan, sit on the balcony with a cigarette and gaze at the Brilliant Palace. Not often do they read, and when they do it is always a book rather than a newspaper.

Above the mellow old buildings, the sky is lit by a full moon, tickled by the fingers of a thousand feathery clouds. As far as the eye can see, the roofs are red tile. It makes the city more vivid from the air than are Chinese cities where the tile is gray. The red ones, a Wuhan official explains, are inferior, since they have not been baked like the gray ones. "We needed so many new buildings that we could not afford the time to bake the tiles like that."

Where you do not see red tiles, you see people eating, sleeping, and playing on flat concrete rooftops. Some are close enough to smile, or wave a greeting with their chopsticks as they eat an early supper. From the street below rise the ring of bicycle bells and the toot of a bus horn — sound effects for the mime of our rooftop fraternization.

The pavements, still like hot plates from the day's sun, are now dotted with cane beds ready for an eventual attempt at sleep. Bedtime is still a way off, and the beds are being used as tables for a snack or a game of *bai-fen,* as chairs for a group conversation. From my balcony the cane oblongs look like yellow rafts, laden with arms and legs, afloat on the gray stream of asphalt.

At night the mood in Hankow is as relaxed as it is businesslike around breakfast time. I slip out from the Brilliant Palace at 9:00 P.M., past a doorman whose face conveys that he would rather I stayed in. The streets are so gloomy, and so packed with strollers, that the doorman may think I will get lost.

There are small street stalls, where fruit drinks and hot snacks sell briskly. Silent groups sit on their haunches at the religion of *bai-fen.* Fifty or sixty people stand chattering at each bus stop in Sun Yat-sen Road, waiting to clamber on the overcrowded red-and-white buses. The crying and shouting of children and the horseplay of youths are uninhibited.

Two workers in their twenties appear beside me. They seem to be out for a lark; hair combed with style and faces flushed with a few drinks. I watch them go into a provision store. They each pull out a ten-yuan note. You have the impression they are flaunting the money just a bit. Into the night they carry off three quarts of beer and half a dozen packets of cigarettes.

The small alleys are now a vortex of half-private, half-public activity. Some people rush by with bundles or a bowl of rice. Others lounge against a wall and absorb the kaleidoscope of sights. Quite a

323

Delivering fish from East Lake to the kitchens of the Brilliant Palace Hotel

few are lying on their cane beds, though with no intention for the moment of going to sleep. In alleys which are roofed in brick, electric lights shine down on the polished cane, and catch with a yellow shaft the waving of a hundred fans.

Some of the old shops look charming by night. Above their windows are glass panels in varied hues, made brilliant by the light within the store. A number of alleys have a similar colored glass panel in a semi-circular shape above the entrance to the alley. From the dim streets, the stained glass makes a cathedral of Hankow's night life.

Evening uniform in the alleys is a shirt and a singlet. On the larger streets, girls have pretty skirts, and younger men wear bright but single-colored T-shirts. Many older women sport a satin blouse, buttoned to the throat in traditional style. No one over fifty is without a fan.

Signs exist of an easy relation between the generations. A softness is shown toward old folk. A youth chats in a relaxed way with someone four times his own age. I come upon no arrogant interference by an old person in young ones' pleasures.

I listened earlier in the day to a radio pep talk about the "two lines" in culture. The gist was that there are two kinds of morality in creative work and daily conduct alike. One is the morality of a society where the workers rule. It is "people's morality." The other is that of a class-ridden society where the bourgeoisie is still in the box seat. This is "bourgeois morality."

324

Now as I watch Hankow people in their off-duty moments, I wonder: what kind of morality lies behind the moods, the words, the gestures of these vivacious folk? I cannot tell; yet one thought leaps up.

What the radio called "people's morality" is a straitlaced code of conduct. In the West we would call it precisely *bourgeois morality!* What the radio called "bourgeois morality" is a swinging, even libertarian way of living. This is what we in the West think of as the new "people's morality" of the counterculture!

The CCP in Wuhan and the opinion makers of Peoria, Illinois, could easily agree on a practical differentiation between "square" and "swinging."

The finer issue is this. Which of the two is a natural expression of the people? Which of the two is imposed by some force, authority, or tradition from outside the ranks of the people? And who indeed, by any standard that could bridge the chasm between Wuhan and Peoria, *are* the people?

I come back to the Brilliant Palace, sit down to a Wuchang fish, and ask myself what looks different in Hankow compared with Asian cities better known to Westerners. Taking Hong Kong, Djakarta, and Bangkok, this is how it seems.

There are fewer streetlights in Hankow, so you seldom have the feeling of being in a big city that is showing itself off. There is far less traffic, especially autos; the press of the evening is a matter of crowds on foot. At no point does the danger of being mugged or robbed even cross the mind. Nor do you feel that wary inner expectation — hardly to be avoided in Djakarta — of coming across at any moment a beggar or a sick person on the pavement.

In many alleys of Hankow, you could imagine yourself to be in the central district of Hong Kong island. It is no less noisy and not much cleaner. It is just as lively a theater of social perambulation. Yet fifteen minutes in one spot suggests two contrasts. Almost any sign you see in Hankow has to do with politics; in Hong Kong you may not find a political notice during a whole night.

And the products in the Hankow stores are much more modest in style and narrow in range. Walk till your shoes wear through but you

325

won't see an item which in Hong Kong would be called a luxury. Only in food stores is there little difference between the two cities.

There is a blandness about the Hankow crowds. The clothes are not less colorful than those along Silom Road in Bangkok. But they are less flashy, more monotonous in texture. And no stylistic surprises pop up. You feel no coil of excitement, that a grand sight might appear at the next corner.

You know that economic distress does not lurk beneath the evening's surface. In this respect Hankow is another world from Djakarta, where 85 percent of the city residents lack electricity and sewers; where about 25 percent of the school-age children go to school (virtually 100 percent go in Wuhan); where there is one hospital bed for every fourteen hundred Djakartans (Wuhan has one for every two hundred people). Equally you know that no one is living like a king, fifty or a hundred times as well off as the man who cuts your hair or sells you a bus ticket.

The foreigner in Hankow feels like a gnat on the broad back of a social body that is solid, complacent, living utterly within itself. He sees the Chinese people going about their affairs with crisp purpose, settled confidence. The foreigner impinges on them — in any basic way — no more than does a tree. As if through a two-way mirror, he watches a materially simple, organizationally complex, culturally unshakable way of life. He gains respect for the quarter of mankind which is Chinese.

PEKING

北京

You FEEL AT ONCE the dry air and sense the high, open sky of north China. The heavens are stark as in Italy. The light is soft, not a relentless glare as in steamy south China. Peking's climate is harsh, with icy winters, hot summers, dust storms in spring. Seasons are as extreme as those of North America; the contrast is taxing, but maybe it makes northern people sharp and resourceful.

The bone-dry texture of Peking days, too, makes for physical well-being. You hardly need the statistics which long showed Peking folk to be highly resistant to epidemics. Only look around at the razor eyes and the silky complexions. Even when features are not fine — beauty is less prodigal in Peking than in Hangchow — faces seem to radiate freshness.

Not that every face in the streets is a Peking one. The capital is a magnet drawing people from all China. They come for work or meetings, on behalf of their province or as a step up from a previous local post. The "floating population" from out of town is almost half a million.

On Peking buses you hear accents from all over China. Peking's four thousand eating houses have plates to satisfy every Chinese culinary taste. "Fragrant chicken" of Kiangsu; "red-sauce" meat of Fukien; dishes of Tibet, Mongolia, of the Moslem people. Peking is a national city, a hearth of all the provinces.

The city's reach is more than territorial. Peking is perhaps the one city in the world which presumes to relate itself to the cosmos. It was built to partner the planets and stars of the firmament. If Peking didn't care much about the earth beyond China, it did care about the heavens.

The Temple of the Sun was built in the eastern city. The Temple of the Moon faced it from the west. To the Temple of Heaven, in the south, emperors would go to pray for a good harvest. On a north-south axis lay most of the great buildings, facing south to snare maximum sunlight. Even ordinary houses made this same arrangement with nature; their best rooms faced south to a courtyard.

Pekinese have been for centuries — and still are — as much oriented to "east" and "west" as to "left" and "right." Taxi drivers talk of turning north; they enter a street from its "west mouth." The winds have a say in where factories are built. Since the main winds come from the north and the northwest, the city government has steered new industry east and south of the city center — to cut down air pollution.

The seasons, too, are treated as if they achieve a physical unity with the city. Sights are described, and esteemed, with nature's time dimension included: Fragrant Mount in autumn dress; Kunming Lake frozen hard for winter skating; the ocher walls of the former Imperial Palace garnished with the first green shoots of spring. The city lives with sun, moon, and the calendar on the edge of its mind.

Long-time residents of Peking seem part of the city, as the city seems part of nature. They dwell in the shadow of a rich past. It is a place, someone has said, "where ghosts might walk with men." This lends a touch of class to Peking.

Not only the elite of Peking have a sense of history about their city. Like a tangible mist, Peking's culture touches every resident with its cloying power. Even in old Peking, the man in the street had a cultural pride, as if by osmosis or inheritance. Even more so today is Peking's culture pervasive; as everyday energy, as an awareness of quality. The very walk of a Peking man — erect, unhurried, square-footed — expresses his assured place in the large compact of things.

Peking folk are daily conscious of a certain prestige. They sometimes look at other parts of China with a condescending eye, the way old-style Chinese used to view the world beyond China. Living in Peking confers status, even in the People's Republic of China.

This prestige has its reasons. Pekinese share walls and willows with Chairman Mao, as great a leader as China has ever had. They speak the Chinese accent — once called Mandarin or "Peking speech," now known as "ordinary speech" — which the whole country is required to master. The hands of their watches show a time which, despite China's five-thousand-kilometer breadth, the whole nation must call

330

its own (a great change, this, from past Chinese respect for nature, for western provinces have to flout the signs of sun and moon and stars).

People in other cities of China do their part to sustain Peking's prestige. They look up to "China's capital, Peking," as they term it. During the Cultural Revolution, Red Guards in the provinces, alienated from the establishment as they were, marched off in good faith to "tell Peking" their views. During the recent campaign against the influence of Confucius and Lin Piao, citizens from Dairen traveled to Peking, expressly to register their grievances in wall posters which they stuck plaintively to the gate of the Peking city government. It was like coming to address a trusted elder whose nobility would guarantee a fair hearing.

One afternoon in 1971 I was lying in a hot spring near Sian — following a regimen that goes back to the empresses of the T'ang dynasty — when a messenger arrived to disturb my lazy bath. "Peking has phoned. You must return first thing tomorrow morning." But I have two more days of activities in the Sian area! The Sian official swept aside my hesitations. "Peking requires your return — we will make all necessary arrangements immediately."

I could not even find out the reason for Peking's summons. Nor did the Sian cadres know, or feel it appropriate to ask Peking (it turned out that Prince Sihanouk had set a time to talk with me). No logic was needed, much less pressure, for Sian to rally to the voice of the capital. No trouble was too much, for dozens of people involved in my Sian stay, in order to answer Peking's call.

We put aside our towels, left the languor of the hot springs, and drove into Sian. My Peking companion and local officials alike kept referring to "Peking's instruction" and "the call from the capital." I was most impressed with the power of this message from the east. There were almost echoes of imperial days in the awe with which these folk spoke of Peking, as if the city were a personification of authority.

To me as a foreigner, Peking exudes another kind of authority. It seems to be the rocklike core of Asia. Absurd! What of Tokyo's wealth, Calcutta's throng, Singapore as a pivot of communications? In a different sense is Peking the pure heart of Asia. It is Asia's last big-league holdout against the seduction of Western civilization.

331

There are several "Asias" which are mirror images of a particular Western impact. A British Asia, where London used to rule, English is widely spoken, ready access is given British religion, ideas, and products; a French Asia, which looks to Paris, where French culture is esteemed by an elite, where trousers are narrow and shoes pointed (compared with those in London's outposts); and, since World War Two, an American Asia, mostly never ruled from Washington, but recipient of U.S. troops and dollars during the effort to "contain" China (a very *self*-contained nation!)

Peking is outside the West's tamed Asia. It looks up to nobody, rests content with its own values and culture. Not foreign products, but Chinese, fill the fast-selling spots in the department stores. No Pekinese, planning a fine meal or a special occasion, would choose a cuisine other than China's own. Peking intellectuals do not make their high flights in a Western tongue; it is considered enough for a Chinese sage to express himself in Chinese.

As these lines are written an ad appears in the *New York Times* about life in Taiwan, inserted by the Chiang Kai-shek regime. "The dictates of couturiers in Paris and Rome," it boasts, "are followed as slavishly in Taipei as in New York or Los Angeles." Peking's self-esteem is not based as Taipei's seems to be. Fashions, newspapers, investments from the West? They do not exist in Peking. The most recent foreign suitor — Russia — made hardly more impact than did the West. Moscow "lost" China no less than did the United States before it. Peking still lacks an inferiority complex toward anything non-Chinese, still has lost little of its conscience to the West.

In the present era when the West declines in Asia, China, the hold-out against Western seduction, emerges carrying the torch of Asia's confidence in itself. Peking which was never really part of the "Asias" turns out to be the heart of Asia.

Though there are two to three thousand foreigners in Peking, they live on the margins of the city's life. This is a double change from pre-Liberation Peking. In the heyday of the old Legation Quarter, the "Powers" policed the area, even kept troops there, and Chinese had to keep a sharp eye out for foreign authority. Though Peking knew no foreign presence on the scale of that at Shanghai — was never a treaty port — it had to cede enclaves of privilege to nations mightier than China.

After Liberation, when China first stood up and then turned inward, the prestige of foreigners in Peking melted like butter in a pan. In Peking during 1964, I sometimes found it hard to credit that here was a major capital city. The few Western diplomats huddled together like sad birds in an unsuitable clime. Dinner parties of foreigners had a stoic, flat, ironic spirit about them.

By 1973 the foreigners are so much more numerous that Peking seems part of the international community again. Twice as many embassies exist as in 1964; many times more foreign journalists are in residence (forty-odd in 1974). The twenty-five long-term and unofficial Americans living in Peking have been joined by fifty official Americans at the United States liaison office.

Peking sees a far broader array of foreigners than it *ever* did before. Here is a leathery old waiter at the Peking Hotel. Yang has worked at this best of Peking hotels since 1927. He recalls that guests all used to be Europeans or Americans (by the late 1930s, Japanese also). During the 1950s and 1960s he noticed a big change. Customers at the Peking Hotel — whether diners from embassies, or room guests who were on official delegations from abroad — were mostly from Third World lands. "Algerians, Syrians, Laotians," he observes. "No one from these countries ever came to the hotel before Liberation."

Yet it remains true that foreigners impinge little on Peking. They seem less forlorn, if only because more numerous, than a decade ago. But their life in no way recalls the power and social privilege of envoys in the years of the Unequal Treaties. The old Legation Quarter is a Chinese area now, its embassies turned into schools, bureaus, hostels. The foreign community is kept at arm's length in the dusty eastern suburbs. Before Liberation many spots in Peking were forbidden to Chinese. Now it is the foreigner who occasionally sees notices forbidding his entry, as near military zones in the Western Hills.

Ordinary Peking citizens have little contact with foreigners. Their lives are surely less affected by foreign presence than those of people in any other major world capital. You do notice, however, a certain pride among the Pekinese that foreigners gather again at Peking. A remark, a smile, a nod of the head conveys the mood. Foreigners once plundered Peking; they were driven away. Back they come but on quite different terms; with respect this time. It is natural that foreigners should clamor to come to Peking; they are welcome . . .

Stately as it may be, Peking is informal in the rhythm of its days. People go about their business with purpose; a high degree of organization marks all that is done. Yet the crowds are relaxed to the point of being homespun.

It is six o'clock on a warm afternoon. We are not far from Tian-an men, the Gate of Heavenly Peace, Peking's heart. The street is dappled from the shadows of a hundred trees. Youths wander home after a game of basketball in the park north of Legation Street (where the foreign troops once drilled). Couples with bulging string bags return from shopping in Wang-fu-jing Street, the city's commercial hub, across the Boulevard of Eternal Peace. An army man squats on the pavement to feed his tiny child from a bottle. Some people just sit on benches by the curbside, watching the lengthening shadows, eyeing the passersby, feeling the last rays of a generous sun.

I walk a couple of blocks to Tian-an men Square. Museums and lofty gates; tablets of the great; the sweep of public grandeur. The gate itself is the nerve center of People's China, official emblem of the post-1949 government, crimson perch from which Chairman Mao views parades. In front are stone lions and pillars; my Chinese guidebook calls them "a masterpiece of art marked by a sense of power and beauty." The lions are framed against a wall which screams: "Ten Thousand Years to the People's Republic of China."

But look closer and here are two scenes from another world. Three small boys sit astride the noble lions. One tumbles off and laughs at his misfortune; one playfully pats the smooth mane; another pauses to piss at a lion's feet. To three unawed youngsters these lions at the doorstep of the Imperial Palace are a toy for good fun.

The square is speared by an obelisk called the Monument to the People's Heroes. "The material embodiment of the spirit of heroism," says the Peking guidebook. Its bas-reliefs survey a hundred years of revolutionary struggle. Just beside the monument rises a flagpole where Mao Tse-tung, on a day of joy in 1949, hoisted the flag of the People's

Republic of China. I begin to read the monument's inscriptions, which are done in the hand of Premier Chou.

Then out of the corner of my eye I see a young couple. In body they are close to the people's heroes; in spirit maybe not. Hands interwoven, they gaze at each other as if the two sets of eyes were programmed to engage. The monument is no more than a spot for these lovebirds to occupy. I stare at a caption — "The People's Heroes Are Immortal" — but somehow the characters do not electrify me.

Under a grove of pine trees at the southern tip of the square I sit and listen to the radio. The sun has sunk low. A brilliant sunset is budding above the orange bricks of the Great Hall of the People. A public affairs program begins from the loudspeaker. There is a studio debate about the "revolution in education," and letters from listeners on "how to practice self-reliance in concrete ways" and how to apply Mao Tsetung's thought.

Ah, here is what the West knows as "Maoism." These phrases are the bread of ideology by which Peking lives. I glance back across the square and toward Legation Street. The basketball players, the shoppers, the father with his infant, the lovers at the monument, the small boys outside of time and care. It is all Maoism, yes.

It is also a way of living together in society. A way in which some things bulk large — like collective purpose — and other things are minimized — like private ownership. The radio program is no more than a lesson in this kind of civics. The sunset now lends a gentle pink to the huge flagstones of the square. I walk back to the New Traveler Hotel and reflect on the blandness of Maoism's modes.

No Chinese city is as many-sided as Peking today. Haven of emperors ever since the Mongols ruled China, it is now a major industrial center; officials say industrial output is today one hundred times what it was in 1949. In a thousand shrines, built before the birth of most Western nations, pure Chinese tradition is distilled. Yet the only more-than-tiny foreign community in China lives in this grand, proud town. It is a beehive of bureaucrats, but also a place where culture is pervasive.

In 1973 I visit the Peking Underground Railway. The line is still an infant — sixteen stations spread over twenty-three kilometers, open

335

only from 6:00 A.M. to 7:30 P.M. — but it is a glimpse of the future. You forget you are in Peking of the emperors when you go down from the Boulevard of Eternal Peace to the metallic clatter below, from the glare of a hot morning to the fluorescent cool of a steel-and-marble cavern. The only underground things in Peking used to be tombs and wells; technology has intruded on nature and the monarchs.

You pay ten fen and pass a decor of plastic flowers and poems in Mao's hand. You are swallowed into a crowd of nonchalant commuters. The trains are Chinese-made to the last screw (built in *dong bei*). Their square fawn heads whiz between the marble stations each fifteen minutes, at a top speed of eighty kilometers per hour. The carriages have lightly padded seats with chrome frames, plenty of standing room, long metal bars to hang on to. No ads or notices on the walls.

Clinging to a metal bar as we speed toward Front Gate (Qian men) station, I reflect how much more complex life in Peking has become since my first visit a decade ago. No real surprise that the Pekinese are going to work in an underground; that they like to do so; that they pulled down remaining bits of the city wall to build it. The Chinese are no less enticed by modern conveniences than any other people.

Yet somehow the sight of the trains lingers in my memory. A sharp reminder of something nation-blind and inexorable about the "modern world." An underground was until yesterday a thing which most world cities had, which Peking did not have but wanted. The gulf narrows between life in Peking and life in the cities of the West and Japan.

Like Shanghai, Peking is now a municipality with the status of a province. It forms an enclave of some twenty-four-thousand kilometers within Hopei ("North of the River"). Peking's name simply means "Northern Capital." Further north than our other four cities, its latitude is the same as Philadelphia's.

Peking draws little beauty from its setting. Not on the sea like Dairen; without a lovely lake like Hangchow's; not at the confluence of two great streams like Wuhan. It does not even have a river as big as Shanghai's modest Whangpu.

336

Peking does have hills, though set well back. At the top end of the North China Plain, the city is not far from the Mighty Range (Tai-hang) Mountains to the west and the Shadowy (Yin) Mountains to the north.

These lofty peaks — acting as a fence against monsoon winds from the south, which causes the humidity to condense — ensure a good summer rainfall. With sixty centimeters of rain a year, Peking is less dry than its sister cities on the North China Plain.

But winds sweep down with force from the north. Just as Mighty Range and Shadowy Mountains rise to merge with the Mongolian plateau, so the dust of Mongolia descends to blend with Peking's purer air. The specks of loess put an orange carpet over the city. Things look as if seen through a yellow pane of glass. One good result of the CCP's promiscuous tree planting has been to modify this golden curse put on Peking each spring by Mongolia.

Peking is only two hundred kilometers from the border of Inner Mongolia, nine hundred kilometers from Outer Mongolia. In between, marking off the far grasslands from the nearer cultivated fields, stands the Great Wall of China. Its Chinese name means Great Wall of Ten Thousand Li. An hour's drive from downtown Peking brings you to its nearest bend.

When you stand on it the wall looks like a rough-hewn Roman road. From afar, it twists across the velvet ridges like a gray chain tossed down by the gods. The hills and valleys ripple away without end, one patch sunlit, the next seaweed green in shadows.

Nearby runs a railroad, seal of the wall's obsolescence as a separa-tor of Han civilization from an alien world. Gazing out from atop the wall you see the odd train, like a toy hardly moving on a crumpled rug. It chugs off to Mongolia and Russia, its whistle echoing through the gorges.

In ancient times Peking drew importance from the wall. Inside the wall; thus secure against barbarians. Yet far enough north to be a stepping-stone for trade between China's fertile belly and the Eurasian world. Today Peking thumbs its nose at all the wall ever stood for.

Two memories of the Great Wall of Ten Thousand Li. First, a picnic with a Chinese diplomat in 1971. We sit on a grassy mound

337

and sink a lunch of chicken, eggs, warm beer. We walk along the top of the wall, between the ramparts on the inner side and the battlements facing outward. PLA men are enjoying a day off, brown camera straps pulling out of shape their unruly green jackets.

Suddenly a group of Japanese appear over the next hump of the wall. It is a delegation of the Komeitō (Clean Government Party). Now that the Komeitō has taken a friendly stance toward China, I remark, surely it is time the ruling party of Eisaku Sato (premier at this time) did the same. The Chinese diplomat makes a grand gesture with his fan. "They should and they will. But China is not in a hurry. We can wait for them to change." I look up at the stony twists of the wall, its battlements like an infinite row of dragon's teeth. A people that could build five thousand kilometers of that *must* be patient.

Another day I chat about the wall with a Chinese leader who is a member of the Central Committee of the CCP. I throw into the conversation Moscow's notion that the Great Wall ought to be the boundary of China. My companion flashes an ironic smile as he draws himself up to reply. "We began this wall twenty-five hundred years ago, during the Chou dynasty. Who — what — were the 'Russians' then? My friend, they were not even a nation!"

Southwest of Peking begin the crops — winter wheat, maize, sorghum — of the North China Plain. Most yield three harvests in two years. Here is the village, Zhoukoudian, where the bones of 450,000-year-old Peking Man were found. A short drive in a similar direction leads to Marco Polo Bridge, flash point of World War Two in Asia.

The bridge spans the Stable Forever (Yong-ding) River. Locals long ago came up with the nickname Unpredictable (Wu-ding) River because it often flooded. The river was also once called Reedy Moat (Lu-gou), and this is the Chinese name which stuck to the 780-year-old bridge. Two signs of the times near today's Reedy Moat Bridge: a reservoir which has put an end to floods; red glare from a steel plant at nearby Stony View Hill.

Europeans have called the graceful span "Marco Polo Bridge," because the Venetian saw it in the 1270s and left an exuberant account. "A very great stone bridge . . . there are few of them in the world so beautiful . . . I tell you that it is quite 300 paces long and quite 8 paces wide . . . all of gray marble very well worked and well founded."

The marble arches have known two famous inscriptions. One was a tribute to the bridge's early role in north-south traffic. Travelers heading for Peking often reached Reedy Moat before daybreak, when the view of the stream was said to be superb. The tablet reads: "Morning Moon at Reedy Moat Bridge." The second inscription is to the first as a bomb is to a moonbeam. Japanese soldiers who hacked their way here in 1937 left a self-revealing epitaph: "Birthplace of Peace in East Asia."

Leaving Peking's southern gates you are soon among market gardens (and an occasional "May 7 School," where, in accord with an idea Mao had on May 7, 1966, white-collar types go to the fields for a while and do a little work). Here is Red Star commune, which feeds the capital with grain and meat and vegetables. I see it in the middle of a political campaign. Big-character posters attack leftists who pay more attention to Marx than to melons.

The answer to my request to take a poster home is fair enough: "The man who wrote it would not be happy. He had a grievance — he made out his case. Now he awaits a reply from the Party. The poster ought to stay there until he gets it."

But the current style (1971) is to be useful and correct at the same time. Onions, pears, melons, grapes are being loaded on trucks, to go to Peking's Bridge of Heaven shopping area for sale tomorrow. Peking ducks are being fed, with ugly coercion, to fatten them for the table.

Wheat is being threshed while red flags flutter over the stacks of husks, and loudspeakers blare out "Three Eight," a song about the PLA's three rules of discipline and eight points to watch. Beside the sweating farmers is a row of giant Chinese characters, each one in red on a yellow board, stuck into the ground like a target for rifle practice. The array adds up to a slogan: "Prepare Against War, Prepare Against Drought, Serve the People."

Peking's thousand fruit and vegetable stores are nearly all supplied by the city's own outskirts. In 1949, the area that is now Peking had 5,250 acres of vegetables; today, 27,500 acres. Fresh and dried fruit production was 20,000 tons; today, about 125,000 tons a year. At Liberation, 3 percent of what are now Peking's suburbs was irrigated;

now 34 percent is. As a result of all this, daily fresh vegetable supplies to the city of Peking now average half a kilogram per man, woman, and child.

Four months of the year are ruled out by climate for growing, which leads to ingenious schemes by farmers and scientists who work together. Tomatoes and cucumbers are now planted at nine different times of the year. Cabbages stored in bunkers (*bai-cai jiao*) taste as fresh in March as when picked in November. All kinds of seasonal vegetables are grown in beds under plastic sheet. Produce from the off season — when farmers' costs are higher — is subsidized. Every urban citizen gets an average vegetable subsidy of 1.5 yuan a year from the municipality.

Much traffic from Peking heads east. To the nearby port of Tientsin, China's number three city, Peking's sea outlet. To a pleasant beach at Peitaiho, 240 kilometers due east, the capital's stylized summer holiday spot.

Tientsin (the only city to which foreigners may drive from Peking) is a pivot for travel to the Northeast. I have seen it while on the way from Shantung to Dairen. I have also made the train ride from Tientsin to Peking, which may be the only ninety-minute train trip in the world linking two cities of more than four million population each.

No hills enliven this approach to Peking. The even skyline of crops is broken only by gray chimneys of industry and masts of vessels at Tientsin port (China's number two port, after Shanghai, before Dairen).

Peitaiho has more to offer the jaded foreign diplomat than does Tientsin. Its sandy seashore is also a retreat for Chinese officials, or the few who prefer the sea to hills and lakes. It was from this resort on the Bay of Pohai — only two hundred kilometers across the water from Dairen — that Lin Piao made his night flight to oblivion in 1971.

Defense Minister Lin had been seeking a more important role for the PLA, and for himself. He may even have been plotting against the life of Chairman Mao. He was at Peitaiho with his wife during September when his feud with Mao and Chou reached its climax.

Lin was listening to a Peitaiho concert when a phone call from Premier Chou came to his villa. Chou had been tipped off (by Lin's daughter) that the Lins were about to fly out of China. It was the beginning of the end. Mrs. Lin took the call, then sped to Peitaiho concert hall to warn her husband. In a haste which proved fatal, the Lins took off from Peitaiho and headed toward Russia. Their Trident had not been properly fueled. It crashed over Mongolia and all aboard were killed.

Many air routes link Peking, at last, to the outside world which has sometimes seemed beyond its care. No national airline expanded so much over the past two years as China's flag carrier (CAAC). Income, passengers carried, and volume of freight all rose more than 200 percent in 1973 as compared with 1972.

There are now eight major air routes between China and other countries. CAAC offers short-range service to three friendly neighbors: Hanoi (via Nanning), Pyongyang (via Shenyang), and Rangoon (via Kunming). Now that it has ten Boeing 707s, CAAC also goes nonstop to Tokyo and to Moscow, serves Paris via Pakistan, and Tirana and Bucharest via Teheran.

Until 1973 most foreign airlines were confined to Shanghai, but now seven of them fly into Peking. Aeroflot and the Korean airline have for years landed at Peking. New are the Air France flights from Paris, Ethiopian service from Addis Ababa via Bombay, a Japan Air Lines time-saver to Tokyo, Pakistan's reasonably well-patronized hop to Karachi, and the service begun by Swissair in 1975 to Zurich.

Meanwhile Boeings and British Tridents pep up CAAC's domestic service. New routes have been opened from Peking to Chungking, Urumchi in Sinkiang, and other far-flung cities. Nonstop service to Canton is now a matter of course (it did not exist when I first flew CAAC in 1964).

Peking airport is still no jet hub. China makes its big leap forward in aviation from a long way back. There are still more flights each day from Boston to Europe than from Peking to the vast population centers of south and southwest China.

One day in 1973, waiting at Peking airport for a plane to Wuhan, I consult the notice board of flights. It is not easy to read this chalked blackboard — all in Chinese — since every city has a nickname; Shanghai is "Hu," Canton is "Sui." Seventeen planes are scheduled

341

Here is Red Star commune, which feeds the capital with grain and meat and vegetables (the author at the pigsties)

Tian-an men is Peking's flat smooth stomach; the big characters say "Unite to Win Still Greater Victories"

for today. Ten coming in, seven going out, one of them an international flight, Aeroflot to Moscow.

But CAAC is full of plans for the near future. Peking has with a rush signed no fewer than thirty-six foreign civil aviation accords. CAAC has made test flights on a Peking–New York route, via Anchorage. It has its eyes on a link with Vancouver.

The air boom provides more jobs for young Chinese with an interest in machines. It is a sign of the times that the son of waiter Yang, the veteran of forty-seven years and a revolution in style at Peking Hotel, is a CAAC ground technician.

Airports are great liars. Bland and abstract and functional, they reflect little of life twenty kilometers away. They express an apparent "international technical culture" which really does not exist. Peking's bare, remote airport is no exception. Except for Mao photos, and music which is designed to inspire rather than soothe, it could be a small city terminal anywhere. Peking begins to trade the melody of isolation for the banal chords of intercourse.

Peking is a lovely city to approach by air from the far north. In 1964 a CAAC flight of four hours brings me in from the Siberian city of Irkutsk. Lake Baikal appears, shimmering in the warm August afternoon, surrounded by wooded mountains. When its last tentacles have receded we reach the fringes of the Gobi Desert. Utterly barren, an unrelieved ginger waste, baking in the sun. Here is no-man's-land between Europe and the Far East.

Within an hour or so of Peking the desert is behind us. Peaked mountains rear high into the sky. In their lap nestle streams, the yellow water gleaming silver in fierce sunlight.

The odd village can be seen, often on a grassy eminence, always intensely cultivated. Soon you recognize the large straw hats and blue costumes of farmers. The scene becomes lush, a galaxy of greens merging into yellows.

The first thing I see over the city is a parade ground full of military and civilians. After we land I learn what is going on. One million Chinese are protesting — we are still in the bitter days of 1964 — American naval aggression in the Gulf of Tonkin. It is my baptism to Peking. A first glimpse of mass politics in the land of the masses.

❀ ❀ ❀

It is 11:00 P.M. — a late hour in Peking — as I leave the New Traveler Hotel* in old Legation Street. I have been drinking ginseng wine with Wilfred Burchett, the Australian writer on Asia. (He is only half unpacked from Pyongyang, where Kim Il-sung dined with him last night and presented him with three bottles of Korea's unique brew. The taste is faintly medicinal, but if, as President Kim says, this potent root can add ten years to your life, who will let a funny flavor keep him from a double bonus of good spirits and good health?)

The summer night is soft and I decide to return on foot to my own hotel, the Nationalities. The two hotels lie east and west of the main public buildings of Mao's Peking. An hour's walk shows me much of "new state Peking."

Flashes of lightning make Tian-an men Square seem like a vast white skating rink, its big surrounding buildings like pink hills. Built during the early Ming, the square has been the heart of empire, republic, and people's republic alike. It is China's national emblem; the motif on CAAC's air tickets; the "red sun" in people's hearts. It is Peking's flat smooth stomach.

During the Great Leap Forward (1958) Tian-an men Square was rebuilt and enlarged from twenty-seven acres to a hundred acres. A staggering ten thousand trees were planted around it. Graceful willows; solid pines; maples with a rosy surprise up their sleeves for the autumn.

As one series of jumps within the Leap, Peking put up ten new buildings in ten months, to celebrate ten years of liberation. Most of the "triple ten" projects are near the square. The entire skyline of Peking today is made up of new public buildings, including the clocks of the railway station, the spire of the TV center, the Agricultural Exhibition Center, the Cultural Palace of Nationalities, the red star on top of the Military Museum.

Emperors used to hand down edicts at the northern fringe of the square, near the palace moat. An edict was held in the mouth of a

* The two characters of the hotel's name, *xin qiao,* are short for *xin hua-qiao,* which means "new overseas Chinese." In fact, overseas Chinese do not generally stay at the hotel. But the idea of the name continues, i.e. a new type of visit, or visitor, to post-Liberation China; hence my translation, "New Traveler Hotel."

344

gold-painted wooden phoenix. Down from the Gate of Heavenly Peace the bird was lowered. A mandarin of the Board of Rites took the edict on a tray decorated with clouds, carried it off to be copied on yellow paper and sent to every corner of China.

Here I am at the moat, and it is still called Golden Water River as under the Ming. Edicts, though, are handed down these days through the *People's Daily* rather than a golden phoenix. Ceremony is still frequent, and now an affair of the masses. A streak of lightning suddenly turns the paving beneath my feet into a silver lake. Each flat square flagstone has a number on it. So *that* is why China's parades go like clockwork!

On the square's eight-hundred-meter eastern flank, where the old Board of Rites and Board of Astronomy stood, I pass two new museums. Both the Museum of Chinese History (up to 1840) and the Museum of the Chinese Revolution (since 1840) were part of the "triple ten" project, shooting up like mushrooms after spring rain during 1959.

They are done in the quite pleasing style of new state Peking. Long (three hundred meters) in relation to height (forty-five meters), they do not chop off the view, or take away Tian-an men Square's sense of deep space. They match the Great Hall of the People, which faces them from the western flank, where the Court of Censors and Board of Punishments used to be. Pink granite at the base; fawn walls relieved by simple colonnades; upturned eaves of green- and gold-glazed tile.

There are few idlers around — unlike Shanghai's Nanking Road at the same hour — though some groups crouch at chess or *bai-fen*. A trickle of people in work clothes hurry to or from a night shift. It is a surprise to see two girls who seem to be just out for a stroll. Passing people on vast Tian-an men Square at 11:30 P.M. is hardly like passing them in a street; no need to "pass" anyone at all. But these snazzily dressed girls edge their way into my path. They do not merely smile then look away. When I glance at them, they gaze back intently, with a cool half smile.

I look across to the museums, closed for the evening, and for most of the last decade. Both of them I visited in 1964. My guide at the

345

Museum of the Chinese Revolution was a girl on whom the passion of the exhibits had rubbed off. Tight-lipped and prim in her white smock, she became more intense with each hall that we inspected.

I have never forgotten the shock of learning so bluntly in those halls what imperialism did to China, and how anti-imperialist the Chinese became as a result. The museum exhibits were judged soft and weak, though, during the Cultural Revolution. Since 1966 the museums have been under "rearrangement" (*zheng-li*).

The Great Hall of the People was the star of the "triple ten" spasm. It can hold a meeting of ten thousand delegates, mount a dinner party for five thousand, provide a chic salon for a quiet interview. There is an air of the grandness of public life inside this Parthenon of new China.

In August 1964 the hall was in full preparation for the fifteenth anniversary of Liberation. It seems a while ago, now that the twentieth and twenty-fifth anniversaries have also gone by, but I well recall the fine quality of sound in the main auditorium. Engineers showed me the reason for it; ten thousand loudspeakers, one at each chair, which give you the feeling of being in the middle of the stage.

Once I used the hall's southern entrance for a meeting with Kuo Mo-jo, China's top cultural politician. I came in from a lobby; he glided in from behind a curtain the height of a theater stage. As we stood for photos in front of a wrought-iron landscape in Anhwei style, Mr. Kuo explained that the hall has at least one room decorated in the style of each of China's provinces. For our conversation a small room of bare elegance had been chosen. Thick rug of cherry red; paneled walls; drapes of golden silk. Deep wicker armchairs for Kuo Mo-jo and myself, as well as for three people writing down what we said.

On another occasion, for a session with Premier Chou, we entered from the north door. It seems so far from the south door — 310 meters in fact — that you feel you are in a different part of Peking. Things are on a grander scale at this end. Up the big flight of steps which Chinese architects still consider essential. Corridors; chandeliers; red carpets.

The Premier is not quite ready so we wait in an anteroom the size

346

of a basketball court, its wooden doors like lofty pines. The room for the session itself is not one of the Great Hall's biggest but it is immense. From our seats the photographers and tea girls against the walls seem like miniature figurines. Sunk in a wicker chair, I have the sense of sitting on a deck chair at the beach.

New state Peking is everything that old dynastic Peking was not. Its buildings are fairly high; the old city was very low. They are only half-Chinese in style; roofs alone identify them with their dynastic sisters. Inscriptions used to be allusive ("Pavilion of Pleasant Sounds"). Today they are direct and assertive ("People Alone Are the Motive Force of History"). They used to evoke a purely Chinese range ("Salute the Son of Heaven"). Now an international strain has entered ("Working Class of the Whole World Unite!").

The buildings of new state Peking seem to point beyond themselves to something else that is new: the creation in China of a state mentality. During most of the dynasties the Chinese were not a very state-conscious people. They were led by an emperor; image of a family head writ large. They were bossed by mandarins; image of cultural gurus, rather than political operators.

This new Peking is made of transformed values as well as piles of smooth fawn marble. The family; the pull of a ripe culture — these are still strong bonds. But lying over them, squeezing them into new patterns, is the new entity of a national state bent on reforming the old society.

It is near midnight as I reach the northern side of the Great Hall of the People. The hundred-acre square looks even vaster than usual as lamplight reflects from sheets of rainwater on the flagstones. Red Flag limousines — the premier Chinese brand — are lined up at the steps to the hall, their chauffeurs smoking in groups. Smaller Shanghai cars come and go, bearing documents or lesser officials. Under way is the round of meetings leading up to the CCP's Tenth Congress.

There is a small stir as a woman comes out the northern door, attended by half a dozen aides. It appears to be Chiang Ch'ing, wife of Mao Tse-tung. Chauffeurs stub out cigarettes, dissolve their groups, polish the already gleaming bodies of their long black vehicles. The woman strides to her curtained Red Flag, is whisked away with a

347

bodyguard seated beside the driver. The car turns into the entrance of nearby South and Central Lakes, the government compound where the Chinese leaders live and work.

A flutter of self-importance surrounds the Great Hall as plans are laid for the congress. It is a special moment for new state Peking. Low-key, done at night — like so many political things in China — and with the feel of steel about it. Firm hands have a grip on China, and the present is a political age par excellence.

For the people this means that they are not only fathers or daughters, and sharers in the ability to read and write Chinese characters, but also citizens of a new Leviathan. They do not goggle from a distance at the golden phoenix; they join in and shout slogans at Tian-an men's orchestrated rallies.

I leave Tian-an men — feet tired by now — and walk to the Number Ten bus stop in Boulevard of Eternal Peace. No bus arrives; I approach a PLA man for advice. He is one of a line of soldiers with fixed bayonets who are guarding the strip between the Great Hall and South and Central Lakes during the meetings leading up to the Tenth Congress. "Comrade," I ask, "will there be another Number Ten bus?" The lean, fresh-faced army man is friendly, almost bashful. He tells me with a rueful smile that the last bus went at 9:30. Some buses keep going all night, he adds, but only on limited routes serving factories on shift work.

So I head on foot for the Nationalities Hotel. The occasional street-lamps look ghostly through the gauze of a fine mist. Sanitation trucks with sprinklers and high-pressure pumps spurt jets of water at the curb. There is a clatter of garbage cans being emptied into refuse trucks (the compost becomes fertilizer for thirty communes near Peking). Watching these clean-up operations I recall that not a single mosquito has bothered my summer stay in Peking.

On the sidewalk there are piles of melons which will go on sale tomorrow. They are loosely covered from moisture by straw mats; but no one thinks it necessary to guard them against pilfering. The Palace of Nationalities looms up and beyond it my hotel, named also for China's minority peoples, those other than Han. In style the Palace is Chinese flesh hung on international bones. A green-tiled Chinese roof

In style the Palace of Nationalities is Chinese flesh hung
on international bones; a green-tiled Chinese roof sits
on a modern hotellike block

sits on a modern hotellike block. In its aim the Palace of Nationalities is a fitting part of new state Peking. It stands for the power of a reforming state pitted against narrow loyalties from the past.

The city of Peking is unusual for having its highest buildings mostly on the fringes. Except for new state Peking, the center is low as well as flat. Homes are one story; shops rarely more than two. Trees planted since Liberation already top the roofs.

I speak of the forty square kilometers which used to be ringed by walls and a dozen gates. The northern part was called the Inner City (Nei-cheng); foreigners knew it as the Manchu or Tartar City. The southern part was called the Outer City (Wai-cheng); to foreigners, the Chinese City.

Two reasons explain why central Peking became a low gray jumble flecked with palaces. Within the Inner or Manchu City lay the Imperial City. The Imperial City, in turn, enclosed the Forbidden City, China's White House. No emperor since the Mongols would allow anyone to build a home which might overshadow his own.

And Peking bourgeois liked courtyards and privacy. Anyone who built a tall house would be able to see into the courtyard of his neighbors — unacceptable to all concerned. The middle classes built antisocial homes. Rooms issued onto a courtyard; a blank wall was turned to the outside world.

Even today the architectural staple of inner Peking — one can hardly call it downtown Peking — remains these Ming and Manchu houses. But they are old vessels into which new wine is being poured.

Each house used to serve one family circle; each courtyard was a sibling's hearth. The northern wing, facing south to catch the sun, was naturally set aside for the head of the family. Rooms facing east and west were for married sons. The meaner southern wing comprised the kitchen, servants' quarters, and rooms for lesser relatives who came to stay.

Today such a house has become a locality. It is no longer the preserve of one family but a slice of rebaked Peking society. Half a dozen

Even today the architectural staple of inner Peking remains these Ming and Manchu houses

nuclear families live where one extended family once lived. Working-class folk have taken over courtyard living from the middle classes, and they have made it communal instead of tribal.

Here is a neighborhood called West Eternal Peace, a cluster of streets close to the Boulevard of Eternal Peace. Morning sunshine lights up the yellow tiles of the old Imperial Palace as I leave the boulevard and enter the lanes of a residents' area within the neighborhood.

Most of these homes are a century old. In gray brick with red lacquered doors and pillars, they resemble smoky cats with bright bows at the neck. Latticed windows reach high to eaves decorated with tableaus of birds. They are filled with paper — glass is a new thing in China — which is replaced twice a year. Roofs are made of U-shaped, overlapping gray tiles, Spanish in appearance except that the gable is not so sharply angled.

Mr. Cha of West Eternal Peace's office leads me into a courtyard of his choice. It is large and yet cozy. Spaced around the flagstones are flowers in porcelain pots. Fruit trees twist their way toward the block of light offered by the courtyard. In the middle there is an old well with a pump. Over raised thresholds, heavy brown doors lead to half a dozen single-family apartments.

I sit on a stone doorstep to chat with Mr. Cha. He is a Peking man from way back. High cheekbones; piercing eyes; handsome features; a pale and soft complexion. Under a peach tree opposite us, four old men play *bai-fen*. With a frank grin, Cha admits that the game is getting more popular. It is far more common here, he says, than is Chinese chess (*xiang-qi*).

Cha explains that we are in one of West Eternal Peace's thirty-five residents' areas (each is broken down again into four or five lane areas). The whole neighborhood has twenty thousand families — as Cha chooses to put it — or eighty thousand people.

Some families have roots in early Manchu times. This single dynasty, it takes an effort to recall, runs back as far as the English settlement of America. West Eternal Peace's five factories occupy converted houses from the Manchu. Their workers, 78 percent of them women, make buttons and do tailoring; they fold book leaves; they make locks and magnetic motors for farm implements.

Civic pride seems high. A woman died not long ago, leaving the husband with four children, aged three to nine. The man did not have to devise an individual scheme for coping, since the residents' committee pitched in with a plan. X would cook a meal for the family three times a week. Y would mind the small child. Z would keep an eye on the household's sewing needs.

When I remark that the stone yards and dirt lanes are clean, Cha tells me about garbage collection. As well as penalties against a household that does not put out its rubbish daily, there is a cunning rule to prevent smell and litter in the lanes. Garbage cans may only be brought to the lane once the streetlights go on! (pickup is soon after).

Cha says that in old Peking most people cleaned their house once a year, before Spring Festival, which is the Chinese New Year. Now residents' committees call the tune on when and to what standard cleaning is done. It is more frequent and it is more collective. The whole city also proclaims mass "cleanups" seven or eight times a year. Gone is the spirit of "each man looks to his own" (*ge xing qi shi*).

Electricity is being used in these low gray homes as if they had always known it. Here is a boy whose mechanical dump truck has flashing lights. There a tiny girl puts her arms around a big blue bird that waddles and chirps. Since one family's toys cannot be sharply more costly than the next one's, the general standard is apparently lavish.

I ask to choose another courtyard for myself. We wander into one that turns out to be similar to the first. In fact we hit upon a man with a very high salary, a cadre in the Bank of China's head office. He brings home 150 yuan a month, spends four yuan of it for the rent of his three tasteful rooms. (I see only two rooms, one very big, but Cha points to the ceiling, where a beam runs across the waist of the large room. "In Peking we always count rooms *by the beam*.") The rent, which includes water and electricity, is extra low and I ask Cha about it.

His answer gives an interesting glimpse of Peking's housing setup. Most houses are owned by the municipality's Bureau of Real Estate

A market in the western part of old Peking

Administration. (With its branches in each of Peking's six urban districts, it employs thirty thousand people, has its own training college.) But a sprinkling of houses are owned by work units, like this one belonging to the Bank of China. The rent for these homes is cheaper.

The banker smiles with modest pleasure when we talk about his good housing deal. Cha and I move out from the living room, lined with more than a fair share of Chairman Mao's works, into the well of sunlight which is the courtyard. A child is ready to sing us a song, but Cha turns to me with a further remark. "Before the Cultural Revolution," he says quietly, "most of Peking's houses, except for those owned by a work unit, were privately owned."

We enter the lane with a cortege of kids behind us. I say nothing — I am not sure of Cha's opinion about the change in house ownership — but Cha resumes. "During the Cultural Revolution the houses were handed over. But maybe they will be handed back." I bend down to shake the hand of a tot who has broken away from a game of jumping-the-rubber-band to present me with a flower. I am eager to let Mr. Cha say what he wants to say. "You know," he adds, "the constitution of China permits private ownership — have you read it carefully?" He looks at me with a steady eye. "It is now being discussed whether homes should go back to private ownership."

A knock on the door and in bounces Wang Hsi, deputy editor of China's worldwide weekly, *Peking Review*. I had asked for the meeting, having found Miss Wang on a previous occasion to be frank and amusing. Usually one interviews people at their place of work or in a reception room; certainly I did not expect Wang Hsi to come rapping at my room in the Nationalities Hotel. It is a sign of the relaxed air of 1973 — as is a call that evening from a Chinese diplomat I know, who "heard I was in town" and phoned to see if we could get together.

Miss Wang is fifty-six, stocky, gregarious. Her round kind face is cheerful when there is no good reason to be gloomy. She has no airs and could pass as readily for a bus conductor as an editor. Working as a journalist on a magazine sent abroad, she is more aware of foreign ways than the average Chinese cadre. One hand busy with a fan, she

355

sits in a bedside armchair and declares: "I don't know much, but I'll talk about anything you like." We start on the Peking publishing scene.

Wang Hsi has charge of the Chinese version of *Peking Review,* before it is translated into English, French, Spanish, German, and Japanese. Not published in Chinese, the *Review* began in English only in 1958 (successor to *People's China*), added the extra tongues later. It sells 200,000 copies in its five editions, 10,000 of these in the United States.

Miss Wang has been to America and is interested in U.S. reading habits. "You know," she says with a frown, "many Americans write and say they do not find it easy to get our magazine. The problem is an odd one. Our price is so low that the news dealer's proportion does not make it worth his while to stock the *Review*." I suggest a bigger cut to the dealer, on the ground that it would still be far less expensive than the airmail postage on copies sent to American mail subscribers.

Miss Wang sighs at the problem but remarks with satisfaction: "*China Reconstructs* [a pictorial which began in 1952] should sell far more than the *Review* in America. In fact its circulation is no higher than ours." Later, there comes a gentle barb at this other magazine for foreigners. When she asks for suggestions to improve the *Review,* I urge use of interviews. "Oh, *China Reconstructs* prints interviews — do you really think they're any good?"

I hastily move on to Miss Wang's view of America. Hawaii intrigues her; sympathetic halfway house between the United States and Asia. She once wrote these words about it: "Only after visiting Hawaii did I get a deeper understanding of the time-honored friendship between the Chinese and American peoples."

Drugs, unemployment, the surge of religious feeling. Wang Hsi raises these U.S. phenomena with an air of wonder, as an American might take note of the alien laws of gravity on the moon. It had stuck in her mind that one U.S. worker likened to a "lottery" the chances of getting on in America. But editor Wang's main point about the United States concerns her trip there in the spring of 1973, and comes as a small bombshell.

She begins with a question: "Is America really so dangerous that the Secret Service has to protect Chinese visitors every moment of the day?" Then she launches into a discussion of "overprotection" that could have dropped from the lips of many an American visitor to China.

"In New York they forbade us to ride the subway. We only met people at receptions and banquets. I never sat down with a single blue-collar worker. Here we are, you and I, chatting like two friends in your hotel room. In the United States this was impossible for us. The State Department was, I suppose, trying to be hospitable. We were disappointed."

I can only guess at the reply if a Peking friend should ask Wang Hsi the question I have been asked a hundred times about China: "In America, do you only see what they want you to see, or can you wander around freely?" Are you listening, State Department?

Wang Hsi brings me up to date on the froth and bubble of life in Peking. The affectionate prefix "old" — as in "Old Chen" or "Old Teng" — is no longer used only for men, but is just as common now as the term of address for an older woman. Yes, it's true that an egg costs the same, nine to twelve fen, whether you buy it raw in the shell, or cooked and ready to eat. As a new antipollution step, separate chimneys for heating individual buildings are on the way out, in favor of a few vast central heating systems in key districts. At middle schools, boarding and "busing" are far less common than before the Cultural Revolution, and schools now serve only their immediate environs.

Politics is not Miss Wang's cup of tea but she has her views. The fan moves fast, like a flapping bird between her face and mine, as she sums up Liu Shao-ch'i and Lin Piao. "Look, they were both the same, as far as I am concerned — they departed from socialism."

But isn't it hard to know ahead of time what is a departure from socialism? "I have that same problem," comes the matter-of-fact response. "I had not considered Liu's *How To Be a Good Communist* a bad book. Then our *Review* ran a piece criticizing it; I saw things I had not seen before. Such is the power of revolutionary criticism."

Peking journalists get tip-offs which help them find high points in the plateau of official prose. Miss Wang tells me to take good note of Premier Chou's speech last week at the banquet for President

N'gouabi of the Congo. "It contains China's first statement on the Superpowers since Brezhnev visited the U.S. in the summer." But is Chou's speech so fresh . . . ? Wang Hsi is philosophic: "We have been told it is very important."

The time ticks by and I have the feeling Wang Hsi needs to get home and cook dinner. I cast a final line into broad waters: what is the most important problem facing China? "Our economy. After the Cultural Revolution, to push ahead with economic development." I wonder if China's growing prosperity and security will not cause people to slacken from the efforts of the past twenty-five years. "I don't think so," says Wang Hsi quietly. "It may spur new advance."

When I meet the political writer Hu Sheng, he tells me it is the first time he has received a scholar from a foreign university. Though not visible to foreigners — he has traveled hardly at all except for lengthy trips in Russia — Hu Sheng has been one of the CCP's leading propagandists: deputy director of the Propaganda Department of the Party, a top man at *Red Flag* magazine, writer of important works of history, influential voice in the Department of Philosophy and Social Sciences of the Academy of Sciences.

We sit among electric fans and tea mugs in a reception room of the Nationalities Hotel. Hu is above middle age, slow and polite in gesture, with a stiff bearing more common in Prussia than in China. A native of Kiangsu, he has the flat face of east China, and eyes that are big, expressive, easily amused. There are moments when he simply gazes at me and offers a smile in place of an answer.

One reason I wanted to see Hu was that his book *Imperialism and Chinese Politics* is one of the works published in Peking that I most frequently suggest to students at Harvard, and some of his articles in *Study* (a forerunner to *Red Flag*) and *Historical Research* have been much discussed in China and abroad.

Winds of change have blown over China since Hu wrote these things. Hu fell from favor during the Cultural Revolution. He tells me that *Imperialism and Chinese Politics* is now a "reference book" — which means it has errors. This does not lessen my interest in his opinions. And I want to know what is wrong with his book (which my Harvard students had thought of as a pillar of Peking orthodoxy).

358

Hu coolly remarks that Marx's five stages of historical development are not always fulfilled. "In China, for example, some of our minorities have gone directly from slave society to socialist. No feudal or capitalist stage in between. Marx did not predict it, but it has happened." This does not make Hu believe in a special Asian mode of development. Marx's laws "basically" apply to the whole world.

If this is a wavering from strict Marxism, it is Hu's only one. I soon feel, in fact, that Hu is an old-fashioned Marxist, that this fidelity itself brought him troubles after 1965.

Was Liu Shao-ch'i a "pessimist?" Hu asks if we may leave that subject and move to another. How does he feel, looking back on Moscow's role in the Chinese revolution? "I think the Soviet Union made a great contribution to our revolution." When we talk about the Sian Incident of 1936 Mr. Hu makes no criticism of Soviet policy.*

Hu Sheng's book, written in Hong Kong during 1947, deals with imperialism in China from the Opium War until the 1920s. What about the decades since; where is the cutting edge of imperialism today? This does not lead Hu to attack "social imperialism" (Russia) as one might expect. It is U.S. imperialism on which he concentrates.

I tell Hu Sheng that I have been struck by a relative soft-pedaling on Japan in his writings about China's suffering from imperialism. "When I wrote a lot of that," he replies, "during the late 1940s, Japan's imperialism had become clear to all. Not enough attention, though, was being paid to rising U.S. imperialism."

Two days before, Chang Wen-chin, Assistant Foreign Minister, made the same point to me about the late 1940s, but he went on to say: "From the late 1960s, the rising imperialism is that of the Soviet Union. Asian people were slow in the 1940s to see that America was the new problem; now they are slow to see that America is past its peak and Russia is the ambitious one." But Hu Sheng does not draw this parallel.

History is always written, says Hu, under the influence of the historian's own direct experience. "I could not have written my book about imperialism but for what I learned as a journalist and organizer

* Moscow did not approve of the capture of Chiang Kai-shek by his own disgruntled colleagues.

in the anti-Japanese struggle of the 1930s and 1940s." The Cultural Revolution, too, is having an influence on how Chinese history gets written.

Because the nature of the influence has yet to be clarified, Hu has written nothing since 1966. He and his colleagues at the Institute of Modern History, within the Academy of Sciences, are still thinking things through. Stress in the near future will be on the period 1912–1927, for which there exist many unexamined materials.

Hu apologizes for *Imperialism and Chinese Politics,* says it was a hasty job, based on very limited sources. He had been isolated in Chungking as a journalist on *New China News (Hsin-hua jih-pao),* came to Hong Kong in 1946, and wrote the book quickly from documents available there.

But the real problem with Hu Sheng's book, after 1966, was "revisionism." Hu had been criticized before for mechanical interpretations. For being too tough on the Boxers, whose movement he called a "perversion." Too unappreciative of the policies of "national and race salvation" of the 1898 reformers. Too rigidly opposed to private enterprise (in some 1952 articles about the Five Anti Movement). His plodding 1950s-type Marxism was apparently called too close to the Soviet line during the Cultural Revolution.

I talk more with Hu two evenings later, when Yang Kung-su, who has been ambassador to Nepal and is now head of China Travel Service, invites the two of us to dinner, along with Professor Chou I-liang, Tu Chih-kuo, the Foreign Ministry's specialist on Australia, and other friends.

But it was one year later that I pondered most carefully Hu's words. For on the occasion of National Day 1974, Hu Sheng sprang back to favor. At a grand reception in the Great Hall he, along with other key "revisionists," made his first reported public appearance since the Cultural Revolution. Then in January 1975, Hu was not only a delegate at the National People's Congress, China's parliament, but was elected to its standing committee. An interesting straw in the wind.

A visit to America's new toehold in Peking for lunch with Ambassador Bruce, then shopping in the lanes outside Front Gate. From one island of old-world quality to another.

David Bruce, so uninhibited by Peking that he wears purple trousers, crimson shirt, and blue shoes, handles his chopsticks and the fiery *mao-tai* liquor with determination. Mrs. Evangeline Bruce, not cast down by a muddle of packing cases and workmen hammering, comes to the table with a plastic bag of macaroons she picked up from an old German baker at Peitaiho.

There are no purple trousers at Palisade Street (Da-zha-lan) and Glazier's Shop (Liu-li-chang), two shopping lanes beyond Front Gate. But these redeemed feudal enclaves seem almost as removed from new state Peking as does Mr. Bruce. Here is a slice of central Peking famous for shops and theaters since Ming times. Low dark brick buildings that are scarred with the wires and poles of an electric age. Roofs at all angles; few trees. On larger streets like Outside Trumpet the Military Gate, a few villas in Western style, in brown and orange bricks with fancy windows and battlements on the top floor.

One shabby building is the original Peking Duck Restaurant. Here food quality is in inverse ratio to that of decor. A nontipper would once be dealt an ear-piercing cry from the headwaiter: "Guests leaving. No-o-o T-i-i-ip." Today a tip is considered an insult.

A giant among pygmies is the massive Front Gate. Curved eaves are piled one on top of the other; the arch is like a gaping mouth; the worn bricks bear a banner which cries "Raise High the Great Red Flag of Mao Tse-tung's Thought." In earlier days this gate was a barrier between the order of the Tartar City and the scramble of the Chinese City.

Mrs. Chia, my companion on this shopping trip, is as calm a Chinese official as you will find. Her eyes are wise and tired for a woman in her thirties; a streak of humor is ready at the mouth; her expression suggests patience without limit. The husband is a teacher at middle school, and there is a young son. Mrs. Chia gives the boy lessons in classical Chinese, "so that he won't be cut off from knowing China's past." On topics from art and sex to politics, Mrs. Chia never tries to inject me with correct thoughts. This does not reduce the mark she makes on me as a convincing voice of new China.

Palisade Street was once the Broadway of Peking except that it was narrow. It has lost its intimate theaters, since theater in China turned monumental, and all ninety of its pre-Liberation brothels. But its nooks exude variety and bustle, and seven theaters have made it into the era of socialist art. Two movie houses remain, and both are showing foreign films — from Hanoi and Pyongyang.

Here Chinese socialism meets Old Peking. The freewheeling social genius of the city; the unscrubbed face; a few loose ends; the unabashed stare at a foreign face; an old guy caught between tradition and the new norms. One feels far removed indeed from the official reserve of the diplomatic quarter, from the banner by Tian-an men which cries "Ten Thousand Years to the Unity of All Peoples of the World."

Misty rain creeps down on people scurrying under sheets of blue or green plastic. Some stop to buy a slice of melon and eat it on the run. Everyone is dressed in loose, floppy clothes which conceal the body but are comfortable. We pass a shop-front noodle factory. Its loud machines emit the long white strings that once were squeezed by hand.

A spacious textile store with a marble porch does a brisk trade in silk, cotton, serge, synthetics. It has been here for eighty years. Ten thousand customers a day go in its graceful wooden doorway, coming out with sixteen thousand yuan worth of fabrics. The store has not changed for decades, but its spirit and the goods have. Every second roll of cloth seems to be a synthetic fiber, especially vinyon, and 30 percent of the clerks are women (none before Liberation).

I want a pair of Chinese-style cotton shoes and Mrs. Chia says this is a good moment to get them, for Palisade Street has the best *bu di xie* shop in all Peking. In we go and I secure a blue pair — no giveaway at five and a half yuan — which prove a dream to wear. (But they came to a quick bad end, for I got them damp, which one should not do. In Wuhan a luxurious green fungus appeared on the uppers. By the time I reached Canton, it was clear the shoes had to be discarded. But how? Anything you throw away in China that has a 10 percent chance of life comes back to you like a boomerang. It was the morning of my departure from China. I left my seventh-floor room

362

at the Hotel of the East, but instead of taking the elevator went down the stairs. On a fifth-floor window ledge I placed a parcel neatly wrapped in an old *People's Daily*. I hope those rotten *bu di xie* didn't cause anyone a struggle session.)

Into a Chinese medicine shop we plunge to look for ginseng ("person tonic"). An air of concentration at the crowded counters. A smell of roots and herbs that I feel I won't be able to stand for long. Looking at the mostly older customers I recall two things said by the doctor at West Eternal Peace neighborhood: Chinese drugs are often cheaper than Western; old people favor the Chinese while young people lean to the Western.

A young clerk tells me that for maximum effect I should buy ginseng root, then boil it or stew it in wine. But it is more practical to take the extract, at three yuan for a small bottle. I ask on behalf of a relative about potions for arthritis. A jungle of leaves, insects, even deer antlers is brought out for our inspection. But I would need to charter a plane to take enough for a lengthy treatment.

Glazier's Shop got its name during the Ming, when tile makers gathered in this cluster of lanes. In Manchu times it opened its low archways to old books, antiques, paintings. Luxurious and exotic items were gradually weeded out after Liberation. With the Cultural Revolution most of the curio shops closed. To ram home the sensitive point, the main lane was in 1966 renamed Antifeudalism Street.

Culture being the nagging problem it is for the CCP, Glazier's Shop is a rather faded flower. Yet many of its shops have reopened, as after a typhoon, and Mrs. Chia and I have fun in them. We stroll in from Palisade Street, which is just to the northwest, past the Wide Harmony Theater and innumerable repair shops. The first thing we see is a fine sweet shop. Firecrackers and sweets used to be by-line specialties of Glazier's Shop. The firecrackers seem to have gone up in smoke but the candies certainly have not.

Everything is a dusty color, lit up by red signboards and outcrops of green roof-moss. The weaving lanes are piled with pipes, bricks, timber on makeshift shelves. Glazed work is no longer produced, we find, only ordinary gray bricks, which are superior to red ones because they are baked longer.

363

The boutiques still have style. In a scroll and pottery shop the clerks seem ready to talk for hours about the origin of their wares. Prices are no longer cheap as before the Cultural Revolution, but I buy some nice paper cuts of scenes from the T'ang dynasty.

A branch of the China Bookstore is a haven of antiquities. Just off the press are some superb tomes which reproduce cave drawings from Loyang and other regions of China. Books are stored flat on the shelves in the traditional way. There is a table with a green cloth for browsers to look with care at a fragile volume.

Posters on sale at China Bookstore are by no means all political. Here are landscapes; flowers and fruit; children playing. A rare pose has Chairman Mao sitting casually in an armchair. But Mrs. Chia and I are almost the only customers in both these cultural shops. The anti-feudal campaign in Glazier's Shop, like the average Chinese political campaign, no doubt won a bit and lost a bit.

❋ ❋ ❋

If Tian-an men Square is Peking's stomach, Eternal Peace Boulevard is a belt drawn across it. North of the square and a little east of the former Imperial Palace lies another old commercial quarter. Its core street is Wang-fu-jing (Well of the Princes' Residences). Once it was known as Morrison Street, after an Australian who wrote from Peking for the London *Times*. The *People's Daily* is written and printed where the well to which the street's name refers used to stand.

Ordinary people of old Peking were crowded into the north and south. Better-off folk built their homes to east and west. Here we seem to be in a fringe area. It is more solid, better paved, more blessed with trees than the Front Gate area. It has more Western buildings, fewer shanties, a lot of squat bourgeois chimneys. And Wang-fu-jing lacks the naughty traditions of Palisade Street. It is not smart but has an air of prosperity.

A magnet in the street is Peking's largest department store. The Wang-fu-jing has the informal air of a church bazaar. It serves each day 100,000 customers, whose purses are fatter in 1973 than they used to be. Goods are more various; shopping baskets are fuller; the counters are more crowded than two years ago. A long line of people wait to buy sets of festive electric light bulbs in multiple colors. I am tempted only by a pair of crisscross Peking sandals, the most comfortable kind I know.

A new extension to Peking Hotel protrudes like a long molar at the southern mouth of Wang-fu-jing. Nearby a handsome new arts and crafts shop is almost completed. Here, too, is CAAC's central office, in a cool colonial building. I once arrived there to check in for a flight to Canton, to find that south China was gripped by a storm. "Try again in four hours," said the agent with a cheerful smile.

Several of Peking's fifty-odd twenty-four-hour shops are in Wang-fu-jing. Mellow old shops for seals, too, and junk shops which the ever-curious Chinese love. White sheets are spread across display windows to subdue the bone-dry heat of midday. The store's name is printed across them in red characters. Trash cans in aqua porcelain stand out against the sidewalk's sea of white shirts and silver bicycles.

Eastern Market sells seventeen thousand kinds of products, including single socks, gloves, and shoes. The stalls are better stocked and laid out than two years ago. But the secondhand book section is a shadow of what I recall from 1964. The foreign books are mostly dictionaries and technical manuals, with a scattering of noncontroversial titles like *Familiar Trees of Hopei* by F. H. Chow.

North of Lantern Market Street and Pig Market Street, the establishments are less solid, even scraggy. There are curbside markets which are a whirl of apples, babies, cabbages, bicycles. The leathery faces of farmers, up from a commune to sell their fruit, stand out from the pale radiant Peking faces.

An ample matron in black pants elbows her way through to assess a box of cucumbers. A boy with bunches of scallions tied to the handlebars of his bike is too eager to get near the melons. He knocks a four-wheeled wagon in which sit a baby and a sack of flour. The baby begins to cry; brows furrow.

The boss of one little mart is about seventy but firm and energetic. A long black apron reaches almost to his bare spindly ankles which shine like lizard skin. Above his darting eyes a bald strip runs back

In Wang-fu-jing Street white sheets are spread across display windows to subdue the bone-dry heat of midday

A baby's cart shares the road with heftier vehicles, in a commercial sector northeast of Tian-an men

between two close-cropped sides of an oval head. He dispenses pears and peppers with the speed of a computer, calling out their virtues as he does so.

A store that will sell a single sock! Is this a supreme badge of poverty? To me, it is at any rate a badge of China's high standard of practical, flexible service. Shops have been relocated so that most residential areas are very close to what they need. Opening hours are adjusted to suit the work patterns of the neighborhood. There are shops-on-wheels, mounted on pedicabs, which visit out-of-the-way lanes. Shops are not allowed to raise prices just because demand soars.

No simple item exists that you cannot get repaired in Peking. Things lost in this city of seven million amazingly often can be retrieved at lost-and-found depots run by Public Security. Some theaters carry flexibility to the point of selling tickets on the basis of small time segments — two fen per ten minutes — so that patrons can come and go as mood and schedule require. Peking even sent to Shanghai for tailors, hairdressers, cleaners, window dressers, to lift services to Shanghai's unbeatable level.

Buses have a "Suggestion Book" hanging on the wall. Conductors call out the time when they announce a destination, and they are trained to live up to the proud slogan "Every Conductor a Walking Map." The Peking consumer, in brief, is by no means an unheeded victim of Moscow-type bureaucratism.

Through a small wooden door in Wang-fu-jing I find my way to the Bright and Flowery Bathhouse. It is a refreshing spot after shopping or on the way home from work. Though wintertime is its busy season, the tiled halls are crowded even on a summer day. Hours are 8:30 A.M until 8:30 P.M. I have come at noon, to purge my body instead of gorging it with one more Rabelaisian lunch.

The blackboard by the entry is scrawled with a complex list of services available, many of which I cannot decipher. A well-scrubbed boy of fifteen rescues me, leads me through glass doors and up a stone staircase. Little Ma (as he introduces himself) swings a small cloth and whistles an aria from *Taking Tiger Mountain by Strategy*. Into a small bathroom he puts me and says it will be "comfortable and convenient."

But this is not what I have come for; my hotel has such a Western bath. I ask Ma to slow down his rapid Shensi accent. We consult. Soon I have a ticket for the Public Room (thirty fen), which turns out to be a big clean hall with sixty or seventy bathers.

Little Ma seems pleased, after all, that I have chosen to join the masses. Dozens stare with interest and amusement as he shows me around with grand gestures. Finally he leads me to my couch and leaves me with two towels.

Each bather has a wooden couch draped in a towel. There are cloths, sandals, and a teapot on a small table beside the couch. Each bather also has a locker for valuables; an attendant keeps the key.

The hall accommodates three long double rows of couches and there is, I find later, a similar hall downstairs. It is all modern; Little Ma says Bright and Flowery was built after Liberation. Corridors lead off to other rooms for massage, haircutting, foot care, laundry — done in the time it takes you to bathe and rest.

My feet half in straw sandals that are too small, I go to the bath itself (*chi-tang*). The scene is one of steam, soapsuds, brown bodies tinged pink with the heat. I slip off the sandals, hang up my towel, take a shower before choosing a pool. There are three pools with a label in red characters on a small board: Warm, Hot, Most Hot.

Little Ma rushes up to suggest I do not try Most Hot. I have already made a mental note to the same effect. Six or seven people lie around in both Warm and Hot, smiles of well-being on their faces. Most Hot has only one, a wizened old guy who seems to be making a supreme effort to stay in the water. Heat waves rise from the surface in slow undulations.

For a long time I wallow in Warm and Hot — not even a foot will agree to stay in Most Hot — and watch the action. Here are two mates about eighteen years old, one a factory worker and the other a middle-school student. At the Warm pool they scrub each other's back. Later they read comic books on their couches.

A middle-aged man comes in who is not a manual worker. His hands are soft, he walks with a certain dignity, he is not in good shape. He is with a lithe youth, who soaps him down as he lies on the edge of the Hot pool.

One thing is clear about age differences at Bright and Flowery. The older men are smaller than the younger. It is not just that some are wizened and shrunken; that some betray malformations (a limp, a spine problem). The young workers, students, and PLA men are simply bigger in stature.

Their floppy clothes off, most of these youths turn out to be well built. Chinese garments, like the walls of old Chinese houses, conceal a good deal. The average guy is wiry and half-muscular in a curved way. Faces are angular and shoulders are broad. There are no obvious southerners — round and short-legged — at Bright and Flowery today.

Soft and pink I retire to my couch. It is the custom to linger. There is no extra charge if you stay a long time or use more towels. Some swathe themselves in a towel and sleep. A group near me lie smoking cigarettes and chatting from their couches.

A few read books but no one has a newspaper. A man of forty across the aisle is absorbed in *Red Flag,* which I have rarely before seen anyone in China reading. He may be a cadre; hard to tell in the reclining naked state.

There is an air of peace and renewal. No trace of tension in the room; a pleasant chance to converse. But the accents are often thick. Are these men out-of-towners, cleaning up, perhaps, during a few hours stopover at the Peking railway station? I meet one such, but many are regulars. The majority are working-class; sunburn marks follow the line of their singlet straps.

One evening I go to another bathhouse in the cramped lanes outside Front Gate. A PLA man on a bus told me about it. I have passed a long session with a Chinese Minister and am weary after the excitement of it.

Great Fragrant Garden is close to Palisade Street and Glazier's Shop. The setup is similar to that of Bright and Flowery but the tone is different. The environment is a bit raffish, if not quite sleazy. From a barber's chair I look out on gray roofs, ill-lit lanes, houses that have known better days. This bathhouse dates from pre-Liberation and is shabby; but it's clean and has a friendly air.

The price is twenty-eight fen, a little cheaper than Bright and Flowery. At the showers you stand on a board, which starts the water as you step on, stops it when you leave. Typical of China's backyard ingenuity in pursuit of economy.

Instead of lockers for one's valuables, Great Fragrant Garden has an easy, safe, and cheap system. An attendant takes your clothes and bag and hoists them with a long pole to a railing high toward the ceiling. No fuss, no keys, no delay, yet safe as a church. Everyone can see the things; only the attendant has a pole to get them down.

I am fiercely massaged by a grinning giant from Liaoning. He talks at me as I grit my teeth. Great Fragrant Garden closed up, he says, for eighteen months during the Cultural Revolution. "There were criticisms," he declares as he stands triumphant on my spine. "We came in every day and discussed things. But there were no customers."

The steamy informality of Bright and Flowery and Great Fragrant Garden gives the foreigner a fresh angle on Peking. He will enter few homes in a purely social way. The bathhouse is the best place I know to relax with ordinary folk, without prior arrangement or agenda. The PRC naked, after all, is not less a part of Chinese life than the PRC on parade.

❁ ❁ ❁

New Peking impinges at Three Mile River (San-li-he), a few kilometers from Tian-an men, a bit west of the Nationalities Hotel.

The Temple of the Moon once stood in this neighborhood, near a green park with a pool. It was built in the late Ming for the emperor to make sacrifices at autumn equinox. White jade and white silk were put on the tablet of the moon. White sheep, pigs, and oxen were killed at the setting of the sun. Around the Jade Pool the royals would romp when not occupied with cosmic ritual. Surrounding it was a Moslem slum and a large cemetery.

Three Mile River is the site of a spanking new housing estate. Some of its twenty-odd blocks are prefabricated; the Chinese call this "simple

370

and easy housing" (*jian-yi-lou*). The tallest are ten stories, Peking's highest apartments.

Each building has a small box for the requests and suggestions of residents. Streets have been laid out where only kingly paths used to exist; trolleybuses come right to the estate. Most remaining low gray houses (*ping-fang*) were recently sacrificed — not like pigs to the moon — but to the geometric logic of the underground railroad.

Three Mile River has cast off the robes of a feudal past for the tunic of modernity. Cosmos, kings, corpses; their grip has loosened. Kids of the 1970s who get curious about the moon are only two minutes by trolley from the exhibits at the Peking Planetarium. As for the Jade Pool, it is part of the Stable Forever River irrigation project!

Let us go to Peace Zone (He-ping li), one of ten neighborhoods in East City district. Here too is a new Peking on which nostalgia lays no claim. Before Liberation it was wasteland; today it is an industrial suburb of sixty-five thousand moderns. The veterans among its population were all in service trades before 1949. Now most of the people in Peace Zone's twenty-three residents' areas work in machine plants and textile mills.

In the east and to a degree in the southeast and west, Peking has become what it never seemed cut out to be: an industrial city. It is home to 1.2 million factory workers. It offers employment to thirteen times the people it did twenty-five years ago. Its industrial production has leapt up a hundred times since then. Can these rows of blocks and chimneys still echo Peking's old self-understanding?

Within a year of the CCP victory Peking had changed in spirit and organization. Civic pride arose as if from thin air; a net of control fell over each citizen; streets were cleaned up and began to buzz with purpose. Physical changes to the city took longer but have been very great.

Because they impeded traffic, the city walls were torn down, and most of the gates too. New round-the-city roads were built, which "checkerboard" Peking hadn't known before. Public transport took a quantum jump forward; a mere 164 vehicles in 1949 has turned into 2,500 (trams losing out en route to buses and trolleys).

Columns of smoke soon announced that Peking, for the first time in its highly political history, was making steel, chemicals, machines, cotton yarn. The city no longer had to buy all needed manufactures, except handicrafts, from Shanghai and Tientsin. Each year new products appear. Among the latest in the light industry area are ultra-high-pressure xenon lamps, and a durable fabric which is part polyester and part goat hair.

Completely new, too, are the five- and six-story housing blocks, into which 700,000 Peking households have moved. Already by the *end of 1954,* total floor space in Peking — much of it residential — had increased by half as compared with 1949. The new blocks have wrought a revolution in the daily life of Peking man.

Residents used to courtyard living find themselves thrown together, yet in a way more alone than before. For lucky families who had a lot of space, the old homes were wells of privacy. The new blocks have no walls to keep out the eyes and cries of neighbors.

Yet for ordinary families the new blocks give more room space than they had before enjoyed. Modern apartment living helps make them true individuals, encourages a sense of oneself, an awareness of capacity, a feeling that there is an open path ahead. Links with other people are broader, more arbitrary, more stimulating. And rents have come down. Twenty fen per square meter is the standard rate, which finds the average family paying only 6 percent of its income on rent.

That new Peking man has more yuan in his pocket than his father did is shown by a few simple figures. Retail sales in Peking during 1973 were 10.5 times what they were in 1949. Bank deposits for 1973 topped those for 1949 by 867 times! (and for the first half of 1974 they were up 16.5 percent over the first half of 1973). Two hundred twelve times as many bicycles were sold in 1973 as in 1949.

As factories and apartments went up the *People's Daily* spoke of a "great high tide of Industrial Revolution." Such a mood does stalk these avenues of brick oblongs, blue overalls, young trees. Here is the buoyancy of a generation that by its own hand has changed its way of life. Here, too, is a certain parochialism and self-preoccupation, as these newly moderns delight in things which are taken for granted in most big industrial cities.

There is a sense of involvement in what has been achieved which is

The petrochemical plant is a
city of steel and dust amid
the rocky foothills of Mighty
Range Mountains

the result of endless mutual consultation. No more is the Chinese
worker asked to do only what he is ordered to do. Told the purpose
of what's going on, he gets prizes and publicity if he suggests useful
improvements. "Exchange of technique" meetings give the worker a
chance to demonstrate to others a new method he has hit upon. He is
dared to think, to make connections, to be a poor man's Prometheus.

I sense this participant's pride at Peking General Petrochemical.
This plant, started in 1968, is refining 2.5 million tons of oil a year
by the time of my 1971 visit. I drive south and west from the city, past
the Peking Man site, by some old ladies whose bare breasts hang like
shopping bags in the hot afternoon. The plant is a city of steel and
dust amid the rocky foothills of Mighty Range Mountains — which
protect it against easy air attack.

Except for tea tanks — rather than water fountains — the workshops could be those of an American plant. There are ten thousand
workers, 35 percent of them women; most are ex-peasants who have
made a leap from rural torpor to industrial routine. The plant is
headed by a PLA man who tells me he never had a day's formal
schooling. It is all-Chinese in design and execution, with a few parts
bought from Romania.

In turning the wilderness into a refinery, workers met disheartening
problems by sheer social willpower. A manganese steel tower had to
be welded in a temperature above zero degrees centigrade, but the task
arose in midwinter with the mercury twelve degrees below zero. Would

373

the tower have to be sent off to a factory for welding? A team decided to whip up a mat shed heated by three stoves made of oil drums. The tower was welded inside it, on time, without flaw.

I walk out among pipes and red banners to the unlikely sight of pools of goldfish and Peking ducks in cane pens. There are smiles when I ask how these can stand the polluted environment. "You have seen the point," says a PLA cadre with a knowing grin, "but upside down." The fish and ducks are the living fruit of ingenious efforts to beat pollution.

The plant emits waste water, the PLA man explains, which contains harmful sulfides and phenols. If allowed to run away it would damage crops and foul rivers. The best way to get rid of evil, it was reasoned, is to turn evil into good.

Here is a tower where sulfides are removed from the waste water. Over there a cement pool where the residue of oil is skimmed off it — and sent back for refining. Nearby, an aeration tank where compressed air and a flotation agent are added to the water.

The water then flows into pools in which the emulsified oil and flotation agent are scooped off. Still left are the phenols, but with the aid of a rotary beater they are absorbed by microorganisms. Now the water is ready for the fish and ducks, as well as vegetable plots which help feed the plant's workers. Everyone grins with satisfaction as we survey this cunning sequence.

A moment later I see a young worker in the plant's instrument control room. He is encircled by red and white tributes to the power of Mao's thought. Can there be a link, I wonder aloud, between these sleek control panels and the puffery of political philosphy? He swivels around and points to a quotation on the green wall behind him: "We Stand for Self-Reliance." "You see," he says with simple logic, "we made this control room ourselves. Relying on our own efforts, looking up to no authorities, we designed it and built it at the same time."

Back at Peace Zone, I find the neighborhood on the move to new ways and higher levels. New bicycles, elaborate toys, transistors, fancy skirts. All spring from a recent rise in wages. The press doesn't talk much about wage questions but the folk of Peace Zone do.

Before the Cultural Revolution the seven neighborhood factories

374

were rather makeshift, like today's residents' area workshops. They paid low piece wages (*ji-jian gong-zi*). This "did not suit a socialist society" so monthly wages were introduced. The average wage in Peace Zone's factories rose to a healthier but uninspired thirty yuan. This still fell far short of wages in large factories, because it was not based on the national eight-grade scale.

In 1972 the sun burst through the clouds for local industry. Peace Zone's thirteen hundred workers went onto the eight-grade scale. Average wage jumped overnight to forty yuan. Medical treatment became totally free, instead of 50 percent subsidized as before. Hence those bikes and radios and toys. Forty yuan is still a cut lower than in the big plants, but not unfairly so, perhaps, given the convenience of neighborhood work.

Another boon is that the much-criticized bonus of pre-1966 days has crept back in modified, less unequal form. The magic word is "auxiliary wage" (*fu-jia gong-zi*).* Given unless there is reason not to do so — taking a lot of leave of absence, working poorly — the living allowance can amount to four to five yuan a month. It nicely fills out the purses of Peace Zone's on-the-spot workers.

For housewives, the latest things are radiators and gas stoves. The stoves do away with the use of dirty and inconvenient briquettes. They are fueled partly with liquefied petroleum gas that is a by-product of Peking General Petrochemical. Also used are pure natural gas, firedamp, oil-field gas, and coke-oven gas from coking plants.

* or "living allowance" (*huo gong-zi*). A note on these new supplements may be useful for students of Chinese industry. During visits to a few cities in the summer of 1973 I found four variants:

1) *Huo gong-zi,* in Dairen factories, averaging about five yuan per worker per month, and at Anshan Steelworks, averaging nine yuan.

2) *Fu-jia gong-zi,* in Peking factories, including neighborhood ones, and in Canton factories; average five to six yuan, slightly lower in neighborhood plants. This term (auxiliary wage) plays the same role as *huo gong-zi* (living allowance) as far as I could see.

3) Instances where *fu-jia gong-zi* recently underwent the name change to *huo gong-zi* — as in Peking's Peace Zone neighborhood. The amount in yuan did not undergo any clear change.

4) Places where neither exist, as in Wuhan factories.

One day I asked Chang Wen-chin, Assistant Minister of Foreign Affairs, about the two terms. His reply, that he had never heard of them and that they must be "local" terms, underlines the new and fluid nature of this supplementary wage. Peking journalists told me the allowances go only to factory workers, not to office workers and professionals.

Family patterns have changed out of recognition since Manchu days. Here I am in the neat bright living room of Mrs. Heng. She is a cylindrical woman with a heavy jaw but sparkling eyes. As an official of Peace Zone, Mrs. Heng (her name means "persistent") keeps a finger in many pies and knows the social scene well.

Most mornings she helps in the "breakfast parlor" (*zao-dian-bu*) of one of Peace Zone's twenty-three residents' areas, dispensing two pancakes and a bowl of bean-curd milk for fourteen fen per person. The local phone is in the parlor; Mrs. Heng sometimes stays on after breakfast to tend it. From the window Mrs. Heng points to a shop opposite her apartment. It is called an "agency shop" (*dai-xiao dian*) and she has a voice in it. Goods are supplied by a state shop in the district, sold here with 4 percent commission going to the local organizers.

For the seven factories of Peace Zone, which employ 1,170 women and 130 men, Mrs. Heng serves as liaison with East City district. This work comes under the "enterprises department," one of seven units into which the neighborhood revolutionary committee activity is divided (the others are general office, political, culture and education, militia, civil defense, residents' committees).

Mrs. Heng helps arrange payment to the district of two taxes on Peace Zone's enterprises: a 7 percent tax on total income (before wages are deducted); a tax on profit, which is 30 percent if the profit is below ten thousand yuan per year, 50 percent if it exceeds ten thousand yuan. Now and then a special problem has to be solved. Recently one factory irritated East City by piling iron materials in the street. Mrs. Heng defended it before the district; where else could the iron be left? But she had to give in and get the factory to move it.

Mrs. Heng says divorces among the fifteen thousand households run at seven to nine per year — still a low rate, because of social pressure to "patch up," and because bad conduct can be explained away as a hangover from the old society. As the divorce rate slowly rises, the birthrate quickly falls. Last year it was eleven per thousand; the district wants it brought down to ten per thousand.

When we talk about unmarried mothers Mrs. Heng deals me a small shock: "The girl no longer has to kill the child, nor get an abortion unless she wants to." Have I misheard the Chinese terms — confusing

376

killing with aborting? No mistake; Mrs. Heng is harking back to infanticide. She recalls it from her girlhood. "Bathing the baby" was the chilling euphemism for drowning an unwanted infant.

At a stroke I am reminded of the leap Mrs. Heng's generation has taken from feudalism to factory. Indeed there is a new Peking, pushing through the relics of the old.

A strange shock it would be for landlords — who used to pile a "key money" fee on top of already high rents — to see the masses living in smart new homes at a rent that is 6 percent of their incomes. Hardly to be imagined by the mandarins that an ordinary woman like Mrs. Heng could be an arbiter of social norms and a leader of economic enterprises.

The city that made only handicrafts and specialty goods is now a city whose coinage is machine tools, chemicals, polyester. And what has become of the stagnant dumps of garbage and sewage? They are now a park which resounds to the thump of basketball and the shouts of tots on swings.

I am curious to see South Church (Nan-tang), near the gate called Trumpet the Military. It is Peking's orphan cathedral; the city's only operating Catholic church. At the Nationalities Hotel service desk, I ask which bus will take me to South Church for tomorrow's Sunday service.

Next morning the Number Fifteen bus lands me at the door, a few minutes before Mass begins. Two men of about forty greet me with a smile. One of them, a layman who is a clerk at a factory, startles me by asking: "Are you perhaps from the Nationalities Hotel?"

The building is quite graceful, in gray brick, ornamented in the fulsome style of a century ago. On top is a cross which can be seen throughout the district, and there are crosses over each doorway. Both the sanctuary and the courtyard are well kept; a big effort on behalf of a small flock. There are shrubs and crimson flowers in the grounds, but no political slogans anywhere in the compound.

Inside South Church you see at once how Christianity in China was cursed with an alien face. To enter the high arched door is like leaving

To enter the high arched door of
South Church is like leaving
China, going back into a past
world of European piety

Rice Market Church is an old YMCA building in relaxed semi-Chinese style

China, going back into a past world of European piety. Saints with white faces; a Western ceiling; stained-glass windows; Madonnas with Italian noses.

The most famous Catholic missionary to China, Matteo Ricci (1552–1610), lived in a house on this spot, and the first Catholic church in Peking was built here in 1650. There were many later tribulations, however, chiefly the Boxer Rebellion of 1900, in whose bitter battles the church was largely destroyed.

This morning there are fifty-four people in the congregation, sparse like winter leaves against the brown benches and fawn marble panels. Twelve are Chinese. Half of the forty-two foreigners are black Africans. At 9:30 A.M. two priests enter and switch on the lights. Electrically lit candles spring to life on the altar. The Mass begins. From my pew near the back the mumble is quite inaudible. I move twenty rows toward the altar; still all I can tell is that the priest is using a mixture of Latin and Chinese.

The service drawls on with no high or low point. It seems quickly over and we troop out. The morning's only excitement occurs when an African child throws a tantrum, rolls on the tiled floor with white teeth bared. My eye lights on a blackboard at the rear of the dark sanctuary, which gives details of the Gospel and the Epistle for the day. An offering box stands hopefully beside it; its contents surely cannot maintain even this ghostly parish.

Another morning I look for Peking's Protestant parish. No accident that it is in the Rice Market district, which used to be upper class. A golden sun grips Peking as I set out. Ask a hundred people in the street, but no one has heard of the church. Luckily I know that it is near Red Star Cinema. I clamber on to a bus, buy my ticket, tell the conductress I'm going to Red Star.

It is a Sunday morning but the bustle is almost that of a weekday. Not a single shop seems closed. Piles of fresh melons, cabbages, onions, mushrooms, are being sold on the sidewalk.

My bus is crowded and the girl who patrols it has a trying time. Her hair is cut short and square; the nose is dumpy. She elbows her way through the bus. At each stop she hops off and takes up a position on the sidewalk. There she collects the ticket of each alighting passenger. Anyone who hasn't got one must pay on the spot.

The conductress does a good job by me. When I climb on she tells a couple of passengers to make sure I don't miss the Red Star. As we enter Rice Market Street, one of them informs me that my stop is near. I alight and soon find myself at the green wrought-iron fence of the church. Then comes a tug at my elbow; a schoolgirl looks up brightly into my face. She says with a smile that is shadowed by puzzlement: "Don't you want the Red Star Cinema?" The conductress has been even more thorough than I realized.

Although I recognize the church, I need to meet someone in order to find a proper way of entry. I stop a youth as he comes out of a gate next door to the church. "Is that building a church?" He seems a little nervous as he replies that it is. When I ask about the time of the services, he excuses himself, hops on his bike, pedals off.

Rice Market Church is an old YMCA building in relaxed semi-Chinese style. It is three stories, with airy windows and wide, turned-up eaves in green tile. (The Protestants do not, like the Catholics, have the disadvantage of a Gothic ecclesiastical bastion.)

Suddenly I see a congregation of a dozen or so people quietly coming out of the church's doorway. In a moment I am chatting with the pastor, Yin Chi-chen. Yin used to work with the American Brethren Mission in Shansi province, later with American Presbyterians in Peking. He looks up into my face with big steady eyes.

As we begin to talk, I think back over the decade since I first went to a service in Rice Market. The situation during my three visits is a measure of its ups and (mostly) downs.

I recall a service here in 1964. The sanctuary is a typical YMCA hall, with small hard wooden chairs. There is a simple brass cross at the front, beside a piano made in England. At the piano is sheet music with a title in English: "Concert Transcriptions of Favorite Hymns (Pennsylvania)." About a hundred people attend; 80 percent of them look over fifty. The singing is lusty. A vigorous thirty-five-minute sermon is preached on a biblical theme with Marxist punctuation. Bibles and mimeographed hymnbooks are available.

During this 1964 visit I have a long interview with Dr. Chao Fu-san,

380

head of the Protestant organization in Peking. It is arranged with the cooperation of government officials. In these calm days 40 percent of Peking's one thousand Protestant families regularly come to the city's four parishes. (Twenty Protestant parishes are active in Shanghai.)

Dr. Chao speaks of "a great rebuilding to be done" by Peking's forty pastors and its laymen. He stresses that the Christian church became almost a foreign institution in old China; that in the new China "Christians must become Chinese again." The Christians of Peking, he tells me, are trying to find new ways of holding their faith in new circumstances. "You must realize that we need time to understand the new situation. . . ."

None of Peking's churches remained open during the height of the Cultural Revolution. Like nearly everything else in China, churches felt the barbs of an attack on "the four olds." Red Guards held Rice Market Church for several weeks and gave political lessons to the Christians.

One Sunday morning in 1971 I came again to Rice Market Church. No sound of "Holy, holy, holy" pouring from the open windows, as in 1964. There have been no meetings in public of Christians for several years. Chao Fu-san is "not available" to see me. People in Peking wonder now if the Christian church in China is finished.

I do not believe that the Cultural Revolution has "finished" the churches. Christians' experience at the hands of the Red Guards has not been so different from that of many other people judged guilty of clinging to "old" and "bourgeois" ways. Many people will come back from a pit of disrepute to an orderly life again, Christians among them.

When the dust settled after the Cultural Revolution, Rice Market Church and South Church did open their doors again. They were the only two churches in Peking to do so; two last pools on a terrain heated by a blazing sun . . .

I look back at the grave, calm face of Pastor Yin as he briefs me on the 1973 Peking Protestant scene. Apart from Rice Market, all church buildings have been rented to banks, bureaus, welfare agencies. "It is true," says Yin, "that the number of believers is less than ever before, and that most of the Sunday congregation are foreigners. Maybe there are five hundred believers in Peking." A small seed in a city of seven million. Pastor Yin also points out that since the Cultural Revolution there are no sermons, baptisms, weddings, or funerals at Rice Market Church.

The pastor does not say, as Chao Fu-san did in 1964, that the church has deliberately made itself lean in order to prepare for future advance along fresh lines. He simply gives a frank explanation of why the trend of attendance is downward. "So many people are working on Sundays now" — he gestures toward the busy street beyond the gate — "that Sunday is no longer a day for extra activities."

The pastor's last point is a key one. If the Christian church in China seems doomed, the reason lies deeper than the Cultural Revolution. Chao Fu-san said in 1964 that the state had been good to the pastors. In a way that is true. It has been good to them because in the long run it does not fear them.

The church is a dying force since it never took root in the new society. I ask Yin where is Chao today. "He is ill from a heart attack; he is tired. He is gone from Peking; he will not be back again." There is no one to replace Chao. That is a more important reason for the decline of the church than the grilling and book burning of the Red Guards.

Chao Fu-san said in 1964 that the Christians need time. It is truer to say that the Communists need time — and nothing else. Time only for the pre-Liberation pastors to pass on.

Since there are only five hundred Protestants in Peking, and about five thousand Catholics, is it not perverse to dwell on such a tiny minority? In a way it is. The Western observer in China finds it hard to stop himself from a special curiosity before the relics of Western influence.

Chinese Communist friends are always polite about religion. But they quickly sniff — when Westerners show interest in Chinese churches — the old effort by foreigners to remake China's soul. They also point out, quite correctly, that toward religions other than Christianity the CCP has been no more hostile than was the Republican government of Chiang Kai-shek (1928–1949). And that the CCP — this is seldom recalled in the West — has been less disdainful of non-Christian religions than were the cocky Christian missionaries.

At the same time, the bleak agony of religion in a Marxist society does raise the fundamental issue of individual freedom. A Christian believer may be the final swallow of a sinking summer; he is also a human being. The Bible he would read is not compatible with Marxism; but does it reduce his value as a Chinese citizen if he reads it?

A talk with Pastor Yin is in one basic respect no different from a 1964 talk with Chao Fu-san. It leaves an impression of a Christianity which is fading. First, because its ideals have lost their power. Chao talked with passion about Saint Paul and the Fourth Gospel, but Yin never gets to hard-core religious matters. Second, because the sociology of new China leaves no niche for a church.

Pastor Yin's predicament is just an extreme form of one shared by Christian clergy in dozens of countries. The church as an organization is ebbing. Christianity evaporates from its institutional vessel, becomes a diffuse world view.

❀ ❀ ❀

A "city of learning" has grown up northeast of Tian-an men, on leafy boulevards between the Manchu City and the Western Hills. Colleges such as Iron and Steel, Geology, Peking Medical College, are housed in functional oblongs built after Liberation. The floor space of education buildings erected in Peking between 1949 and 1954 alone was *five times* the figure for the previous forty years.

But in this part of Peking there was also much to build on from the Manchu period. A favorite quarter for the pleasure of court and mandarins, it was dotted with big homes, well off for paved roads and running water. Quite a few schools, among them Peking University, learn socialism in mansions and gardens of the feudal era.

Cultural sentry at the northwest tip of the old city, Peking Library occupies a classical Chinese mansion on the fringe of the City of Learning. I spent a 1964 afternoon in its sunny reading rooms (and found there all the books of C. Wright Mills). I strolled in the gardens with the library's director, who told me that only organizations, not individuals, may borrow Peking Library books.

Staffed by six hundred people, this best of China's libraries has eight million books and ten thousand periodical series. Also manuscripts of

Buddhist sutras dated A.D. 416, books printed centuries before Europe "invented" printing, and rare revolutionary magazines such as *Youth* (*Shao-nian*), which Chou En-lai edited in Paris half a century ago. I am not able to visit the library in 1971 or 1973, but its new director — on a recent trip to Harvard — says the library is growing fast.

I wander from the library to see more of the City of Learning. The old North Church — compass companion of South Church — has been turned into a middle school. The former site of Peking University, Red Mansion, is now the editorial offices of several magazines. Here Mao Tse-tung worked as a librarian, and his boss, Li Ta-chao, fired youth with lectures on socialism. You see two student exam papers, to which Professor Li gave 95 marks out of 100, from a course on historical materialism. On the wall hangs a poem of Kuo Mo-jo:

> *A single spark of fire can start a prairie fire,*
> *A trickle may expand into an ocean.*
> *In the Red Mansion, once filled with*
> *   youth and teaching,*
> *The ink-slabs and brushes*
> *   of Comrades Mao and Li remain.*
> *Powerful are things newly born,*
> *Great are achievements that posterity remembers,*
> *For they will live as long as the people,*
> *Unfading as eternal spring.*

Peking Hospital of Chinese Medicine occupies the former estate of a Ming princess, with a Buddhist temple for its acupuncture wing. Here I meet paralyzed patients who say they are determined to "recover for the sake of revolution," and I hear views about smoking and the impact of the Cultural Revolution on health care.

As we sit down in the old temple several hospital personnel light up a cigarette. They laugh when I ask if no one fears lung cancer. True though, say the smiling doctors as smoke curls around the red pillars, that doctors trained in Western medicine are more inclined to criticize smoking than they are. "We only say — don't smoke when you're sick, or have a cough."

The Cultural Revolution had the effect of upgrading *Western* medicine at this hospital. The best health care combines Western and Chinese medicine, ran the line, and since these doctors had specialized in the second, they had to catch up a bit with the first. The storm of 1966–1969 brought, too, an out-of-the-ordinary contribution from the military. It is de rigueur at this time (1971) to learn from the PLA. What has the hospital learned?

"When PLA men came here in 1967," a frail old acupuncturist replies, "they asked doctors to experiment on their bodies — to find, for instance, the roots of nerves for placing acupuncture needles — in order to improve methods of treatment. This was done; advances were made. The hospital was much affected by this PLA spirit of service. Now we doctors test new ways on our own bodies, too."

I drive out past the Temple of the White Dagoba and Lu Hsün's old Peking home — marked by a silhouette of the writer at the lane's entrance — to Peking University, apex of the City of Learning. The way runs by shady Revolutionary Friendship Road, called Science Road when I first went along it in 1964.

Here are the towers and dorms of People's University and Central Academy for National Minorities. Colleges of music, petroleum, aeronautics, afforestation. Sections of the Academy of Sciences, where tens of thousands of scholars work free from the burden of students. Nearer the hills I notice market gardens and the uninviting gates of military barracks.

Here is one of many middle schools in the area, Second Middle School Attached to Peking Normal University. I go inside to hear about its partnership with a metals factory (designed to give pupils industrial experience) and with a brigade called Horse Country (to lend a rural perspective). I find at Second Middle that the grading scale in Peking schools is no different from that in "bourgeois" schools of the West: Excellent; Good; Pass; Fail.

Peking University lost little when it left the cramped Red Mansion in 1952 and came to its present park setting, then the home of U.S.-sponsored Yenching University. It was once a pleasant outpost for the Manchu court, visited by Lord Macartney when the king of England sent him in 1793 to "open up" China to British exports. It seems in keeping with the calm grandeur of the place that the Chinese emperor replied to Macartney: "Our celestial empire possesses all things in prolific abundance . . . we have no need of the products of outside barbarians."

The lakes and graceful pavilions are now interspersed with basketball courts and ten factories. New since 1973 is a simple memorial to Edgar Snow, America's best friend of China who once taught at Yenching University and died in 1972. His widow chose to scatter half Snow's ashes here — one-half also in the Hudson River — rather than in the Cemetery of Revolutionary Martyrs, which was offered by Chou En-lai.

Red slogans light up the trees like lanterns. One of them sums up a perennial issue at the university: "Do Not Let a Class Brother Fall from the Team." Today's students mostly lack intellectual family backgrounds, a change from the university's elitist past. They are better at being "red" than at being "expert." It's not easy for a great school to strike a balance between political needs and its own high standards.

Complicating the picture has been disagreement among China's leaders over education policy. Liu Shao-ch'i, according to my sources at the university, put forward the slogan: "If the father is a hero the son will be a good guy; if the father is reactionary the son will be a stupid egg." Such a sentiment is a long way from the values of the Cultural Revolution.

A great deal goes on at Peking University other than what is trumpeted from the propaganda boards. From these you would not know that students write a ten-thousand-character thesis in their final year. You would get no clue to the stress on foreign-language teaching — what other Asian university offers eleven oriental tongues besides its own? You would wonder why the university has started to build a new library (the present one, with 2.8 million books, is judged too small for today's needs). No institution sounds its best when talking about things other than what lies at the heart of its work. And this is what Chinese schools often do.

A 1973 chat about Chinese political thought with two historians is the best I can recall on the topic. Professor Chou I-liang, one of China's best-known historians, has brought along a young colleague who specializes in the May Fourth Movement. No formalities — clapping, opening remarks, briefing on the education line — stiffen our meeting. We simply sit down one summer morning in a musty pavilion that is brushed by fine bamboo and exchange views on the theory of socialism.

Chou is a silver-haired man with a vigor and fresh face that belie his middle years. He has an easy charm and a well-stocked mind. A Harvard PhD from the 1940s, he has written on Buddhism and general Chinese and Asian history. Chang P'ei-sen is a younger man, with crew cut, glasses, and a crisp manner. He teaches a course on the history of the CCP; ideology is his cup of tea. Later we are joined by Robert Winter, an American octogenarian who has worked here for some years and lived in China for decades.

When the question of the individual and socialism comes up, my mind darts back to a poster at this same campus in 1971. The occasion for it was the fiftieth anniversary of the founding of the CCP. "It is a perilous danger," said the brush strokes in several colors, "that the THEORY OF HUMAN NATURE will result in the restoration of capitalist dictatorship." Part of our 1973 conversation centers on this Marxist view that there is no such thing as human nature.

It is no good to judge socialism by the yardstick of what will fit human nature, Chang asserts. Human nature varies with class, changes with the development of history. It was a weakness of May Fourth, especially of the "radical democrat" Ch'en Tu-hsiu, to fail to see this. Ch'en was a rationalist who lacked both class analysis and a historical way of thinking.

I ask if socialism is not tested in the end by what it does for the individual. The historians don't quite answer this — they talk of what is wrong more than of what is correct — but they make two interesting distinctions. When exalting "development of the individual," says Chou, the radical democrats of May Fourth meant the bourgeois individual. "We cannot accept this as a test." Chang chimes in with a historical point. "It is only a tiny minority who get the chance to fulfill themselves in the dog-eat-dog conditions of capitalism."

"Individual personality" (ge-xing) flourishes under socialism, Chang explains, but not "individualism" (ge-ren ju-yi). Twins may have dif-

387

ferent personalities though identical class background; such differences will never be eliminated and are a good thing for society. Peking University, adds Chou, certainly takes into account the temperament and wishes of each new student: what interests him, where his talents lie, his tentative job preference.

Individualism, on the other hand, is a world outlook. It is that of the bourgeoisie, opposed to that of socialism. A student may express his individual personality to the full, yet still study for the sake of the revolution. But a student in the grip of individualism studies only to build up his own career.

Again, while individualism is a relic of a past social order, "individual interest" (*ge-ren li-yi*) is respected under socialism. A citizen has his possessions — in the countryside, this probably includes a house — which Chou says is proper. But an individualistic outlook, which leads a person to exploit others for his own benefit, is not proper. Happily it has been "largely" undermined by public ownership of productive units. In China today, individualism is just "not apposite" (*bu he fan*).*

When we leave the cool old pavilion Professor Chou walks with me through lush bushes to my Shanghai car. His mood is more buoyant than when I saw him last in 1971. A recent trip to Japan gave him a lift ("a far more hopeful place than the Japan I used to know"). Thanks to the twist of international political events, he has been able to resume research on early historical links between China and Japan. I had sensed from letters he wrote in the spring that the sap was flowing again; now I see why.

Robert Winter strikes a discordant note at the end. He is present because I brought a message for him from I. A. Richards, the literary philosopher, who is seeking to help Peking University with its English teaching. Winter has slowed down quite a bit now — he is eighty-six — and he had a sour time during the Cultural Revolution. A bolt of tension runs through the midday air as he says loudly in the presence

* The day before at Tsinghua University, a professor quoted to me, as a different kind of example of the individualistic world view, the notion that without Isaac Newton there would have been no theory of dynamics. In fact, he said, all discoveries emerge from social development.

of Chou and Chang: "They give me nothing to do; they won't give me anything to *do*."

Above the gray tiles of inner Peking rise the golden tiles of imperial Peking. Coal Hill Park, on the north-south axis, is a good vantage point for the spectacle. From its summit, in the Pavilion of Everlasting Spring, you have a bird's-eye view of the Forbidden City to the south.

This former seat of the emperors is now a museum and park, a sleepy place even though it borders on Tian-an men. The orange palaces seem endless. Set in groves of pine and cypress, they look from above like heavy goldfish on the surface of a deep green pond. Beyond the Forbidden City you see the marble blocks of new state Peking. Their orange cornices match the orange tiles of the imperial buildings, a nod of recognition from the new fawn oblongs to the old vermilion walls.

A blend of the grand and the simple meets the eye: salons where four hundred servants at a time put dinner before a Manchu emperor; a woman washing clothes in a tub by the gray wall of a nearby lane. Turn your back to the Forbidden City and the Drum Tower and Bell Tower peer through a smoky haze, jewels on the north of the axis. Gray roofs of gates and temples dot the horizon, like elephants browsing at a respectful distance from the flames of empire.

On Coal Hill's east slope stands an old locust tree from which the last Ming emperor hanged himself in 1644, as Li Tse-ch'eng's peasant army bore in on Peking to topple the dynasty. A little to the west are the willows and red enamel pillars of South and Central Lakes, where Mao Tse-tung has lived since leading *his* peasant army to Peking.

Peking is not set in a park, like Hangchow, but it draws a lot of its character from parks. Without them, much of the city would be a brick jungle. As most of Peking's palaces date from the Ming — Peking replaced Nanking as the capital in 1420 — most of its parks stem from the Ch'ing. Though stiff with the memory of emperors, they have a place in daily life as well as in history. Not set aside for

389

the rich, or claimed only by derelicts and mischief-makers, they are places to chat and read and stroll. Parks play as much part in Peking life as homes and schools and factories.

The Children's Park is an informal spot near the new diplomatic quarter. Kids like it for games, gourmets because of its restaurant for *jiao-zi* (meat dumplings with chives). People from every walk of life ride here, check their bicycles at the gate, and give way to a pile of these irresistible, indigestible doughy sacks, soused in vinegar and soy sauce.

North Sea (Peihai) Park is a charming retreat first laid out early in the tenth century (Liao dynasty). Some ancient trees here are so valued that lightning rods have been placed in them. One lace bark pine was planted eight hundred years ago. Fang Shan (Imperial Style) restaurant serves — or did in 1964* — fine dishes to holiday makers who have worked up an appetite skating or rowing on Peihai.

This hall of a hundred smells copied recipes and inherited chefs from the Empress Dowager. The "Old Buddha" liked maize rolls (*wo-wo-tou*) — she picked up the taste from north China peasants, when fleeing Peking in 1900 as foreign troops invaded — and "thousand-layer" cakes. After Liberation Fang Shan started to turn out these delicacies for the masses on Sunday afternoons. One old cook says he used to be called a "greasy rat" in the old days but is now known as a "culinary expert."

Alone I walk by the former Imperial Palace toward the park which was named after Sun Yat-sen in 1928. Rays of sun catch rows of fat brass nails on the crimson doors. Two men in shorts and T-shirts are doing repairs on the giant gold characters of a billboard which reads: "The People and Only the People Are the Motive Force in Creating World History." The two characters for "history" have fallen down. As I walk by, each man is holding one character with both arms. In the morning sunshine the three-foot-long frames look less like words than golden harps.

Back on Tian-an men Square, the snowy marble balustrades dazzle a naked eye. Most strollers on the vast expanse are equipped with

---

* Peihai Park has been closed in recent years, but Fang Shan has moved and is open for business at Friendship Hotel in western Peking.

At Sun Yat-sen Park you are greeted by a big arch in white marble with a forehead of blue ceramics

sunshades and cameras. The gray hulk of Front Gate glares from the distance, like a mountain on the far side of a glass lake.

A ten fen admission fee and then Sun Yat-sen Park engulfs me. Superb trees keep the paths and pavilions serene despite a crowd of many thousands. Juniper (pink wood); arbor vitae (yellow wood); the widest variety of peonies in Peking. Some of the cypresses are a hundred years old, and so fat that it takes four people to encircle the trunk with arms at full stretch. The arbor vitae has a long life; Pekinese give small branches of it to friends at New Year's as a spur to longevity.

You are greeted by a big arch in white marble with a forehead of blue ceramics. It was originally built by Europeans to commemorate their losses in the Boxer clashes. Red Peking has calmly accepted it, with a new inscription that simply says "Defend Peace." Weeping pagodas cast a scratch of shadows on the pale flagstones. The Chinese call this tree "dragon's claw" pagoda, and the black pattern of shadows is indeed like a tangle of dragons' claws.

Tubs of goldfish are shaded by straw mats against a fierce dry sun. Here is a giant bronze tortoise, ringed with red hibiscus, its head tossed to heaven in a snarl of pain or triumph. Above the cypresses and fancy lampposts, the vermilion walls and egg-yolk tiles of Tian-an men seem to keep watch on the relaxed scene.

Taking pictures is the favorite activity, but some quiet souls bend at charcoal sketching or watercolors. Willows, pavilions, rock gardens are a more common artistic theme than workers, peasants, soldiers. The northern end of the park stops at the back moat (*hou-he*) of the Imperial Palace. Here youths row boats against a backdrop of gingko trees, grotesque rocks, and the glittering tiles of the palaces.

On the lattice balustrade of an ornamented corridor, two men in work clothes take a nap. One's hands are outstretched above his head, gripping a green pillar to keep him on his narrow bed. The other has taken care to plant one foot down on the pavement. A fat stomach supports his clasped brown hands, and a water bottle sits under his right knee.

Children ride in toy boats and planes which whiz in a circle at the end of shafts attached to a noisy motor. Three little girls in floral dresses, hair like mops, play at an old copper vat. They take turns to sit inside its smooth bowl, while the other two dance around the three legs singing a ditty whose words I do not catch.

The park restaurant looks humble, with its dirty concrete floor and metal chairs. The diners are in singlets and shorts, their limbs the same color as a straw roof which is held up by bamboo scaffolding. But everyone is eating fish and meat, eased with *man-tou* (rolls) and the odd bowl of rice. I sit down beside a youth who is reading the famous old novel *Saga of Wanderings in the West* (*Xi-you ji*).

More grand than Sun Yat-sen park is the Temple of Heaven. Indeed, I find it the noblest of all China's monuments. The surrounding park, though near the city center and now fringed on the south by new housing blocks, has the atmosphere of a forest. Not hard for picnickers to find a secluded spot here for reading, cards, or intimate things.

A good season always has been, and still is, crucial to China's wellbeing. In the temple's chief sanctuary, Hall of Prayer for Good Harvests, emperors came to ask Heaven's help. Terraces in milk-white marble lead up to the sharp neat splendor of the hall. It is conical, its three blue-tile roofs like three coolies' hats in a stack. On top is a gold knob, as if the deity might pick up the dainty building and twirl it at his pleasure.

The inside is beautifully painted with frescoes. You see, too, that the hall is quite a feat of construction. It stands by virtue of twenty-eight wooden pillars and a scatter of rafters. No cement or steel, not one nail, has been used to put up the forty-meter-high cone. Each of the four central columns ("dragon well pillars") represents one of the seasons. The simple lines, the well-bred plainness, the *confidence* of it, make even the Taj Mahal seem by comparison as contrived as a Disneyland turret.

Nature has been respected. No city noise detracts from its spell. You are awed by the sky, toward which the hall seems to soar, and by the broad spaces rimmed by foliage, as much as by architectural style and craftsmanship. A promenade 360 meters long leads to the

TEMPLE OF HEAVEN

Terraces in milk-white marble lead up to the sharp
neat splendor of the hall. It is conical, its three blue tile
roofs like three coolies' hats in a stack. On top is a gold
nob, as if the deity might pick up the dainty building
and twirl it at his pleasure

Imperial Vault of Heaven, which is like a blue umbrella in conversation with the clouds.

Objects in four colors everywhere answer your gaze. Sky-blue glazed tiles, pearly marble, walls in rosy flesh, bushes and trees in green. The south wall of the park is straight while the north wall is semicircular; this expresses the old Chinese view that the earth was square while heaven was round. You feel like an ant before the cosmic aplomb of it all.

Double rows of cypresses run away as far as the eye can see. Pigs, sheep, and bullocks used to graze here, before being put in a green porcelain furnace as a whole-burned offering for Heaven's pleasure. I gaze across from the marble promenade to a grassy spot shaded by these same cypresses. A group of girls and boys — students, to judge by the books beside their water bottles — are playing cards in silence.

Near the Imperial Vault of Heaven a photographer is at work, taking visitors' pictures and mailing the prints for fifty fen. Under his red and white umbrella a board displays the choice of spots at which he will take your photo. Few young couples hold hands — far fewer than in Shanghai parks — but teen-age girls interlock fingers, as do pairs of boys.

Children love the long curved Echo Wall, built so that a remark whispered close to one part can be heard clearly at any other part. An amazing Triple Sound Stone (*san-yin-shi*) lies by the steps leading from the Imperial Vault of Heaven. If you stand on the first stone and call out, one echo is heard; the same call on the second stone produces two echoes; on the third stone, by God, the sound comes back three times.

People like to go to the hills west of Peking for picnics, amid shrines that in many cases outdistance the whole of West Europe's history by centuries. I see the T'ang dynasty Temple of the Sleeping Buddha, which is set in a grove of twisting trees. On Fragrant Mount, the chief peak, I climb up a slope called Sight That Discourages Devils (Gui jian chou).

But in summertime I do not find Fragrant Mount as attractive as locals say it is when laden with snow. The most fun is chatting with

395

Mrs. Chia over a bottle of beer in a hillside cafe, and hearing from her about the penurious last days of the author of *Dream of the Red Chamber,* spent in numb obscurity on these slopes.

It is the Summer Palace which draws most visitors to Western Hills. The Empress Dowager had much of it built after the previous Summer Palace — by Peking University, now the campus of Number 101 Middle School — was burned down by the British in an angry effort to make the Ch'ing court "see reason."

This corner of Peking is China's Heidelberg. The palaces are set in a park of 660 acres on the shores of Lake Kunming. Hills rising above the satin lake offer peaceful nooks and large vistas. On a ridge of Longevity Hill, named by emperor Ch'ien Lung as a sixtieth birthday gift to his mother, I feel refreshed by the beauty and balance of what lies below.

The shapely curve of Jade Belt Bridge; colored pleasure boats dotting the lake like bright beetles on a rug; the pencil pagoda on adjacent Jade Spring Hill. The Palace Piercing the Clouds and other pavilions, their tiled roofs like scaly lizards in the sun. The chimneys of new industrial Peking in the far hazy distance. Two gardeners at my feet, one snipping dead shoots off a bush with scissors, the other neatly putting them in a straw bag.

The years since Liberation have not added to the Summer Palace any new luxuries, but they have brought it an everyday spirit. It's a good spot for swimming in summer, skating in winter, climbing all year round. Older folk peer at historical sights — some remember the death of the Old Buddha in 1908 — but youths bother little with these ashes of the past.

Hardly less dated, now, is Sun Yat-sen Hall, just beyond the Summer Palace in the Temple of Azure Clouds. The walls are inscribed with Sun's letter of 1925 to the Soviet government: "I want to express my warm hope that the day will soon come when, as a good friend and ally, the USSR will welcome a mighty, independent China. . . ." Guides do not any longer, as they used to in the early 1960s, tell visitors that "Sun Yat-sen's hope has now come true."

❁ ❁ ❁

You can think of Peking as an *abstraction*. Peking opens its arms to Sihanouk of Cambodia; Peking does not believe in peace. You can think of the city as a *mecca*. Peking is the red sun of our hearts; Peking will not fail the oppressed peoples of the world.

I have been speaking of Peking as a *functioning city,* as a place where people live, get up in the morning, do the jobs of the 1970s, go to sleep or make love. This Peking does not stand still — whether as implacable monster or shimmering image — but moves on as the result of its own eager zeal to shake off the past.

Back in 1964, the new buildings of Peking seemed like fish on the broad sands of an old city. New state Peking had arisen with the Great Leap Forward, but there were far fewer plants and apartment blocks than there are today.

There were many old touches to the face of the city. Handcarts and donkeys near Front Gate. Peddlers with baskets hanging from a pole, selling everything from dumplings to goldfish. Veteran barbers with a pair of scissors and a wooden chair in dirt lanes.

Niches remained into which the red blood of ideology had not seeped. On TV there was a folk opera, *The Butterfly Lovers,* which might now be thought idle, and a circus film, *The Knife Thrower,* which would certainly be judged a risk for boys with itchy fingers. Women made a big thing of going to the hairdresser, parents of steering their children down a path of career success. Saturday night dances brought students into the arms of jaded cadres and foreign experts. You could buy *Tom Sawyer* and *David Copperfield* in the bookstores; even *Fifty Ways to Slice Meat* and a fifty-thousand-character treatise on aspects of Peking duck.

Parties other than the CCP — "democratic parties" — still had a voice on issues other than fundamental ones. Unreconstructed classical Peking opera was being played (as music to work by) at construction sites. Social relations — in the family, in colleges — were still tinged with the unequal ways of the Confucian tradition.

Peking had not yet burned its bridges with Russia. Underlying the passionate arguments with the Soviets was a note of care and sorrow. It was a marital quarrel; not two ships firing at each other in the night. East Europeans made up a majority among foreign residents. Anxiety about Russia's intentions was growing, though, adding to Peking's jittery view of the outside world.

There was deep fear and resentment toward the United States. The Chinese felt pressured by U.S. military activity on their doorstep, outraged by Lyndon Johnson's aggression in Indochina. Even the fact that I had once *visited* the United States brought on some delicate moments in Peking. And when I tried to tell an official that LBJ was not as bad as Goldwater would be, the angry reply was that "Johnson and Goldwater are jackals of the same lair."

By 1971 Peking seemed a different city in body and spirit. Not only had factories sprung up, but inside them you sensed a fresh self-confidence. No more "directors" whose word was law; no automatic awe for "sacred" foreign parts and techniques.

In every way the city was living through "post–Cultural Revolution" times. This storm lay in the background as a trauma that everyone had known but not everyone wanted to talk about. Peking seemed a more serious city in 1971 than in 1964.

It had been shaken up. It had pulled up the roots of its socialism to check whether the growth was healthy. It felt a mixture of strength and doubt as a result of the experience.

Intense participation had been exciting; it gave people a heightened sense of citizenship. At the same time, the twists and turns of the campaign had made some people wary about committing themselves too ardently.

Parks had been neglected and were overgrown; fences and walls were shabby with the shreds of posters whose day was long done. PLA men ran half Peking. Mao had brought them in as caretakers, but some had grown all too comfortable and had the air of guardians.

The firebrands of the Left who had preceded the PLA in the revolving door of Cultural Revolutionary politics were flat on their face. Student leaders of 1966 were picking tea in 1971. The lust for "communes" had cooled into a compromise on three-legged committees, which could not possibly walk without bias or collapse.

It was beginning to be said that the fiery leftists were really rightists. During a talk at Peking University about the 1966 fighting with spears and homemade tanks, Feng Yu-lan, the eminent philosopher, re-

398

marked to me that "extreme leftists were responsible for the violence." But a young politico broke in to bluntly correct Professor Feng: "No, they were reactionaries."

Politics had caught up with certain realities of cultural and social life — churches, rich households, study without the rudder of ideology, museum exhibits that failed to draw a political lesson from the record of the past — that had evaded official norms until 1966. A Mao badge was no less a part of dress than shirt and trousers. Officials welcomed me to a school or factory with a copy of Mao's *Quotations* in hand.

The unfolding of Ping-Pong diplomacy lent an air of expectation. The West, not the East, teased the imagination of Chinese diplomats. Ties with Russia had settled into a muffled pit of animosity. It was the United States which Peking cadres insistently asked me about. It was Henry Kissinger who was — during my 1971 stay — the capital's most keenly awaited visitor.

By 1973 Peking has again known interesting changes. Wages are up, people spend more. There is almost a big-city atmosphere on the Boulevard of Eternal Peace. It's quite a battle now to cross the road. Mostly bicycles, rather than cars, bar your way, but there are lots of commercial vans and swampy-green Corona taxis from Japan.

Daily life is more relaxed than in 1971. Cardplaying; spitting in the street (or over the back of the chair at a dinner); a tendency to take it easy on the job from time to time. A few museums, a mosque, a church or two have opened their doors again.

At West Eternal Peace neighborhood Mr. Cha is frank about the fate of Mao badges. Why are there no more badges? "In summer we change our clothes often," he first ventures, "so it is not convenient to wear a badge." I gently say that during the summer of 1971 every man, woman, and child wore a Mao badge. Cha smiles and comes to the point: "In those days the political temperature was high; now it is down a bit."

In the eased-up mood there is a tendency to evade responsibility. "The state will decide," says a factory chairman who does not want to commit himself on a question of policy. Who will take the initiative when the crucial signals from on high are unpredictable? The "in"

A testimony to changes in China between 1971 and 1973: the same wall in the same room of Futan University in Shanghai. In 1971 (above) there is a quote from Mao on the wall, a PLA man to the fore, the *Quotations* in each hand. By 1973 (below) the wall has a landscape, no PLA man briefs the author, and no Red Books are on hand

term "responsible person" is a giveaway. If a few leaders in any unit are the "responsibles," the rest by definition do not and cannot take any responsibility.

Before your eyes there takes place an evolution away from the "institutions" of the Cultural Revolution, and toward renewed Party authority over spontaneous impulses. The Communist Youth League eclipses the Red Guards. Trade unions are back. Party cadres dust themselves down after a spell at a May 7 School and generally find their desk and chair warm. The PLA has resumed a low profile; no chance is missed to say that the army is under the leadership of the Party.

Even the stage has responded to the vogue of Party regularity. With Mrs. Chia I go to the Workers' Club near Front Gate for a performance of the new model piece *Azalea Mountain*. It is set in the 1920s, an opera about the need for the Party to control the army. Chairman Mao, leader of China, commander of the PLA, is referred to throughout as "committee member Mao" (*Mao wei-yuan*)!

Foreigners are more numerous in Peking and visitors are spread in many hotels. A resident cannot any more ask simply "What room are you in?" — taking for granted that the hotel is the New Traveler — as an ambassador asked me in 1971.

Being an Australian visitor to Peking is quite different from before, for Peking and Canberra now have full and cordial ties. On the 1964 visit I ran out of money in Peking and had to turn to the British Office for a loan. Nineteen seventy-one was the year of the Australian Labor Party's effort to bring the two lands together. But it was the gamble of a party out of power, its results unclear in the short term. Mr. Whitlam had no idea how he would be received or by whom; and Australia still had an ambassador chasing history backward in Taipei.

But here at last is an Australian embassy in Peking, and already it is too small for the swelling tasks before it. China has been demystified a bit for Australians. Settled diplomacy has replaced the illusion-breeding vacuum of the past.

Few things are more striking after two years than the new official warmth toward Japan. No more talk of Japanese "militarism"; trade and visits are on the rise. One Chinese official, just back from Tokyo

where technology had dazzled him, tells me with enthusiasm how the
Japanese used *cranes* to whisk away right-wing demonstrators from
his Chinese delegation's hotel.

And the issue of the United States has come out from behind the
curtain, where it was in 1971, to a central place on Peking's official
stage. A lot of the old tension has gone. My U.S. links are no longer
a liability. You fly from Canton in a U.S. Boeing, instead of a Russian
Ilyushin as before.

It is quite moving to see the Americans in their liaison office, in
busy harmony with a Chinese staff. One looks at the scene and recalls
the faith of Mr. Dulles twenty years ago that the CCP government
would "pass away" (Peking has the same premier now, Chou En-lai,
as it did then, while Washington has gone through five presidents).

Here in a defense shelter at Peking Construction Tool Plant I
sniff the new Sino-U.S. atmosphere. Who might attack China, I ask,
and the answer is, "Imperialists." But since there are two major types
of imperialism I decide to press my question through a back door.
Have any Americans visited this shelter? "Mr. Edgar Snow came here,
and later on Mr. Joseph Alsop." Have you had Russian visitors? The
chairman of the shelter dismisses the idea crisply: "This place is only
for visitors from friendly countries."

That Peking keeps changing means more than that one must bustle
to keep up, and that portraying five cities has more value than gen-
eralizing about a fluid and diverse nation. The *way* Peking changes
is a clue to China's condition.

In most of Asia the change you notice over a decade is economic,
especially that which results from the movement of the international
capitalist economy. Manila gets bigger; Hitachi signs multiply over
Taipei; cars increase in Bangkok. The changes I see in Peking are
mostly not economic, and the steady development of the economy
which has taken place owes nothing to international forces.

The change is *social:* role of women, spread of education, firmer
local community. It is *psychological:* students lose their awe for teachers, a feeling of pride in China's new world stature arises, a controlled
theater constrains people to embrace the political myths of the CCP.
And it is *political:* Mao makes a fresh analysis of America; the PLA

is called in and then called off; the high are brought low and the low ushered into their places.

All this is change with a purpose, not change as a result of the onward march of economic mechanism. Some moves have been ill-advised — assigning Red Guard impulse to do the job of Party organization — and have had to be canceled. But the purposive change the CCP brings about speaks strength, independence from fashions and pressures in the world, leadership that uses political power in the service of values, minds that believe society can progress far beyond today's levels.

And it is change that does not just produce new *things* but new ways of living in society. Maybe this makes change in Peking more basic — because more self-moving — than change in most of Asia. Some call it the making of a "new man." I do not think the CCP has made a new man. But it has called into being new social circumstances which make men and women able to behave in new ways. This is true social development, beside which all the gadgets of "growth" are dross.

And who cares if communism obviates itself by the self-moving nature of the change it sets in motion. Isms cannot matter as much as the minds and bodies that invent them for a purpose.

SOURCES

The book is based mostly on material gathered during visits to China, when I set my own program and traveled as an individual. The present tense is used for a 1973 journey, and generally the past tense for visits of 1971 and 1964. Supplementary documentary sources are really those used over a decade of studying China. The following is a brief roundup of works which I have specifically used or quoted; these are mostly primary sources from the PRC.

For all five cities I have extensively used China's premier newspaper, *Jen-min jih-pao*, and also these PRC periodicals: *Lü-hsing chia* [Traveler], an especially rich source; *China Reconstructs; Ti-li chih shih* [Geographic Knowledge]; *Li-shih yen-chiu* [Historical Studies]; *Li-shih chiao-hsüeh* [History Teaching]; *Ch'eng-shih chien-she* [Urban Construction]; *Chien-chu hsüeh-pao* [Building Journal]; *Chung-kuo kung-jen* [Chinese Worker]; *Chung-kuo ch'ing-nien* [Chinese Youth]; *Chung-kuo kung-yeh* [Chinese Industry]; *Hsin-hua pan-yüeh-k'an* [New China Fortnightly], later *Hsin-hua yüeh-pao* [New China Monthly]; *Lao-tung* [Labor]; *Hung-ch'i* [Red Flag].

Also, *Ta-kung pao* [Impartial Daily] of Hong Kong; broadcasts from various regions of China, as recorded and translated by the Foreign Broadcast Information Service of the United States government; dispatches of Hsinhua (the official Chinese news agency); *Ta-lu tsa-chih* [Mainland Magazine] (Taipei).

For Shanghai I note the following: *The Gateway to China* by Mary Gamewell (New York, 1916); two periodicals of today's Shanghai, *Wen-hui pao* [Literary Currents] and *Hsüeh-hsi yü p'i-p'ing* [Study and Criticism]; several unpublished essays by Professor Lynn White of Princeton University; Lu Hsün's *Ta-hsu Hsu Mou-yung ping kuan-yu k'ang-jih t'ung-yi chan-hsien wen-t'i* (see page 37) and other pieces of his in *Lu Hsün tsa-wen-hsüan* (Shanghai, 1973); Hao Ran's *Yen-yang t'ien* [Bright Sunny Days]; an article by Wang Cheng-lung (see page 23) on his visit to San Francisco in *Wen-hui pao*, August 13, 1973; four memoirs of various stages of Shanghai's past: *Shanghai Journal* by Neale Hunter (New York, 1969), *Shanghai: City for Sale* by E. Hauser (New York, 1940), *Story of Shanghai* by J. W. Maclellan (Shanghai, 1889), *Red Shadows over Shanghai* by M. Ezpeleta (Manila, 1972); *Shanghai: Key to Modern China* by R. Murphey (Cambridge, Mass., 1953); *Shang-hai chieh-fang yi-nien* [One Year of Liberated Shanghai] (Shanghai, 1950); the rich unpublished autobiography of Randall Gould, kindly shown me by Mr. Gould; *Hsin Shang-hai pien-lan* [Guide to New Shanghai] (Shanghai, 1951); E. Kovalev's "Novye materialy o pervom s'ezde kommunisticheskoi partii Kitaia," *Narody Azii i Afriki* [Peoples of Asia and Africa], 6, 1972; translated in *Chinese Studies in History*, Spring 1974 (material on CCP founding meeting, see pages 31 to 33).

For Dairen I have leaned on the following: "Manchuria as a Political Entity," a PhD thesis by R. B. Stauffer (University of Minnesota, 1954); articles in the Peking magazine *Jen-min pao-chien* [People's Health]; *Liao-ning shih-nien* [Ten Years in Liaoning] (Shenyang, 1960); *Liao-ning hua-pao* [Liaoning Pictorial] (Shenyang); *Lü-shun Ta-lien ti-chu 1949 ti shi-zi yün-tung* [The Learning to Read Movement in Lushun-Dairen Region in 1949] (Shanghai, 1950); "Ta-lien chung hua kung hsüeh hui chi ch'i ling-tao ti kung jen yün-tung" [The Dairen Industrial Association and Its Workers' Movement] in *Chi-lin ta-hsüeh jen-wen k'o-hsüeh hsüeh-pao* [Kirin University Journal of Humanistic Sciences], 3, 1959.

On Hangchow I have drawn on the work of Jacques Gernet (see page 161); *Hsi-hu tsa-t'an* [Random Chats About West Lake] (Hangchow, 1956); *The Middle Kingdom* by S. Wells Williams (New York, 1883); various essays by the veteran New Zealand writer Rewi Alley, including those in his *Travels in China* (Peking, 1973); *Mei-li ti Hsi-hu* [Beautiful West Lake] (Hong Kong, 1956); *T'ai-p'ing t'ien-kuo ch'üan-shih* [Complete History of the Taiping] by Chien Yu-wen (Hong Kong, 1962); numerous articles in *Lü-hsing chia* [Traveler]; Siao-yu's *Mao Tse-tung and I Were Beggars* (New York, 1973) for the account of Mao in Hangchow.

For Wuhan: *T'ai-p'ing t'ien-kuo: Chung-kuo chin-tai shih tzu-liao* [Taiping Rebellion: Materials on the Modern History of China] (Shanghai, 1952); *Chin-tai shih tzu-liao* [Materials on Modern History], no. 1 (Peking, 1955); *China in the Twenties,* a memoir by M. Kasanin (Moscow, 1973); "The Urban Bureaucratic Elite in Communist China: A Case Study of Wuhan, 1949–65," by Ying-mao Kau, in *Chinese Communist Politics in Action,* ed. A. Doak Barnett (Seattle, 1969); *Two Years in Revolutionary China, 1925–27,* by Vera Vishnyakova-Akimova (Cambridge, Mass., 1971); *Wu-han shih-chien tzu-liao chüan-chi* [Special Collection of Materials on the Wuhan Incident] (Hong Kong, 1969); *La Voie Chinoise* by G. Étienne (Paris, 1962); *Hsin kuan-ch'a* [New Observer] (Peking), Feb. 1, Feb. 16, and March 1, 1957 (articles on the strike incident of February 7, 1923); *Ch'ang-chiang ta-ch'iao* [Great Yangtze River Bridge] (Hong Kong, 1956); *Ke-ming yi-shih* [Informal History of the Revolution] (Changsha, 1939); *P'ing-chou k'o-t'an,* by Chu Yü, vol. 2 (see story on frogs, page 242); *Hsiu-chien chung ti Wu-han ch'ang-chiang ta-ch'iao* [The Great Yangtze River Bridge at Wuhan in Process of Construction] (Peking, 1955); *Ch'ang-chiang jih-pao* [Yangtze River Daily] (Wuhan); *Hu-pei jih-pao* [Hupei Daily] (Wuhan); Abbé Huc's *l'Empire Chinois* (Paris, 1854); *Narrative of the Earl of Elgin's Mission to China and Japan,* by Elgin's secretary Laurence Oliphant (New York, 1860); *China's Millions* by A. L. Strong (New York, 1935); a memoir by Li Shao-ch'en, "Tsai pai-se k'ung-pu ti jih-tzu li" [In the Days of the White Terror], in *Hung-ch'i p'iao p'iao* [Red Flag Flutterings], vol. 6; "The Wuhan Cities" by E. F. Weil, in *Asia,* May 1917; *Wu-han shih chien-chih yen-ke* [Making Rules for the Revolution in Wuhan] (Wuhan, 1956); *Hsin-hai ke-ming hui-yi lu* [Memoirs of the Revolution of 1911] (Peking, 1961); *Pao-lo-t'ing yü Wu-han cheng-ch'üan* [Borodin and Political Power in Wuhan] by Chiang Yüan-ching (Taipei, 1963); Father Du Halde's *Description de la Chine* (Paris, 1735).

For Peking the sources particularly used include: *Chin-jih Pei-ching* [Peking Today] (Hong Kong, 1971); two memoirs by foreigners, J. Blofeld's *City of Lingering Splendour* (London, 1961) and *The Years That Were Fat* by G. Kates (New York, 1952); *Yi-ho-t'uan yün-tung* [The Boxer Movement] by Chin Chia-jui (Shanghai, 1957); *Kuang-ming jih-pao* [Brilliant Daily]; article by Hu Sheng (see page 358) in *Li-shih yen-chiu,* no. 1, 1954; several issues of *Ching-chi yen-chiu* [Economic Research]; articles on Liu-li-chang and other cultural sites in *Wen wu* [Cultural Relics]; *Pei-ching wen-yi* [Literature and Art in Peking]; Wang Hsi's article on the United States (see page 356) in *Peking Review,* Sept. 7, 1973; other articles by Chinese journalists about their visit to America, in *Kuang-ming jih-pao,* July 27 and August 5, 1973; a number of the fiction writings of Lao She, which deal intimately with the city of Peking, in *Lao She hsüan-chi* [Selected Works of Lao She] (Peking, 1951).

ACKNOWLEDGMENTS

People I have met in China have made this book possible, including Liu Yun-kuo, Yang Kung-su, Chia Ai-mei, Wang Cheng-lung, Chang Wen-chin, Chou I-liang, Wang Hsi, Wu Pai-yang, Hu Sheng, among many others.

For acute comments and suggestions I am grateful to the professionalism of Li-li Ch'en and Donald Gibbs, and the experience of Neale Hunter and Gerald Tannebaum. Help on certain points also came from Ch'üan Ju-hsiang, Ho Ping-ti, Ying-mao Kau, Colin Mackerras, Samson Tu, Hak Wong, Ezra Vogel, William Holland, Bruce Liang, and Lynn White.

Harvard's East Asian Research Center has been a splendid base for my work; I am especially in debt to the knowledge and wisdom of John Fairbank, Dwight Perkins, Jerome Cohen, and Benjamin Schwartz.

At the Atlantic I have benefited from Upton Brady's vigor, Melissa Clemence's care, and the friendship and the light but powerful touch of Robert Manning. Lisa Nekich has been at all times a staunch helper.

The idealism, open-mindedness, and curiosity about China that I have found in meeting ordinary citizens throughout the United States has inspired me to try to make life in one great land more vivid to the people of another.

Phannarong Salirathavibhaga has lit my path with his own special light.

Harvard, April 1975

INDEX

411

Drasnin, Irv, 93
Dream of the Red Chamber (historical
novel), 41, 70, 136, 396
dress, 197, 369; in Dairen, 106, 113; in
Hangchow, 175, 188–189, 195–196,
201, 209, 227; in Peking, 362; in
Shanghai, 14, 58, 63; in Wuhan, 242,
324
Du Halde, Father, 249
Dulles, John Foster, 402

"East Is Red, The" (song), 57, 111, 194
East Lake, Wuhan, 235, 248, 281
East of the Bank, Shanghai, 59
East Sea Fleet, 276
education, 301, 386; in Chekiang, 210–
215; CCP policy on, 215, 218; cost of,
27–28; in Dairen, 145; in Peking, 383;
and politics, 150–151; and practical
experience, 282; for workers, 28, 149,
295; *see also* political study groups;
youth, reeducation of
"Electric Shovel" (poem), 297
electricity, 123, 310, 353
Elgin, Lord, 190, 244, 246, 249–251, 280,
299
Empress Dowager, 390, 396
emulation, *293*, 293–294
energy, 97, *98*, 123, 160, 353, 375; solar,
16; *see also* electricity; oil
Engels, works of, 69, 148, 151, 183
Episcopal Mission to Wuchang, 256
Establish Virtue neighborhood, Hangchow, 180–184, 187–189, *191;* factories of, 184–185
Eternally Red neighborhood, Dairen, *98*,
121, 124–127, 145; factories of, 128–
129, 130; housing in, 97–98
Ethiopian airline, 341

Facing the Sun neighborhood, Dairen,
121–123, *122*, 129
factories, *293*, 375n; in Dairen, 128–130,
131, 135–139, *136*, 139–142, *141;* in
dong bei, 109; handicrafts, 135–139,
136, 139–142, *141*, 185, 186–187; in
Hangchow, 184–185, 186–187; in Hankow, 320; in Peking, 352–353, 374–
375, 376; in Shanghai, 8, 25, 75, 85;
in Shenyang, 130–134, *131*
family, 5, 139, 295
family planning. *See* birth control
Fang Shan restaurant, 390, 390n
Feast of Lanterns, 194

Feng Hsüeh-feng, 39
Feng Yu-lan, 398–399
ferries, 26, 318
Festival for Sacrifices to the God of the
Soil, 195
Field of the Eight Trigrams, Hangchow,
192–193
First Five-year Plan (1953–1957), 286
Five Anti Campaign, 83
Five Dynasties period, 223
Five One (movie), 200, 201–202
food, 63, 314; cost of, 111, 204; *see also*
dishes
Forbidden City, Peking, 389
foreign language study: by broadcast, 18;
English, 18, 215; Japanese, 108; in uni-
versities, 146, 212–213, 386
Foreign Languages Press, Shanghai, 18,
19
Foreign Literature Bookstore, Shanghai,
68
foreign trade. *See* trade
foreigners; 333–334; restrictions on, 24;
travel arrangements for, 164
CHINESE ATTITUDE TOWARD, 93; in
Dairen, 106–107, 113, 133, 154; in
Hangchow, 162–163, 176, 188–189; in
Shanghai, 77, 87; in Wuhan, 273–274,
299–300, 326
Fortune, Robert, 208–209
Fragrant Mount, Peking, 395
French, in Shanghai, 45, 47, 71
From Emperor to Citizen (P'u Yi), 108
Front Gate, Peking, 361
Futan University, *400*

Gamewell, Mary, 49–50, 53, 67
games and sports: "army game," 198–
200; *bai-fen*, 72, 114, 197, 198, 323,
345, 352; chess, 72, 196, 345, 352; in
Dairen, 106, 111, 114, 123, 126; in
Hangchow, 196–197, 198–200; *mah-
jong*, 198; in Peking, 345, 352; in
Shanghai, 37, 54–57, *55*, 58, 72; *tai-ji-
quan*, 37, 54–57, *55*, 111; *wu-shu*, 56,
58; in Wuhan, 323
garbage collection, 348, 353
Garden Bridge, Shanghai, 61, 61n
General Headquarters of Revolutionary
Rebel Workers (GHRRW), 89
Glazier's Shop, Peking, 363–364
Gobi Desert, 343
Gorky, Maxim, works of, 204
grain, 30
Grand Canal, Hangchow, 169